Lessons from Pension Reform in the Americas

Lessons from Pension Reform in the Americas

EDITED BY

Stephen J. Kay and Tapen Sinha

OXFORD
UNIVERSITY PRESS

OXFORD
UNIVERSITY PRESS

Great Clarendon Street, Oxford OX2 6DP

Oxford University Press is a department of the University of Oxford.
It furthers the University's objective of excellence in research, scholarship,
and education by publishing worldwide in

Oxford New York

Auckland Cape Town Dar es Salaam Hong Kong Karachi
Kuala Lumpur Madrid Melbourne Mexico City Nairobi
New Delhi Shanghai Taipei Toronto

With offices in

Argentina Austria Brazil Chile Czech Republic France Greece
Guatemala Hungary Italy Japan Poland Portugal Singapore
South Korea Switzerland Thailand Turkey Ukraine Vietnam

Oxford is a registered trade mark of Oxford University Press
in the UK and in certain other countries

Published in the United States
by Oxford University Press Inc., New York

First published 2008

British Library Cataloguing in Publication Data
Data available

Library of Congress Cataloging in Publication Data
Lessons from pension reform in the Americas / edited by Stephen J. Kay
and Tapen Sinha.
p. cm.
ISBN-13: 978–0–19–922680–1
1. Pensions–Government policy–Latin America. 2. Social security–Latin America.
I. Kay, Stephen J. II. Sinha, Tapen.
HD7130.5.L47 2008
331.25′22098–dc22 2007028399

Typeset by SPI Publisher Services, Pondicherry, India
Printed in Great Britain
on acid-free paper by
Biddles Ltd., King's Lynn, Norfolk

ISBN 978–0–19–922680–1

1 3 5 7 9 10 8 6 4 2

Preface

It has been over a quarter of a century since Chile introduced a series of radical changes to its pension system. Many other countries, especially in the Americas, have followed Chile either fully or, most often, partially.

In an era when policy major reforms are being re-evaluated, and countries like Chile are pursuing a 'reform of the reform', this is the first volume to evaluate pension reform in the Americas in the 'postprivatization' era. This book assesses both successes and failures. It considers the breadth of the region's reforms from the privatizations inspired by Chile's landmark reform that have captured so much attention to the parametric measures of Brazil's recent reforms. The section containing country studies covers not only reforms undertaken or proposed by large countries like Canada, Mexico, and the USA, but also critical yet understudied reforms in smaller countries like Costa Rica and Uruguay. This book also examines universal policy challenges, regarding the impact of pension reform with respect to gender, decision-making processes surrounding reform, and the role of default choices in program design. A foreword by Nobel laureate Robert W. Fogel on evolving demographic challenges and a chapter on World Bank policies, written by three current and former World Bank specialists, complete the picture and provide cues and clues for future directions in pension reforms around the world.

The Americas have been the site of the world's most significant pension reforms. The analyses presented here by leading experts provide valuable insight as governments everywhere consider how best to proceed with pension reform. This book is written for anyone with an interest in social security and pension reform, and is geared to be accessible to both specialists and nonspecialists alike.

The Pension Research Council

The Pension Research Council of the Wharton School of the University of Pennsylvania is an organization committed to generating debate on key policy issues affecting pensions and other employee benefits. The Council sponsors interdisciplinary research on the entire range of private and social retirement security and related benefit plans in the US and around the world. It seeks to broaden understanding of these complex arrangements through basic research into their economic, social, legal, actuarial, and financial foundations. Members of the Advisory Board of the Council, appointed by the Dean of the Wharton School, are leaders in the employee benefits field, and they recognize the essential role of social security and other public sector income maintenance programs while sharing a desire to strengthen private sector approaches to economic security. More information about the Pension Research Council is available on the Internet at http://pensionresearchcouncil.org or send email to prc@wharton.upenn.edu.

Acknowledgments

The editors thank all the contributors for their enthusiastic participation. This book was truly a collective effort, and we thank all authors for writing it with us. We are grateful to the Federal Reserve Bank of Atlanta's Americas Center, the Instituto Tecnologico Autonomo de Mexico (ITAM), and The Pension Research Council of the Wharton School of the University of Pennsylvania for their institutional support. The views expressed here are those of the authors and not necessarily those of these three institutions.

We also want to thank our Atlanta Fed colleagues Galina Alexeenko, Michael Chriszt, Tom Cunningham, Sarah Dougherty, Julie Hotchkiss, Vanessa Jordan, Monica Ospina, Myriam Quispe-Agnoli, John Robertson, Diego Vilán, Vivian Wilkins, Elena Whisler, and especially Robert Eisenbeis, for encouraging us to undertake this project. We thank Arturo Fernandez, Enrique de Alba, and Diego Hernandez in ITAM. Tapen Sinha would like to acknowledge the support of the Asociación Mexicana de Cultura AC. We owe a special debt of gratitude to Nancy Condon, who provided invaluable help in editing and preparing the manuscript. At various points, Daniel Béland and Fabio Bertranou provided insightful comments, as did three anonymous readers. We also thank Larissa Bocanegra for her translations of two chapters. We are grateful to Tanya Dean, Matthew Derbyshire, and David Musson at Oxford University Press for all their attentive assistance throughout the editing process.

Our deepest heartfelt gratitude goes to Olivia S. Mitchell of Wharton's Pension Research Council, whose enthusiastic support helped shape this project, and who provided us with valuable advice from start to finish. We are honored that this book is being published in the Pension Research Council's Oxford University Press series.

This book is dedicated to the memory of Michael Wallerstein, a teacher and friend, and to the people of the Americas who will live the unfolding drama of pension reform in the decades ahead.

Contents

Part II. Country Studies

List of Figures

List of Tables

Notes on Contributors

Alberto Arenas de Mesa is Chile's Budget Director.

Jere R. Behrman is the W. R. Kenan Jr. Professor of Economics at the University of Pennsylvania.

John Beshears is a Ph.D. Candidate in business economics at Harvard University.

David Bravo is on the faculty of the department of economics at the University of Chile.

Robert L. Brown is a professor of statistics and actuarial science at the University of Waterloo.

Eliana Carranza is on the faculty of the Universidad del Pacífico in Peru.

James J. Choi is an assistant professor of finance at the Yale School of Management.

John F. Cogan is the Leonard and Shirley Ely Senior Fellow at the Hoover Institution, and a professor in the Public Policy Program at Stanford University.

Michelle Dion is an assistant professor at the Sam Nunn School of International Affairs at the Georgia Institute of Technology.

Alejandra Cox Edwards is a professor of economics at California State University, Long Beach.

Robert W. Fogel is the Charles R. Walgreen Distinguished Service Professor of American Institutions and director of the Center for Population Economics at the Graduate School of Business of the University of Chicago. He won the Nobel Memorial Prize in Economic Sciences in 1993.

Robert Holzmann is director of the Social Protection Department of the World Bank.

Estelle James is a consultant to the World Bank and the United States Agency for International Development.

Stephen J. Kay is the Americas Center coordinator in the Research Department of the Federal Reserve Bank of Atlanta.

David Laibson is a professor of economics at Harvard University and a research associate with the Programs on Aging, Economic Fluctuations, and Asset Pricing, at the National Bureau of Economic Research.

Brigitte C. Madrian is the Aetna Professor of Public Policy and Corporate Management at the John F. Kennedy School of Government at Harvard University.

Juliana Martínez Franzoni is a researcher at the Social Research Institute at the University of Costa Rica.

Milko Matijascic is director of the Salesian Center for Public Policy at the Salesian University in Americana, Brazil.

Olivia S. Mitchell is the International Foundation of Employee Benefit Plans Professor of Insurance and Risk Management, the executive director of the Pension Research Council, and director of the Boettner Center on Pensions and Retirement Research at the Wharton School.

Eduardo Morón is an associate professor in the department of economics at the Universidad del Pacífico in Peru.

Truman Packard is a senior economist for Social Protection in the Latin America and Caribbean Regional Office of the World Bank.

Rafael Rofman is a senior economist for Social Protection in the Latin America and Caribbean Regional Office of the World Bank.

Rodolfo Saldain is the principal partner of Saldain and Igarzábal and the former president of Uruguay's Social Security Bank.

Tapen Sinha is the ING Comercial America Chair Professor in the department of actuarial studies at the Instituto Tecnológico Autónomo de México (ITAM) in Mexico, and Special Professor of the School of Business, University of Nottingham, UK. He is also the founder and director of the International Center for Pension Research.

Petra E. Todd is a professor of economics at the University of Pennsylvania.

Kurt Weyland is a professor of government at the University of Texas, Austin.

Rebeca Wong is a senior research scientist and the associate director of the Maryland Population Research Center at the University of Maryland.

Maria de los Angeles Yañez is on the faculty of the department of actuarial studies at the Instituto Tecnológico Autónomo de México.

List of Abbreviations

AEPS	Anuário Estatístico da Previdência Social, Social Security Statistics Annual (Brazil)
AFAP	Administradora de Fondos de Ahorro Provisional, or pension savings fund administrator (Uruguay)
AFIP	Administración Federal de Ingresos Públicos, or Federal Public Revenue Administration (Argentina)
AFORE	Administradora de Fondos de Retiro, or retirement fund administrator (Mexico)
AFP	Administradora de Fondos de Pensiones, or pension fund administrator (Chile, Peru)
AFJP	Administradora de Fondos de Jubilaciones y Pensiones, or pension fund administrator (Argentina)
ANEP	Asociación Nacional de Empleados Públicos y Privados, or National Association of Public and Private Employees (Costa Rica)
ANFIP	Associação Nacional dos Fiscais de Contribuições Previdenciárias, National Social Security Auditors Association (Brazil)
ANSES	Administración Nacional de la Seguridad Social, or National Social Security Administration (Argentina)
APRA	Alianza Popular Revolucionaria Americana, or Popular American Revolution Alliance Party (Peru)
BHU	Banco Hipotecario del Uruguay, or Mortgage Bank of Uruguay
BPS	Banco de Previsión Social del Uruguay, or Social Security Bank of Uruguay
BONOSOL	Bono de Solidaridad, or Solidarity Bond (Bolivia)
BROU	Banco de la República Oriental del Uruguay, or Central Bank of Uruguay
BSE	Banco de Seguros del Estado, or State Insurance Bank (Uruguay)
CAP	Caixas de Aposentadorias e Pensões, or Pension and Retirement Funds (Brazil)
CAPREDENA	Caja de Previsión de la Defensa Nacional, or National Defense Pension Fund (Chile)
CCSS	Caja Costarricense del Seguro Social, or Costa Rican Social Security System

CEPAL	Comisión Económica para América Latina y el Caribe, or Economic Commission for Latin America and the Caribbean
COFINS	Contribuição Social para Financiamento da Seguridade Social, or Social Contribution to Finance Social Security (Brazil)
CONSAR	Comisión Nacional del Sistema de Ahorro para el Retiro, or National Retirement Fund System Commission (Mexico)
CPMF	Contribuição Provisória sobre Movimentação Financeira, or Temporary Contribution on Financial Transactions (Brazil)
CPP	Canada Pension Plan
CPPIB	Canada Pension Plan Investment Board
C/QPP	Canada/Quebec Pension Plans
CSLL	Contribuições sobre o Lucro Líquido, or Contribution on Profits (Brazil)
CW	contribution wage
DB	defined benefit
DC	defined contribution
DIPRECA	Dirección de Previsión de Carabineros de Chile, or Chile Police Pension Fund
DL	decreto ley
EAP	economically active population
EAPC	Entidades Abertas de Previdência Complementar, or open complementary private pension program (Brazil)
ECLAC	Economic Commission for Latin America and the Caribbean
EFPC	Entidades Fechadas de Previdência Complementar, or closed private pension programs (Brazil)
EPS	Encuesta de Previsión Social, or Social Protection Survey (Chile)
EPV	expected present value
FAP	Fondo de Ahorro Provisional, or pension savings fund (Uruguay)
FCN	Foro de Concertación Nacional, or National Concertation Forum (Costa Rica)
FOPC	Fondo Obligatorio de Pensión Complementaria, or Mandatory Complementary Pension Fund (Costa Rica)
FINSOCIAL	Fundo de Investimento Social, or Social Investment Fund (Brazil)
FUNRURAL	Fundo de Assistência ao Trabalhador Rural, or Rural Worker Assistance Fund (Brazil)

GDP	gross domestic product
GIS	Guaranteed-Income Supplement (Canada)
HHI	Herfindhal-Hirschmann index
HLSS	Historia Laboral y Seguridad Social, or History of Labor and Social Security (Chile)
HRS	Health and Retirement Study (United States of America)
IAP	Institutos de Aposentadorias e Pensões, or Retirement Pension Institutes (Brazil)
IBGE	Instituto Brasileiro de Geografia e Estatística, or Brazilian Institute of Geography and Statistics
IDB	Inter-American Development Bank
ILO	International Labour Organization
IMF	International Monetary Fund
IMSS	Instituto Mexicano del Seguro Social, or Mexican Social Security Institute
INAMU	Instituto Nacional de la Mujer, or National Women's Institute (Costa Rica)
INARSS	Instituto Nacional de Recaudación de los Recursos de la Seguridad Social, or National Institute for Collection of Social Security Revenue (Argentina)
INDECOPI	Instituto Nacional para la Defensa de la Competencia y de la Protección de la Propiedad Intelectual, or National Institute for the Defense of Competition and Protection of Intellectual Property (Peru)
INEGI	Instituto Nacional de Estadística, Geografía e Informática or National Institute of Statistics, Geography and Information (Mexico)
INFONAVIT	Instituto de Fondo Nacional de la Vivienda para los Trabajadores, or National Workers Housing Fund (Mexico)
INP	Instituto de Normalización Provisional, or Social Security Normalization Institute (Chile)
INPC	Indice Nacional dos Preços ao Consumidor, or National Consumer Price Index (Brazil)
INPS	Instituto Nacional de Previdência Social, or National Social Security Institute (Brazil)
INSS	Instituto Nacional de Seguro Social, or National Social Insurance Institute (Brazil)
IPASE	Instituto de Previdencia e Assistencia dos Servidores do Estado, or State Employees Social Security Institute (Brazil)
IPSS	Instituto Peruano de Seguridad Social, Peruvian Social Security Institute

IRA	individual retirement account
ISSB	Instituto de Serviços Sociais do Brasil, or Brazilian Social Service Institute
IV	Seguros de Invalidez y Vida, or Life and Disability Insurance (Mexico)
IVCM	invalidez, vejez, cesancía, en edad avanzada y muerte, or disability, old-age, retirement, and death insurance
IVM	invalidez, vejez y muerte, or disability, old-age, and death insurance
IVS	invalidez, vejez y sobrevivencia, or disability, old-age, and survivorship insurance
LOPS	Lei Orgânica da Previdência Social, or Organic Law of Social Security (Brazil)
LPT	Ley de Protección al Trabajador, Worker Protection Law (Costa Rica)
MHAS	Mexican Health and Aging Study
MPAS	Ministério da Previdência e Assistência Social, or Ministry of Social Security and Social Assistance (Brazil)
MPG	minimum pension guarantee
MRA	minimum retirement age
MTSS	Ministerio de Trabajo y Seguridad Social, Labor and Social Security Ministry (Uruguay)
NDC	notional defined contribution or non-financial defined contribution
OAS	Organization of American States
OECD	Organisation for Economic Co-operation and Development
OIT	Organizacíon Internacional del Trabajo, or International Labour Organization
ONP	Oficina de Normalización Previsional, or Office of Social Security Normalization (Peru)
OSFI	Office of the Superintendent of Financial Institutions (Canada)
OSS	Orçamento de Seguridade Social, or Social Security Budget (Brazil)
PAP	Prestación Adicional por Permanencia, Additional Benefit (Argentina)
PASIS	Pensión Asistencial de Ancianidad, or Old-Age Welfare Pension (Chile)
PAYGO	pay-as-you-go
PBU	Prestación Básica Universal, or Universal Basic Benefit (Argentina)
PEC	projeto de emenda constitucional, or constitutional amendment proposal (Brazil)

PNAD	Pesquisa Nacional por Amostra de Domicilios, National Household Survey (Brazil)
PRORURAL	Previdência do Trabalhador Rural, or Rural Worker Social Security (Brazil)
QPP	Québec Pension Plan
RGPS	Regime Geral de Previdência Social, or General Social Security Regime (Brazil)
RB	recognition bond
RCV	Seguro de Retiro, Cesantía en Edad Avanzada y Vejez, or Retirement and Old-Age Insurance (Mexico)
RIVM	Régimen de Invalidez, Vejez y Muerte, or Disability, Old-Age, and Survivorship Regime (Costa Rica)
RNC	Régimen No Contributivo, or the Non-Contributory Pension Regime (Costa Rica)
ROE	return on equity
RPP	Regime Próprio de Previdência, or Special Retirement System (Brazil)
SA	Spouse's Allowance (Canada)
SAFP	Superintendencia de Administradoras de Fondos de Pensiones, or Superintendency of Pension Fund Administrators (Chile)
SAFJP	Superintendencia de Administradoras de Fondos de Jubilaciones y Pensiones, or Superintendency of Pension Fund Administrators (Argentina)
SAR	Sistema Para el Retiro, or Retirement System (Mexico)
SICERE	Sistema Centralizado de Recaudación, or Centralized Collection System (Costa Rica)
SIEFORE	Sociedades de Inversión de Fondos para el Retiro, or retirement investment fund (Mexico)
SIMPLES	Sistema Integrado de Pagamento de Impostos e Contribuições das Microempresas e Empresas de Pequeno Porte, or Integrated Tax Payment System for Small and Medium Enterprises (Brazil)
SNP	El Sistema Nacional de Pensiones, or National Pension System (Peru)
SPC	Secretaria de Previdência Complementar, or Secretary of Supplemental Pensions of the Ministry of Social Security (Brazil)
SPP	Sistema Privado de Pensiones, or Private Pension System (Peru)
SQ	Social Quota (Mexico)
SUPEN	Superintendencia de Pensiones, or Superintendency of Pensions (Costa Rica)

SUS	Sistema Único de Saúde, or Unitary Health System (Brazil)
SUSEP	Superintendência de Seguros Privados, or Superintendency of Private Insurance (Brazil)
UF	Unidades de Fomento (Chile)
UN	United Nations
WB	World Bank
YBE	year's basic exemption (Canada)
YMPE	year's maximum pensionable earnings (Canada)

Foreword: Toward an Era of Longevity and Wealth

Robert W. Fogel

I begin this foreword on economic forecasting with a brief history because forecasting necessarily involves history: it is an extrapolation of past trends into the future. There are, however, many different ways of extrapolating; which of these many possible forecasts an investigator favors depends on his or her theories of future economic growth and future improvements in health and longevity. Greater longevity, in turn, will have dramatic implications for pension reform policies.

The period between 1800 and 1950 was a remarkable era for the now developed countries. In 1800 the nations of Western Europe and North America were poor agricultural countries by current standards, and barely 5 percent of the population was urban. Life expectancy at birth in the emerging cities was so low that the growth of these cities was due mainly to immigration from rural areas or abroad rather than from natural increase.

As the cities increased in size, problems of health intensified and mortality rates soared. Problems of waste disposal outran the ability of authorities to provide pure water and uncontaminated food. Although scientists and engineers struggled with the problems, solutions did not come quickly. Not only did many false theories have to be disproved, but also correct theories were expensive to implement. Implementation required an educated public, more commodious housing, new methods of water purification and delivery, and expensive new technologies to cleanse the air of the haze of pulverized horse manure that enveloped cities and provided a rich diet for the dense population of flies. The main new technology that solved the horse problem was, of course, the automobile, which has been transformed from savior to villain now that memories of past problems have faded.

Severe and persistent inequality was still another problem of urbanization during the nineteenth and early twentieth centuries. Mortality rates in the large cities varied greatly by wards. In the worst wards of large American cities, the infant death rate averaged about 50 percent in 1890 and 1900, while in the best wards it was about 8 percent. However, such disparities declined rapidly during the early decades of the twentieth century. What we now decry as severe differences in infant mortality rates by socioeconomic class in the rich nations are a minute fraction of what they were a century ago, although it is appropriate and urgent that we seek to eliminate the remaining differences.

Death rates were exceedingly high among the poor during the early nineteenth century not only in the cities but also in the countryside. In countries such as England and France in the late eighteenth century, food production was so inadequate that the bottom 20 percent of the population was excluded from production and the next 20 percent had enough energy for only a few hours of light work. Moreover, the majority of those in the active labor force were so stunted and wasted that their capacity to work, and the duration of their active working life, was quite limited by modern standards. It has been estimated that half of the English growth rate in per capita income between 1790 and 1980 was due to improvements in human physiology made possible by better nutrition.

The course of global economic growth over the next generation or two is bright. The foundation for such optimism is the remarkable economic growth in East and South Asia since the late 1970s in countries that together represent a population much larger than Europe and the USA put together. These countries, which are growing at three or four times the long-term rates of Europe and America, are likely to overtake the Western nations in total income by 2020 and may equal them in per capita income by 2040. The two largest Asian countries, China and India, which together represent 40 percent of the world's population, have both been growing quite rapidly since 1980.

The development of the Chinese economy over the past three decades has been particularly impressive. Its real per capita income increased at an average annual rate of 7.7 percent, exceeding the best rates of such previous long-term pacemakers as Japan, Korea, and Singapore. Several factors suggest that China will continue to grow at high rates for at least another generation. One is the very heavy investment China is making in education, not only extending primary and secondary education to almost all of the school age population but also dramatically extending tertiary education. From 1998 to 2003, the number of students enrolled in 4-year colleges increased from 3.4 to 9.0 million. India has experienced a similar increase in college education. It is estimated that in 2006, China will produce 3.3 million college graduates; India 3.1 million; and the USA, 1.3 million.

There are other reasons why China, India, and other high-performing Asian economies are likely to continue to grow at high rates. First, these countries have large shares of their labor force in agriculture, where labor productivity is low compared to labor productivity in industry and services. Hence, about one-third of their projected growth rates can be obtained by shifting labor from agriculture to the sectors with much higher value added per worker. Additionally, these countries are not yet at the global frontier of technology in any of the three main sectors of an economy and therefore do not have to advance the global frontier of technology to raise labor productivity within each sector. They can do so merely by adapting the existing global technology to their own specific conditions.

My estimate for the long-term growth of the rich nations—designated here as OECD, for nations of the Organisation for Economic Cooperation and Development—is that during the twenty-first century they will grow in excess of their average during the second half of the twentieth century, which was about 3.3 percent per annum in gross domestic product (GDP), or about 2.8 percent in GDP per capita. I expect the rate of growth to increase because technological change is accelerating.

Rapid technological change is confined to a tiny fraction of the 200,000 years since the origin of our species. For most of its existence, *Homo sapiens* lived in small, far-flung hunting-and-gathering communities that teetered on the edge of extinction. It was not until 9,000 years ago that humankind discovered agriculture, which broke the tight constraint on the food supply. However, it took 4,000 years after this discovery for agriculture to supersede hunting and gathering as the main source of food, 5,000 years for the first cities to emerge, 6,000 years to develop writing, and 7,000 years to invent mathematics. Despite these advances, which permitted a more rapid increase in population than in the past, it was not until 1700 that humans obtained a degree of control over their environment so great that it set them apart not only from all other species but also from all previous generations of *Homo sapiens.*

During the past three centuries, a remarkable synergism has emerged between technological and physiological improvements that has produced a form of human evolution that is biological but not genetic, rapid, culturally transmitted, and not necessarily stable. MIT economist and biodemographer Dora Costa and I call this process, which is ongoing in both developed and developing countries, *technophysio evolution.* Because of technophysio evolution, human beings have been able to increase their average body size by more than 50 percent, increase their average longevity by more than 100 percent, and improve greatly the robustness and capacity of vital organ systems.

One of the aspects of technophysio evolution is the substantial delay in the onset of chronic diseases during the course of the twentieth century. American men aged 60–64 years in 1994 were two-and-a-half times more likely to be free of chronic diseases than their counterparts a century earlier. Among those who turned 65 between 1983 and 1992, such chronic conditions as arthritis, heart disease, and respiratory disease began 9 to 11 years later than those who turned 65 between 1895 and 1910.

What is the outlook for the current generation of college students? James Vaupel recently estimated that this generation has a 50-50 chance of living to a hundred—a considerably longer life expectancy than that projected by the US Census Bureau, the United Nations, OECD, and other national and international agencies. These official agencies believe that the increase in life expectancy during the twenty-first century will be less than half of what it was in the twentieth century.

This same sort of pessimism prevailed at the start of the twentieth century. No authority in 1900 had the slightest inkling that life expectancy at the end of the century would be older than 75 years. Indeed, authorities persistently underestimate the potential for increases in longevity. Many experts today argue that the longevity gains of the twentieth century cannot be replicated because the main causes of death today are from chronic diseases at old ages and not from the infectious diseases that were the main killers in the past. However, as already noted, the onset of chronic diseases has already been delayed by a decade or more and further delays are likely because those born after 1950 were healthier during their developmental ages than were their parents. Moreover, the decline in age-specific disabilities among the elderly has accelerated in recent years. Between 1984 and 2000, the rate of decline in age-specific disabilities among Medicare enrollees increased by 50 percent.

I expect the decline in chronic conditions and disabilities to continue, partly because of continuing improvements in human physiology and partly because globally we have the economic resources and the inclination to invest heavily in health improvements. In OECD countries, the long-term income elasticity of the demand for health care is about 1.5, and it appears to be even higher in China and other newly industrial countries (NICs), which implies that if economic growth continues at past rates, the share of GDP expended on health care could double (to 30% in the case of the USA) by 2030 or 2035.

Will such a vast expansion of expenditures on health care pay off? There are reasons to be optimistic here also. The onset of disabilities has not only been delayed a decade or so, but when they do appear, they are milder and easier to treat. Moreover, technophysio evolution appears to be making us better candidates for evolving medical interventions. The outlook for new and more effective technologies to deal with chronic disabilities is very promising, both in drug therapies and in the marriage of biology and microchip technology. Indeed, some devices that combine living cells and electronics to replace failed organs are already at the stage of human trials. Somewhat farther off, but even more promising, are advances in genetic engineering that will produce cures for what are now untreatable diseases.

The future health of the young generation is quite bright, provided that they adopt an appropriate lifestyle to go with the new technological opportunities.

This of course has implications for social security policies. Policymakers in both the industrialized and developing countries must consider potential changes in longevity when it comes to planning pension systems. As policymakers engage in pension reform, they must incorporate demographic changes, including revising mortality tables and retirement ages and ensuring that benefits are adequately financed.

Chapter 1

Overview: Lessons from Pension Reform in the Americas

Stephen J. Kay and Tapen Sinha

Well over a century ago, Chancellor Otto Von Bismarck introduced a state-sponsored pay-as-you-go (PAYGO) pension system in Germany with a single purpose: to reduce poverty among the aged. This primary goal is true today, even as policymakers struggle to address changing demographics and aging populations amid much disagreement regarding the best path for reform. This situation holds especially true in the Americas, which, since Chile's pension reform, have become a global laboratory for pension reform.

In 1981 Chile took the unprecedented step of switching from a PAYGO to a substitutive prefunded pension system. It continued to pay benefits promised under the old system by issuing recognition bonds and running budget surpluses during the initial years to finance these bonds. In 1994 Argentina and Colombia followed suit. With the publication of the landmark study *Averting the Old-Age Crisis* that same year, individual prefunded accounts were now officially encouraged by the World Bank and other leading international organizations (WB 1994). Since then, the World Bank has helped more than eighty countries make changes in their pension systems (Holzmann and Hinz 2005). Of these, about a dozen countries in Latin America have passed laws introducing mandatory saving, while a similar number in Europe and central Asia—mainly in the post-Soviet 'transition economies'—have also made legal provisions for individual accounts.

Beginning in 2004, a fundamental shift in thinking became evident in the process of pension reform in international organizations such as the World Bank and the International Monetary Fund, as well as in countries such as Chile that have undertaken reform. The first element of such a shift became evident with the watershed publications of *Keeping the Promise of Social Security in Latin America* (Gill, Packard, and Yermo 2005) and the 2006 World Bank Independent Evaluation Group (IEG) report, which explicitly states, 'The Bank should pay greater attention to parametric reforms and to exploring options to expand the safety net for those not covered by

Opinions and errors are solely those of the authors and do not reflect views of the institutions with whom the authors are affiliated.

the pension system' (p. xii). Holzmann and Hinz (2005) maintain that the motivation for the Bank to support pension reform did not change from 1994 to 2004, but rather was strengthened by the experiences of that decade: most pension systems in the world do not deliver on their social objectives, create significant distortions in the operation of market economies, and are not financially sustainable when faced with an aging population.

This evolution in thinking is most evident in Chile. In the introduction of a report by her pension reform commission (called the 'Marcel Commission', after its chairman, Mario Marcel), Chilean President Michelle Bachelet notes that the pension system faces numerous challenges:

> The system has low coverage, low density of contributions, it leaves almost ninety-five percent of the independent workers outside the system, it shows very little competition and high commission charges, it does not take into account the complexities of modern workplace, high turnover, high level of informality... and discriminates against women... among other shortcomings (Consejo 2006: 5–6). [authors' translation]

The Marcel Commission report, which was the basis of reform legislation introduced in December 2006, addresses the particular challenges that developing countries face with respect to their sizable informal sectors, which in many countries comprise over half of the economically active population. It argues that instead of expecting a reform to formalize the informal sector workers, pension reform should serve all workers, both informal and formal, and proposes a universal solidarity pension aimed at alleviating poverty (Consejo 2006: 47). Because Chile's reform has influenced so many other governments in the region, measures that address these policy challenges will be watched closely throughout Latin America and beyond.

In other words, after more than a decade, the dominant policy prescriptions in vogue in the 1990s are being re-evaluated. With the euphoria of the initial phase of pension reform clearly over and with a decade or more of experience to review, policymakers and scholars now have access to important new evidence to analyze the efficiency and equity of switching to individual accounts.

This volume is among the first to assess these reforms in this new 'post-privatization' era. Three influential policymakers either now or previously connected to the World Bank reflect on pension policies since the landmark publication of the World Bank's 1994 report *Averting the Old Age Crisis* (WB 1994), of which Estelle James, one of the panelists, is a primary author. James argues that we now have a clearer grasp of some of the implementation problems inherent in multipillar systems and outlines potential solutions. Truman Packard, an author of the 2005 book *Keeping the Promise of Social Security in Latin-America* (Gill, Packard, and Yermo 2005), which assessed reform since the publication of *Averting the Old-Age Crisis* and generated considerable debate, stresses that the book's most distinguishing and overlooked feature is its application of a microeconomic framework of insurance and savings and its focus on the primary policy objectives of old-age income security: ensuring efficient consumption smoothing and preventing poverty in old age. Robert Holzmann notes that the extensive experience in implementing pension reforms in a range of settings since the early 1990s has motivated a review and refining of the framework with respect to appropriate objectives and path of reform efforts, and he describes the World Bank's current approach.

The perspectives of these three authors provide insight into the evolution of pension policies at the World Bank since the mid-1990s. *Averting the Old-Age Crisis* suggested a three-pillar system: the first pillar would be a PAYGO component, the second a prefunded scheme, and the third a voluntary saving component. Today, by contrast, the World Bank espouses a *five*-pillar format. The additional pillars are the 'zero pillar', which is a noncontributory and universal pillar, and a pillar that includes not just direct monetary benefits for retirement consumption but also nonmonetary benefits such as access to housing and health care in retirement.

This volume also offers a chapter on Chile that focuses on the results of the first-ever micro-level longitudinal study of worker behavior linked with administrative records conducted in Latin America. The study links the results of the survey, which tested the accuracy of people's knowledge of their own retirement savings, to the actual pension records of each individual. This study, conducted in 2002 and 2004, and every two years thereafter as long as funding continues, addresses universal issues of worker behavior and financial literacy—a problem in developed countries (e.g. Lusardi and Mitchell 2007) and, *a fortiori*, for developing countries. This research will have wide impact on policymaking in Chile and other countries that have switched to prefunded individual accounts.

The chapter on Mexico's pension reform exemplifies how the country studies in this collection address key issues, including coverage, competition, costs, investment performance, and projected benefits. In particular, the chapter compares important counterfactuals about what would have been the costs had there been parametric reforms and compares them with the costs of the currently implemented change. It also discusses important results of the payout stage, concluding that most retirees in the formal sector under the new system will not have enough money to buy a pension equivalent to the minimum wage, which has been guaranteed by the government.

Also included in this collection are analyses of parametric changes in pension systems, as in Costa Rica, which reformed its system in 2005, and Brazil, where President Lula initiated a significant reform in 2003.

Parametric changes have typically received short shrift, as discussion of individual accounts had dominated the policy agenda since the 1990s. Moreover, past publications have tended to focus on the big three reforms—Argentina, Mexico, and Chile—omitting smaller countries such as Uruguay and Peru as well as Costa Rica. The countries examined in this volume, including the USA and Canada, are more representative of the range of reforms in the hemisphere. The country studies also provide a thorough assessment of policy performance since reforms have taken place.

Part I: System Design and Policy Implications: Demographic Trends, Financial Education, Importance of Psychological Considerations, and Gender

Part I of this volume addresses issues of system design that have significant implications with respect to compliance, coverage, financial literacy, and gender issues. These are universal issues that all countries contemplating reform face.

In his foreword, Robert W. Fogel provides an overview of demographic development during the past three centuries, as life expectancy and per-capita growth of the GDP have increased dramatically. Due to the intense interplay between physiological improvement and technological advances, humans have increased their body size by more than 50 percent in the past two centuries, and the betterment of general sanitation, reduction of air pollution in the cities, and higher food intake have improved life expectancy. According to Fogel, demographers have consistently underestimated the impact of such improvements and, consequently, have underestimated gains in life expectancy. With more workers living longer and healthier lives, men in Western countries have four times more leisure than they did a century ago, and this trend will continue. Paradoxically, this achievement has devastating financial implications for already overburdened social security systems and calls for a careful re-examination of social security to ensure future sustainability.

A team of researchers led by David Bravo designed and implemented the Encuesta Previsión Social (EPS, or Social Protection Survey), a household survey designed to gather microeconomic data on the Chilean labor market and social insurance system (see www.microdatos.cl). The findings from the first two rounds of this longitudinal study are analyzed in the chapter that Bravo co-authored with Alberto Arenas de Mesa, Jere R. Behrman, Olivia S. Mitchell, and Petra E. Todd. The authors note that they found significant differences between individuals' self-reports and the administrative records of the individuals interviewed. Not all respondents could estimate the balances in their private savings accounts but those who could were quite accurate and, significantly, their balances were four times higher than those who could not. The results highlight considerable information gaps among the workers participating in the Chilean pension system. The authors stress that greater financial literacy is essential in enhancing the system. Furthermore, for the government to make useful budgetary projections, better data are necessary on who is in the system, who is contributing, and who is likely to try to obtain the minimum pension guarantee or social assistance.

In general, defined contribution (DC) savings plans require employees to make complex decisions, including how much to contribute and how to distribute their contribution among a variety of investment funds. In their chapter on default options, John Beshears, James J. Choi, David Laibson, and Brigitte C. Madrian provide evidence that refutes a standard notion from economic theory that posits that if transaction costs are small, default choices should not matter. They note that the psychology literature has documented the tendency of individuals to put off making decisions as the complexity of the task increases, a factor that would tend to lower participation in retirement savings plans. To assess the impact of defaults on retirement savings, the authors examine the impact on worker savings when workers are automatically enrolled by their employers and when they must actively opt in to a retirement savings plan.

Among their findings, the authors note that with automatic enrollment in retirement plans, participation rates are much higher than with opt-in enrollment. Furthermore, many individuals view the employer default savings option as an implicit endorsement of both the contribution rate and the distribution of funds. They find that default choices are *not* neutral; they play a role in every stage of the lifetime savings cycle, including savings plan participation, contributions, asset allocation, rollovers, and decumulation. They become even more crucial as pension fund plans in the Americas introduce more investment options for workers. Because they carry such significant consequences for retirement saving, default options merit close attention from policymakers.

The chapter by Kurt Weyland analyzes the decision-making process surrounding pension reform, arguing that decision-makers in Latin America did not systematically process information when they evaluated pension reform but rather used three principal shortcuts of bounded rationality documented by cognitive psychologists: *availability*, *representativeness*, and *anchoring*. With respect to availability, Chile's pension privatization captured the attention of decision-makers in Latin America in its boldness, obscuring other sources of relevant information such as the notional DC scheme developed in Europe. Representativeness induces people to base their judgments on logically irrelevant similarities, overestimating the significance of patterns that appear in small samples and mistaking short-term trends as proof of structural tendencies. Consequently, initially high returns may have led policymakers to attribute other Chilean outcomes (like the rise in domestic savings and investment) to the privatization. Finally, anchoring leads people to base their judgments on any given clue, even a logically arbitrary one. Even when they adjust their opinions with additional information and experience, they diverge from this accidental starting point much less than full rationality would require. Thus, according to Weyland, decision-makers in many Latin American countries may have followed the Chilean model more closely than they should have. In short, countries with limited domestic expertise, including Bolivia, El Salvador, and Peru, followed the Chilean model even though doing so may have not been reasonable given their particular circumstances.

Although gender issues are just now beginning to appear on policymakers' radar screens—as *The Economist* put it, 'Forget China, India and the internet: economic growth is driven by women' (*The Economist* 2006)—the role of gender in pensions is still not getting the attention it deserves. Chile's President Bachelet commented that the Chilean pension system to some extent 'discriminated against women' and, in its evaluative analysis, the Marcel Commission agreed. The commission notes that women receive annuity benefits equivalent to only 42 percent of what men receive due to a variety of factors, including women's differential participation in the labor market (with lower wages), the division of household and reproductive work, demographics, and such pension system regulations as the earlier retirement age and the fact that insurance companies are permitted to use differential mortality tables. The Marcel Commission's frank assessment of the impact of pension reform on women—and the accompanying set of policy prescriptions, including subsidized childcare and a measure that would pay women retiring at age 65 years a bonus for the birth of each child (see Consejo 2006)—represents the first of its kind in Latin America and is destined to receive considerable attention from other countries that have followed Chile's path.

The two chapters on gender and pension reform in this book are critical contributions to this important debate. In their chapter, Estelle James, Alejandra Cox Edwards, and Rebeca Wong present the results of their investigation into the effects on gender of the reformed pensions systems in Chile, Mexico, and Argentina. They note the arguments of reform critics, who say the tight link between payroll contributions and benefits in the DC pillar will produce lower pensions for women, and of supporters, who say that multipillar systems remove distortions favoring men and permit a more targeted public pillar that will help women. James, Edwards, and Wong set out to test these conflicting claims by asking the following questions:

- What are the relative monthly and lifetime benefits and redistributions to men versus women under the new systems?
- What are the relative gains or losses of men versus women due to the shift from the old to the new systems?
- Which subgroups within each gender benefit or lose the most from the reform and redistributions under the new systems?
- What are the key policy choices that determine these gender outcomes?

These are important questions for the following reasons. First, the majority of senior citizens are women. Second, poverty among the old is most severe among women aged 85 years and older. Third, the system may reward or penalize formal labor market work. Finally, cash transfers compete with other uses for public funds.

For their analysis, the authors used household survey data available for these three countries to simulate employment histories. Although they find that women accumulate retirement funds and private annuities from the DC pillar of the multipillar systems that are only 30–40 percent of those of men, they suggest that this effect can be mitigated by introducing two critical elements into the new systems: (*a*) targeting the new public pillars toward low earners, because the majority of low earners are women, and (*b*) restricting payout provisions such as joint annuity requirements. With these modifications, total lifetime retirement benefits for women would reach 60–80 percent of those for men. For 'full-career' married women, they would equal or exceed benefits of men. The authors propose that low-earning women are the biggest gainers from the pension reform. For women who receive these transfers, female/male ratios of lifetime benefits in the new systems exceed those of the old systems. They also find that gender difference in lifetime benefits would fall substantially if women were to delay retirement until aged 65 years. Currently, the retirement age for women in Chile and Argentina is 60 years; in Mexico, 65 years.

Michelle Dion proposes some alternative interpretations to issues of gender inequality in her chapter. She notes that whether outcomes for women can be considered positive, negative, or neutral depends on whether publicly mandated pension systems are seen as insurance or redistribution. With these different perspectives come different criteria for evaluating gendered outcomes of pension privatization, which explains why assessments of gender effects differ. Her chapter begins with a brief overview of the sources of gender inequalities and discusses elements of pension policy that affect gender welfare. It then critiques the insurance-based criterion for evaluating the gender effects of pension reform that emphasizes lifetime benefits, actuarial fairness, or consumption outcomes. Dion offers an alternative set of criteria for evaluating gender outcomes based on three dimensions: women's ability to claim social citizenship rights, gender stratification, and the distribution of welfare responsibility among the market, the state, and the family. She concludes with a discussion of the ways in which pension privatization is likely to affect women's welfare in Latin America.

Part II: Country Studies

Part II of this volume comprises case studies. A common theme among these studies is that all pension systems face political risks because all schemes depend on effective governance. The political abuses in the old PAYGO systems, whereby pensions were often traded for political support, are well documented (e.g. Piñera 1991: 5). However, DC accounts also present political risks (see Barr 2002). 'Political risk' can be defined narrowly as the risk of ineffective governance with respect to pension funds, or more broadly as any government action (or inaction) that adversely affects the interests of pension fund account holders. For example, governments can fail to provide adequate supervision and regulation of funds, or they can initiate inflationary macroeconomic policies that erode the value of pension fund investments. More directly, governments can default on bonds that are a significant portion of pension fund investment portfolios, or they can seize pension fund assets in order to finance government spending. That pension funds remain subject to political risk and uncertainty should not come as much of a surprise, because the same governments that now regulate these funds have historically mismanaged their public PAYGO systems.

Political risk is ameliorated to the extent that governments act as the guarantors of the new private pension systems. If pension funds face a crisis, political pressure is likely to compel governments to provide some form of protection to pensioners or, as Nicholas Barr says, 'the larger the share of the population with private pensions and the greater the fraction of pension income deriving from private sources, the greater the pressure on government in the face of disaster' (2002: 20). The crisis in the Argentine system in 2001 exemplifies a worst-case scenario, when the government seized pension fund assets as a source of financing in a desperate (and ultimately unsuccessful) effort to stave off default and devaluation. In his chapter, Rafael Rofman suggests that the pension system in Argentina survived the worst of the crisis in relatively good condition and, although political risk is unavoidable, the extremes of the Argentine crisis have not been repeated elsewhere.

While the financial and actuarial conditions of the US and Canadian social security systems are not easily compared to the policy challenges of their Latin American neighbors, they still provide evidence of many universal lessons that pertain to pension reform, and are discussed in this part. These countries—indeed, countries throughout the hemisphere and beyond—confront the same issues of coverage, investment choice, fees, and transition costs.

Part II begins with reflections by John F. Cogan and Olivia S. Mitchell on the work of US President Bush's Commission on Social Security Reform. The commission endorsed a two-tiered approach, whereby a modified version of the traditional social security system would be augmented by prefunded private accounts intended to improve the program's overall transparency and equity. The commission's report was the culmination of a major initiative that, though it failed to gain political traction, constituted the most significant effort yet to reform the US Social Security System, and would have introduced private individual accounts.

For those familiar with the process of reform in Latin America, this account of the president's commission seems quite familiar. The commissioners were dealing with many of the same issues that policymakers in Latin America have been confronting since the 1990s. Like those in Latin America, the US policymakers were charged with keeping administrative costs low while still providing adequate service and suitable investment options. They had to take into account risk/reward tradeoffs and consider the long-term costs of instituting individual accounts. These issues of efficiency and equity remain vital in the region and throughout the world: from economic education to the institution of multiple funds, from gender equity to wage versus price indexing, the commission was treading the same path as that taken by policymakers in Latin America, suggesting that the challenges of social security reforms are in many ways universal.

In his chapter on Canada's 1997 pension reform, Robert Brown describes how a modest package of measures placed the system on a healthy foundation for at least the next seventy-five years. Canada stands in marked contrast to the other cases in that its reforms were parametric rather than structural, and they received widespread political support despite a steep rise in the contribution rates from 6 to 9.9 percent over a 6-year period. In addition, Canada's Pension Plan Investment Board, a government-created entity, has been investing pension funds in the financial markets since 1999. This model differs dramatically both from reform proposals in the USA, where centralized pension fund investment was rejected, and from the Latin American model, which is based on individual accounts. Canada's relatively harmonious political debate over reform and its strong commitment to the state-sponsored PAYGO model makes it unique in the hemisphere.

When Mexico's government instituted individual accounts in 1997, it more or less followed the Chilean model that inspired so many of the Latin American reforms. Reformers hoped that the new system would increase coverage by bringing more workers into the formal sector, provide greater incentives for individuals to save for retirement, and deepen capital markets. In their analysis, authors Tapen Sinha and Maria de los Angeles Yañez find that the system faces a number of challenges, including a reduction in the ratio of contributors relative to affiliates, high commission charges, and a likelihood that the government will have to support the old-age poor when lower-income individuals retire with insufficient funds in their accounts. On the other hand, they note, the government bond market has deepened, bringing more financial security to the pension system.

Within the context of Latin America, Brazil is an outlier. In their chapter, Milko Matijascic and Stephen J. Kay point out that while much of the rest of the region moved toward individual accounts, Brazil, like Canada, instead engaged in parametric reforms. Recently, the country introduced the *fator previdenciário*, a system akin to a notional DC system, whereby contributions and benefits are strictly linked but contributions do not go into individual-funded savings accounts. Although a few political leaders have favored private accounts (most notably ex-President Cardoso), individual accounts never received much political support, and the transition costs are considered potentially prohibitive, reaching as high as 201 percent of GDP (ECLAC 2006: 127). Structural reform is complicated by the fact that the social security system is codified in the 1988 constitution, which means that any structural reform requires going through the laborious and politically costly constitutional amendment process. Matijascic and Kay argue that administrative and legislative reforms that would make the system more efficient and equitable are possible even when support for constitutional reform is lacking.

Costa Rica's recent reforms differ from regional reforms in that they maintain continuity with the defined benefit (DB) system that began in the 1940s while also introducing a complementary DC second pillar. In her chapter, Juliana Martínez Franzoni describes this hybrid system that reflects both the continuity of a parametric reform and the structural reform of a system of individual accounts smaller in scale than in other Latin American countries. The 2005 reform improved the system's financial equilibrium (and averted near-term financial crisis) and introduced a more progressive PAYGO benefit. Martínez Franzoni describes how, on the political side, various stakeholders struggled to shape reform outcomes. As in the other countries in this study, reform in Costa Rica remains a work in progress.

Peru's reform introduced private savings accounts while maintaining a fiscally unsustainable public pillar that authors Eduardo Morón and Eliana Carranza say must eventually be fixed. The authors note a number of factors that led to slow acceptance of the new system, including the fact that workers had more incentive to remain in the old PAYGO system, which offered a lower contribution rate, a lower retirement age, and a minimum pension guarantee. However, eventual adjustments allowed the new system to compete more effectively for workers. The authors analyze how well the Peruvian system has performed with respect to investment, fees, competition, and coverage, and argue that reducing political interference is critical to its future success.

Rodolfo Saldain describes Uruguay's 1995 structural reform, which is based on a multipillar, or mixed, system, with contributions and benefits linked to both a state-managed PAYGO system and privately managed individual savings accounts. Since its implementation, the reform faced challenges arising from its design, turbulent financial markets, and difficulties with respect to political and social acceptance. Saldain notes that Uruguay is unique in its reserving a strong role for a state-owned institution administering private funds. He points to legal regulations that led to the homogenization of investment policies and the lack of appropriate investment instruments, which in turn contributed to a concentration of investment in instruments issued by the public sector. He also notes that the new pension system emerged in good condition from the country's worst financial crisis, which occurred in 2002. The system now faces renewed political challenges after the election of a political coalition that had opposed the creation of the new mixed system. However, the lack of a viable alternative to the 1995 reform suggests that current policies will be maintained, though it is likely that policymakers will make advisable and necessary adjustments.

Argentina instituted a major pension reform in 1994 following an extremely serious macroeconomic crisis. Partly inspired by Chile's experience, Argentina replaced its purely PAYGO system with a mixed model that incorporated elements of both public and private systems. Rafael Rofman suggests that the pension reform was actually a combination of four separate but interdependent reforms: parametric changes, which resulted in stricter requirements for receiving benefits, shifting from a DB formula tying benefits to previous earnings to a DC structure; re-introducing a funded scheme; and institutional changes that created both pension fund management firms and public supervisory agencies. His chapter includes a look at coverage rates as well as indirect economic effects, such as the impact on capital and labor markets, and a review of key policy challenges with respect to coverage, institutional design and efficiency, and system fragmentation. While these issues were exacerbated by the 2001–2 financial crisis, he notes that the pension funds have produced reasonable returns over time.

Conclusion: Looking for Lessons

Ultimately, the test of these pension reforms and their impact on poverty reduction among the aged will occur when these systems mature—which,

Fogel reminds us in his chapter, is occurring in the context of a global demographic transition. All the reforms centered on individual prefunded accounts were implemented relatively recently, beginning with Chile in 1981 and followed by several other countries in the 1990s. In the meantime, indicators like coverage rates, annual returns, and administrative and transition costs provide some perspective on how well these systems are performing with respect to efficiency and equity.

This collection illustrates the wide range of reforms in Latin America—indeed, throughout the hemisphere—and suggests some of the key lessons of pension reform. As Olivia Mitchell writes in the epilogue, political actors have often focused on the 'front end' of the reform so that accounts are set up and funds begin to accumulate, deferring to later, and sometimes neglecting, tax, health care, and capital market reforms. As this volume makes evident, it is important for governments to follow through with necessary complementary measures after the adoption of major pension reforms. Whether it is investment rules and capital market reforms in Mexico, administrative fee structures in Peru, or lax disability and survivorship rules in Brazil, reformers often failed to put adequate legal rules and regulatory frameworks in place to support reforms.

Clearly, pension reform is an ongoing project. Over its twenty-five-year-plus history, the Chilean pension system has been continually modified, as policymakers have changed investment rules and added worker choices, and is now moving toward a basic solidarity pension and improved gender equity. Furthermore, economies and labor markets evolve over time, requiring an effective response to changing conditions. For practical political reasons, political leaders will find it rational to pass reform measures piecemeal and to postpone the most politically costly measures, even if this approach can actually serve to undermine reforms. The critical question is whether policymakers will accept the challenge of continuing and deepening the reform process, with its many costs and obstacles, even after the initial 'front-end' reforms have been implemented.

In some instances, however, governments may choose to return to state-sponsored PAYGO systems at the expense of individual accounts. This process appears to be taking place in Argentina, where the legislature approved measures that would raise the benefit in the state-run system, allow workers to return to the public system from the private, place a ceiling on commission costs, and steer new workers who neglect to choose a pension fund into the public rather than private system. As Rofman notes in this volume, these measures could result in a smaller private pillar limited to providing complementary benefits to a relatively small percentage of upper- and middle-income workers.

In the Western hemisphere, it is apparent that policymakers are increasingly putting pension reform at the top of the agenda. First, we have seen movement toward retrenchment with respect to recent pension reforms after the election of administrations that opposed, or at the very least did not lend their support to, systems of individual accounts. As mentioned above, Argentina has moved to roll back some of its reforms, and a range of proposed measures to retrench individual accounts have surfaced elsewhere in the region, including Bolivia and Uruguay. Second, Chile, which pioneered individual accounts, is engaged in its most serious attempt yet to correct the perceived shortcomings in its system of individual accounts and to universalize coverage to incorporate the significant percentage of workers who fail to accumulate sufficient funds in their accounts. Just as governments turned to Chile for inspiration when developing their reforms in the first place, policymakers in the region will no doubt watch Chile's ongoing reform efforts closely. Finally, even amid the wide variation in the scope of pension reform in the region, the chapters in this book indicate that there is a wide range of policies and rules that affect pension adequacy, coverage, competition, costs, and minimum guarantees, where governments can learn lessons from their neighbors.

References

Arenas de Mesa, Alberto, David Bravo, Jere R. Behrman, Olivia S. Mitchell, and Petra E. Todd (2008). 'The Chilean Pension Reform Turns 25: Lessons from the Social Protection Survey', this volume.

Barr, Nicholas (2002). 'Reforming Pensions: Myths, Truths, and Policy Choices', *International Social Security Review*, 55(2): 3–36.

Beshears, John, James J. Choi, David Laibson, and Brigitte C. Madrian (2008). 'The Importance of Default Options for Retirement Saving Outcomes: Evidence from the USA', this volume.

Brown, Robert (2008). 'Reforms to Canadian Social Security, 1996–7', this volume.

Burkeman, Oliver (2005). 'Retirement—A Very Modern Notion', *The Guardian*, November 29, 2005.

Carranza, Eliana and Eduardo Morón (2008). 'The Peruvian Pension Reform: Ailing or Failing?', this volume.

Cogan, John J. F. and Olivia S. Mitchell (2008). 'Perspectives from the President's Commission on Social Security Reform', this volume.

Consejo Asesor Presidencial para la Reforma Previsional (2006). *El Derecho a una Vida Digna en la Vejez: Hacia un Contrato Social con la Previsión en Chile*. Santiago: Presidencia de la República de Chile.

Dion, Michelle (2008). 'Pension Reform and Gender Inequality', this volume.

Economic Commission for Latin America and the Caribbean (ECLAC) (2006). *Shaping the Future of Social Protection: Access, Finance, and Solidarity*. Santiago: ECLAC.

The Economist (2006). 'Women in the Workforce: The Importance of Sex', April 15, 2006.

Fogel, Robert W. (2008). 'Foreword: Toward an Era of Longevity and Wealth', this volume.

Gill, Indermit, Truman Packard, and Juan Yermo (2005). *Keeping the Promise of Social Security in Latin America.* Stanford, CA: Stanford University Press.

Holzmann, Robert and Richard Hinz (2005). *Old-Age Income Support in the Twenty-first Century: An International Perspective on Pension Systems and Reform.* Washington, DC: World Bank.

James, Estelle, Alejandra Cox Edwards, and Rebecca Wong (2008). 'The Gender Impact of Social Security Reform in Latin America', this volume.

—— Alejandra Cox Edwards, and Robert Holzmann (2008). 'Reflections on Pension Reform in the Americas: From "Averting the Old-Age Crisis" to "Keeping the Promise of Old-Age Security" and Beyond', this volume.

Lusardi, AnnaMaria and Olivia Mitchell (2007). 'Financial Literacy and Retirement Preparedness: Evidence and Implications for Financial Education Programs', *Social Science Research Network,* http://ssrn.com/abstract = 957796

Martínez Franzoni, Juliana (2008). 'Costa Rica's Pension Reform: A Decade of Negotiated Incremental Change', this volume.

Matijascic, Milko and Stephen J. Kay (2008). 'Pensions in Brazil: Reaching the Limits of Parametric Reform in Latin America', this volume.

Mitchell, Olivia S. (2008). 'Epilogue: The Future of Retirement Systems in the Americas', this volume.

Piñera, Jose (1991). *El cascabel al gato: La batalla por la reforma previsional.* Santiago: Editora Zig-Zag.

Rofman, Rafael (2008). 'The Pension System in Argentina', this volume.

Saldain, Rodolfo (2008). 'Uruguay: A Mixed Reform', this volume.

Sinha, Tapen and Maria de los Angeles Yañez (2008). 'A Decade of Government-Mandated Privately Run Pensions in Mexico: What Have We Learned?', this volume.

Weyland, Kurt (2008). 'Bounded Rationality in Latin American Pension Reform', this volume.

World Bank (WB) (1994). *Averting the Old-Age Crisis: Policies to Protect the Old and Promote Growth.* Washington, DC: World Bank.

—— Independent Evaluation Group (IEG) (2006). *Pension Reform and the Development of Pension Systems: An Evaluation of World Bank Assistance.* Washington, DC: World Bank.

Part I

System Design and Implications

Chapter 2

The Chilean Pension Reform Turns 25: Lessons from the Social Protection Survey

Alberto Arenas de Mesa, David Bravo, Jere R. Behrman, Olivia S. Mitchell, and Petra E. Todd, with assistance from Andres Otero, Jeremy Skog, Javiera Vasquez, and Viviana Velez-Grajales

Global aging trends pose bankruptcy threats to many conventional PAYGO social security systems around the world. Accordingly, analysts are looking with keen interest at Chile's funded individual-account DC pension plan, a system that was adopted in 1981 and remains in place after twenty-five years. Numerous other Latin-American countries followed Chile in embracing funded individual-account pensions, and the Chilean model has received substantial attention in the USA and other countries as well.[1] Commentators have showered the Chilean pension reform with both praise and criticism, and numerous studies have analyzed dimensions of the reform, including its impact on the macroeconomy, capital markets, and aggregate savings.[2] Despite the prominence of the Chilean approach to old-age security and continued debate about the pension system's impacts, however, there has been little attention to microeconomic aspects of the new retirement program. In part, this lack of research is attributable to the lack of longitudinal microeconomic data with which to conduct such analyses.

This chapter introduces the Encuesta de Previsión Social (EPS, or Social Protection Survey), a recently developed longitudinal survey of individual respondents that provides invaluable new information for microeconomic analyses of key aspects of the Chilean pension system, and illustrates some of the analyses possible with these data. Initiated in 2002, the EPS fielded a follow-up round in 2004; additional survey waves were scheduled for 2006 and every two years thereafter (funding permitting). In addition, the

Lead authors are listed alphabetically. The authors acknowledge research support from NIA grant AG023774-01; a grant from the Mellon Foundation to the Population Studies Center on Latin American demographic issues; awards from the Population Aging Research Center (PARC) of the University of Pennsylvania Population Studies Center, and the Boettner Center for Pensions and Retirement Security and Pension Research Council at the University of Pennsylvania. Opinions and errors are solely those of the authors and do not reflect views of the institutions supporting the research nor with whom the authors are affiliated.

research team has worked to link respondent records to a wide range of historical administrative files on contribution patterns, benefit payments, and other program features. Accordingly, the EPS represents a substantial advance for analysts interested in important micro questions related to the operation of the Chilean retirement system. To illustrate some of the richness of the new information available, this chapter discusses new analyses regarding three key policy questions:

1. Who participates in the Chilean retirement system, and what do lifetime contribution patterns look like?
2. What have people accumulated in the Chilean retirement system, and what benefits may be anticipated?
3. How financially knowledgeable are Chileans about their retirement system?

These three interlinked questions are of interest as they pertain to the central purpose of a retirement system: namely, to provide adequate resources for a secure retirement. The subject of pension coverage and who contributes to their pensions over their work lives is important in the Latin-American context as well as in many other nations where pension system nonparticipation is currently a topic of active debate (see, for instance, Gill, Packard, and Yermo 2005). Whether and how individual workers and their families participate in the system can only be studied with microdata of the sort we are developing. Anticipated retirement benefits from the system are also of key policy interest, as these will vary with lifetime contribution patterns as well as socioeconomic status, retirement ages, and other factors. In the Chilean context, it is also worth recognizing that the funded individual-account program is backstopped by safety net components to protect those who accumulate little in their personal accounts. Improved projections of future financing burdens will require detailed data on patterns of contributions and assets accumulated over the lifetime. Finally, learning more about workers' financial literacy regarding their pension system is of interest in the Chilean case, as lack of knowledge may possibly explain participation and other choices related to the system, as well as whether the system favors certain types of people over others—for example, those with more rather than less schooling.

To preview, the results show:

- Over their work lives, men self-report contributing to the pension system about half the time since aged 18 years, with lower levels for women. Thus, men in their 40s report contributing for a total of about 14 years since aged 18 years; women, about 10 years.

- Self-reports of payments into the new pension system indicate higher contribution levels than do administrative records for the same people over the same period. For instance, administrative records for men currently in their 40s indicate about 13 years of contribution since aged 18 years, and for women, about 6 years.
- Spells of noncontribution appear mainly to be periods when people held no jobs, were unemployed, or were self-employed (self-employed persons are not required to contribute to the system). In other words, contribution patterns during periods of work as employees (particularly in wage employment) are very high.
- Account balances reported by respondents who claim to know their accumulations in the AFPs (Administradoras de Fondos de Pensiones, or pension fund managers) are remarkably similar to those derived from administrative records, averaging around $3 million Chilean pesos (~US$5,600). However, only 40 percent of the respondents are able to provide an estimated balance—and administrative data for the entire sample suggests that those who offer estimates have larger accounts than respondents who cannot estimate their AFP assets.
- Retirement payments for those currently reaching retirement age also depend on recognition bonds (RBs) from the old PAYGO system. Those RBs are worth as much as the AFP system assets for respondents entitled to them. Accordingly, any analysis of retirement assets and eventual benefits must recognize both sources of retirement support.
- Knowledge of the new Chilean pension system is far from perfect. For instance, most workers cannot accurately report contribution requirements under the new system, how much they pay in commissions, what the rules are for minimum pensions, and how they have their funds invested. Lack of knowledge is concentrated among those employees with poorer backgrounds and less education and among women.
- Among retirees, knowledge is more satisfactory. Most people who are retired according to administrative records also self-report they are retired (84%). Some two-thirds of the retirees know what kind of pension they are receiving, and about 64 percent know the benefit amount (give or take 20%), though they tend to report smaller amounts than are indicated by the administrative data. In general, people who know their pension amounts also are those receiving larger benefits than the median.

Some of these findings appear to be matters of concern to the newly elected Chilean president, who confirms that pension reform is high on her policy agenda.

The Evolution of Chile's Retirement System[3]

Chile was among the pioneers of social security in Latin America, establishing its first national social insurance fund in 1924. The subsequent evolution of Chile's social security system had three stages. The first, between 1924 and the 1970s, was based on the Bismarckian model of occupationally segmented social insurance schemes. The second, from the 1970s to 1980, reflected the Beveridge plan's proposal for universal social security coverage. The hallmark of the third, which began in 1980, was the development of a funded system with privately managed individual accounts, supplemented with a social safety net, described below.

The Chilean Retirement System before 1980

The Chilean old-age system began in the 1920s. By the mid-1950s, three main pension funds (or *cajas*) provided benefits for most salaried workers, and two separate funds covered the police and armed forces. As time went on, other funds were created and the menu of regimes within the three main pension programs expanded. At the end of the 1970s, the retirement system included as many as 150 individual regimes and substantial institutional fragmentation, with 35 different funds (see Castañeda 1990). Consequently, coverage was stratified, was only moderately progressive, and threatened the nation with a rising fiscal burden. Several different governments tried unsuccessfully to reform the structure over the years, but their attempts were repeatedly blocked by powerful interest groups (Arellano 1985; Mesa-Lago 1994). Benefit eligibility varied across sectors and depended on a minimum number of work years in that sector. Retirement payouts were set according to DC formulas that granted higher payouts for more years of work and higher pay in that sector. Many workers were not covered by any retirement plan, and those who were faced very uncertain benefits due to the increasing insolvencies of the programs.

Issues Regarding Coverage

The core objective of an old-age system is to ensure an adequate income for retirees, with most modern systems also providing social insurance for disabled persons, surviving spouses, and orphans. Effectiveness in fulfilling these objectives, therefore, relies heavily on the system's ability to collect contributions or taxes when individuals are in the economically active population. Accordingly, assessing a pension system's success is at least partly measurable by inquiring what percentage of active workers pays into the program. Table 2-1 summarizes the fraction of the employed population

TABLE 2-1 Pension System Contribution Patterns: 1975–80

Year	*Contributors/Employment*			*Contributors/Labor Force*		
	AFP	*INP*	*Total*	*AFP*	*INP*	*Total*
1975	n/a	71.2%	71.2%	n/a	61.9%	61.9%
1980	n/a	53.3%	53.3%	n/a	47.8%	47.8%
1985	44.0%	12.8%	56.9%	38.8%	11.3%	50.1%
1990	50.6%	8.1%	58.7%	46.8%	7.5%	54.4%
1995	57.2%	5.5%	62.7%	53.5%	5.1%	58.6%
2000	59.4%	4.2%	63.6%	54.5%	3.9%	58.4%

Source: Derived from Arenas de Mesa, Behrman, and Bravo (2004).
Note: n/a = not applicable.

and the fraction of the labor force that has paid into the retirement system over time. The table shows that the highest ratio of contributors was seen in the mid-1970s, with a downward trend thereafter. When the new system was introduced in 1980, the fraction of workers and the overall labor force that contributed to the national pension fund (the Instituto de Normalización Provisional, or INP) fell precipitously, while the contribution rate to the AFP system rose steadily. Other authors report similar patterns over the period, although levels of coverage differ from one study to the next (Arellano 1985; Cheyre 1988).

The downward trend in effective coverage that began in the early 1970s can be accounted for in part by rising unemployment, since jobless workers have not been expected to pay into the system. But increasing unemployment was not the only reason, since coverage within occupations (among workers with jobs) also declined in the mid-1970s, falling from 86 to 71 percent over the period 1975–80 (Cheyre 1988) or from 71 to 53 percent (Arellano 1985). Some experts contend that much of the coverage declined during the 1970s was attributable to increased evasion (Cheyre 1988). Others emphasize the complex interaction of higher unemployment, greater incentives for evasion, and more precarious labor relations (Marcel and Arenas de Mesa 1992).

Financing the Old PAYGO System

Another measure of a retirement system's effectiveness has to do with its ability to provide benefits to those eligible to receive benefits. In Chile, the number of retirees and others eligible to receive benefits climbed from approximately 500,000 people in the late 1960s to more than 1 million people by the end of the 1970s, for an average annual growth rate during that decade of 5.7 percent (Arenas de Mesa 2000).

Before 1980, the system was for all intents and purposes a PAYGO system; returns on the few invested assets amounted to only 2.5 percent of the system's total annual revenues. As a result, the system's financial equilibrium depended on economic growth, since in a PAYGO program, economic growth, along with trends in the ratio of contributing members to noncontributing members, determines wage levels and hence revenues from contributions.

Assuming constant conditions in terms of replacement ratios and contribution rates, the contribution ratio is in turn determined by demographic factors such as the age composition of the population, economic factors such as unemployment, the relative size of the informal sector in the economy, evasion rates, regulatory and policy-related factors such as the established retirement age, and pension eligibility requirements for early retirement. In Chile, the ratio of contributing to noncontributing members had trended downward between 1965 and 1980, falling from 3.6 to 2 contributing members for every pensioner. At the time of the reform, government revenues averaging 2 percent of GDP per annum had already been required to finance the system (see Table 2-2). Further, it seemed clear that maintaining pension promises would have required further infusion of large amounts of government revenues to the old-age system.

The 1980 Chilean Pension Reform

Thus, Chile's pension system, like those of many other Latin-American countries that undertook reforms later, was institutionally fragmented, included a vast number of different regimes, and faced problems regarding finances, coverage, equity, and administrative efficiency (Arenas de Mesa 2000). Both the Frei and Allende administrations attempted to standardize

TABLE 2-2 Pre-1980 Old-Age System Revenues and Expenditures: 1974–80

Year	*Millions of 2003 pesos*			*% of GDP*		
	Revenues	*Expenditures*	*Deficit*	*Revenues*	*Expenditures*	*Deficit*
1974	344,523	698,866	−354,342	3	6.2	−3.1
1975	310,985	422,261	−111,276	3.4	4.6	−1.2
1976	360,509	662,877	−302,369	3.4	6.2	−2.8
1977	454,651	831,933	−377,282	3.6	6.7	−3
1978	556,642	1,027,681	−471,039	3.7	6.8	−3.1
1979	937,063	1,241,874	−304,811	5.2	6.9	−1.7
1980	1,017,362	1,336,172	−31,881	5.5	7.2	−1.7

Sources: Marcel and Arenas de Mesa (1992) and Central Bank of Chile (BCCH).

the pension regimes and do away with privileges enjoyed by limited groups, but both failed to achieve the necessary consensus.

Several years after the military government of General Pinochet took power, it launched a national retirement system reform. The first phase sought to stabilize the PAYGO system by raising retirement ages, increasing contribution rates, and eliminating some special schemes. Subsequently, the government moved in 1980 to reform the system dramatically by closing the old system to new workers and replacing it with a new system that placed at center stage a system of funded DC individual accounts. In addition, the government standardized eligibility and benefit requirements.

While many non-Chileans focus primarily on the individual-account element of the pension system, it must be recognized that the resulting structure is a 'three-pillar public/private' system, in the terminology of the World Bank (1994).

The *first pillar* has three key components:

1. A noncontributory public system provides welfare-based pensions (*pensiones asistenciales*, or PASIS) for the indigent. The system is means-tested and operated centrally for both the determination and payment of PASIS benefits.
2. A state-guaranteed minimum pension guarantee (MPG) for AFP participants who have twenty years of contributions. The purpose of the MPG—a key element of Chile's social protection policy—is to ensure that all eligible participants will receive a basic level of minimum old-age income. In practice, the federal government makes transfer payments to the AFP accounts of retirees who have insufficient balances to pay the minimum pension.
3. The public DC system, the old INP, that administers the old PAYGO DC program was closed to new entrants by the 1980 reform.[4]

The *second pillar* of the Chilean pension system consists of the mandatory contributory program known as the AFP system. This is a national savings program aimed at all wage and salary workers, intended to provide participants with old-age benefits. (It also provides life insurance and disability benefits as part of the mandatory program.) When the new program was announced, existing workers were required to decide whether to remain in the old INP system or to move to the new system. Those who moved to the new system received credit for INP contributions in the form of the transferable RB.[5] The new AFP system is mandatory for all new wage and salary workers joining the labor force as of 1981, but affiliation remains optional for self-employed workers.

Wage workers in the AFP system establish individual pension accounts by affiliating with one of the privately managed pension funds. By law, workers must contribute 10 percent of their monthly earnings, plus an additional contribution (currently 2–3% of monthly wages) to cover administrative costs as well as disability and survivor insurance.[6] Workers may only participate in one AFP at any given time, but they may periodically switch between AFPs with proper notice.[7] Initially, all AFP monies were invested in government bonds, though more recently pension fund managers have been permitted to offer a broader, albeit regulated, array of investment choices. They also offer a lifecycle investment strategy that automatically moves assets into more conservative investments as workers age. At retirement, retirees may use their accumulated funds, including the RBs, to purchase a lifetime income stream.[8]

Affiliates who have contributed for at least twenty years but who have accumulated funds insufficient to reach the MPG level are entitled to receive a government subsidy financed from general tax revenues.[9] Workers cannot receive their pensions until the legal retirement age (currently age 60 years for women and 65 years for men), but early retirement is allowed under some conditions.[10] Naturally, as with any DC plan, retiree benefits depend directly on AFP balances at retirement, and hence benefits are a function of workers' lifetime earnings, contribution histories, and AFP investment choices. For this reason, retirees' benefits depend more closely on individuals' risk preferences and behavior, whereas in a DC, or PAYGO, plan, solvency risks are more prominent.

The *third pillar* of the Chilean system, like the second, operates on the basis of individually funded DC accounts. However, in keeping with the World Bank model that gained in popularity during the 1990s, it is a voluntary program. Affiliates who wish to pay more than the mandated pension contribution may do so, and such contributions receive some tax benefits.

The new AFP system and the old PAYGO system differ in key ways. Most importantly, workers' AFP accumulations represent funded, individually owned accounts, over which affiliates have some investment and bequest decision-making power. By contrast, the PAYGO structure of the old Chilean system faced bankruptcy. In moving to the new plan, the hope was that workers would become more aware of the value of participating in the system, the size of their own accumulations, the opportunity to make investment choices, and the options regarding retirement payouts. Further, under the AFPs, workers would have a chance to save more than the 10 percent required contribution, which might be attractive to those who truly value access to funded individual investment-based accounts. Also, AFP savings and pension payouts are inflation-adjusted, addressing a well-known deficiency of the old PAYGO plan.[11] Finally, the fact that AFP affiliates are guaranteed a minimum wage-indexed retirement benefit—worth twice the welfare benefit—if they pay into the new system for twenty years was anticipated to draw more workers into formal sector jobs.

Transition Issues

More than twenty-five years of experience with the new reform finds the Chilean transition process in full swing. Both the old and the new systems continue, with the old one gradually winding down over time and the new one growing at a steady pace. Contributors to the old system will cease being active workers in about 2025, and retirement pensions will stop being paid in approximately 2050.[12]

It is interesting that the reform was intended to confine the government's role to that of pension system regulator, inspector, supervisor, and guarantor of the AFP system. In particular, via the Superintendencia de Administradoras de Fondos de Pensiones (SAFP, or Superintendency of Pension Fund Managers), the government is charged with regulating, inspecting, and supervising the management of the AFP system (SAFP 2002). In addition, the government plays a significant role in several key areas:

- Administration and payment of benefits under the old INP system;
- Administration, calculation, and payment of RBs for those who transferred to the AFPs;
- Administration and payment of pension benefits under the public plans for the armed forces and the police;
- Administration and payment of the MPG under the AFP system; and
- Administration of the PASIS system for indigents and those lacking pension coverage.

The first two of these governmental duties are time-limited, but the others are ongoing.

Furthermore, the government serves as the guarantor of last resort in the event of the bankruptcy or default of any AFP or insurance provider, as well as by ensuring that the yields for plan members remain above an established floor rate. Each of these responsibilities imposes an actual and potential financial burden on government coffers, the amount of which is an area of continuing research.

Economic Impacts of the Funded Individual Accounts

The accumulating pension funds have played a growing role in the Chilean economy since 1980. By 2003, the assets had grown to around 60 percent of GDP (see Table 2-3). The pension funds have acted as an engine of growth for various sectors of the economy and for the capital and life-insurance markets, among others. The AFPs, now the largest institutional investors

TABLE 2-3 Cumulative Value and Rates of Return on Chilean Pension Fund Assets: 1981–2003

Year	*Pension Fund Assets under Management*		*Returns on Fund Assets*
	Value[a]	*% of GDP*	*Average Yearly Real Return (%)*
1981	11,695	0.9	12.8
1982	44,495	3.7	28.5
1983	99,474	6.5	21.3
1984	159,576	8.4	3.6
1985	281,807	10.3	13.4
1986	433,377	12.7	12.3
1987	644,728	14.1	5.4
1988	885,875	14.7	6.5
1989	1,329,268	17.5	6.9
1990	2,244,481	23.3	15.6
1991	3,769,243	29.7	29.7
1992	4,736,462	29.4	3
1993	6,830,788	35.4	16.2
1994	8,983,563	38.8	18.2
1995	10,230,990	36.1	−2.5
1996	11,555,632	37	3.5
1997	13,405,826	38.6	4.7
1998	14,552,547	39.8	−1.1
1999	18,093,003	48.7	16.3
2000	20,343,371	50.1	4.4
2001	22,955,974	52.8	6.7
2002	25,227,058	54.4	3
2003	29,176,611	58.6	10.5
1981–91	—	—	14.2
1991–2003	—	—	8.7
1981–2003	—	—	10.4

Source: Arenas de Mesa (2005).
[a]Millions of current pesos.

in the financial market, finance five out of nine new mortgages (SAFP 2002).

Over time, the asset mix of these funds has changed considerably, becoming more diversified (see Table 2-4). In 1981, the bulk of these investments were in financial papers (71.3%) but in 1989, the share of such instruments began to shrink, falling to 26 percent by 2003. Meanwhile, the share of corporate bonds—that is, bonds issued by nonfinancial institutions—and equities expanded, rising to 7.7 and 14.5 percent (13.5% in business

TABLE 2-4 Distribution of Investment Portfolio: 1981–2003

Year	*Government*	*Financial Institutions*[a]	*Nonfinancial Institutions*[b]	*Equities*[c]	*Mutual Funds and Others*[d]	*Foreign Assets*[e]	*Other*[f]
1981	28.1	71.3	0.6	0	0	0	0
1985	42.4	56.0	1.1	0	0	0	0.5
1990	44.1	33.4	11.1	11.3	0	0	0.1
1995	39.4	22.4	5.2	30.1	2.6	0.2	0.1
2000	35.7	35.1	4.0	11.6	2.5	10.8	0.2
2003	24.7	26.3	7.7	14.5	2.9	23.8	0.1

Source: Derived from Arenas de Mesa (2005).
Note: Totals should sum to 100% except for rounding error.
[a]Financial sector less the equities of financial institutions.
[b]Business firms less equities and quotas of investment funds.
[c]Stocks of financial institutions plus those of the business sector.
[d]Investment funds of the business firms plus others from the external sector.
[e]Foreign issuers less others from the external sector.
[f]Disposable assets.

enterprises and 1% in financial institutions), respectively, by 2003—about 13 percent of GDP. Investment in foreign assets began in 1993, three years after the law creating this option was passed. In that year, such investments amounted to 0.6 percent of the funds' total value; by 2003, their share had grown to 23.8 percent. These changes in AFP portfolios have been made possible by the growth of the pension funds, the development of the capital market, and the relaxing of regulations that place limits on investments (SAFP 2002).

The Social Protection Survey and Linked Administrative Data

In 2002, the Micro-data Center of the Department of Economics of the Universidad de Chile under the directorship of David Bravo conducted a new household survey, called the Encuesta de Previsión Social (EPS), or the Social Protection Survey. This survey has been an invaluable research tool, providing researchers much useful new individual-level information—information that previously was unavailable—for addressing numerous research questions, including the main issues of this chapter.[13] The interview sample was drawn from a sampling frame of approximately 8.1 million current and former affiliates of the Chilean old-age systems compiled from official databases obtained from the Chilean Ministry of Labor and Social Security. The frame included about three-quarters of the population aged 15+ in 2001. The survey, fielded between April and December 2002, collected data from individuals who were working, unemployed, out of the labor force, receiving pensions, or deceased (in which case information was collected from surviving relatives).

The 2002 EPS survey included sociodemographic information and current labor market data for each member of the household, detailed information about receipt of pensions and types of pension plan participation, and retrospective labor market history going back to 1980. Ultimately, the survey contains data on 17,246 individuals (937 of them were reports by surviving relatives) affiliated with the old or the new retirement system for at least 1 month at any time during 1981–2001.[14]

In 2004 surveyors administered another round of the survey, which included a second wave for previously surveyed respondents as well as new surveys for a subsample of individuals not affiliated with the social security system (individuals never employed in the formal sector) and a subsample of new entrants into the AFP system between 2002 and 2004. The survey, in addition, introduced a host of new health and wealth questions.[15] Consequently, the 2004 survey is representative of the entire Chilean population.[16] Furthermore, the research project received permission to merge responses with administrative records on pension contributions and earnings in the PAYGO and AFP systems since 1980; data on the amounts of RBs; and monthly data on account changes in the individual investment accounts, switches between AFPs, AFP commissions charged, and investment returns earned on all AFP accounts. The survey data has also been merged with monthly social security records available since 1981.[17] In what follows, we provide details about the specific variables central for each analysis.

Informing the Policy Debate Using the Social Protection Survey

As noted, the 2002 and 2004 surveys, linked to administrative records, provide the essential database for answering the critical micro questions about the current Chilean pension system posed in the introduction of this chapter. Next we turn to the evidence.

Contribution Patterns under the Chilean Retirement System

This section characterizes retirement system contributions made by EPS respondents. The information used to track contributions is derived from two sources. First, EPS interviewees were asked about their employment and old-age system work histories and contribution patterns from 1980 onward. Specifically, Module II of the 2002 EPS survey asks, for each job held since aged 15 years, whether the respondent contributed to some retirement system and, if so, which system. Second, it asks respondents to report earnings, hours of work, labor force status, occupation, and industry for each job. We use this survey information to derive the respondents' self-reported months of contribution over time. This information may be further classified according to each respondent's labor market status at the time, which we identify as working, unemployed, or not in the labor force. To derive the self-reported months of contributions to various retirement systems, we first turn to the labor history section of the 2002 EPS. Here we count only months of contributions reported for respondents between the ages of 18 years and 60 years, inasmuch as there is little formal work prior to age 18 years, and some individuals, particularly women, retire at age 60 years.

The results of this tabulation may be seen in Table 2-5. Panel A contains both self-reports and administrative records on months of contributions to the AFP system, for those for whom we have both sets of records.[18] Panel B indicates total months of contributions to all retirement systems, including the old INP as well as the AFP programs. In the self-reports on AFP contributions, men report more months of AFP contributions, on average, than do women. This finding is not surprising, given that many Chilean women leave the paid labor force for childrearing. Also clear is the rising pattern of contributions by age, such that workers in their late 20s report 64 months of contributions to the AFP system (5.3 years on average) since 1981, while workers in their 50s report more than double this level (14.1 years). It is worth recalling that workers older than 39 years in 2002 would have been exposed to the old INP system prior to the 1980 reform and hence are likely to have had periods of contributions under the old system as well (more on this below).[19] Somewhat surprising is the result that months of contributions do not vary much by education, at least for the self-reported tallies.

The second column in Panel A of Table 2-5 indicates mean months of contributions to the AFP system derived from administrative records over the same calendar period, while the third column displays the ratio of self-reported months to administrative data.[20] Overall, self-reported contribution months exceed the administrative data counts by 20 percent, no doubt in part due to recall error.[21] Those in the 30–50 age range seem to be most optimistic regarding their self-reported months of contribution, with lesser differences for younger and older individuals. The third column shows that men are less likely to over-report than women, compared to administrative records; younger workers less than middle-aged workers; and educated workers less than the lesser-educated. Figure 2-1 plots the months of contribution patterns and differences by more detailed age groups, for the AFP system alone and for (self-reports of) contributions to all

Table 2-5 Contribution Patterns to the Chilean Retirement System by Sex, Age, and Education: Number of Months Contributed by EPS 2002 Respondents

	Mean Self-Report	*Mean Admin*	*Ratio Self/Admin*	*N*
A. Respondents with Linked Records: Months of AFP Contributions Only				
Total	113	90	126%	12,108
By sex				
Men	129	103	125%	6,722
Women	94	73	127%	5,386
By age				
18–20	12	13	97%	208
21–5	32	27	117%	1,252
26–30	64	51	123%	2,013
31–8	107	84	128%	3,190
39–45	150	114	131%	2,571
45–50	161	129	125%	1,257
51–5	170	141	121%	964
56–60	169	141	120%	653
By education				
<Elem	114	82	139%	2,064
<HS	112	83	135%	3,267
HS	110	88	126%	3,725
>HS	117	103	113%	3,052

	*Mean Self-Report**	*N*	*Mean Self-Report***	*N*
B. All Respondents: Months of Contributions to All Retirement Systems				
Total	121	12,128	120	13,397
By sex				
Men	137	6,728	136	7,330
Women	101	5,400	100	6,067
By age				
18–20	12	213	11	245
21–5	33	1,255	33	1,319
26–30	66	2,016	65	2,057
31–8	112	3,193	111	3,271
39–45	161	2,575	156	2,781
45–50	176	1,259	169	1,459
51–5	185	964	174	1,251
56–60	184	653	166	1,014
By education				
<Elem	126	2,065	122	2,629
<HS	120	3,276	118	3,625
HS	117	3,733	117	3,938
>HS	122	3,054	122	3,205

Source: Authors' computations from the EPS 2002 and administrative records linked with EPS respondents.

Notes: EPS respondents in 2002 aged 18–60; all results weighted. * = Respondents with a linked administrative record; ** = All EPS 02 respondents. Number of months of contributions counted from the date of the first self-reported contribution to AFP system.

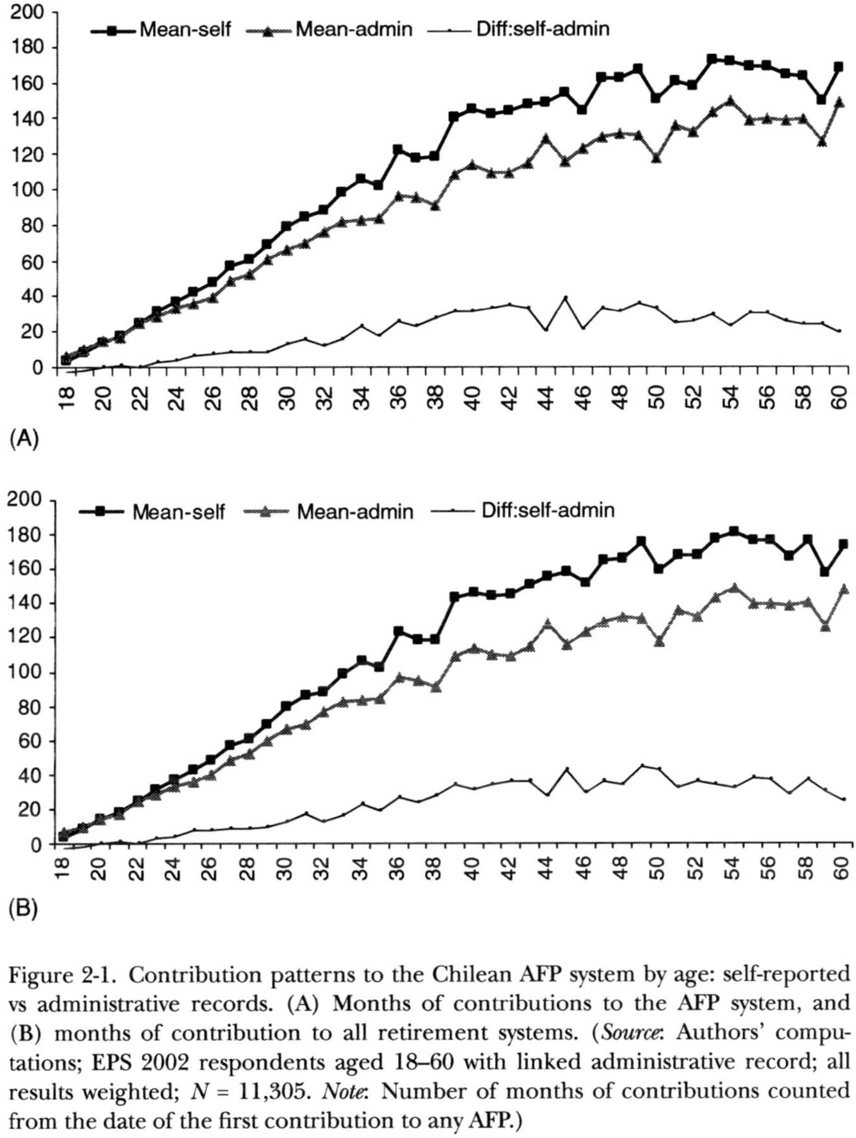

Figure 2-1. Contribution patterns to the Chilean AFP system by age: self-reported vs administrative records. (A) Months of contributions to the AFP system, and (B) months of contribution to all retirement systems. (*Source*: Authors' computations; EPS 2002 respondents aged 18–60 with linked administrative record; all results weighted; N = 11,305. *Note*: Number of months of contributions counted from the date of the first contribution to any AFP.)

retirement systems. Overall, the patterns appear similar to those depicted in Table 2-5.

For purposes of comparison, Panel B of Table 2-5 provides self-reported months of contribution data for all retirement systems, including the old INP, various public sector *cajas*, and the new AFP system. The first two

TABLE 2-6 Pattern of Contribution Months to All Retirement Systems by Sex, Age, and Education: Labor Market Status at Time of Contribution

	Mos. While Working	*Mos. While Unemployed*	*Mos. While NILF*	*N*	*% of Mos. Contributing in that LF Status*			
					Working	*Unempl.*	*NILF*	*Wage wrkr*
By sex								
Men	135	0.5	0.7	7,330	78.72	5.44	3.67	89.30
Women	97	0.6	2.2	6,067	81.86	4.00	2.92	90.56
By age								
18–20	10	0.1	0.3	245	80.92	1.95	3.86	81.69
21–5	32	0.2	0.4	1,319	82.26	2.79	1.91	86.31
26–30	65	0.2	0.6	2,057	80.89	2.48	1.47	86.87
31–8	110	0.4	1.2	3,271	77.89	3.28	2.40	87.63
39–45	154	0.6	1.4	2,781	79.32	4.68	3.24	89.93
45–50	166	1.0	2.1	1,459	79.87	11.04	5.98	91.65
51–5	171	1.2	1.6	1,251	82.03	7.56	4.55	93.30
56–60	161	0.8	4.1	1,014	82.73	4.70	7.39	93.54
By education								
<Elem	119	1.0	1.8	2,629	71.34	5.49	2.41	85.29
<HS	116	0.6	1.4	3,625	76.07	4.59	3.59	88.22
HS	116	0.4	1.2	3,938	84.09	4.30	3.31	91.29
>HS	121	0.3	1.4	3,205	85.96	4.27	2.92	92.26

Source: Authors' computations from the EPS 2002 and administrative linked data.
Notes: EPS respondents in 2002 aged 18–60; all results weighted. NILF = not in labor force. Number of months of contributions counted from the date of the first self-reported contribution to the AFP system.

columns focus on respondents with linked records only, while the third column focuses on all EPS 2002 respondents, whether they had linked records. Not surprisingly, overall patterns are similar to those previously described by age, sex, and education. One difference is that self-reported months of contributions to all systems are higher than those to the AFP system alone, mainly due to the fact that older (age 40+) workers report more contribution months. This is probably accurate, inasmuch as the older workers could have been contributors to the old INP system and we lack accurate contribution history data from that system.

Table 2-6 breaks down the pattern of workers' months of contributions in the retirement system by labor market categories—specifically, working, unemployed, and not in the labor force. The data reveal that the majority of contribution months coincides precisely with those months when respondents were working, particularly in the wage labor force. Contribution patterns (particularly wage employment) are very high during periods of work. Put differently, lapses in contributions appear associated mainly with periods of nonemployment rather than outright nonpayment of retirement contributions during employed periods. This finding suggests that analysts concerned with low levels of retirement accumulations would do well to focus on non- or unemployment. Furthermore, contribution months are very high for periods of wage work, in the 80–90 percentile range, which implies that the problems of low contribution months are not concentrated among the self-employed. Although self-employed persons are not required to contribute to the system, this does not seem to be a major source of nonpayment.

Retirement Accumulations in the Chilean Retirement System

Previous research has focused on whether workers are contributing enough to the Chilean retirement system to obtain adequate benefit levels in retirement. As a result, analysts have based projected replacement ratios for AFP participants on the assumption that workers would contribute 70–90 percent of their work lives (cf. Arenas de Mesa and Gana 2003). The replacement rate is defined here as the percentage of the worker's last pay divided by his or her monthly pension (assuming the partnered retiree takes a joint-and-survivor benefit). However, in a more recent study, Arenas de Mesa, Llanés, and Bravo (2005) recomputed projected replacement ratios using the self-reports of contribution patterns taken from the 2002 EPS. These new findings are important, as they rely on actual patterns of contributions reported over workers' lifetimes rather than on assumed contribution patterns on average. In addition, the findings provide evidence at the individual worker level, allowing the projection of patterns by earnings, sex, and age. The above-mentioned studies project likely AFP balances at retirement as well as replacement rates implied by these projections for a male age-65 retiree with female partner 5 years younger, and a lifetime contribution pattern of 80 percent of the work life (also known as 'density of contributions'), or 60 percent; and a female age-60 retiree with a density of contributions of 80 percent, or 43 percent.[22] A man at age 65 years who has contributed 80 percent of his work life would be expected to accumulate an AFP balance of $37 million, which Arenas de Mesa and Gana (2003) expect would finance a joint-and-survivor annuity amounting to about 60 percent of pre-retirement pay. A single woman who retires earlier after the same contribution pattern would accumulate an AFP balance of $29 million, which implies a replacement ratio of 43 percent. However, having lower lifetime contributions reduces projections substantially. For instance, if men contribute only 60 percent of the time and women, 43 percent, estimated AFP balances would be lower by 25–46 percent, and the pension annuity would drop from 60 to 44 percent for men, and from 43 to 23 percent for women (see Figures 2-2 and 2-3).

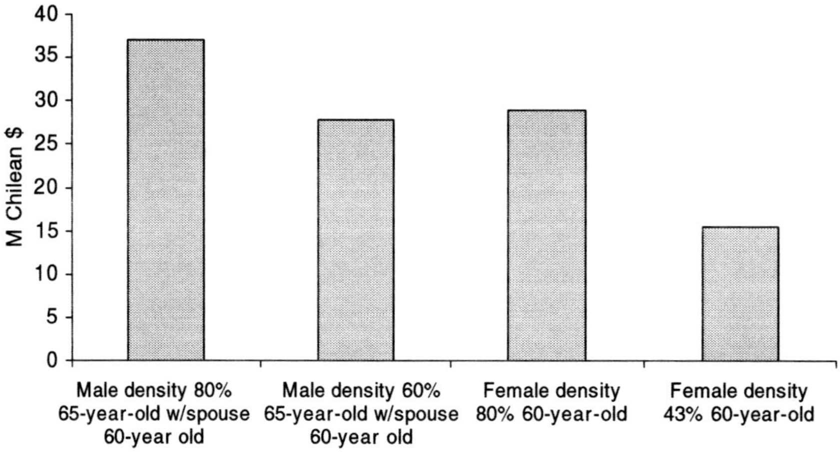

Figure 2-2. Projected accumulations in AFP accounts at retirement age given alternative density of contribution assumptions (*Source*: Arenas de Mesa, Behrman, and Bravo 2004).

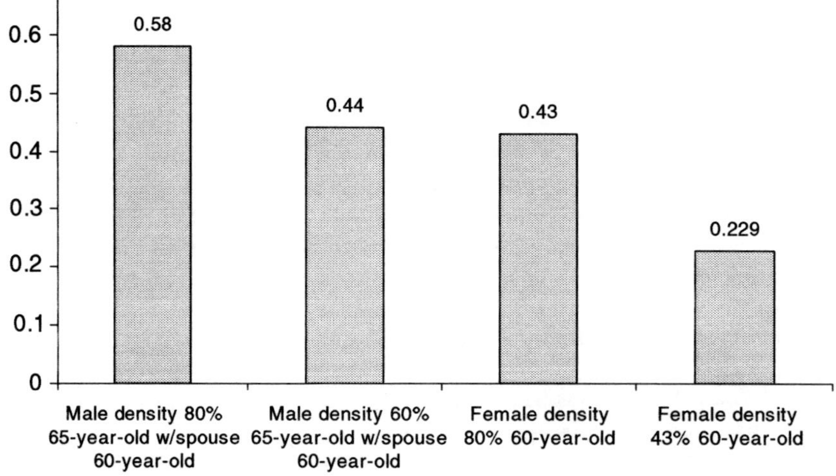

Figure 2-3. Projected replacement rates under alternative density of contribution assumptions (*Source*: Arenas de Mesa, Behrman, and Bravo 2004).

This chapter does not include new projections of accumulations and replacement rates using the administrative data, though that is the goal of future work. However, the information presented in this chapter informs that analysis by reporting on retirement system assets accumulated by participants to date. Panel A of Table 2-7, for instance, shows that AFP account balances reported by respondents who state that they know their accumulations are accurately measured compared to AFP balances from administrative records, with the median at around $3 million Chilean pesos (~US$5,600). On the other hand, only 40 percent of the EPS respondents could provide an estimated AFP balance, which might imply that these individuals are likely to have more assets than those unable to provide an estimate. Indeed, over the entire EPS sample, the median respondent offering a balance estimate appears to have four times the accumulation compared to the median respondent unable to estimate his or her AFP assets, according to administrative records. Across the entire sample, the median AFP accumulation derived from administrative records totals about $1.5 million Chilean pesos (or about US$2,800).

Retirement payments for those currently reaching retirement age also depend on RBs from the old PAYGO system. Panel B of Table 2-7 shows that these RBs are worth as much as the AFP system assets for respondents entitled to them, with the median account worth about $4 million Chilean pesos (about US$8,000). Clearly, analyses of projected retirement benefits under the Chilean retirement system must recognize both sources of retirement support. Panel C indicates that AFP accruals for those without an RB are lower, in part because individuals in this group are much younger than those who accumulated substantial benefits under the system that was closed to new entrants in 1980.

Financial Literacy Regarding the Chilean Pension System

What workers know about their old-age benefit system can have a major impact on how effectively they prepare for retirement and how they determine their retirement plans. For example, if people believe their benefits rise with deferred retirement, they may be more likely to respond to incentives to continue work. On the other hand, if they systematically misperceive the costs and benefits of the system, then their misinformation (e.g. about the number of years required for eligibility) can shape the system's popularity as well as the perceived effectiveness of specific reforms. Yet very little is known about how people develop the necessary level of financial literacy to understand their pension systems, particularly when workers have personal DC pension accounts. Studies based on the United States' experience suggest that many workers arrive at retirement with little knowledge of

TABLE 2-7 Retirement Balances Accumulated under the AFP and RBs: Self-Report vs Administrative Records

Percentile	*For Those with a Self-Reported AFP Balance (N = 4,677)*				*Does Not Know (N = 7,686)*	*Total (N = 12,363)*
	Self-Report Amt	*Admin. Amt*	*Diff.*	*Percentage*	*Admin. Amt*	*Admin. Amt*
A. Individual Account Balances, AFP System: Self-Report vs Administrative Records (2004 Chilean Pesos)						
p25	820,000	906,000	−86,000	−10	125,443	324,300
p50	3,000,000	2,929,800	70,200	2	738,300	1,531,100
p75	8,000,000	7,087,800	912,200	11	2,549,900	4,574,200
Percentile	*AFP Balance*	*Bond*	*Total*			
B. Individual Account Balances Plus RBs: Administrative Records Only (2004 Chilean Pesos; N = 2,458)						
p25	86,800	748,857	5,800,972			
p50	4,263,400	4,491,373	12,700,000			
p75	10,700,000	13,000,000	23,800,000			
Percentile	*AFP balance*					
C. Individual Account Balances for Those with No RBs: Administrative Records Only (2004 Chilean Pesos; N = 9,905)						
p25	341,700					
p50	1,293,000					
p75	3,561,700					

Source: Authors' computations from the EPS 2002 and administrative linked data.
Notes: EPS respondents in 2002 aged 18–60; all results weighted.

their retirement system. (See, for instance, Mitchell 1988; Gustman and Steinmeier 1999; Lusardi and Mitchell 2006.) As a result, they often fail to plan well for their retirement and may be ineffective advocates for retirement system changes. Little is known about whether similar problems arise for workers in a national DC system. As they bear greater responsibility for their own retirement and pension options through personal accounts, workers may be better informed about retirement risks and rewards.

This section investigates to what extent Chilean workers understand and make sense of the pension institutions covering the workforce. We posit that those better informed about their pensions are more likely to make sensible provisions for old age, possibly by contributing more, paying more attention to plan investments, and making appropriate payout options. Accordingly, we investigate the factors associated with being informed about the pension system's characteristics, focusing on, for example, the association with age, schooling, occupation, sex, birth cohort, and socio-economic class. Answers to these questions are important for understanding how people perceive their pension system and whether they value the future benefits it will provide. This issue was important in the recent national elections in Chile and is a key source of discussion throughout all the Latin-American nations that have moved toward systems similar to Chile's (Gill, Packard, and Yermo 2005). The results of the EPS help identify which workers can most efficiently understand and maneuver under such plans, how the plans might be made more effective, and what the distributional implications of such plans are.

Table 2-8 summarizes the results on knowledge of key aspects of the Chilean pension system. Across the top of the chart are the data source, sample, and number of included observations in each cell. Columns (b) and (c) refer, respectively, to the responses for the 2002 survey, first for the entire 2002 sample, and second for affiliates. Column (d) refers to all EPS interviewees in 2004, while columns (e)–(g) break the total down into the panel subset, new entrants (affiliates) to the pension system, and nonaffiliates.

Row A in Table 2-8 reports respondents' answers to whether they received a statement from the AFP system (the quarterly cartola, which reports past contributions and projects future benefit amounts). It must be noted that the questions differed slightly across the two years: 2002 respondents were asked whether they had received their AFP quarterly report, whereas 2004 respondents were asked whether they had received an AFP cartola in the past twelve months. In either case, the results are comparable. In 2002 60 percent of respondents said they received the statement, whereas in 2004 the fraction was 69 percent, with a similar change for the subset of panel members. Three-quarters of new affiliates, who are likely to be younger than the average respondent, affirmed they received it.

TABLE 2-8 Knowledge of Chilean Pension System Attributes

Variable[a]	*2002 Survey*				*2004 Survey*							
	All Respondents[b]		*2002 Affiliates*		*All Respondents*		*2002 Affiliates*		*2004 New Affiliates*		*2004 Nonaffiliates*	
	%	*n*	%	*n*	%	*n*	%	*n*	%	*n*	%	*n*
A. Receipt of AFP statement												
1.1. Receives AFP statement	60.7	12,367	60.6	5,942	—	—	—	—	—	—	—	—
1.2. Received AFP statement past 12 mos	—	—	—	—	69.2	10,131	68.8	9,324	74.3	807	—	—
B. Knowledge regarding contributions												
1. Claims knows AFP amt contrib.	52.2	13,397	51.5	10,659	38.0	13,711	46.2	10,009	39.9	828	8.8	2874
2. Gave correct amt AFP contrib.	28.0	13,397	27.0	10,659	30.9	13,711	34.3	10,009	34.9	828	17.8	2874
C. Knowledge regarding prices (commissions)												
1. Claims knows fixed AFP commiss	1.5	12,367	1.5	9,805	1.7	10,131	1.7	9,324	1.5	807	—	—
2. Claims knows var AFP commiss	2.7	12,367	2.5	9,805	2.1	10,131	2.1	9,324	1.7	807	—	—
3. Claims knows both commissions	0.6	12,367	0.5	9,805	0.5	10,131	0.5	9,324	0.5	807	—	—
D. Knowledge regarding accumulations												
1. Claims knows AFP accum.	44.9	12,367	45.5	9,805	52.7	10,131	53.7	9,324	42.1	807	—	
2. Gave correct amt AFP accum. (±20%)	—	—	—	—	21.6	10,124	—	—	—	—	—	—
E. Knowledge regarding investments												
1. Knows how pension funds are invested (only 2002)	10.3	12,367	9.9	9,805	—	—	—	—	—	—	—	—
2.1. Knows about multifunds	—	—	—	—	47.4	10,131	47.5	9,324	46.8	807	—	—
2.2. Knows how many are the multifunds	—	—	—	—	32.8	10,131	33.1	9,324	30.3	807	—	—

2.3. Knows correctly number of multifunds	—	—	—	—	20.2	10,131	20.2	9,324	20.4	807	—	—
2.4. Knows his/her type of fund	—	—	—	—	32.8	10,131	33.1	9,324	28.9	807	—	—
2.5. Knows correctly his/her type of fund	—	—	—	—	15.8	10,131	16.1	9,324	13.0	807	—	—
2.6. Knows the riskier fund	—	—	—	—	38.1	10,131	38.8	9,324	30.0	807	—	—
F.1. AFP system												
1.1. Knows female legal retirement age	83.2	13,397	82.8	10,659	76.5	13,711	79.0	10,009	73.3	828	68.5	2,874
1.2. Knows male legal retirement age	86.1	13,397	85.9	10,659	80.0	13,711	82.7	10,009	77.0	828	71.4	2,874
1.3. Knows how AFP calculates pensions	14.2	12,367	13.8	9,805	9.3	13,711	11.1	10,009	8.3	828	3.5	2,874
1.4a. Claims spouse gets survivor pension benefit[a]	66.4	13,397	66.7	10,659	65.2	9,755	64.1	7,319	61.0	384	69.8	2,052
1.4b. Claims spouse gets survivor pension benefit[b]	69.3	9,931	69.6	7,910	66.1	9,037	64.9	6,818	62.6	287	71.1	1,932
1.5a. Claims kids get survivor pension benefit	61.4	13,397	60.9	10,659	32.8	11,061	40.7	8,272	30.5	444	5.3	2,344
1.5b. Claims kids get survivor pension benefit[b]	61.4	13,397	60.9	10,659	33.3	10,599	41.3	7,944	33.0	387	5.1	2,268
F.2. Guaranteed benefits												
2.1. Claims knows reqs for min pen	22.2	13,397	22.5	10,659	31.1	13,711	34.3	10,009	19.8	828	23.2	2,874
2.2. Knows reqs for min pen	0.2	13,397	0.2	10,659	0.2	13,711	0.2	10,009	0.1	828	0.2	2,874
2.3a Knows there is minimum pension	—	—	—	—	44.9	13,711	49.0	10,009	38.1	828	32.9	2,874
2.3b Claims knows min pension amt	20.3	13,397	21.0	10,659	32.8	13,711	36.0	10,009	25.9	828	23.9	2,874
2.4. Gave correct value min pension amt	4.9	13,397	5.1	10,659	3.4	13,711	3.7	10,009	2.5	828	2.6	2,874

(*cont.*)

TABLE 2-8 (*Continued*)

Variable[a]	*2002 Survey*				*2004 Survey*							
	All Respondents[b]		*2002 Affiliates*		*All Respondents*		*2002 Affiliates*		*2004 New Affiliates*		*2004 Nonaffiliates*	
	%	*n*	%	*n*	%	*n*	%	*n*	%	*n*	%	*n*
F.3. Welfare benefits												
3.1. Claims knows reqs for welfare pension	19.3	13,397	20.3	10,659	19.6	13,711	20.5	10,009	12.3	828	18.4	2,874
3.2. Gave correct reqs for welfare pension	2.7	13,397	2.7	10,659	3.8	13,711	4.0	10,009	1.4	828	3.9	2,874
3.3. Claims knows welfare pension amt	17.0	13,397	18.0	10,659	17.5	13,667	17.8	9,972	10.4	828	18.6	2,868
3.4. Gave correct amt welfare pension	11.2	13,397	11.9	10,659	11.9	13,667	11.5	9,972	6.9	828	14.6	2,868

Source: Authors' calculations from respondents to SPS 2002 and 2004 surveys.
Notes: Affiliation status comes from administrative data. Sample is restricted to population aged 18–60 (ages in year 2002). N = refers to the number of people who were asked the question.
[a]2002 and 2004 surveys have different questions, making F1.4 and F1.5 not comparable.
[b]F1.4b and F1.5b apply to more comparable subsets of people among 2002 and 2004 surveys.

Whether the effort to provide pension information translates into useful knowledge about the pension system is quite another matter. Row B.1 of Table 2-8 shows whether respondents knew the contribution (or payroll tax) rates required for AFP accounts. Row B.2 then indicates whether the responses are correct. In 2002 slightly more than half (53%) of the respondents claimed that they knew the payroll tax rate, but just over one-quarter (28%) were correct. In 2004 fewer of the panel members (46%) claimed to know the rate, though more (34%) got the tax rate correct. Not surprisingly, new affiliates are less well informed, and nonaffiliates know little to nothing about required contributions.

Another topic of recent policy interest has to do with the commissions charged by the AFPs. If AFP participants pay little attention to investment costs, it is likely that AFPs will not need to compete among themselves to drive down prices and enhance service (Berstein and Ruiz n.d.; Valdés Prieto 2005). The results from the EPS analysis show, in Row C, that fewer than 2 percent of the respondents (panel members as well as new affiliates) know either the fixed or variable commissions in either year. Only half of 1 percent of all respondents claim to know both the fixed and variable commissions. The fact that workers and savers know virtually nothing about the costs of investing their funds suggests that there is much work to be done to educate Chileans about this key aspect of their retirement system.

Financial information regarding amounts accumulated in workers' retirement accounts, and how the funds are invested, is reported in rows D and E. Line D.1 indicates that 45 percent in the 2002 survey claimed to know their AFP balances, with the fraction thus knowledgeable rising to over 50 percent 2 years later. Among panel members interviewed in both waves, 20 percent had more information in the second period than in the first. It is also of interest that new affiliates are relatively well informed, with 42 percent saying they knew their balances. Line D.2 indicates how accurately respondents in 2004 reported their AFP balances compared to administrative records. Estimated balances are within 20 percent of administrative amounts for 21 percent of the sample. Overall, it would appear that Chilean AFP participants are about as informed as their US counterparts in corporate pensions. For instance, Gustman and Steinmeier (1999) find that US workers tend to understate their DC assets by about 30 percent, at the median, as compared to administrative records, and by half in the middle and upper tiers. Furthermore, the low fraction of those who can offer accumulation estimates suggests that many workers are not well apprised of a key retirement asset.

For the first two decades of life of the Chilean AFP system, affiliates could decide only which AFP they wanted to invest with but could not diversify their holdings across AFPs, nor could they choose asset allocations. In 2000 the government permitted the AFPs to open a more conservative account for retirees or those within ten years of legal retirement. In 2002 each fund administrator was permitted to expand the number of investment offerings from two to five to allow participants to diversify their asset allocations. Under this new 'multifund' structure, each AFP must offer a so-called Fund A, which invests 80 percent of the portfolio in equities; Fund E, which holds 100 percent fixed income; and Funds B–D, which hold intermediate fractions of equities. Workers may elect to hold up to two funds in a single AFP at a time.

What Chileans indicate that they know about their pension investments is summarized in Section E of Table 2-8. Line 1 shows that respondents in 2002 did not know much about their pension investments (10% claimed to know), but this finding is not surprising given that affiliates had not yet been granted access to a variety of fund choices. By 2004 almost half of the respondents claimed that they knew about the multifund setup, though only one-third said they knew the number of funds, and only about one-fifth could give the correct number of total funds. Further, in 2004, only one-third of respondents said they knew which funds they held, but only 16 percent were accurate and only 38 percent were aware of which fund was the riskiest.

Regarding retirement system payouts, Section F of Table 2-8 breaks the results into three topic areas. The first part summarizes what people know regarding the AFP system payouts. The second part reviews what individuals know about the MPG. The third part illustrates what people know about the minimum welfare benefits, or PASIS.

Several key questions arise regarding the rules pertaining to eligibility and access to benefits. For instance, the legal minimum retirement age refers to the age at which eligible retirees may claim benefits. In 2002 knowledge about the legal retirement age for men and women appeared widespread—roughly 83–86 percent accurately reported these ages (lines F1.1–1.2). By 2004 the percentages fell a bit, mainly due to the inclusion of nonaffiliates in the overall sample, though the percentages for panel members also showed a decline. Line 1.3 shows that few people responded that they knew how AFP benefits were calculated, with 14 percent of the panel in 2002 falling to 11 percent 2 years later. Almost two-thirds of respondents claimed to know the rules for spouse and dependent benefits, but again the percentages fell between years for the same panel sample. It must be acknowledged that many are simply unaware of the social insurance coverage that spouses and children receive when the worker contributes to the AFP system.

Also of interest is the question of whether respondents know about requirements for the MPG as well as the benefit level. Some pundits have suggested that requiring twenty years of contributions for eligibility might induce workers to drop out of formal sector jobs, and recently some analysts have opined that the minimum benefit might need to be raised (Rohter 2006). The EPS research shows (lines F2 in Table 2-8) that very few respondents in 2002 knew the requirements for the minimum pension benefit, and only a very tiny minority could accurately report the requirements for the MPG (0.2% or fewer). Regarding financial literacy, there was an increase in the panel's awareness of the minimum pension between 2002 and 2004, rising from 22 to 34 percent, but the accuracy of their knowledge declined.

The final section of Table 2-8 focuses on respondents' knowledge of PASIS, which is a means-tested payment to the indigent. Interestingly, about 20 percent of the respondents in both 2002 and 2004 claimed they knew the eligibility requirements, with no important difference between affiliates and nonaffiliates in 2004 (new affiliates knew the least). In addition, only 3–4 percent of the respondents actually knew the correct eligibility requirements for these payments. Similarly, a relatively large percentage (approximately 17%) claimed to know the value of the welfare payment. However, only about 11 percent accurately stated the value. Those most likely to need the PASIS benefit—namely, nonaffiliates—were no more likely to be aware of program eligibility rules than others. However, those nonaffiliates who did know that there was a welfare pension were better informed about the benefit level than were others. Nonetheless, the low level of awareness among the population who are most likely to need the benefit is striking.

Among retirees, knowledge is generally more accurate than among workers (see Table 2-9). Most people who are retired according to administrative records also self-report they are retired (84%). Some two-thirds of the retirees know what kind of pension they are receiving, and about 64 percent know the benefit amount (with an accuracy of ±20%), though the retired tend to report smaller benefits than are indicated by the administrative data. Using the EPS, we can compare respondent questions about payouts with the administrative records. Comparing those for whom we have both self-reports and administrative data linkages, and focusing first on those who say they took the programmed withdrawal payout option, Panel A indicates that beneficiaries understated the value of their payouts by about 7 percent. That is, at the median, retirees self-reported benefits of only $69,000 pesos, compared to $74,000 pesos from the administrative records. For those receiving life annuities, the degree of understatement was even more substantial, with retirees reporting benefits about 10 percent lower than actually paid. The degree of understatement was less at the low end. Panel B shows that retirees who said they knew what type of income they received generally had lower actual benefits than did those who did not know. Panel C contains official data that show that, as of December 2005, the Chilean pension system had some 377,000 old-age retirees, of

TABLE 2-9 Pensions under the AFP System: Self-report vs Administrative Records

Percentile	*Self-Report Amt*	*Admin. Amt*	*Diff.*	*Percentage*
A. Pensions, AFP System: Self-Report vs Administrative Records[a] *(04 Chilean Pesos)*				
For Those with Self-Reports and Administrative Records in AFP: Phased Withdrawal (Median of the Percentile) (N=148)				
p25	65,000	60,667	4,333	6.7
p50	69,420	74,175	−4,755	−6.8
p75	70,000	74,883	−4,883	−7.0
For Those with Self-Reports and Administrative Records in AFP: Life Annuity (Median of the Percentile) (N=604)				
p25	70,000	73,454	−3,454	−4.9
p50	85,000	93,041	−8,041	−9.5
p75	130,000	142,361	−12,361	−9.5

For Those with Self-reports and Administrative Records in AFP	*%*	*N*
B. Pensions in the AFP System: Knowledge[b]		
B.1. Know that have a retirement pension	84.4	1,092
Life annuity	92.8	702
Phased withdrawal	72.6	440
Temporary income	95.5	64
Median pension of those that know	78,602	
Median pension of those that don't know	129,430	
B.2. Claim knows his/her type of pension	82.0	911
Life annuity	89.4	648
Phased withdrawal	68.1	308
Temporary income	92.4	60
Median pension of those claim know	81,126	
Median pension of those claim don't know	92,256	
B.3. Know correctly his/her type of pension	66.0	911
Life annuity	74.9	648
Phased withdrawal	52.1	308
Temporary income	73.2	60
Median pension of those that correctly know	91,085	
Median pension of those claim don't know correctly	110,998	
B.4. Know his/her amount of pension (±20%)	63.9	676
Life annuity	68.2	539
Phased withdrawal	57.0	179
Median pension of those that know their amount of pension	91,760	
Median pension of those that don't know their amount of pension	121,013	

Source: Authors' computations from the EPS 2002 and administrative linked data.

[a]Old-age pension, phased withdrawal, and annuities.

[b]Panel 2002–4, old-age pension include phased withdrawal and life annuity.

TABLE 2-9 (*Continued*)

	Phased Withdrawal	*Life Annuity*	*Temporary Income*
C. Number of Benefits in the AFP System: Official Figures			
Old Age			
1990	16,893	12,689	84
2000	76,710	142,446	6,217
2005	115,236	256,107	5,786
Disability			
1990	4,095	2,645	45
2000	12,045	7,840	396
2005	22,496	14,475	1090
Survival			
1990	15,176	4,857	19
2000	55,229	38,402	19
2005	71,057	62,507	40

Source: SAFP.

whom almost 70 percent were receiving benefits in the form of a life annuity.[23]

Implications and Conclusions

It is fitting that the Chilean pension reform is receiving much attention as it celebrates its Silver Anniversary. Despite the attention and continued debate about the system's impacts, little attention has been paid to the microeconomic aspects. The EPS is a recently developed longitudinal survey of about 20,000 individual respondents that has provided valuable new information for microeconomic analyses of key aspects of the Chilean pension system. Significantly, strengthening the EPS data are the links between respondent records and a wide range of historical administrative files on contribution patterns, benefit payments, and other program features. Accordingly, the EPS represents a substantial advance for analysts interested in important micro questions related to the operation of the new Chilean retirement system.

To illustrate some of the richness of the new information available, this chapter presents new analyses regarding three key policy questions:

- *Who participates in the Chilean retirement system, and what do lifetime contribution patterns look like?* We find that, on average, men report almost 40 percent higher months of AFP contributions than do women, which is not surprising, given that many women interrupt their labor force careers to rear children. Men report about one-fifth and women report about one-quarter higher months of contributions than indicated in the administrative records, which suggests that self-reports underestimate the extent of shortfall in coverage for sufficient months to satisfy the twenty-year minimum contribution requirement for the MPG for participants in the AFPs, somewhat more so for women. Thus, the probable extent of dependence on the PASIS is greater than would be indicated by self-reports. Also not surprising is the positive relation between reported months of AFP contributions and age, with an increase on average in reported months of contribution of one-third of a month for every additional month of age over the prime working years between the age groups 26–30 and 51–55 years. What is somewhat surprising is that self-reports do not differ with schooling attainment. On the other hand, administrative records indicate a positive association with schooling attainment, at least for those who have completed high school or more. It seems, therefore, that self-reports are likely to overstate somewhat the relative extent to which those with less schooling are likely to satisfy the twenty-year minimum contribution requirement. Finally, spells of reported noncontributions are strongly associated with nonemployment, which suggests that to increase coverage, efforts might best be directed toward reducing these nonemployment spells.

- *What have people accumulated in the Chilean retirement system, and what benefits may be anticipated?* The 2002 EPS shows that reported contributions must take place over a high percentage of an individual's work life to have replacement rates of over half. For example, a 65-year-old man would have to contribute for 80 percent of his work life to have a replacement rate of 60 percent. When the percentage of the work life during which an individual makes contributions falls, the replacement rate falls on average by as many or more percentage points. The findings cited earlier show that the EPS respondents who claimed to know their AFP accumulations report balances that are close to those in the administrative records. In contrast, those who did not know their AFP balances according to the administrative records have much lower balances on average. The findings also indicate that for respondents entitled to RBs, such bonds are worth about as much as are their AFP assets. It is therefore important that assessments of probable financial position on retirement include the RBs with AFP balances.
- *How financially knowledgeable are Chileans about their retirement system?* While about two-thirds of AFP affiliates affirmed that they receive periodic reports on past contributions and projected future benefits, much smaller proportions know critical details such as payroll tax rates and commission rates. That such a small percentage of AFP contributors know the rates suggests that work is needed to increase the effective competition among AFP providers. The majority of AFP

plan participants also do not know their AFP balances, details on the multifund system, or details of the eligibility requirements for minimum pensions. On the other hand, among those who claimed to know their AFP balances, they appear better informed about their accumulations than their US counterparts in corporate pensions, and the fraction of respondents who claimed to know their AFP balances increased between 2002 and 2004. It is clear, however, that knowledge about retirement benefits is far from perfect. Although most people retired according to administrative records also self-report they are retired, only two-thirds of the pensioners know what kind of benefit they receive and 64 percent know the amount of the benefit (give or take 20%). In other words, it appears that information gaps are considerable, which necessarily limit the effectiveness of the system.

Ultimately, to have a more resilient pension system, people will need a better appreciation of exactly what is required for eligibility to each of the pillars. In addition, greater financial literacy would enhance contribution and investment patterns. Greater knowledge of commissions and related matters is also essential in making a more competitive AFP system. Finally, for the government to make useful budgetary projections, better data are needed on who is in the system, who is contributing, and who is likely to try to obtain the MPG or PASIS benefits.

If the system is to survive to its next quarter-century mark and beyond, then it will have to be politically resilient—a difficult goal to attain if few Chileans obtain AFP benefits or if replacement ratios prove low. It is likely that political pressures will grow to raise MPG and PASIS pensions, with negative fiscal implications. And if people do not accumulate enough, there will also be pressures to allow phased withdrawals instead of annuitizing the payoffs—another significant financial risk for the government.

It is essential, of course, at this quarter-century mark, a time of taking stock of the Chilean pension system, to recognize that the system is still very young and in transition. Most people retiring now were actually not covered by the new system over their entire work lives. Rather, today's retirees continue to rely more heavily on RBs than on AFP accumulations. It is still unknown how well future retirees who spend their entire lives under the system will do. Initial analyses of the EPS data suggest both the value of further analysis and that there are some concerns that must be addressed to help the system to become more effective and efficient.

Notes

[1] Other Latin-American countries that implemented similar changes to their pension systems include Peru (1993), Colombia (1994), Argentina (1994), Uruguay (1996), Bolivia (1997), Mexico (1997), El Salvador (1998), Costa Rica (2001), the

Dominican Republic (2003), Nicaragua (2004), and Ecuador (2004). Cogan and Mitchell (2008) discuss prospects for funded individual DC account pensions in the USA.

[2] Many have written on the Chilean pensions system (cf. Cheyre 1988; Iglesias and Acuña 1991; Baeza and Margozzini 1995; SAFP 1996, 2002). Implementational and operational aspects have been explored by Diamond (1993), Diamond and Valdés Prieto (1994), Arenas de Mesa (1997), and Mesa-Lago and Arenas de Mesa (1998). Fiscal aspects of the reform are the focus of other work (cf. Ortúzar 1988; Marcel and Arenas de Mesa 1992; Arenas de Mesa 1999*b*). Arenas de Mesa and Marcel (1999*a*) have estimated the financing costs associated with the transition (from the old PAYGO to the new funded system) and minimum basic pension guarantees. Yet a common characteristic of these studies and most studies on the Chilean pension reform is the use of aggregate and macroeconomic information. In fact, the implications of the pension reform on aspects such as private savings are usually deduced from simple aggregate correlations of macroeconomic indicators (even though Chile experienced a significant number of concurrent economic reforms) or from simulations carried out on general equilibrium models (the pioneering application in this respect was Arrau 1991). Even when analysts looked at specific aspects such as the minimum basic pension, they have simulated representative individuals because they lacked microeconomic data. Accordingly, they did not consider individual heterogeneities critical for questions of equity (cf. Wagner 1991; Zurita 1994).

[3] This section draws heavily on Arenas de Mesa (2005).

[4] This institution also manages the retirement systems of the armed forces (Caja de Previsión de la Defensa Nacional, or CAPREDENA) and the police force (Dirección de Previsión de Carabineros de Chile, or DIPRECA).

[5] This is a lump sum paid to workers at retirement by the government. The sum is based on the last twelve monthly contributions before June 1979 and is adjusted by the proportion of total years under the public system and an annuity factor. The RBs are expected to cost around 1% of GDP per year for the period 2000–20 (Arenas de Mesa and Marcel 1999).

[6] Mandatory system contributions are capped at a ceiling earnings level of approximately US$1,500 per month; fewer than 5% of AFP contributors earn over that ceiling.

[7] In response to high levels of churning across AFPs, the Superintendency of the AFP system in 1997 required participants to file paperwork in person at their AFP, a move that greatly diminished the rate of fund switching.

[8] Additional factors influencing pension amounts are the worker's life expectancy (derived from age- and sex-specific official life tables) and the worker's number of survivors at the time of retirement. Retirees have three withdrawal options: (*a*) Retiro Programado, or 'Programmed Retirement', which allows a system of phased withdrawals from the accumulated funds and where the pension amount is recalculated every year; in this case, the pension is paid by the AFP; (*b*) a real lifetime annuity from an insurance company (Renta Vitalicia)—in this case, the AFP transfers funds to the insurer, which in turn makes monthly payments; and (*c*) some mix of phased withdrawals for a determined period and a deferred lifetime annuity.

[9] The current minimum monthly pension is US$105, while the minimum wage is about US$150 per month.
[10] Early retirement may be permitted if the worker can demonstrate that his or her early retirement benefit would be at least 110% of the minimum pension benefit level and 50% of his or her average monthly contributions over the past 10 years (currently, 60% of pension benefits paid by AFPs are for early retirement).
[11] All pension system variables (pension funds, yields, and benefits) are measured in unidades de fomento (UF), an accounting unit indexed to inflation. That the pensions are automatically inflation-adjusted solves a longstanding and serious problem of Chilean social insurance. Unlike regular pensions, however, the minimum pension is not indexed against inflation but is instead periodically adjusted by the government.
[12] The AFP system currently covers nearly half as many pensioners as the INP system, has more beneficiaries than the welfare PASIS pension, and includes three times as many beneficiaries as the public pension system for the armed forces (Arenas de Mesa 2004).
[13] The 2002 survey was initially called the 2002 Historia Laboral y Seguridad Social (HLSS) survey, or History of Labor and Social Security. But the follow-up 2004 and 2006 longitudinal surveys are called Encuesta de Previsión Social (EPS), or Social Protection Surveys. To avoid awkward terminology, in this chapter we refer to the 2002 data as well as the subsequent rounds of data as EPS, or Social Protection Surveys. The interested reader is referred to http://www.proteccionsocial.cl/english/presentacion2002.htm for access to the public use data, codebooks, and documentation of the survey.
[14] Information on the methodology and extent of the survey can be found in Bravo (2004). Members of the armed forces or police covered by separate government pension systems were excluded, as well as a very small percentage of the Chilean population residing in inaccessible or sparsely populated areas (e.g. islands).
[15] A number of the questions were adapted from the US Health and Retirement Study (HRS) with the intention of providing cross-national comparisons.
[16] The sample is reweighted using sampling weights, so it represents the national population.
[17] Further rounds of the survey were planned for 2006, 2008, and 2010.
[18] The sample size for which we can currently link self-reports and administrative AFP records for the EPS 2002 is 11,305.
[19] The reader should be reminded that as the AFP system has been in place only since the early 1980s and tabulations run to mid-2002, the maximum possible number of months in the chart can total only about 260.
[20] Data on AFP contributions are available only from 1981. INP contribution patterns may become available in the future but to date these are unavailable for analysis.
[21] Another reason that the self-reports of contribution months are higher is that the EPS labor history asks for job beginning and end dates. Our calculation assumes that contributions were made without interruption on each job, which may produce an overstatement of contributions if layoffs or other interruptions occurred but are not accounted for in the reported beginning and end dates.

[22] That analysis assumes that workers' initial taxable earnings were CP$200,000 (below twice the current minimum wage); that real earnings would grow at 2% per year to 50 years of age; that pension investments would earn 4% real per year; and that the worker would pay fixed monthly commissions of CP$500.
[23] This data confirms recent findings by James, Martinez, and Iglesias (2006) on payouts under the Chilean pension system.

References

Arellano, José Pablo (1985). *Políticas sociales y desarrollo: Chile 1924–1984.* Santiago: CIEPLAN.

Arenas de Mesa, Alberto (1997). 'Learning from the Privatization of the Social Security Pension System in Chile: Macroeconomic Effects, Lessons and Challenges', Ph.D. diss., University of Pittsburgh.

—— (1999*a*). 'Proyecciones del déficit previsional chileno: Gasto público en pensiones asistenciales 1999–2010', paper presented at the XI Seminario Regional de Política Fiscal, CEPAL, Brazil, January 26–28.

—— (1999*b*). 'Efectos Fiscales del Sistema de Pensiones en Chile: Proyecciones del Déficit Previsional 1999–2037', paper presented at the Conference 'Responsabilidades Fiscales de los Sistemas de Pensiones', Ministerio de Hacienda y CEPAL, Santiago, Chile, September 2–3.

—— (2000). 'Cobertura Previsional en Chile: Lecciones y Desafíos del Sistema de Pensiones Administrado por el Sector Privado', in *Serie de Financiamiento del Desarrollo.* Santiago: CEPAL.

—— (2004). *El sistema de pensiones en Chile: Principales desafíos futuros.* Santiago, Chile: International Labour Organization.

—— (2005). 'Fiscal and Institutional Considerations and the Chilean Prescription', in Carolin A. Crabbe (ed.), *A Quarter Century of Pension Reform in Latin America and the Caribbean: Lessons Learned and the Next Steps.* Washington, DC: Inter-American Development Bank, pp. 83–126.

—— —— (1999). 'Fiscal Effects of Social Security Reform in Chile: The Case of the Minimum Pension', in *Proceedings of the Second APEC Regional Forum on Pension Fund Reforms,* Ministerio de Hacienda de Chile and Asian Development Bank, Viña del Mar, Chile, April 26–27.

—— and Pamela C. Gana (2003). 'Protección Social, Pensiones y Género en Chile', in F. Bertranou and A. Arenas de Mesa (eds.), *Protección Social, Pensiones y Género en Argentina, Brasil y Chile.* Santiago, Chile: OIT, pp. 137–225.

—— Jere Behrman, and David Bravo (2004). 'Characteristics of and Determinants of the Density of Contributions in a Private Social Security System', Michigan Retirement Research Center Working Paper, www.mrrc.isr.umich.edu/publications/papers/pdf/wp077.pdf

—— Maria Claudia Llanés, and Fidel Miranda Bravo (2005). *Protección social efectiva, calidad de la cobertura y efectos distributivos del sistema de pensiones en Chile.* Santiago, Chile: CEPAL.

Arrau, Patricio (June 1991). 'La reforma previsional chilena y su financiamiento durante la transición', *Colección Estudios*, 32: 5–44.

Baeza, Sergio and Francisco Margozzini (eds.) (1995). *Quince años después. Una mirada al sistema privado de pensiones*. Santiago: CEP.

Banco Central de Chile (BCCH), http://www.bcentral.cl/eng/

Berstein, Solange and Jose Luis Ruiz (n.d.). 'Sensibilidad de la Demanda Con Consumidores Desinformados: El Caso de Las AFP in Chile', working paper, www.sbs.gob.pe/Journal/Bernstein.pdf

Bravo, David (January 2004). 'Evaluación de los resultados del sistema de pensiones. Informe Final', Departamento de Economía, Universidad de Chile.

Castañeda, Tarsicio (1990). *Para Combatir la Pobreza: Política Social y Descentralización en Chile Durante Los '80*. Santiago: Centro de Estudios Públicos.

Cheyre, Hernán (1988). *La previsión en Chile ayer y hoy. Impacto de una reforma*. Santiago: Centro de Estudios Públicos.

Cogan, John F. and Olivia S. Mitchell (2008). 'Perspectives from the President's Commission on Social Security Reform', this volume.

Diamond, Peter (June 1993). 'Privatization of Social Security: Lessons from Chile', *Revista de Análisis Económico*, 9(1): 21–33.

—— and Salvador Vadés Prieto (1994). 'Social Security Reform', in B. Bosworth, R. Dornbusch, and R. Labán (eds.), *The Chilean Economy*. Washington, DC: Brookings Institution, pp. 257–328.

Gill, Indermit, Truman Packard, and Juan Yermo (2005). *Keeping the Promise of Social Security in Latin America*. Stanford, CA: Stanford University Press.

Gustman, Alan and Thomas Steinmeier (1999). 'What People Don't Know About Their Pensions and Social Security: An Analysis Using Linked Data from the Health and Retirement Study', NBER Working Paper No. 7368, Cambridge, MA.

Iglesias, Augusto and Rodrigo Acuña (1991). *Chile: Experiencia con un régimen de capitalización 1981–1991*. Santiago: CEPAL/PNUD.

James, Estelle, Guillermo Martinez, and Augusto Iglesias (Spring 2006). 'The Payout Stage in Chile: Who Annuitizes and Why?', *Journal of Pension Economics and Finance*.

Lusardi, Annamaria and Olivia S. Mitchell (2006). 'Financial Literacy and Retirement Planning: Implications for Retirement Wellbeing', working paper, Pension Research Council, the Wharton School of the University of Pennsylvania.

Marcel, M. and A. Arenas de Mesa (1992). 'Social Security Reform in Chile', Occasional Papers, No. 5, Inter-American Development Bank, Washington, DC.

Mesa-Lago, Carmelo (1994). *Changing Social Security in Latin America: Toward Alleviating the Costs of Economic Reform*. Boulder, CO and London: Lynne Rienner.

—— and A. Arenas de Mesa (1998). 'The Chilean Pension System: Evaluation, Lessons and Challenges', in M. Cruz-Saco and C. Mesa-Lago (eds.), *The Reform of Pension and Health Care System in Latin America. Do Options Exist?* Pittsburgh, PA: University of Pittsburgh Press.

Mitchell, Olivia S. (1988). 'Worker Knowledge of Pension Provisions', *Journal of Labor Economics*, 6: 21–39.

Ortúzar, Pablo (1988). 'El déficit previsional: recuento y proyecciones', in Sergio Baeza and Rodrigo Manubens (eds.), *Sistema privado de pensiones en Chile.* Santiago, Chile: Centro de Estudios Públicos.

Rohter, Larry (2006). 'Chile's Candidates Agree to Agree on Pension Woes', *The New York Times,* January 10.

Superintendencia de Administradoras de Fondos de Pensiones (SAFP) (1996). *El sistema chileno de pensiones,* 3rd edn. Santiago: SAFP.

—— (2002). *El sistema chileno de pensiones,* 5th edn. Santiago: SAFP.

Valdés Prieto, Salvador (Fall 2005). 'Para Aumentar La Competencia Entre Las AFP', *Estudios Públicos.* Santiago, Chile.

Wagner, Gert (June 1991). 'La seguridad social y el programa de pensión mínima garantizada', *Estudios de Economía,* 18(1): 35–91.

World Bank (WB) (1994). *Averting the Old-Age Crisis: Policies to Protect the Old and Promote Growth.* Washington, DC: World Bank.

Zurita, Salvador (June 1994). 'Minimum Pension Insurance in the Chilean Pension System', *Revista de Análisis Económico,* 9 (1): 105–26.

Chapter 3

The Importance of Default Options for Retirement Saving Outcomes: Evidence from the USA

John Beshears, James J. Choi, David Laibson, and Brigitte C. Madrian

If transaction costs are small, standard economic theory would suggest that defaults have little impact on economic outcomes. Agents with well-defined preferences will opt out of any default that does not maximize their utility, regardless of the nature of the default. In practice, however, defaults can have sizable effects on economic outcomes. Recent research has highlighted the important role that defaults play in a wide range of settings: organ donation decisions (Johnson and Goldstein 2003; Abadie and Gay 2004), car insurance plan choices (Johnson et al. 1993), car option purchases (Park, Jun, and McInnis 2000), and consent to receive email marketing (Johnson, Bellman, and Lohse 2003).

This chapter summarizes the empirical evidence on defaults in another economically important domain: savings outcomes. The evidence strongly suggests that defaults affect savings outcomes at every step along the way. To understand how defaults affect retirement savings outcomes, one must first understand the relevant institutions. Because the empirical literature on how defaults shape retirement savings outcomes mostly focuses on the USA, we begin by describing the different types of US retirement income institutions and some of their salient characteristics. We then present empirical evidence from the USA and other countries, including Chile, Mexico, and Sweden, on how defaults influence retirement savings outcomes at all

We thank Hewitt Associates for their help in providing the data analyzed in this and several previous chapters that form the foundation for the arguments advanced in this chapter. We are particularly grateful to Lori Lucas and Yan Xu, two of our many contacts at Hewitt Associates. We acknowledge individual and collective financial support from the National Institute on Aging (grants R01-AG021650 and T32-AG00186) and the US Social Security Administration (grant #10-P-98363–1 to the National Bureau of Economic Research as part of the SSA Retirement Research Consortium). The opinions and conclusions expressed are solely those of the authors and do not represent the opinions or policy of NIA, SSA, any other agency of the US federal government, or the NBER. Laibson also acknowledges financial support from the Sloan Foundation.

stages of the savings life cycle, including savings plan participation, savings rates, asset allocation, and postretirement savings distributions. Next, we examine why defaults have such a tremendous impact on savings outcomes. Finally, we consider the role of public policy toward retirement saving when defaults matter.

Retirement Income Institutions in the USA

There are four primary sources of retirement income for individuals in the USA: (*a*) social security payments from the government, (*b*) traditional employer-sponsored DB pension plans, (*c*) employer-sponsored DC savings plans, and (*d*) individual savings accounts that are tied neither to the government nor to private employers. We briefly describe each of these institutions in turn.[1]

The US social security system provides retirement income to qualified workers and their spouses. While employed, workers and their firms make mandatory contributions to the social security system. Individuals are eligible to claim benefits at age 62, although benefit amounts are higher if individuals postpone their receipt until a later age. Individuals must proactively enroll to begin receiving social security benefits, and most individuals do so no later than aged 65. The level of benefits is primarily determined by either an individual's own or his or her spouse's earnings history, with higher earnings corresponding to greater monthly benefit amounts according to a progressive benefits formula. Benefits are also indexed to the cost of living and so tend to increase over time. They are paid until an individual dies, with a reduced benefit going to a surviving spouse until his or her death.

On average, social security replaces about 40 percent of pre-retirement income, although this varies widely across individuals. Replacement rates tend to be negatively related to income due to the progressive structure of the benefits formula. Benefits are largely funded on a PAYGO basis, with the contributions of workers and firms made today going to pay the benefits of currently retired individuals who worked and paid contributions in the past. There is no private account component to the US social security system, although this is something that has received much discussion in recent years.

Traditionally, the second largest component of retirement income has come from employer-sponsored DB pension plans. These plans share many similarities with the social security system. Benefits are determined by a formula, usually linked to a worker's compensation, age, and tenure. Benefits are usually paid out as a life annuity, or in the case of married individuals as a joint-and-survivor annuity, although workers do have some flexibility in selecting the type of annuity or in opting instead for a lump-sum payout.

Because traditional DB pension plans are costly for employers to administer and impose funding risk on employers, there has been a movement over the past two decades away from traditional pensions and toward DC savings plans. There are now more than twice as many active participants in employer-sponsored DC savings plans as in DB pension plans, with total assets in DC plans exceeding those in DB plans by more than 10 percent (US Department of Labor 2005).

These DC savings plans come in several different varieties. The most common one is the 401(k), named after the section of the US tax code that regulates these types of plans. The typical DC plan allows employees to make elective pretax contributions to an account over which the employee retains investment control. Many employers provide matching contributions up to a certain level of employee contributions. The retirement income ultimately derived by the retirees depends on how much they elected to save while working, how generous the employer match was, and the performance of their selected investment portfolios. At retirement, benefits are usually paid in the form of a lump-sum distribution, although some employers offer the option of purchasing an annuity. Relative to traditional DB pension plans, DC savings plans impose substantially more risk on individuals while reducing the risks faced by employers.

The final significant source of retirement income comes from personal savings accounts that are not tied to an employer (or the government). There are many different ways that individuals can save their own for retirement but one particular vehicle, the IRA (Individual Retirement Account), is very popular because it receives favorable tax treatment. After IRAs were first created, the primary source of funding came from direct individual contributions. Over time, however, restrictions have been placed on the ability of higher income individuals to make direct tax-favored contributions, and the primary source of IRA funding has shifted to rollovers—transfers of assets from a former employer's DC savings plan into an IRA. In general, individuals employed at a firm with a DC savings plan that has an employer match would find that savings plan more attractive than directly contributing to an IRA. Direct IRA contributions largely come from individuals whose employers do not sponsor a DC savings plan, individuals who are not eligible for their employer's savings plan, or individuals who are not working.

The relatively low social security replacement rate (compared to other developed countries) in conjunction with the recent shift toward DC savings plans and IRAs in the USA has spurred much of the research interest into how defaults and other plan design parameters affect savings outcomes. With individuals bearing greater responsibility for ensuring their own retirement income security, understanding how to improve their savings outcomes has become an important issue both for individuals themselves and for society at large.

The Impact of Defaults on Retirement Savings Outcomes: Empirical Evidence

We now turn to the evidence on how defaults affect retirement savings outcomes, discussing first the effect of institutionally specified defaults, then 'elective' defaults—mechanisms that are not a pure default but that share similar characteristics with the institutionally chosen defaults, in terms both of their structure and of their outcomes.

Savings Plan Participation

In a DC savings environment, savings plans—employer-sponsored, government-sponsored, or privately sponsored—are useful only to the extent that employees actually participate. Recent research suggests that when it comes to savings plan participation, the key behavioral question is not *whether* individuals participate in a savings plan but rather how long it takes before they actually sign up. The most compelling evidence on the impact of defaults on savings outcomes comes from changes in the default participation status of employees at firms with DC savings plans.

In most companies, savings plan participation requires an active election on the part of employees. That is, if the employee does nothing, the default is that the employee is not enrolled (standard enrollment). An alternative but less widely used approach is to enroll employees in the savings plan automatically, requiring the employee to actively elect to opt out.[2] This simple change in the default participation status that affects employees who do nothing has a dramatic impact on participation outcomes.

To illustrate the effect of automatic enrollment on both participation and other savings outcomes, we present the experience of a medium-sized US chemicals company (Company A). This particular firm has a standard DC savings plan: employees can direct up to 15 percent of pay into the plan, employee contributions are matched dollar-for-dollar up to 6 percent of pay, and employees have seven investment options from which to choose. This company is interesting to consider because it implemented automatic enrollment in two different ways for three different groups of employees.

Company A initially adopted automatic enrollment in December 2000 with a default contribution rate of 3 percent of pay. The first group of employees affected was new hires going forward, which is how automatic enrollment is most commonly implemented. However, this firm also applied automatic enrollment to previously hired employees not then

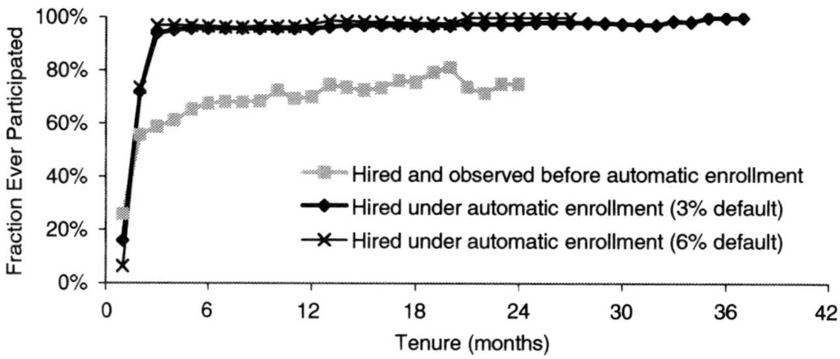

Figure 3-1. Automatic enrollment for new hires and savings plan participation (Company A). (*Source*: authors' calculations.)

participating in the plan. In October 2001, the company increased its default contribution rate to 6 percent, affecting only new hires going forward.

Figure 3-1 shows the effect of automatic enrollment on the participation rates of new hires at Company A. For employees hired and observed before automatic enrollment, savings plan participation is initially low and increases slowly with employee tenure. Under automatic enrollment, however, participation jumps to approximately 95 percent once it takes effect (one to two months after hire) and increases only slightly thereafter. At low levels of tenure, the difference in participation rates under the standard and automatic enrollment regimes is substantial, with a difference of 35 percentage points at 3 months of tenure. As participation increases with tenure under standard enrollment, this difference diminishes but remains sizable even after a long time. For example, at 24 months of tenure, employees under automatic enrollment have a participation rate more than 25 percentage points higher than that of employees hired before automatic enrollment. The impact of automatic enrollment on existing nonparticipants is no less dramatic, as shown in Figure 3-2. These differences are borne out in other firms, as documented in Madrian and Shea (2001), Choi et al. (2002, 2004*a*, 2004*b*), and The Vanguard Group (2001).

Most firms with automatic enrollment have adopted a relatively low default contribution rate, typically 2–3 percent of pay (Profit Sharing/401(k) Council of America 2005). The reason commonly cited for the low rate is a concern that more employees will opt out of the savings plan with a higher default contribution rate. The experience of Company A, as shown in Figure 3-1, suggests that this concern may be unfounded. The participation rate under automatic enrollment is virtually identical

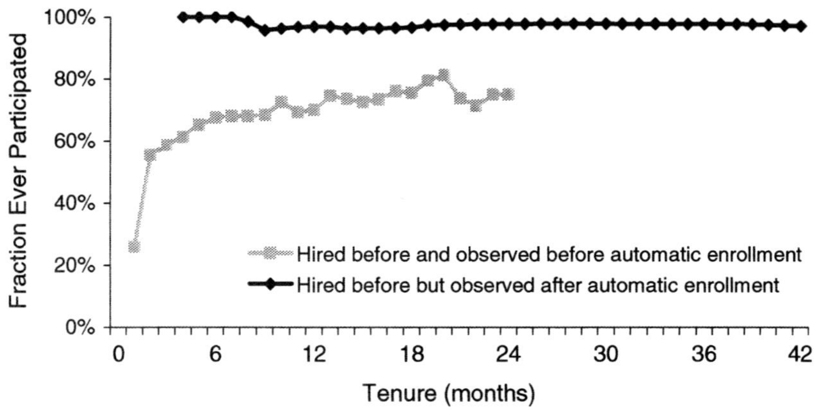

Figure 3-2. Automatic enrollment for existing nonparticipants and savings plan participants (Company A). (*Source*: authors' calculations.)

with either a low 3 percent contribution rate or a higher 6 percent contribution rate, a result corroborated for other firms in Choi et al. (2004*a*, 2004*b*). This finding should not in fact be much of a surprise, as employee contributions up to 6 percent of pay receive a generous dollar-for-dollar employer match at this firm. Most employees should thus have a strong incentive to contribute at least this amount to the savings plan (even if automatically enrolled at the lower 3% default contribution rate!).

Savings Plan Contributions

While automatic enrollment is effective in getting employees to participate in their employer-sponsored savings plan, it is less effective at motivating them to make well-planned decisions about how much to save. Consider, for example, the distribution of contribution rates in Figure 3-3 for employees at Company A hired under automatic enrollment at a 3 percent default contribution rate (the black bars) versus that of employees hired under automatic enrollment at a 6 percent default rate (the gray bars). The sample under both default regimes in Figure 3-3 is restricted to employees with the same level of tenure so that the results are not confounded by differences in the time that employees have had to move away from the default.

The distributions of contribution rates are strikingly different for the two regimes. Under the 6 percent default regime, only 4 percent of employees have a 3 percent contribution rate; 49 percent of employees have a 6 percent contribution rate (the default); and fully 79 percent of employees

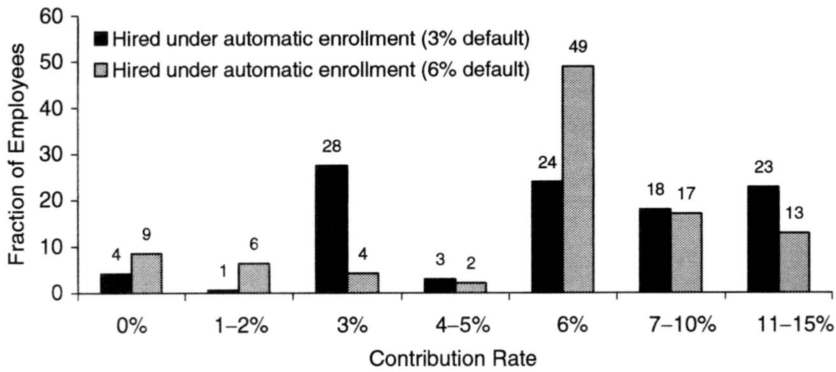

Figure 3-3. Automatic enrollment for new hires and the distribution of 401(k) contribution rates (Company A, 15–24 months tenure). (*Source*: authors' calculations.)

have a contribution rate at or above the 6 percent match threshold. In contrast, under the 3 percent default regime, 28 percent of employees are contributing at the default 3 percent contribution rate (a sevenfold increase relative to the 6% regime), while only 24 percent are contributing 6 percent of pay (half the fraction in the 6% regime). Sixty-five percent of employees overall are at or above the match threshold under the 3 percent regime, which is 14 percentage points lower in the 6 percent regime despite the very strong financial incentive to contribute at least 6 percent of pay due to the generous employer match.

The influence of the 3 percent default contribution rate is somewhat smaller in Company A than in other companies documented in the existing literature on automatic enrollment (Madrian and Shea 2001; Choi et al. 2002, 2004*a*, 2004*b*). This circumstance is likely due to the extremely generous employer match at Company A, which provides a stronger incentive for employees at this firm relative to those at other firms to take action and increase their contribution rate to the match threshold. But clearly, the default contribution rate still has a sizable impact on the savings outcomes of employees hired under automatic enrollment at Company A.

This impact is even more apparent if we examine the distribution of contribution rates for employees subject to automatic enrollment after being hired. Recall that employees not currently participating in the 401(k) plan were subject to automatic enrollment in December 2000 unless they specifically elected to opt out. Figure 3-4 compares the distribution of contribution rates for employees not subject to automatic enrollment in December 2000 because they had already elected to participate in the 401(k) plan (the black bars) with that of employees subject to automatic enrollment with a 3 percent default contribution rate (the gray bars).

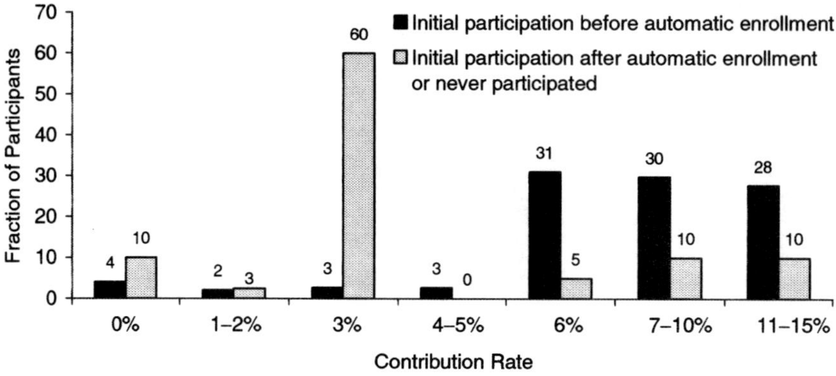

Figure 3-4. Automatic enrollment for existing hires and the distribution of 401(k) contribution rates (Company A, 25–48 months tenure). (*Source*: authors' calculations.)

Among employees who elected to participate in the 401(k) plan before automatic enrollment, only 3 percent chose a 3 percent contribution rate, 31 percent chose the 6 percent match threshold, and fully 89 percent of these employees were contributing at or above the match threshold. In contrast, among employees subject to automatic enrollment, 60 percent contribute at the 3 percent automatic enrollment default, while only 5 percent are at the 6 percent match threshold and 25 percent are at or above the match threshold.

The comparison between the two groups of employees in Figure 3-4 is not as clean as that in Figure 3-3—we might expect the employees subject to automatic enrollment by virtue of the fact that they had not yet enrolled in the 401(k) plan to be different from more savings-motivated employees not subject to automatic enrollment. Nonetheless, the fraction of those subject to automatic enrollment at the 3 percent default contribution is large indeed. The general tenor of these results—the impact of the default contribution rate on the distribution of savings rates, both for new hires and for existing employees—has been corroborated for other firms in Madrian and Shea (2001) and Choi et al. (2002, 2004*a*, 2004*b*).

Asset Allocation

Just as automatic enrollment tends to anchor employee contribution rates on the automatic enrollment default contribution rate, it also tends to anchor employee asset allocations on the automatic enrollment default

TABLE 3-1 Automatic Enrollment and Asset Allocation Outcomes (Company A)

	Hired after Automatic Enrollment (15–24 months tenure)		*Hired Before Automatic Enrollment (25-48 months tenure)*	
	3% Default Contribution Rate (%)	*6% Default Contribution Rate (%)*	*Participated Before Automatic Enrollment (%)*	*Participated after Automatic Enrollment (%)*
Any balances in default fund	33.8	46.5	9.9	86.1
All balances in default fund	25.6	39.5	1.4	61.1
100% default fund + default contribution rate	18.1	32.6	0.0	52.8

Source: Authors' own calculations.

asset allocation. This is shown for Company A in Table 3-1, which gives the fraction of participants with any balances in the default fund, all balances in the default fund, and the combination of having all balances in the default fund along with the default contribution rate (the default automatic enrollment asset allocation in Company A is a money market fund). The employee groups shown are the same as those in Figure 3-3 (columns 1 and 2) and Figure 3-4 (columns 3 and 4).

Consider first the asset allocation of employees who were hired and initiated savings plan participation before automatic enrollment (column 3) and were thus not subject to automatic enrollment. None of these employees is saving at the automatic enrollment default contribution rate of 3 percent in conjunction with an asset allocation entirely invested in the automatic enrollment default fund. Only 1 percent have all of their assets wholly invested in the default fund at any contribution rate. Finally, only 10 percent have any of their assets invested in the default fund. In general, investment in the automatic enrollment default fund is not widespread among employees who actively elected participation in the Company A savings plan.

For those employees subject to automatic enrollment, because they had not initiated participation in the Company A savings plan by December 2000, the picture is very different. A whopping 86 percent have some of their assets allocated to the default fund (compared to 10% for their counterparts not subject to automatic enrollment), with 61 percent having everything invested in the default fund (compared to 1% for those not subject to automatic enrollment). Over half have retained both the default contribution rate of 3 percent and a 100 percent asset allocation in the default fund.

For employees subject to automatic enrollment as new hires, the impact of the default fund on asset allocation outcomes is not quite as stark as that for existing but nonparticipating employees subject to automatic enrollment, but it is nonetheless clear (columns 1 and 2). Between 34 and 47 percent of these participants have something invested in the default fund, and between 26 and 40 percent have everything invested in the default fund. Interestingly, the default investment allocation is much more prevalent among those hired with a 6 percent default contribution rate than for those hired with a 3 percent default contribution rate. The likely explanation has to do with the incentives for moving away from the automatic enrollment defaults. Employees hired with the 3 percent default contribution rate have two reasons to change their savings parameters: first, to choose a higher contribution rate to fully exploit the employer match and, second, to choose a nondefault asset allocation. For employees hired with a 6 percent default contribution rate, the first of these motives is missing and the cost/benefit calculation for making any change shifts toward doing nothing.

The automatic enrollment default asset allocation is not the only type of default that affects employee portfolio outcomes. As noted earlier, most US organizations offering a DC savings plan match employee contributions to some extent. In most of them, the employer matching contributions are invested in the same manner as the employee's own contributions. In many large publicly traded companies, however, the match is directed into employer stock, sometimes with restrictions on when employees can diversify their matching balances out of employer stock and sometimes not.[3,4] Choi, Laibson, and Madrian (2005*b*, 2007) document a strong flypaper effect when it comes to matching contributions directed into employer stock: the money sticks where it lands, even when employees are free to diversify.

A final example of how savings outcomes are impacted by a default asset allocation comes from the DC component of different social security systems. Cronqvist and Thaler (2004) study the asset allocation outcomes of participants in the Swedish social security system and find that despite heavy advertising encouraging Swedes to actively elect their own asset allocation at the time that private accounts were instituted, one-third of the investments of those who were initially enrolled were directed to the default fund. After the initial rollout, when advertising was much diminished, the contributions of over 90 percent of new participants were invested in the default fund. Similarly, Rozinka and Tapia (n.d.) report that in Chile, over 70 percent of participants have retained the default fund.

Pre-retirement Cash Distributions

Another phase in the retirement savings accumulation process is changing jobs. When savings plan participants in the USA leave their employment, they may request a cash distribution, a direct rollover of savings plan balances into a new employer's savings plan, or a rollover of plan balances into a qualified individual savings account (e.g. an IRA). If terminated employees do not make an explicit request, the default treatment of those balances depends on how large their accounts are. For balances in excess of $5,000, balances remain in the former employer's savings plan by default. For balances below the $5,000 threshold, employers can compel a cash distribution.[5] Anecdotally, most employers choose the cash distribution option as their default for terminated employees. Choi et al. (2002, 2004*a*, 2004*b*) document the important relationship between balance size and the likelihood that terminated employees receive a cash distribution. In an analysis of data from four different firms, they find that more than 70 percent of terminated employees with small account balances receive a cash distribution, the default for employees with balances below $5,000, compared to less than one-third of terminated employees with larger account balances. This can have important implications for whether these balances continue to be saved or are consumed. Previous research suggests that the probability of receiving a cash distribution and subsequently rolling it over into an IRA or another savings plan is very low when the size of the distribution is small. Instead, these small distributions tend to be consumed.[6] When employers compel a cash distribution and employees receive an unexpected check in the mail, the path of least resistance is to simply consume the proceeds.

Postretirement Distributions

The final part of the retirement savings process is that of decumulation. There is ample reason to believe that the type of retirement income distributions received by older individuals from their retirement plans impacts economic outcomes. For example, Holden and Zick (2000) find that incomes for older widows fall by 47 percent following the death of their husbands, moving 17 percent of these women into poverty. Presumably, it would be possible to devise a retirement income stream that does not propel one spouse into poverty when the other one dies.

The actual decumulation options available to older individuals vary widely across different types of retirement income vehicles. For example, in the US social security system, payments do not begin until individuals actively sign up, but there are no options when it comes to the structure of the benefits. Recipients essentially receive an inflation-protected life annuity based on an individual's own earnings history and potentially that of his or her spouse. For married couples, social security payments fall subsequent to the death of one partner, but the surviving spouse continues to receive some benefits.

In a typical employer-sponsored DB savings plan in the USA, retired individuals have more options. Married individuals can take their retirement income as a single annuity or as a joint-and-survivor annuity with a lower monthly benefit amount. In addition to these different annuity options, some employers also offer the choice of a lump-sum payout.

The options in an employer-sponsored DC savings plan are different still. In some companies, the only choice is a lump-sum distribution. In others, the employer may retain the account balances, giving individuals the option to take periodic and variable distributions. In still others, the employer may facilitate the purchase of annuities through a private provider.

Just as in the retirement income accumulation phase, defaults also matter for the retirement income decumulation phase. The most telling evidence comes from a government-mandated change in the annuitization options that traditional DB pension plans must offer their beneficiaries. The US regulatory framework established for pensions in 1974 required that the default annuity option offered to married pension plan participants be a joint-and-one-half-survivor annuity. Married beneficiaries could, however, opt out of this default, choosing a single-life annuity with higher monthly benefits during the retired worker's lifetime. In 1984, these regulations were amended to require the notarized signature of the spouse if a retired worker decided to opt for a single life rather than the joint-and-survivor annuity.

Holden and Nicholson (1998) document the effect of this change in the default annuity option on the annuitization outcomes among married men with traditional employer-sponsored pensions. Before the institution of the joint-and-survivor default in 1974, they calculate that less than half of married men elected the joint-and-survivor option. After the move to the joint-and-survivor default, they estimate an increase in joint-and-survivor annuitization among married men of over 25 percentage points. It is not clear how much of this shift is due to the change in the default among retirees at firms that offered both the single-life option and the joint-and-survivor option before the regulatory mandate, and how much is due to the increased availability of joint-and-survivor annuities at firms that were not previously offering them. Saku (2001), however, examines only the impact of the 1984 amendment that requires explicit spousal consent to opt out of a joint-and-survivor annuity. By this time, all firms would have been offering joint-and-survivor options to their pension beneficiaries. He finds an increase in joint-and-survivor annuitization of 5–10 percentage points following this strengthening of the default. One might expect much larger effects from its initial implementation, so that the 25 percentage-point effect estimated by Holden and Nicholson is likely mostly attributable to the change in the default annuity option rather than an increase in the provision by employers of joint-and-survivor annuities.

Elective Defaults

The evidence presented so far all pertains to defaults that specify the savings outcome that will occur if individuals take no action. There are, however, some interesting examples of employer attempts to improve savings outcomes through the use of affirmative savings elections that exploit features of some of the defaults discussed in the previous sections. For lack of a better term, we refer to these as elective defaults, although this does stretch the typical usage of the word 'default'.

One particularly successful elective default is the contribution rate escalator popularized by the Save More Tomorrow (SMarT) plan of Benartzi and Thaler (2004). With a contribution escalator, participants elect to have their savings plan contribution rate increase in the future if they take no further action; in other words, they opt into a default of increasing contributions. The striking results of the first experiment with such a contribution escalator, in which employees signed up for future contribution rate increases of 3 percentage points per year, are reported in Benartzi and Thaler (2004) and Utkus and Young (2004). At the company studied, employees who elected the contribution escalator feature saw their savings plan contributions increase by 10.1 percentage points over 4 years, from 3.5 to 13.6 percent of pay. In contrast, employees who did not sign up for the contribution escalator but who instead elected to adopt immediately a savings rate recommended to them had higher initial contribution rates but increased their savings plan contributions by only 4.4 percentage points over 4 years, from 4.4 to 8.8 percent of pay. Other companies that have subsequently incorporated a contribution escalation feature into their savings plans have also seen increases in employee contribution rates (Utkus 2002). Such contribution escalators are an interesting way to capitalize on the widespread savings plan inertia documented thus far. They are also something that could be easily incorporated as a proper savings plan default.

Hewitt Associates (2003), Choi, Laibson, and Madrian (2005*c*), and Beshears et al. (2006) study another elective default dubbed Quick Enrollment. Quick Enrollment operates by giving employees an easy way to elect a preselected contribution rate and asset allocation from among the many other options that are available within an employer's savings plan. Figure 3-5 shows the impact of Quick Enrollment on savings plan participation

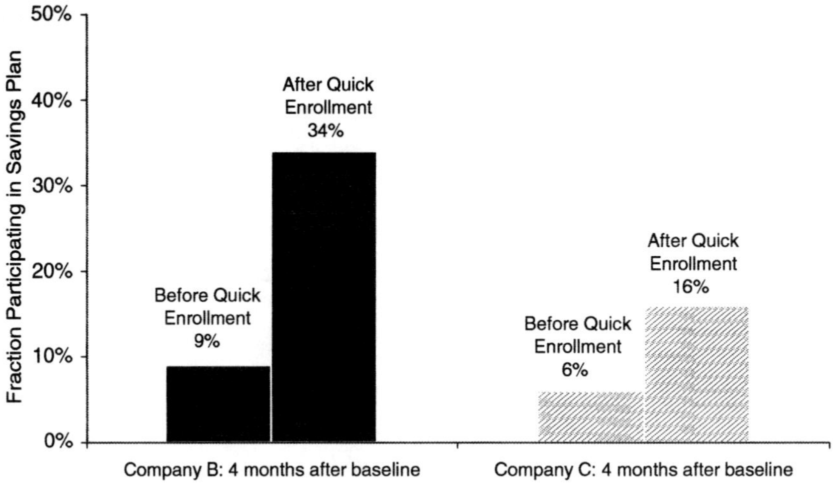

Figure 3-5. Quick enrollment and savings plan participation (Companies B and C). (*Source*: Choi, Laibson, and Madrian 2005*c*.)

at two different firms (see Choi, Laibson, and Madrian, 2005*c*). At Company B, new hires were given Quick Enrollment forms at orientation allowing them to check a box to be enrolled in their firm's savings plan at a 2 percent contribution rate with a preselected asset allocation (50% in a money market fund and 50% in a stable value fund). Participation rates for employees with 4 months of tenure tripled under Quick Enrollment, from 9 percent of new hires to 34 percent. At Company C, nonparticipating employees at all levels of tenure were mailed postage-paid Quick Enrollment response cards allowing them to check a box to be enrolled in their firm's savings plan at a 3 percent contribution rate allocated entirely to a money market fund. Relative to the enrollment trends of nonparticipants a year prior to the mailing, savings plan participation four months later more than doubled, from 6 percent of nonparticipants enrolling to 16 percent. A different implementation of Quick Enrollment at Company B directed toward existing nonparticipants allowed them to choose any contribution rate allowed by the plan with the same preselected asset allocation previously described. Fully 25 percent of nonparticipants signed up for the savings plan over a 4-month period following this version of Quick Enrollment (Beshears et al. 2006).

Beyond its effects on savings plan participation, the impact of Quick Enrollment on other savings outcomes is interesting because, like automatic enrollment, it induces a heavy clustering of enrollees at the employer-selected default contribution rate and asset allocation. At Company B, no savings plan participants affirmatively elected the Quick Enrollment default asset allocation prior to its implementation. Among those participants offered Quick Enrollment at the new hire orientations, 60 percent have the default asset allocation. Among those who enrolled in the savings plan when Quick Enrollment was offered to existing nonparticipants, 91 percent have the default asset allocation. The picture is similar at Company C, where only 6 percent of participants prior to Quick Enrollment affirmatively elected the default asset allocation. In contrast, 75–91 percent of existing nonparticipants who were offered Quick Enrollment and became participants have the Quick Enrollment default asset allocation.

The impact of Quick Enrollment on contribution rates is equally striking. At Company B, the fraction of new hires at the Quick Enrollment default contribution rate of 2 percent of pay increased from 1 percent of employees before Quick Enrollment to 14 percent of employees afterwards. At Company C, the fraction of newly participating employees at the Quick Enrollment default contribution rate of 3 percent increased from less than 1 percent of employees before Quick Enrollment to 12 percent of employees afterwards. In both companies, the fraction of savings plan participants at the Quick Enrollment defaults (as opposed to the fraction of employees overall) is much higher because the participation rates among the impacted groups are relatively low.

Explaining the Impact of Defaults on Retirement Savings Outcomes

The substantial evidence presented in the preceding section on the impact of defaults on savings outcomes is interesting for (at least) three reasons: first, in most of the examples cited, switching from one default to another resulted in very different savings outcomes even though the change in the default did not affect the menu of savings options available to individuals; second, none of the defaults proscribed employees from effecting a different savings outcome; and third, the direct transaction costs (filling out a form or calling a benefits hotline) for making savings plan changes were generally small.[7]

If direct transaction costs are not a plausible explanation for the persistence of savings plan defaults, then what factors are? In this section of the chapter, we consider three alternative explanations: (*a*) procrastination generated by the complexity of the decision-making task, (*b*) procrastination generated by present-biased preferences, and (*c*) a perception of the default as an endorsement for certain savings outcomes. Madrian and Shea

(2001) discuss some alternative explanations, but these three strike us as the most plausible given the existing empirical evidence.

The Complexity of Making a Nondefault Savings Plan Election

There are several sources of complexity involved in making an optimal savings plan decision. Consider, for example, the array of participation options in a typical DC savings plan. Individuals must first choose what fraction of compensation to contribute to their savings plan, which in a typical plan would be anything from 1 to 15 percent of compensation (in some plans even higher contribution rates are allowed). They must then choose how to allocate that contribution among the available fund options. In a plan with 10 funds and a maximum contribution rate of 15 percent, the number of different savings plan options is immense.

For some employees, a second source of complexity is learning how to evaluate this myriad of savings plan options. Surveys of financial literacy consistently find that many individuals are not well equipped to make complicated financial decisions. For example, in a survey of DC savings plan participants, John Hancock Financial Services (2002) reports:

- 38 percent of respondents say they have little or no financial knowledge;
- 40 percent of respondents believe that a money market fund contains stocks;
- two-thirds of respondents do not know that it is possible to lose money in government bonds; and
- respondents on average believe that employer stock is less risky than a stock mutual fund.

Given these results, it should not be surprising that two-thirds of these respondents also report that they would be better off working with an investment adviser than managing retirement investments solo.

The psychology literature has documented a tendency of individuals to put off making decisions as the complexity of the task increases (Shafir, Simonson, and Tversky 1993; Tversky and Shafir 1993; Dhar and Nowlis 1999; Iyengar and Lepper 2000). Evidence supporting the notion that the complexity of the asset allocation task leads employees to delay savings plan enrollment comes from a recent study by Iyengar, Huberman, and Jiang (2004). They document a strong negative relationship between the number of funds offered in a 401(k) plan and the 401(k) participation rate: having an additional 10 funds in the fund menu leads to a 1.5–2 percentage point decline in participation, a result that holds even among firms with a relatively low number of funds. One suspects that this would also act as a deterrent to making asset allocation changes after the initial participation decision has been made.

A likely reason that savings plan participation is so much higher under automatic enrollment than with an opt-in enrollment mechanism is that automatic enrollment decouples the savings plan participation decision from the contribution rate and asset allocation decision. The initial participation decision is simplified from one that involves evaluating a myriad of options to a simple comparison of two alternatives: nonparticipation (consumption or saving outside of the savings plan) versus participating at a prespecified contribution rate with a prespecified asset allocation. Furthermore, Madrian and Shea (2001) and Choi et al. (2004*b*) find that automatic enrollment has its largest impact on participation for those workers who generally have the least amount of financial sophistication—the young and those with low levels of tenure (who would have less knowledge about their own particular savings plan). These are workers for whom the complexity of the participation decision would be a greater deterrent to enrolling in the savings plan under an opt-in regime.

Quick Enrollment works in much the same way as automatic enrollment, simplifying the participation decision by giving individuals a predetermined contribution rate and asset allocation bundle(s) that need only be compared to nonparticipation. The effect of Quick Enrollment on participation, however, is not as great as that of automatic enrollment, suggesting that the participation increases under automatic enrollment are due to more than just the simplification of the decision-making task.

Present-Biased Preferences and Procrastination

Recent research in behavioral economics has fingered another reason for the observed persistence in savings plan outcomes—individual problems with self-control (Laibson, Repetto, and Tobacman 1998; O'Donoghue and Rabin 1999; Diamond and Koszegi 2003). As the adage goes, why do today what you can put off until tomorrow? O'Donoghue and Rabin (1999) propose a model in which, under certain conditions (specifically, *naïveté* about time-inconsistent preferences), individuals may never reallocate their portfolios away from poor-performing investments even when the direct transactions costs of doing so are relatively small. A similar type of argument can be made for delays in savings plan enrollment. The possibility of the latter is suggested by the fact that savings plan participation rates prior to automatic enrollment in Company A and other firms that have been studied (Madrian and Shea 2001; Choi et al. 2002, 2004*a*, 2004*b*) never exceed those under automatic enrollment, even at very high levels of tenure. It is also suggested by the substantial fraction of automatic enrollees at Company A who remained at the relatively low 3 percent default contribution rate 2 years after hire despite a 100 percent employer match on contributions up to 6 percent of pay. Additional corroborating evidence comes from Choi, Laibson, and Madrian (2005*a*), who document that even among older workers with very high average levels of tenure, roughly half fail to exploit the full match in their employer-sponsored savings plan, leaving matching contributions equal to roughly 1.3 percent of pay unclaimed (in companies without automatic enrollment).

The Default as an Endorsement

Default options may also influence outcomes if individuals perceive the default as an endorsement of a particular course of action (an endorsement effect). The lack of financial sophistication on the part of many individuals discussed above may lead them to search for advice without necessarily knowing the best place to find it. Because employer-sponsored savings plans are supposed to be run for the benefit of employees (that, after all, is why they are referred to as 'employee benefits'), some individuals may incorrectly perceive that an employer-specified default must be in the best interest of the firm's employees.[8]

Several pieces of evidence are consistent with the notion that employees perceive defaults in part as some sort of recommendation from their employer. The first comes from companies who have implemented automatic enrollment for only new hires going forward. In these companies, none of the employees hired before automatic enrollment are directly affected (i.e. none are automatically enrolled), but some of them will have affirmatively elected to participate in the savings plan before automatic enrollment was instituted for anyone, whereas others will have affirmatively elected to participate only after automatic enrollment was implemented for new hires going forward. Madrian and Shea (2001) show that the fraction of assets allocated to the automatic enrollment default investment fund is more than three times as high for the latter group as it is for the former (see Table 3-2).[9] Interestingly, Madrian and Shea do not find similar evidence for the contribution rates elected by these two groups of employees: those employees hired before automatic enrollment but who enroll in their savings plan only after automatic enrollment are not substantially more likely to choose the automatic enrollment default contribution rate than are their counterparts who enrolled in the savings plan before automatic enrollment. That the endorsement implicit in the automatic enrollment defaults is more important for asset allocation outcomes than for contribution rate outcomes is consistent with the notion that employees are much more uncertain about choosing an appropriate asset allocation than about

TABLE 3-2 Automatic Enrollment and Asset Allocation Outcomes of Employees Not Subject to Automatic Enrollment (Company D)

	Hired Before Automatic Enrollment and Initiated Participation Before Automatic Enrollment (%)	*Hired Before Automatic Enrollment but Initiated Participation after Automatic Enrollment Applied to Newly Hired Employees* (%)
Any balances in default fund	13.3	28.9
All balances in default fund	2.3	16.1

Source: Taken from Madrian and Shea (2001, Figures IVb and IVc).

choosing an appropriate contribution rate (or, at least, about choosing a contribution rate that garners the full employer match).[10]

Further evidence on the endorsement effect under automatic enrollment comes from the savings outcomes of employees hired under automatic enrollment who choose to move away from the automatic enrollment default. These individuals have overcome the forces of inertia and taken action. Even so, their asset allocation continues to be much more heavily invested in the automatic enrollment default fund than that of employees hired prior to automatic enrollment (Madrian and Shea 2001; Choi et al. 2004*b*). Table 3-3 illustrates this tendency for employees at Company A and Company D. The first column in Table 3-3 shows the importance of the automatic enrollment default asset allocation for employees hired before automatic enrollment (and, for Company A, employees who elected to

TABLE 3-3 Automatic Enrollment and Asset Allocation Outcomes of Employees Not at the Automatic Enrollment Default Asset Allocation and Contribution Rate (Companies A and D)

	Hired Before Automatic Enrollment (%)	*Hired after Automatic Enrollment but not at the Default Asset Allocation and Contribution Rate* (%)
Company A		
Any balances in default fund	9.9	19.4
All balances in default fund	1.4	9.3
Company D		
Any balances in default fund	18.2	71.3
All balances in default fund	5.2	30.8

Sources: Authors' own calculations (Company A) and Madrian and Shea (2001, Table VII) (Company D).

participate before automatic enrollment). The fraction of these employees with anything in the default fund is 10 percent in Company A and 18 percent in Company D. The fraction with everything invested in the default fund is lower still: 1 percent at Company A and 5 percent at Company D. In contrast, those employees hired under automatic enrollment who have made an active election to move away from the automatic enrollment default, changing either their asset allocation or their contribution rate or both, are much more heavily invested in the automatic enrollment default despite having incurred the transactions costs of changing the parameters of their savings plan participation. Among automatic enrollees who have made a change from the automatic enrollment default, the fraction with any balances in the default fund is 19 percent at Company A and 71 percent at Company D, much higher than for the employees hired before automatic enrollment. The proportional differences for those with everything in the automatic enrollment default fund are greater still. Clearly, the default fund exerts an impact on the asset allocation of employees hired under automatic enrollment even after these employees have elected to make a change. A final piece of evidence on the endorsement effect of savings plan defaults comes from the fraction of employee contributions invested in employer stock in companies where employer stock is included in the fund menu. Benartzi (2001), Holden and VanDerhei (2001), and Brown, Liang, and Weisbenner (2006) all find that when the employer directs matching contributions into employer stock, the fraction of the employee's own contributions allocated to employer stock is higher than when the match is allocated according to the employee's direction.

Designing Public Policy when Defaults Matter

There are many goals associated with public policy. When it comes to retirement saving, politicians, economists, and other social planners would largely agree that if governments are to sponsor costly social welfare programs for individuals who are impoverished, they should also promote institutions that provide sufficient income to individuals when retired to reduce the reliance on costly social welfare programs. Because of the risks that DB retirement income schemes impose on employers (through DB pensions) and governments/taxpayers (through social security), there has been a broader trend toward DC savings schemes through both private and government-sponsored institutions (e.g. 401(k) savings plans in the USA and the social security systems in Sweden and Chile). But if defaults have the potential to impact savings outcomes significantly in these types of schemes, what types of defaults should public policy encourage, especially if individuals have heterogeneous savings needs? In this section, we discuss first some of the conceptual issues associated with thinking about an 'optimal' default. We then give some examples of public policy and defaults in practice, both those that seem sensible from the standpoint of promoting better savings outcomes and those that do not.

Is There an 'Optimal' Default?

Choi et al. (2005) model the choice of an optimal default savings plan enrollment mechanism from the perspective of a social planner interested in maximizing individual welfare. In this model, defaults matter for three key reasons. First, individuals face a cost for opting out of the chosen default. Second, this cost varies over time, creating an option value to waiting for a low-cost period to take action. Third, individuals with present-biased preferences may procrastinate in their decision to opt out of the default, even in a low-cost period, if they mistakenly believe that they are more likely to do so in the future. Three different potential enrollment defaults emerge from the model: automatic enrollment, requiring an affirmative participation election (opt-in), and requiring employees to actively make a decision so that there is, in essence, no default (but all employees must bear the immediate transactions costs of deciding what to do). Choi et al. (2005) refer to this latter outcome as the 'active decision' approach. Which of these enrollment regimes is optimal varies according to the parameters in the model.

The conditions under which each of these approaches to savings plan enrollment is likely to be optimal, from both a theoretical and a practical standpoint, are discussed in detail in Choi et al. (2005), but we briefly describe them here. Defaults tend to be optimal when there is a large degree of homogeneity in individual preferences and when decision-makers have limited expertise. In the case of a firm with an employer match, if most employees would prefer to be saving at the match threshold, then automatic enrollment with a default contribution rate equal to the match threshold is likely to be optimal. Requiring an affirmative participation election, on the other hand, is likely to be optimal if most individuals share a preference not to be participating in the savings plan,[11] or if individuals have very heterogeneous preferences and little tendency to procrastinate. Requiring an active decision is more appropriate when individual heterogeneity implies that one choice is not ideal for everyone but individuals do have a tendency to procrastinate.

Although requiring the use of an active decision as an alternative to selecting a default is uncommon in the context of savings plans, Choi et al. (2005) study the effect of just such an approach on savings plan outcomes in one firm. They find that requiring employees to make an active decision leads to substantially higher initial participation rates than those achieved under an opt-in enrollment regime without any perverse effects on the distribution of contribution rates such as is observed with mechanisms like automatic enrollment or Quick Enrollment.

For the purposes of this study, the important point of the modeling effort in Choi et al. (2005) is that there is no single optimal savings plan enrollment mechanism—the optimal default depends on parameters in the model, which are likely to vary across both institutions and individuals. More generally, the framework for thinking about an optimal savings plan enrollment mechanism can be used to think about how sensible other types of economic defaults are likely to be. We turn now to a few specific examples related to savings.

For Better and for Worse: Public Policy and Defaults in Practice

There are many interesting examples of how public policy both encourages and discourages better savings plan outcomes, some that have already been mentioned and others that have not. The first is the legislative mandate that, in DB pension plans, the default payout option for married individuals is a joint-and-survivor annuity. As discussed above, this mandate resulted in a sizable increase in the fraction of married DB pension recipients with joint-and-survivor annuities. This mandate, which was a matter of public policy rather than a matter of choice for pension plan providers, was adopted in order to improve the financial security of widows after their husbands' deaths. Whether it was successful at this objective has not been examined. However, Johnson, Uccello, and Goldwyn (2003) show that those married individuals who have opted out of this default appear to have had economically sound reasons for doing so, such as having a spouse with either his or her own source of retirement income or a shorter life expectancy than the pension beneficiary.

In the context of thinking about an optimal default, there are three particularly interesting aspects of this joint-and-survivor annuity default. The first is that there are actually two different default annuities: one for single individuals (a single-life annuity) and the joint-and-survivor annuity for married individuals. Opt-in versus opt-out savings plan enrollment mechanisms, on the other hand, are blanket defaults that apply to everyone (unless individuals opt out). Clearly, there is a need to think more carefully about the potential role of more nuanced defaults that apply only to some individuals in certain situations. The second interesting feature of the joint-and-survivor annuity default is that the decision to accept the default or to opt out of it is irrevocable—once made it cannot be reversed. The third interesting feature, an extension of the second, is that because the annuitization outcome is irreversible, individuals cannot forever delay the decision about what type of annuity is most appropriate—any opt-out decision must be made before the pension beneficiary can start receiving pension income. These two features reduce the scope for procrastination due to present-biased preferences. Individuals for whom a single-life annuity is better face strong incentives to take action to express those preferences quickly. This consequence shares some similarities with the active decision approach to savings plan participation discussed above. Although there is a default (in contrast to the active decision approach discussed above), it is structured in such a way as to provide strong incentives to take action immediately for those individuals who desire to opt out.

Overall, many features of the joint-and-survivor annuity default seem to work well. The one drawback, perhaps, is that for most individuals, understanding annuity options is no less complicated than understanding asset allocation. Annuity providers are continuing to develop a rich set of annuity products, some of which may be more appropriate to particular individuals than the one-sized joint-and-survivor default specified for married pension beneficiaries. The complexity of evaluating the different available annuity products probably means that any default will significantly influence realized outcomes simply because of the endorsement effect.

Another interesting default to consider from a public policy perspective is the composition of the default investment fund in the DC component of various social security systems. In contrast to the default asset allocation chosen by most employers that have automatic enrollment in the USA, which tends to be a single mutual fund, some countries such as Sweden, Chile, and Mexico have selected a default that is a portfolio of different types of financial assets. For example, in Sweden the default includes exposure to domestic and international equities, bonds, and the money market.[12] Moreover, it is well diversified against geographical, industrial, and asset market shocks, and it comes with a relatively low expense ratio of approximately 0.16 percent. Although it is difficult to say whether the Swedish social security system could have chosen a better default asset allocation, Cronqvist and Thaler (2004) show that the portfolio performance of those in the default fund exceeded that of individuals who opted out of the default and selected their own asset allocation. On this metric, the default would seem to have been relatively well chosen.

The default investment portfolios in the Chilean social security system and in the DC component of the Mexican social security system are interesting for another reason—in both countries the default investment fund for older workers differs from that for younger workers (Rozinka and Tapia n.d.). In Chile, there are three different default asset allocations: one for workers younger than 35 years, a second for men aged 36–55 years and women aged 36–50 years, and a third for men aged 56 years and older and women aged 51 years and older. The Chilean default funds differ in their relative exposure to equities (both foreign and domestic) and fixed income securities, with the default portfolios holding fewer equities and more bonds as participants age. This pattern of equity versus bond holding is certainly consistent with what many financial planners would recommend. In Mexico, the default funds differ largely in the type of fixed income investments they hold. In contrast to the Swedish default asset allocation, the defaults in both Chile and Mexico are heavily weighted toward domestic securities. In Mexico, there are no foreign investments in the default funds; in Chile, the highest foreign investment exposure is 34 percent in the default fund for younger workers (Rozinka and Tapia n.d.). In Sweden, on the other hand, two-thirds of the default portfolio is in non-Swedish stocks, and probably represents inadequate geographic diversification in the Chilean and Mexican defaults.

Another interesting default to consider from a policy perspective is the treatment of savings plan balances following employee termination. This default shares one feature with the default annuity options just discussed. Rather than having a single blanket default option, the default outcome depends on the size of the terminated employee's account balance: balances less than $5,000 are sent to individuals as a cash distribution unless individuals direct the employer to roll over the balances into another qualified savings plan, whereas balances more than $5,000 are retained by the employer unless individuals direct otherwise. However, as previously noted, there is significant leakage from the retirement system for employees with account balances below the $5,000 threshold.

Policymakers in the USA reached an interesting compromise to deal with this issue of leakage. The cash distribution default is costly for employees because it reduces their long-term retirement accumulations, but retaining small account balances is costly for employers because of the fixed costs associated with retaining individual accounts. The public policy compromise applies to the accounts of terminated employees with balances greater than $1,000 and less than $5,000. For these accounts, employers cannot compel a cash distribution. Rather, they can keep the accounts (as was being done all along for accounts of greater than $5,000), or they can roll them over into qualified individual savings plans (e.g. an IRA). Employers retain the option to compel a cash distribution for accounts under $1,000, although they could change the default for these accounts as well and roll the balances into an IRA. Because this change had not taken effect at the time of writing, we cannot assess the outcome, but it at least seems like an example of public policy promoting better savings outcomes. There is a catch, however: the regulations pertaining to the default fund associated with these automatic IRA rollovers make it highly unlikely that any employer will pick anything other than an extremely conservative default fund (e.g. a money market fund). Thus, it is likely that the majority of \$1,000–\$5,000 account balances will be rolled over into an IRA following employee termination, where they will languish over time earning a rate of return that barely keeps pace with inflation. Public policy on this aspect of the default could probably do better.

Another area in which public policy could do better is with employer matches made in the form of employer stock. As already noted, employer matching contributions made in employer stock tend to stick where they land, which imposes greater financial risk on employees—first, because their retirement savings portfolio itself is not well diversified and, second, because much of the risk to their retirement savings portfolio is correlated with the risk to their labor income. Unfortunately, many employees do not seem to understand these risks. The John Hancock Financial Services *Eighth Defined Contribution Plan Survey* (2002) finds that savings plan participants on average rate employer stock as less risky than an equity mutual fund. Similarly, Benartzi et al. (2004) find that only 33 percent of savings plan participants believe that their employer stock is riskier than a diversified stock fund, whereas 39 percent believe it is equally risky and 25 percent believe it is safer. Furthermore, 20 percent of respondents say they would prefer \$1,000 in employer stock that they could not diversify until aged 50 years to \$1,000 that they could invest at their own discretion.

One could view public policy in this area as neutral: the government leaves companies to run their savings plans as they see fit, and some establish a match in which contributions are directed into employer stock. But contrast the approach here with the regulation of DB pension plans, in which employer stock holdings are limited to no more than 10 percent of total plan assets, or to the rather proactive joint-and-survivor annuity default. Public policy could certainly greatly reduce the amount of employer stock held in DC savings plans, either by precluding employer stock as an investment option altogether or by simply mandating that matching contributions be defaulted to the asset allocation selected by the employee.

Conclusion

This chapter has demonstrated the tremendous influence that defaults exert on realized savings outcomes at every stage of the savings life cycle: savings plan participation, contributions, asset allocation, rollovers, and decumulation. That defaults can so easily sway such a significant economic outcome has important implications for understanding the psychology of economic decision-making. But it also has important implications for the role of public policy toward saving. Defaults are not neutral—they can either facilitate or hinder better savings outcomes. Current public policies toward saving include examples of both.

Notes

[1] See the Employee Benefit Research Institute (2005) for a more detailed discussion of the US retirement income system.
[2] In a survey of large US employers, Hewitt Associates (2005) reports that 19% of companies used automatic enrollment in their 401(k) plans in 2005, up from 7% in 1999. In another survey, the Profit Sharing/401(k) Council of America (2005) reports that 8% of firms overall have automatic enrollment, but that the likelihood of having automatic enrollment was much higher in large than in small firms (24% vs 1%).
[3] See Choi, Laibson, and Madrian (2005*b*) for evidence that allowing employees to diversify out of a match directed into employer stock has only a small effect on asset allocation outcomes relative to not being able to diversify the match at all.
[4] Because the companies that offer employer stock tend to be larger firms, 35% of participants in 401(k) plans have an investment menu that includes employer stock (Even and Macpherson 2004) even though only 10% of plans offer employer stock (Mitchell and Utkus 2003).
[5] In January 2005, the threshold at which employers can compel a cash distribution for terminated employees fell from $5,000 to $1,000. For balances between $1,000 and $5,000, employers have two options absent other direction from the affected participants: retain the balances in their savings plan or roll over the balances into an IRA.
[6] Poterba, Venti, and Wise (1998) report that the probability that a cash distribution is rolled over into an IRA or another employer's savings plan is only 5–16% for distributions of less than $5,000. The overall probability that a cash distribution is rolled over into an IRA or another employer's savings plan or invested in some other savings vehicle is slightly higher, at 14–33%.
[7] See Choi, Laibson, and Madrian (2005*a*) for evidence on the magnitude of some of these direct transaction costs.
[8] While this may be true for some employer-specified defaults, in general firms weigh other issues such as cost and legal liability in their selection of defaults, not only the potential benefit to employees.
[9] The data for Company D in Table 3-2 comes from Madrian and Shea (2001). This company implemented automatic enrollment with a 3% default contribution rate invested wholly in a money market fund. The match threshold at this firm was 6%.
[10] Choi, Laibson, and Madrian (2005*c*) discuss in greater detail reasons why the asset allocation task may be more complicated for employees than the decision about how much to contribute to the savings plan.
[11] This could be true in a firm with a largely low-income workforce that has a high social security replacement rate, or in a firm with a generous DB pension as the primary source of retirement income.
[12] The specific asset allocation as reported in Cronqvist and Thaler (2004) is: Swedish stocks (17%), non-Swedish stocks (65%), inflation-indexed bonds (10%), hedge funds (4%), and private equity (4%).

References

Abadie, Alberto and Sebastien Gay (2004). 'The Impact of Presumed Consent Legislation on Cadaveric Organ Donation: A Cross-Country Study', *Journal of Health Economics*, 25(4): 599–620.

Benartzi, Shlomo (2001). 'Excessive Extrapolation and the Allocation of 401(k) Accounts to Company Stock', *Journal of Finance*, 56(5): 1747–64.

—— and Richard H. Thaler (2004). 'Save More Tomorrow™: Using Behavioral Economics to Increase Employee Saving', *Journal of Political Economy*, 112(1): 164–87.

—— —— Stephen Utkus, and Cass Sunstein (2004). 'Company Stock, Market Rationality, and Legal Reform', Mimeo, University of Chicago Graduate School of Business.

Beshears, John, James J. Choi, David Laibson, and Brigitte C. Madrian (2006). 'Simplification and Saving', Mimeo, Harvard University.

Brown, Jeffrey R., Nellie Liang, and Scott Weisbenner (2006). '401(k) Matching Contributions in Company Stock: Costs and Benefits for Firms and Workers', *Journal of Public Economics*, 90(6–7): 1315–46.

Choi, James J., David Laibson, and Brigitte C. Madrian (2005*a*). '$100 Bills on the Sidewalk: Suboptimal Saving in 401(k) Savings Plans', NBER Working Paper 11554.

—— —— —— (2005*b*). 'Are Empowerment and Education Enough: Underdiversification in 401(k) Plans', *Brookings Papers on Economic Activity*, 2: 151–98.

—— —— —— (2005*c*). 'Reducing the Complexity Costs of 401(k) Participation: The Case of Quick Enrollment', Harvard University Working Paper.

—— —— —— (2007). 'Flypaper Effects in Individual Asset Allocation', Yale University Working Paper.

—— —— —— and Andrew Metrick (2002). 'Defined Contribution Pensions: Plan Rules, Participant Choices, and the Path of Least Resistance', in James Poterba (ed.), *Tax Policy and the Economy*, vol. 16. Cambridge, MA: MIT Press.

—— —— —— —— (2004*a*). 'For Better or for Worse: Default Effects and 401(k) Savings Behavior', in David A. Wise (ed.), *Perspectives in the Economics of Aging*. Chicago, IL: University of Chicago Press.

—— —— —— —— (2004*b*). ' "Employees" Investment Decisions about Company Stock', in Olivia Mitchell and Stephen Utkus (eds.), *Pension Design and Structure: New Lessons from Behavioral Finance*. Oxford: Oxford University Press.

—— —— —— —— (2005). 'Optimal Defaults and Active Decisions', NBER Working Paper 11074. Cambridge, MA: National Bureau of Economic Research.

Cronqvist, Henrik and Richard H. Thaler (2004). 'Design Choices in Privatized Social Security Systems: Learning from the Swedish Experience', *American Economic Review Papers and Proceedings*, 94(2): 424–8.

Dhar, Ravi and Stephen N. Nowlis (1999). 'The Effect of Time Pressure on Consumer Choice Deferral', *Journal of Consumer Research*, 25(4): 369–84.

Diamond, Peter and Botond Koszegi (2003). 'Quasi-Hyperbolic Discounting and Retirement', *Journal of Public Economics*, 87(9–10): 1839–72.

Employee Benefit Research Institute (2005). 'The U.S. Retirement Income System', Washington, DC: Employee Benefit Research Institute, October 5. http://www.ebri.org/pdf/publications/facts/0405fact.pdf

Even, William E. and David A. Macpherson (2004). 'Company Stock in Pension Funds', *National Tax Journal*, 57(2): 299–313.

Hewitt Associates (2003). 'Increasing Participation through Quick Enrollment', Lincolnshire, IL: Hewitt Associates.

—— (2005). 'Survey Highlights: Trends and Experience in 401(k) Plans 2005', Lincolnshire, IL: Hewitt Associates.

Holden, Karen C. and Sean Nicholson (1998). 'Selection of a Joint-and-Survivor Pension', Institute for Research on Poverty Discussion Paper no. 1175–98, University of Wisconsin, Madison.

Holden, Sarah and Jack VanDerhei (2001). '401(k) Plan Asset Allocation, Account Balances, and Loan Activity in 2000', *ICI Perspective*, 7(5): 1–27.

—— and Kathleen Zick (2000). 'Distributional Changes in Income and Wealth upon Widowhood: Implications for Private Insurance and Public Policy', in *Retirement Needs Framework*, SOA Monograph M-RS00–1. Schaumburg, IL: Society of Actuaries.

Iyengar, Sheena S. and Mark Lepper (2000). 'When Choice is Demotivating: Can One Desire Too Much of a Good Thing?', *Journal of Personality and Social Psychology*, 79(6): 995–1006.

—— Gur Huberman, and Wei Jiang (2004). 'How Much Choice is Too Much: Contributions to 401(k) Retirement Plans', in Olivia S. Mitchell and Stephen Utkus (eds.), *Pension Design and Structure: New Lessons from Behavioral Finance.* Oxford and London: Oxford University Press.

John Hancock Financial Services (2002). *Eighth Defined Contribution Plan Survey: Insight into Participant Investment Knowledge & Behavior.* Boston, MA: John Hancock Financial Services.

Johnson, Eric J. and Daniel G. Goldstein (2003). 'Do Defaults Save Lives?', *Science*, 302: 1338–9.

—— John Hershey, Jacqueline Meszaros, and Howard Kunreuther (1993). 'Framing, Probability Distortions, and Insurance Decisions', *Journal of Risk and Uncertainty*, 7(1): 35–53.

—— Steven Bellman, and Gerald L. Lohse (2003). 'Defaults, Framing and Privacy: Why Opting In-Opting Out', *Marketing Letters*, 13(1): 5–15.

Johnson, Richard W., Cori E. Uccello, and Joshua H. Goldwyn (2003). 'Single Life versus Joint and Survivor Pension Payout Options: How Do Married Retirees Choose?', Washington, DC: Urban Institute.

Laibson, David I., Andrea Repetto, and Jeremy Tobacman (1998). 'Self-Control and Saving for Retirement', *Brookings Papers on Economic Activity*, 1: 91–196.

Madrian, Brigitte C. and Dennis F. Shea (November 2001). 'The Power of Suggestion: Inertia in 401(k) Participation and Savings Behavior', *Quarterly Journal of Economics*, 116(4): 1149–87.

Mitchell, Olivia S. and Steven Utkus (2003). 'The Role of Company Stock in Defined Contribution Plans', in Olivia S. Mitchell and Kent Smetters (eds.), *The Pension Challenge: Risk Transfers and Retirement Income Security.* Oxford: Oxford University Press.

O'Donoghue, Ted and Matthew Rabin (1999). 'Procrastination in Preparing for Retirement', in Henry Aaron (ed.), *Behavioral Dimensions of Retirement Economics.* Washington, DC: Brookings Institute.

Park, C. Whan, Sung Y. Jun, and Deborah J. MacInnis (2000). 'Choosing What I Want versus Rejecting What I Do not Want: An Application of Decision Framing to Product Option Choice Decisions', *Journal of Marketing Research*, 37(2): 187–202.

Poterba, James M., Steven F. Venti, and David A. Wise (1998). 'Lump Sum Distributions from Retirement Savings Plans: Receipt and Utilization', in David A. Wise (ed.), *Inquiries in the Economics of Aging.* Chicago, IL: University of Chicago Press.

Profit Sharing/401(k) Council of America (2005). '48th Annual Survey of Profit Sharing and 401(k) Plans' (October 10). http://www.psca.org/DATA/48th.html

Rozinka, Edina and Waldo Tapia (n.d.). 'Survey of Investment Choice by Pension Fund Members', Organisation for Economic Co-operation and Development (OECD). http://www.oecd.org/dataoecd/46/61/36553753.pdf, accessed September 7, 2006.

Saku, Aura (2001). 'Does the Balance of Power Within a Family Matter? The Case of the Retirement Equity Act', IGIER Working Paper 202. Milan, Italy: Innocenzo Gasparini Institute for Economic Research.

Shafir, Eldar, Itamar Simonson, and Amos Tversky (1993). 'Reason-Based Choice', *Cognition*, 49(1–2): 11–36.

Tversky, Amos and Eldar Shafir (1993). *Choice Under Conflict: The Dynamics of Deferred Decision.* Stanford, CA: Stanford Center on Conflict and Negotiation, Stanford University.

US Department of Labor, Employee Benefits Security Administration (2005). *Private Pension Plan Bulletin*, October 4. http://www.dol.gov/ebsa/PDF/2000pensionplanbulletin.pdf

Utkus, Stephen P. (2002). *A Recent Successful Test of the SMarT Program.* Valley Forge, PA: Vanguard Center for Retirement Research.

—— and Jean A. Young (2004). *Lessons from Behavioral Finance and the Autopilot 401(k).* Valley Forge, PA: Vanguard Center for Retirement Research.

The Vanguard Group (2001). *Automatic Enrollment: Vanguard Client Experience.* Valley Forge, PA: The Vanguard Group.

Chapter 4

The Gender Impact of Social Security Reform in Latin America

Estelle James, Alejandra Cox Edwards, and Rebeca Wong

Over the past two decades many countries have adopted multipillar pension systems that include both a public DB and a private DC pillar. Critics of these pension reforms argue that the tight link between payroll contributions and benefits in the DC pillar will produce lower pensions for women. In contrast, supporters of these reforms argue that multipillar systems remove distortions that favored men and permit a more targeted public pillar that will help women. This debate is important because the majority of old people are women, pockets of poverty among the old are the largest among very old women, and pension programs affect work incentives for women.[1]

To test these conflicting claims, and to analyze more generally the gender impact of alternative pension systems, this chapter examines the differential impact on genders of the new and old systems in three Latin-American countries: Chile, Argentina, and Mexico. In all three cases, the new social security system includes two mandatory components: privately managed funded individual accounts (DC) and a publicly managed and financed safety net. On the basis of household survey data, we simulate the wage and employment histories of representative men and women. These histories are used to project and compare what their pensions would be under

Parts of this chapter have previously appeared as 'The Gender Impact of Pension Reform' (*2003b*), *The Journal of Pension Economics and Finance*, 2(2):2003, www.pensions-journal.com/articles/v2n2/. Reprinted by permission.

This chapter is part of a joint project carried out by James, Edwards, and Wong. It was financed by the Economics and Gender Trust of the World Bank, for which we express our appreciation. It is heavily based on an earlier version—James, Edwards, and Wong (2003*b*)—but the tables are different. For earlier chapters coming out of this project, see Edwards (2000*a*, 2000*b*, 2001*a*, 2001*b*, 2001*c*, 2002), Parker and Wong (2001), and Wong and Parker (2001). For an earlier expanded version, see James, Edwards, and Wong (2003*a*). A much expanded version is James, Edwards, and Wong (forthcoming).

The authors wish to thank Gustavo de Marco, Rafael Rofman, Hermann von Gersdorff, Augusto Iglesias, and David Madero Suarez for their helpful comments on earlier versions and for answering our endless questions. We owe a special debt to Edward Whitehouse for sharing with us his model for deriving actuarial factors used to convert accumulations to annuity payouts.

the new systems and what they would have been under the old system rules, emphasizing the key design features that determine these gender outcomes.

Why Do Pension Systems and Reforms Have a Gender Impact?

In most public pension programs, workers receive benefits that depend on wages and years of work or more directly on their contributions. These contributory social security systems may have developed because pensions were viewed as a replacement for wages and people are more willing to pay the tax that finances the system if they receive a contingent monetary benefit in return. However, women are likely to have worked and contributed fewer years than men have and earned lower wages when working, which gives them a smaller pension. The labor market and demographic differences between men and women that affect their pensions are well known.

The labor market differences are:

- *Labor force participation rates*: Women, especially married women, traditionally have less continuous employment than do men due to the division of labor within the family. They work roughly 50–70 percent as many years as men in the three sample countries. In industrialized countries the female labor force participation rate is still 10–30 percent below that of men (Ginn, Street, and Arber 2001; OECD 2003). Even when women work, their work is usually part-time, temporary, and informal.
- *Wage levels and age-earnings profiles*: In Chile, Mexico, and Argentina, younger women earn almost as much as men, after controlling for education. However, earnings diverge with age—prime age male earnings rise 2–3 percent per year while female earnings rise 1–2 percent. This may be due, at least in part, to the fact that the experience gap between men and women increases with age. By age 50 women earn only 60–70 percent as much as men, per month worked (James, Edwards, and Wong 2003*a*). In countries like the UK, Canada, and Australia, women's hourly wage rates are 15–30 percent less than men's, controlling for age and education (US GAO 1997; Ginn, Street, and Arber 2001).
- *Different retirement ages*: Social security rules in many countries allow women to retire earlier than men. For example, in Chile and Argentina, women are permitted to retire five years earlier than men. These differential rules started in traditional DB systems and

frequently continue in reformed systems—but the penalty for early retirement is greater in a DC system.

The demographic differences are:

- *Longevity*: In most countries, women at age 60 have a life expectancy that is 3–4 years greater than that of men. In Chile, a woman who retires at age 60 can expect to live 7.5 years more than her husband when he retires at age 65, on average. Thus retirement accumulation yields lower annual pensions for women, especially if gender-specific mortality tables are used for annuitization, as in Latin America. In addition, women are more likely to grow very old, by which time they have used up any voluntary savings and are therefore more likely to live in poverty.
- *Widowhood*: Women tend to be younger than their husbands yet live longer, so are likelier to become widows. (In the USA, 72% of women aged 80–84 years are widows but only 27% of men are widowers.) Hence survivor's pensions are of key importance to women. Without survivor's benefits, widows who did not work in the labor market are likely to find themselves impoverished. Even widows who have a pension of their own would find their household incomes cut by as much as 70 percent without survivor's benefits. Since household costs fall by only 35 percent when the husband dies, due to household economies of scale, widows find their income falls far more than their cost of living. Survivor's benefits fill in this gap.[2]

Given this background, we conjecture that recent reforms designed to link benefits more closely with contributions will produce lower own-annuities for women than for men. Partly to mitigate this effect, the new systems in Latin America contain public DB or guarantees—usually financed by general revenues—which are targeted toward low earners. We expect that these public elements will generate transfer payments that favor women, but detailed arrangements such as degree of targeting, years of work required for eligibility, retirement age, and indexation provisions dictate which women benefit and how much. The Latin-American reforms also contain elaborate restrictions at the payout stage, especially regarding annuitization, that redistribute pensions between the genders. We expect that the common requirement of survivor's benefits and joint annuities will generate an important intrafamily redistribution toward women. We measure the combined gender impact of own-annuities, public transfers, and mandatory joint pensions on monthly and lifetime benefits and redistributions.

Finally, the new systems replaced PAYGO DB systems in which contributions and benefits were only loosely linked, and women must choose between receiving their own benefit or the widow's benefit. The old systems favored women in some ways but hurt them in others; thus, the net impact of the change is uncertain a priori. We examine this question empirically.

Key Design Features of the Old and New Systems

With some important variations, described below, the Chilean system was emulated in Mexico and Argentina, as well as in other Latin-American countries that adopted multipillar systems. A brief discussion follows some of the features of the new systems in Chile, Mexico, and Argentina that affect gender outcomes. For more detailed descriptions of the pension systems in these countries, refer to the chapters in this volume (Arenas de Mesa et al. 2007; Rofman 2007; Sinha and de los Angeles Yañez 2007).

The new system in Chile requires a 10 percent payroll contribution to individual accounts, plus an additional 2.5–3 percent to cover administrative costs and survivor's and disability insurance (James et al. 2000; James, Smalhout, and Vittas 2001; AIOS 2005).[3] Upon retirement (age 65 for men, 60 for women), workers can make gradual withdrawals from their accounts or buy an annuity that must be joint (60% to survivor) for married men. (Lump sums are very restricted.)

A minimum pension guarantee (MPG) is given to those who have contributed at least twenty years. The MPG is currently about 25 percent of the average wage, rising to 27 percent after age 70 and 29 percent after 75. If the worker's pension from private retirement saving does not reach the MPG level, the government uses general revenues to top it up. The MPG is formally indexed to prices and therefore retains a constant purchasing power. However, so far the MPG has risen faster than prices, roughly at the same pace as average wages, due to ad hoc political decisions. Because of productivity growth, wages in Chile have risen 2 percent faster than prices. De facto wage indexation of the MPG means that its purchasing power increases with wage growth over time. In the simulations below we usually assume price indexation but in some cases we show the striking difference implied by wage indexation. While we cannot know what the future holds, it will probably be somewhere between these two extremes.

In Argentina,[4] workers contribute 11 percent of payroll, of which 2.5–3.25 percent is deducted to cover administrative costs and survivor's and disability insurance fees; we use a net investment of 7.75 percent in our simulations (James et al. 2000; James, Smalhout, and Vittas 2001; AIOS 2005).[5] Upon retirement (age 65 for men, 60 for women), the accumulated assets are taken out in the form of gradual withdrawals, annuities (joint annuities with 70% to the survivor), or a lump sum for account balances above the specified threshold. Instead of a Chilean-type MPG, Argentina provides a basic 'flat' benefit that is fixed in nominal terms. It was originally financed by a payroll tax, but general revenues have now been partially substituted. The full flat benefit is paid to all eligible workers, making it much more expensive than the MPG top-up. To contain costs, eligibility is restricted to workers with at least thirty years of contributions—which excludes most women. Workers, mainly women, who reach age 70 with 10 years of contributions are granted a reduced flat pension that is 70 percent of the full benefit. Widows also inherit 70 percent of their husband's flat benefit (the 'widow's flat') when the spouse dies.

In Mexico, a contribution of 6.5 percent of payroll is made to individual accounts. Administrative fees are 1.4–1.9 percent of wages; in our simulations we use a net of 4.6 percent (James et al. 2000; James, Smalhout, and Vittas 2001; AIOS 2005). (Disability and survivor's insurance are financed by separate contribution.) Retirement income is further augmented by a 5 percent contribution of each worker's wage to a housing fund, called INFONAVIT (Instituto de Fondo Nacional de la Vivienda para los Trabajadores). If a worker does not borrow the money in the housing fund to purchase a home, it becomes part of the worker's retirement assets.[6] During the accumulations stage, workers can choose among competing investment managers, as in Chile and Argentina. Upon retirement—at age 65 for both genders—workers choose an annuity (joint with 60% to the survivor) or gradual withdrawals spread over both spouses' lifetimes.

The state helps finance this system in three ways. First, for each day of work it pays a flat 'social quota' (SQ) to each account. The SQ was initially equal to 5.5 percent of one daily minimum wage, which was then 2.2 percent of the average wage. Since it was supposed to be price-indexed, this percentage will decline, as wages rise faster than prices over time. The SQ is designed to increase the accounts of low-income workers and their incentives to join the system. It is financed out of general revenues. Second, workers are guaranteed a minimum pension, initially equal to the minimum wage (40% of the average wage) indexed to inflation—provided they contribute for a total of twenty-four years. Third, although the new system is mandatory for new workers, those who were already in the labor force when the reforms were made can opt back into the old system on retirement. This study focuses on new workers who are not entitled to this opt-back provision.

Methodology

Analysis of how women fare relative to men in the new and old social security systems is made difficult by a number of factors. First, the new systems have not been in place long enough to be mature. That is, current retirees in Chile and Argentina are subjected to a mixture of old and new system benefits. We do not know what will be the benefit of someone who is fully under the new system. In Mexico almost everyone has retired under old-system rules, given the short period for accumulation and the option that current workers have to revert to the old system on retirement. Moreover, in all three countries we do not know the future rate of wage growth and rate of return on investments, on which DC benefits depend. Along similar lines, longitudinal data are not available. Thus, we could not use actual employment histories of current retirees and workers to estimate their retirement accumulations and entitlements.

We addressed these problems by constructing synthetic men and women—using cross-sectional data on current behavior of people at different ages, educational levels, and marital status to proxy the lifetime employment, wage, and contribution histories of 'typical' persons in each category. We then simulated how the average man and woman in each educational category would fare under the rules of the old and new systems, given these histories. Five educational levels are presented, ranging from incomplete primary to several years of postsecondary. The median group has full secondary education in Chile, incomplete secondary education in Argentina, and middle school education (nine years) in Mexico. We use education as a proxy for 'permanent income'.

This methodology assumes that age-specific labor force participation and wage behavior will remain constant through time (except for secular wage growth), separately for each educational level. In reality, female labor force participation rates are strongly positively correlated with education, and educational levels have been rising dramatically over time. This means that aggregate female labor force participation rates will also rise over time. Changing social norms are leading to additional increases in female employment probabilities within each educational category. Moreover, the work incentives and disincentives in the new pension systems may alter work habits, so participation rates may be endogenous. To the degree that rising labor force participation rates are due to increased education, the numbers will remain constant within educational grouping even if the aggregate numbers shift. Our analysis of the relationship between women's education and labor force participation rates over time indicates that one-third to one-half of the aggregate increase is due to changes in educational composition of the population and the remainder is due to other factors (James, Edwards, and Wong forthcoming).

These potential changes in age-specific female labor force participation rates were not taken into account directly. However, in addition to the 'average' woman with average work experience in each educational group, we also calculated pensions for 'ten-year women', women who worked only ten years (prior to childbearing), and 'full-career women', women who had the same labor force participation and retirement age as men. Today's younger workers will probably look more like the full-career women when they retire due to educational shifts and increased work propensities for other reasons. The absence of longitudinal or retrospective data means that we could not estimate wages as a function of experience, so the lifetime earnings and pensions of full-career women are probably understated.

The representative men and women are assumed to be single until the median age of marriage in each country and married thereafter. They marry within their educational class, and the average husband is 3 years older than the wife. The data are not adequate to model pensions of the small proportion of women who remain single throughout their lifetimes. However, the analysis of their work patterns indicates that singles work 50–100 percent more than married women. Thus, our simulations for full-career women may give us a rough approximation of the lifetime earnings and benefits of single women.

Data

We seek to analyze the retirement incomes of women covered by the social security system. (Many women do not work in the formal labor market and hence are not covered by the formal social security system.) In constructing our synthetic men and women, we used national household surveys for urban areas for 1994 (Chile), 1996 (Argentina), and 1997 (Mexico).[7] These data do not coincide precisely with groups that are actually covered by the social security system. While most social security affiliates live in urban areas, some live in rural areas, and some urban residents are not covered by social security. In Chile, the wage and work data primarily cover full-time workers who contribute. The Chilean data allow us to identify social security affiliates and the contributing behavior of affiliates. However, in Argentina and Mexico the data cover full-time plus part-time workers, affiliates plus nonaffiliates. Since many of these are not in the social security system, our data may understate wages and work of women who were covered by social security in these countries. Operating in the opposite direction, we attributed all working time as contributing time, but we know that some part of this work is outside the formal labor sector and social security system, in which case our data would overestimate lifetime contributions, annuities, and eligibility for the public benefit. While our object is to characterize the behavior of men and women who are affiliated with social security and contribute when they work, it is important to remember that a substantial portion of individuals are not affiliated, and many do not contribute much of their working time even if they are—the problem of low density of contributions. We return to this problem later on.

Simulations

In the following sections, we use these employment histories to simulate the accumulations, annuities, and public benefit entitlements that different groups of men and women can expect under the new systems. We simulate the case of young workers, entering the labor market currently and retiring 40–45 years later. Accumulations and annuities under DC plans are very sensitive to rates of return on investments and rates of wage growth. In our baseline simulations, we assume a 'moderate growth' scenario in which economywide real wage growth is 2 percent per year and the real rate of return on investments, net of administrative fees, is 5 percent prior to retirement. (The actual return has been much higher than this so far—for example, it has averaged over 10% real in Chile since the start of the system—but these high rates are unlikely to continue in the long run.) The return during the payout stage is assumed to be 3.5 percent, given the likelihood that many will choose a lower risk fixed-rate annuity (see James and Song 2001; James and Vittas 2001).

Sensitivity analyses assuming a 3 percent real rate of return during the accumulation stage, 1.5 percent during annuitization, and a 0 percent rate of wage growth were also carried out. The gender differentials in this 'slow growth' case were very similar to the baseline, except that the relative role of the public benefit increases dramatically. The tables in this chapter show only the baseline case. (For details on the slow growth case, see James, Edwards, and Wong 2003*a*, 2003*b*, and forthcoming.) Severe portfolio restrictions in Latin America ensure that rates of return will be similar for all workers. If yields were lower for women because they tend to choose a risk-averse portfolio, this would lead to a lower gender ratio.[8] Finally, throughout this analysis we abstract from inflation. As is discussed briefly below, this probably leads us to understate the gender improvement from the new system.

Although both gradual withdrawals and annuities are permitted at the payout stage, to impute a stable annual flow for purposes of this analysis we assume that these accumulations are fully annuitized on retirement. We derive the annuity payouts by dividing the projected accumulation by relevant annuity factors, which depend on the interest and mortality rates. We use World Bank mortality tables that include expected longevity improvement factors for the cohort retiring in 2040, which is the approximate year when young workers today will retire. Gender-specific tables are used by insurance companies in the three countries and by our analysis. These data do not allow us to differentiate longevity by educational or income level, which leads us to overestimate lifetime system progressivity. Men and women are assumed to retire at the age that is specified in each country. In reality, we know that early retirement is common for both genders, which will reduce the size of pension though not necessarily the gender differential. While we start by comparing monthly benefits, to analyze transfers from different sources we shift to a comparison of lifetime benefits, since retirement age and expected age of death vary by gender and country and benefits from the joint annuity start flowing to widows in very old age.[9]

The Old System Counterfactual

We start out by analyzing only the new systems, then move on to compare the gender impact of the new and the old systems. This approach introduces an additional set of methodological problems. The old systems were actuarially unbalanced and so could not have delivered their promised benefits. In the long run, all these countries faced the prospect of raising taxes (which were difficult to collect) and/or reneging on their pension promises. Chile was facing financial insolvency even in the short term, and Argentina was already defaulting on payments to retirees. Given this uncertainty regarding benefit payments in the old system, what is the counterfactual to the new system?

We avoid this problem by applying the DB formulas in place just before the reform and by focusing on relative positions rather than absolute gains and losses to different gender-education-marital groups. We thus abstract from efficiency effects that might lead everyone to be better or worse off. We ask: which groups gained or lost the most in relative terms from the reform? Did gender ratios improve or deteriorate? Implicitly, this means our counterfactual is any system in which the fiscal adjustment to the preexisting insolvency is distributionally neutral—involving equiproportional benefit cuts or tax increases for each group. We compare the new system with this counterfactual.

Retirement Income for Women versus Men in the New System

Using the methodology just described, we estimate the monthly and lifetime benefits representative women and men would receive from private annuities, public benefits, and intrahousehold transfers. All monetary values have been converted to 2002 US dollars. (For Argentina, this exchange rate was about one-third of the rate that obtained during our study period prior to the country's fiscal crisis.)

Income from Women's Own-Annuities

To simplify, we assume here that all workers retire at the legal retirement age: 60 for women in Chile and Argentina, 65 for women in Mexico, and 65 for men in all three countries. Women with 'average' employment experience receive annuities that are only 30–50 percent those of men with similar education because of their lower lifetime work and wages and earlier retirement. The lower benefits for women are partly because of their earlier allowable retirement age in Chile and Argentina. Few women postpone taking their pension beyond age 60, possibly because they do not realize the large difference in the pension amount that would accrue. If women in Chile and Argentina delayed pensioning until age 65, they would collect interest for 5 more years and their annuities would cover 5 fewer years. Tables 4-1a and 4-1b and Figures 4-1a, 4-1b, and 4-1c show that their accumulations would increase by 25–30 percent and their monthly pensions by almost 50 percent, and the gender ratio would narrow substantially. The increase would be even larger if they worked and contributed during this period. The equal retirement ages for men and women in Mexico is the main reason why female/male ratios of annuities are projected to be higher than in Argentina and almost as high as in Chile, despite the relatively lower wages and work histories of Mexican women.

The monthly annuities of 'full-career women', who work as much as men, are higher than those of average women but only 60–75 percent as large as those of men. The remaining difference is due to the lower wage that women have received and the smaller contributions they have therefore made.

TABLE 4-1a Simulated Future Monthly Annuities from Individual Accounts (Based on 5% Real Return in Accumulation Stage, 3.5% in Annuity Stage, 2% Real Wage Growth, Data in 2002 US$)

			Chile		
	Incomplete Primary	*Incomplete Secondary*	*Complete Secondary*	*Up to 4 Post Secondary*	*5+ yrs Post-Secondary*
Average married males, RA = 65					
Annuity	$179	$259	$386	$538	$1,240
Females					
Average women, RA = 60	$59	$83	$146	$241	$444
Average woman if RA = 65	88	121	213	351	661
Full-career woman, RA = 65	136	183	297	408	702
10-year woman, RA = 60	36	42	55	87	140

(*cont.*)

TABLE 4-1a (*Continued*)

	Argentina				
	Incomplete Primary	*Incomplete Secondary*	*Complete Secondary*	*Some Post-Secondary*	*University Degree*
Average married males, RA[a] = 65					
Annuity	$153	$233	$349	$362	$701
Females					
Average woman, RA = 60	$32	$46	$91	$127	$248
Average woman if RA = 65	47	67	132	185	360
FC,[b] RA = 65	101	140	228	238	414
10-year,[c] RA = 60	22	33	42	52	87
			Mexico		
	0–5	6–8	9	10–12	13+
Average married males, RA = 65					
Annuity	$267	$310	$381	$481	$822
Females, RA = 65					
Average woman	$78	$93	$123	$199	$407
FC woman	162	201	247	362	558
10-year woman	47	51	61	86	125

Source: Calculations by authors. See text and James, Edwards, and Wong (forthcoming) for fuller discussion of data and methodology. WB gender-specific mortality tables for cohort retiring in 2040 are used to generate actuarial factors for annuity pricing.

Notes: Joint annuity payouts are given for married men and women in Argentina and Mexico, individual annuities for women in Chile, as required by law. Wives are assumed to be three years younger than their husbands. World Bank gender-specific mortality tables for each country for cohorts retiring in 2040 are used to generate actuarial factors. Wives have three to four years greater longevity than their husbands. MPG in Chile, flat benefit in Argentina, and annuity from the social quota (SQ) in Mexico are not included in this table.

[a]RA: Retirement age.

[b]FC: Full-career woman with same labor force participation rate as men.

[c]10-year woman: Works for ten years, prior to having children.

Women with higher education have higher labor force participation rates than do others, making them more like full-career women. However, they continue to be adversely affected by their lower retirement age, and the wage gap tends to increase for women with the highest education. As a result, female/male pension ratios increase with educational level, until the top level, when they typically fall.

TABLE 4-1b Female/Male Ratio of Simulated Monthly Annuities from Individual Accounts (in Percentages) (Based on 5% Real Return in Accumulation Stage, 3.5% in Annuity Stage, 2% Real Wage Growth, Data in 2002 US$)

			Chile		
	Incomplete Primary	*Incomplete Secondary*	*Complete Secondary*	*Up to 4 post-Secondary*	*5+ years Post-Secondary*
Average married males, RA = 65					
Annuity	100	100	100	100	100
Females					
Average women, RA = 60	33	32	38	45	36
Average woman if RA = 65	49	47	55	65	53
Full-career woman, RA = 65	76	71	77	76	57
10-year woman, RA = 60	20	16	14	16	11
			Argentina		
	Incomplete Primary	*Incomplete Secondary*	*Complete Secondary*	*Some Post-Secondary*	*University Degree*
Average married males, RA = 65					
Annuity	100	100	100	100	100
Females					
Average woman, RA = 60	21	20	26	35	35
Average woman if RA = 65	31	29	38	51	51
FC, RA = 65	66	60	65	66	59
10-year, RA = 60	14	14	12	14	12
			Mexico		
	0–5	6–8	9	10–12	13+
Average married males, RA = 65					
Annuity	100	100	100	100	100
Females, RA = 65					
Average woman	29	30	32	41	49
FC woman	61	65	65	75	68
10-year woman	18	17	16	18	15

Source: Calculations by authors. See Table 4-1a for definitions and methodology.

Notes: The female/male ratio is the ratio of annuities of female to male in the same educational and marital categories.

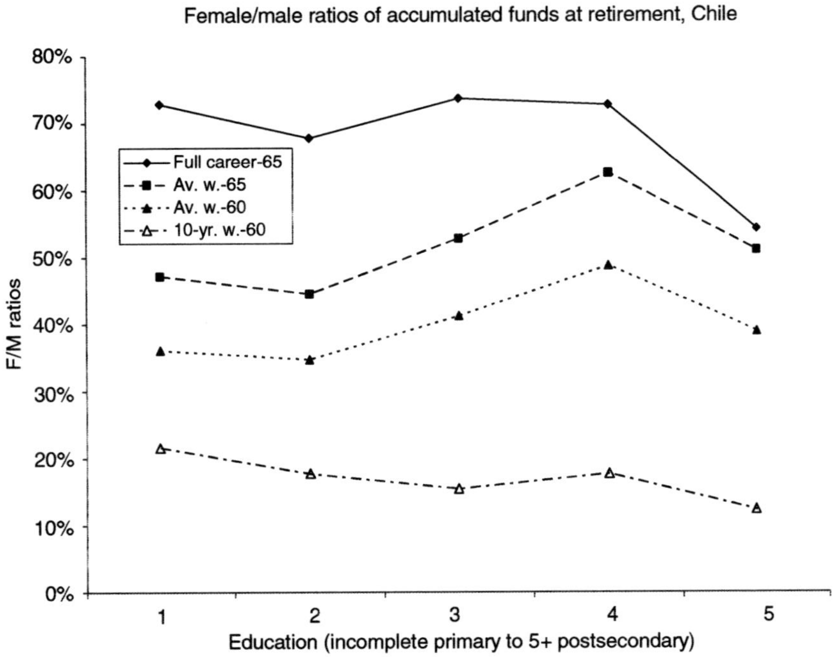

Figure 4-1a. More work and postponed retirement increase female/male ratios of accumulations (Chile).

Income from the Public Benefit

As discussed above, the MPG in Chile, the flat benefit and widow's flat benefit in Argentina, and the SQ in Mexico provide a public benefit that goes disproportionately to low earners. These public benefits raise the total pension of low earners by a much higher percentage than that of high earners, which also means they raise the pensions of women proportionately more than men (Table 4-2). However, the precise effect on women depends on the design of the benefit.

In Chile, if the MPG is price-indexed (as it is formally), it raises the total monthly pension of the average woman who has not completed primary school by 31 percent (Figure 4-2a). Average women in higher educational categories do not receive this benefit, nor do full-career women, because their own-annuity is projected to be above the MPG floor. (For the same reason very few men are projected to receive the public benefit.) Its impact is quite small because a price-indexed MPG that is 25 percent of the average wage today will be only 12 percent by the time today's young workers retire. Because the MPG is currently about double the official poverty line, it will keep all eligible women out of poverty—but it will not help any except the

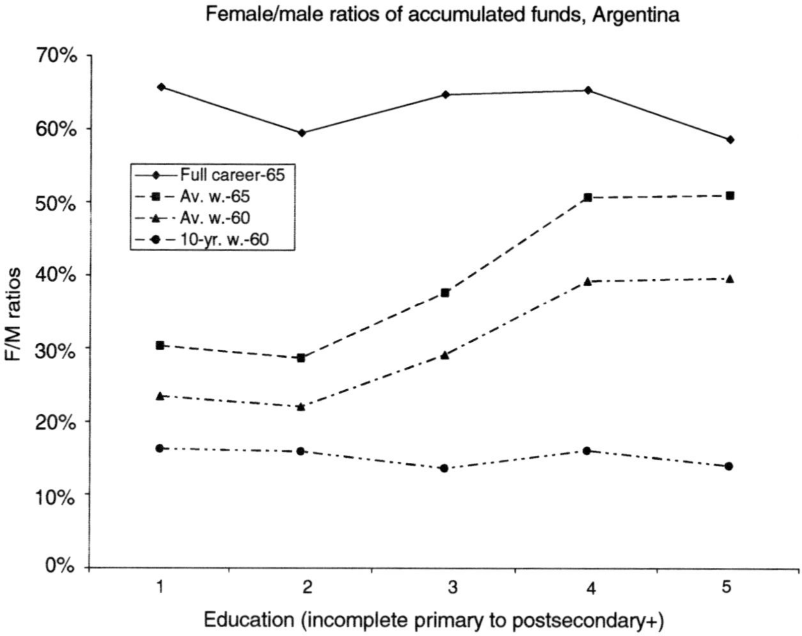

Figure 4-1b. More work and postponed retirement increase female/male ratios of accumulations (Argentina).

lowest earners, it becomes less relevant as it falls further behind the average wage in the economy, and it costs very little.

On the other hand, if the MPG is wage-indexed (as it has been de facto, by political decisions), the story is quite different. With expected wage growth of 2 percent yearly, the MPG will more than double over the working life of today's young worker. Because it grows at the same rate as wages, it remains at 25–29 percent of the average wage. In this scenario, most women (even some full-career women and some men) are likely to receive some MPG top-up. For women with average work histories in the bottom educational category, a wage-linked MPG will almost triple their own-annuities and bring their total retirement income very close to that of their male counterparts. Of course, this increased size of and access to the MPG raises its fiscal cost substantially. Thus the choice between wage- and price-indexation is crucial, as it determines its costs and benefits and how these change for future cohorts. In the discussion below we assume price-indexation, unless wage-indexation is explicitly mentioned. Doing so biases our results against women, whose relative position will improve if the wage linkage continues.

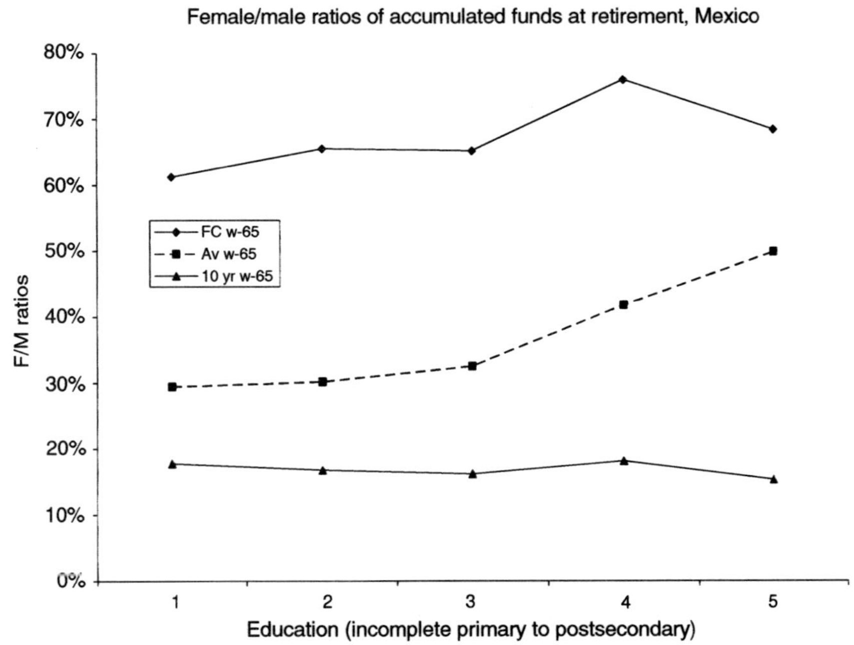

Figure 4-1c. More work increases female/male ratios of accumulations (Mexico).

Whether it is price- or wage-indexed, the MPG does not provide income to high earners. (In this sense, it is more narrowly targeted toward low earners and women than is Argentina's flat benefit or Mexico's SQ.) If it is price-indexed, it narrows the gender gap at the bottom but does nothing at the top or in the middle.

Twenty years of contributions are required to be eligible for the MPG. Although some women do not meet this criterion,[10] the average woman in all educational categories does. Moreover, low-earning women will be encouraged by the MPG to work twenty years even if they did not plan to do so otherwise—but they are discouraged from working marginally more than twenty years because if their own-annuity increases, their public benefit will decrease commensurately. Likewise, low-earning women are unlikely to work past the normal retirement age, once they meet the twenty-year requirement. The incentive for strategic manipulation is greater if the MPG is wage-indexed. An MPG that rises for each year of work would prevent some of these moral hazard problems.

In Argentina, by contrast, most men who contribute when they work are eligible for the flat public benefit and receive it regardless of income.[11] Although most women work fewer than the 30 years required for full

TABLE 4-2 Projected Impact of Public Benefits on Monthly Pensions (2002 US$)

Education	1	2	3	4	5
Chile					
Married Men					
Annuity, RA = 65	$179	$259	$386	$538	$1, 240
% increase-MPG	0	0	0	0	0
Women with average work histories					
Annuity, RA = 60	$59	$83	$146	$241	$444
Annuity + MPG if price-indexed	$78	$83	$146	$241	$444
Annuity + MPG if wage-indexed	$172	$172	$172	$241	$444
% incr.-MPG price-indexed	31	0	0	0	0
% incr.-MPG wage-indexed	192	107	18	0	0
Average female/male ratios (%)					
Own-annuity	33	32	38	45	36
Annuity + MPG if price-indexed	44	32	38	45	36
–if wage-indexed	96	66	45	45	36
Argentina					
Married men					
Annuity, RA = 65	$153	$233	$349	$362	$701
Annuity + flat	$230	$310	426	439	778
% increase by flat	50	33	22	21	11
Women with average work histories					
Annuity, RA = 60	$32	$46	$91	$127	$248
Annuity + flat	$86	$100	$145	$181	$325
% incr. by flat	169	118	60	43	31
Average female/male ratios (%)					
Own-annuity	21	20	26	35	35
Own + flat (at 65)	14	15	21	29	42
Own + flat (at 70)	37	32	34	41	42
Mexico					
Married men					
Own-annuity, no SQ	$267	$310	$381	$481	$822
Annuity incl. SQ	$364	$407	$478	$573	$909
% increase by SQ	36	31	25	19	11
Women with average work histories					
Own-annuity, no SQ	$78	$93	$123	$199	$407
Annuity incl. SQ	126	141	177	260	477
% incr. by SQ	62	52	44	30	17
Average female/male ratios					
Annuity if no SQ (%)	29	30	32	41	49
Annuity incl. SQ (%)	35	35	37	45	53

Source: Calculations by authors. See text and James, Edwards, and Wong (forthcoming) for fuller discussion of data and methodology.

Notes: See Table 4-1a for definition of the five education categories and other notes. The MPG is converted to actuarially equivalent monthly top-up. In Argentina average women in the bottom four educational groups receive a reduced flat benefit at age 70 while in the top education group, they work enough to receive the full flat at age 65, and the flat benefit is treated as if it is price-indexed (although it is not). SQ = social quota.

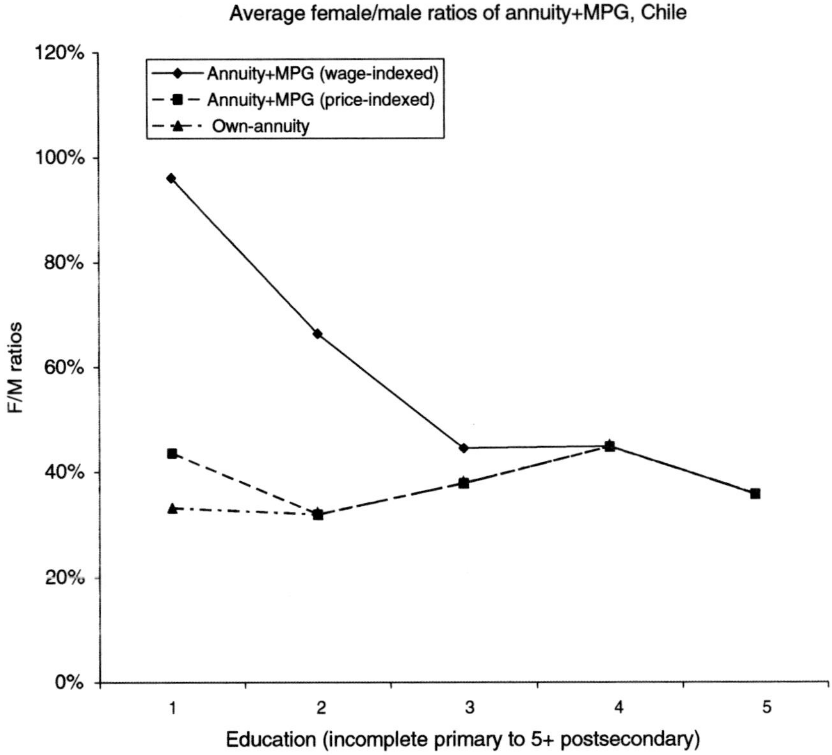

Figure 4-2a. Wage-indexed MPG: larger and broader impact than price-indexed MPG (Chile).

eligibility, they get a reduced flat benefit beginning at age 70 if they have worked 10 years. This situation exemplifies the importance of eligibility conditions in determining the gender impact. Even though the reduced flat benefit for women is a smaller absolute amount than it is for men, it is a much larger increment to women's own-annuity, and more than doubles the pensions of women with primary and partial secondary education. Women with a university degree and full-career women work long enough to get the full flat benefit at age 65 (see Figure 4-2b). Additionally, married women inherit 70 percent of their husbands' flat benefit.

Because the flat and widow's flat benefit are partially financed by a tax on wages, the fact that men earn more than women but get a smaller benefit compared with their wages means that women get a positive net transfer. The largest net transfer goes to women who work only ten years. (For further discussion of imputed taxes and net benefits, see James, Edwards,

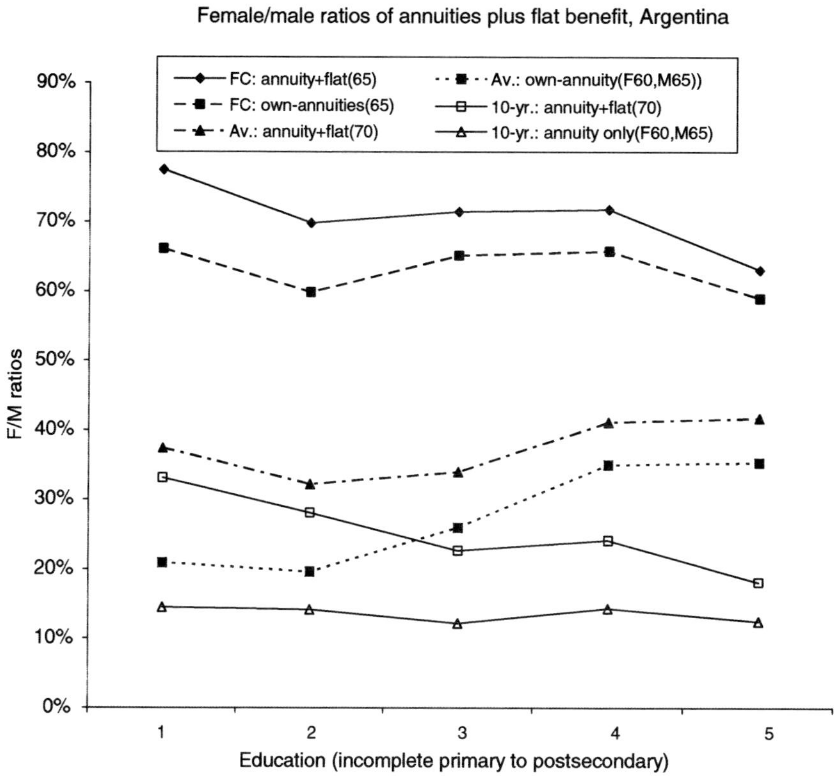

Figure 4-2b. Large % increment to 10-year women and low earners from flat benefit in Argentina.

and Wong 2003*a*, 2003*b*, and forthcoming.) This large benefit for ten-year women makes the Argentine public benefit much like a noncontributory scheme. On the one hand, this transfer provides retirement income to older women who otherwise would have few resources of their own and keeps them out of poverty. On the other hand, it also goes to middle-class women who are far from the poverty line. Moreover, the benefit may discourage market work among women and in the long run make them less financially independent.

Finally, Mexico's SQ adds a flat amount to every worker's account for each day worked: 5.5 percent of the minimum wage. While the public benefits in Chile and Argentina are financed on a PAYGO basis, which may imply a large hidden liability for government, Mexico's SQ is prefunded, paid into workers' accounts long before they retire, and invested by the worker with his or her own contributions.

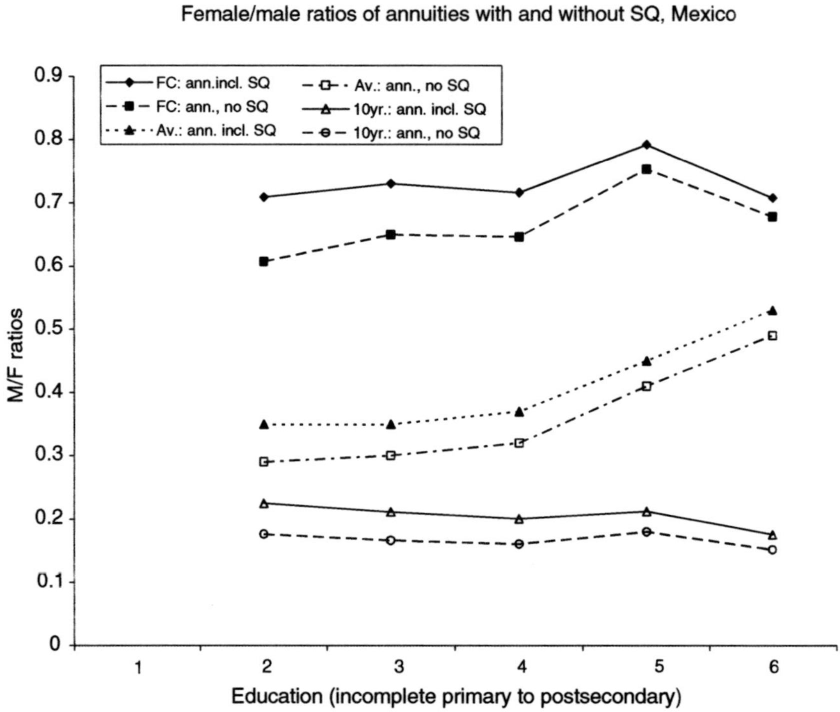

Figure 4-2c. Larger impact of SQ for low earners who work more in Mexico.

The daily size of the SQ is uniform, so the percentage increment to pensions falls for high earners, as in Chile and Argentina. It adds 45–60 percent to the annuities of women with primary or partial secondary education but only 25–35 percent to counterpart men. Women with some university education get a larger total SQ (because they work more) but a smaller percentage increment to their own pensions (Figure 4-2c). Because Mexico's SQ gives an extra benefit for every day of work, it is less tilted toward women than is Argentina's flat benefit, but it encourages work by women more than do Chile's and Argentina's public benefits.

Mexico also offers an MPG for those with twenty-four years of contributions. Initially the MPG was 40 percent of the average wage—a relatively high minimum. However, because it is price-indexed, it will fall to less than 20 percent by the time today's young workers retire. Since most low-earning women work in the formal sector fewer than twenty-four years, and most men will have own-annuities that exceed the MPG floor, our projections indicate that it will have little impact—if it remains price-indexed. The choice between a twenty-year eligibility rule as in Chile and a twenty-four-year rule as in Mexico turns out to be crucial for women, given their current labor force behavior.

Income from Joint Annuities

The gender gap in retirement income from women's own-annuities is offset further by joint annuities (or widow's benefits) that husbands are required to provide for their surviving wives. In Chile and Mexico, the widow gets 60 percent of the husband's annuity amount; in Argentina, 70 percent. The husband pays for this by getting a smaller payout initially. These intrahousehold transfers are an important part of the new systems. They can be viewed as a formalization of the informal family contract, in which men agree to provide monetary support to their wives in return for nonmonetary household services and partial withdrawal from the labor market. Some men may be myopic and fail to arrange for continuing to support their wives after their deaths (Bernheim et al. 2001). The joint annuity requirement is a way to enforce this contract. When the wife is 3 years younger than her husband, joint annuities pay him 17–21 percent less per month than individual annuities, while doubling or tripling the monthly pension that the average widow will receive (see Table 4-3).

The joint annuity is especially important because a widow's cost of living is estimated to be roughly 70 percent that of a couple's cost due to household economies of scale. The widow's benefit plus her own benefit maintains her purchasing power at 70–80 percent of the previous household level, so her standard of living is unchanged when her husband dies. The joint annuity requirement also applies to unmarried mothers of the worker's children. It protects women who did not work at all in the formal market and augments the income of those who did. It does not, of course, protect single, unattached women.

Additionally, since her husband rather than the public treasury has paid for the joint annuity, the widow can keep her own annuity when she gets the survivor's benefit, in contrast to the previous systems in Chile, Argentina, and many other countries. Since women got little or no benefit from their own contributions, their participation in the labor market was penalized and discouraged in many old DB systems. Under the new systems, the treatment of the joint annuity encourages work.

It is also worth noting that, with joint annuities, pensions are similar whether gender-specific or unisex mortality tables are used (James, Edwards, and Wong 2003*b*, forthcoming). Regarding the purchase of individual annuities, unisex mortality tables produce 7–9 percent higher payouts for women and lower payouts for men compared to gender-specific tables, but with joint annuities this choice of mortality tables makes little difference because joint annuity pricing takes into account the combined

TABLE 4-3 The Impact of Joint Annuities (r = 5% during Accumulations, 3.5% during Annuity Stage, Real Wage Growth = 2%, 2002 US$)

Education	*1*	*2*	*3*	*4*	*5*
Chile					
Males, retiring at 65					
Individual	$217	$314	$467	$651	$1,501
Joint	179	259	386	538	1,240
Females, retiring at 60					
Individual	$59	$83	$146	$241	$444
Widow's benefit	107	156	232	323	744
Widow's pensions as % of H + W pensions	70	70	71	72	71
Argentina					
Males, retiring at 65					
Individual	$194	$296	$443	$459	$889
Joint	153	233	349	362	701
Females, retiring at 60					
Individual	$34	$48	$96	$134	$261
Joint	32	46	91	127	248
Widow's benefit	107	163	244	253	491
Widow's pensions as % of H + W pensions	78	77	78	79	79
Mexico					
Males retiring at 65					
Individual	$448	$501	$589	$705	$1,120
Joint	364	407	478	573	909
Females retiring at 65					
Individual	$133	$148	$187	$273	$502
Joint	126	141	177	260	477
Widow's benefit	218	244	287	344	545
Widow's pensions as % of H + W pensions	70	70	71	72	74

Source: Calculations by authors. See text and James, Edwards, and Wong (forthcoming) for fuller discussion of data and methodology.

Notes: See Table 4-1a for educational categories. The MPG and flat benefit are not included in this table. SQ is included, since it is part of annuity. In Chile husbands must purchase joint annuities and wives purchase individual annuities. In Argentina and Mexico, both spouses must purchase joint annuities. Joint annuity assumes 60% to survivor (70% in Argentina). Husbands and wives are assumed to belong to same educational group. The last row for each country gives full public + private pensions of wife after husband dies relative to total pensions of husband + wife while husband was alive. *H + W pensions* means total pensions of husband + wife.

lifetimes of husband and wife. In this way, the joint annuity requirement defuses the sometimes controversial issue of whether to require unisex tables. This applies only to married couples or registered partners; the issue remains important for single men and women.

Total Lifetime Pension from Own-Annuity, Public Benefit, and Joint Annuity

The discussion now shifts to total lifetime rather than monthly benefits because the widow's benefit and Argentina's reduced flat benefit start at a much later age than benefits based on own earnings. Moreover, the retirement age for women in Chile and Argentina is earlier than that for men and for Mexican women (the normal retirement age sometimes changed as part of the reform). To compare benefits across subgroups, countries, and time, therefore, it is necessary to calculate their expected present value, taking into account life expectancy and age when the benefit starts. Expected present value of lifetime benefits is measured as of age 65 using a 3.5 percent discount rate (the rate of return on annuities) and World Bank gender-specific mortality tables for each country. In general, lifetime gender ratios are higher than monthly ratios because women live longer than men and, in Chile and Argentina, retire earlier. Also, in general, lifetime gender ratios are higher for low educational categories because of the equalizing effect of the public benefit and the relatively greater compound interest earned by workers with flat age-earnings profiles.

The addition of the public benefit and joint annuity bring the present value of lifetime benefits for women much closer to that of men than does the own-annuity alone. Among women with an average work history, the public benefit adds 20–80 percent to lifetime income stemming from their own-annuity, and the joint annuity adds another 40–100 percent (Figures 4-3 and 4-4 and Table 4-4). The joint annuity more than doubles lifetime retirement income for ten-year women who did little market work. In general, the joint annuity is larger than the public benefit.

Taking into account all 3 income sources, the lifetime retirement income of the average married woman is 65–95 percent that of average men with similar education (even higher in Chile if it continues to wage-link its MPG). This ratio becomes 100 percent or more for full-career married women—working longer and retiring later has the largest impact of all. Of course, single women do not get the joint annuity. Therefore, their female/male ratios are much lower (Tables 4-4 and 4-5, Figures 4-5a, 4-5b, and 4-5c).

While these generalizations hold for all three countries, formal labor force attachment is rewarded differentially in each case. The own-annuity rises with incremental work in each country. However, very different patterns apply to the public benefit. In Chile, only average women in the lowest educational groups, who retire early with about twenty years' experience, will get a public benefit. Neither ten-year women, full-career women, women who postpone retirement, nor highly educated women who work more get the MPG. In Mexico, by contrast, full-career women get the largest

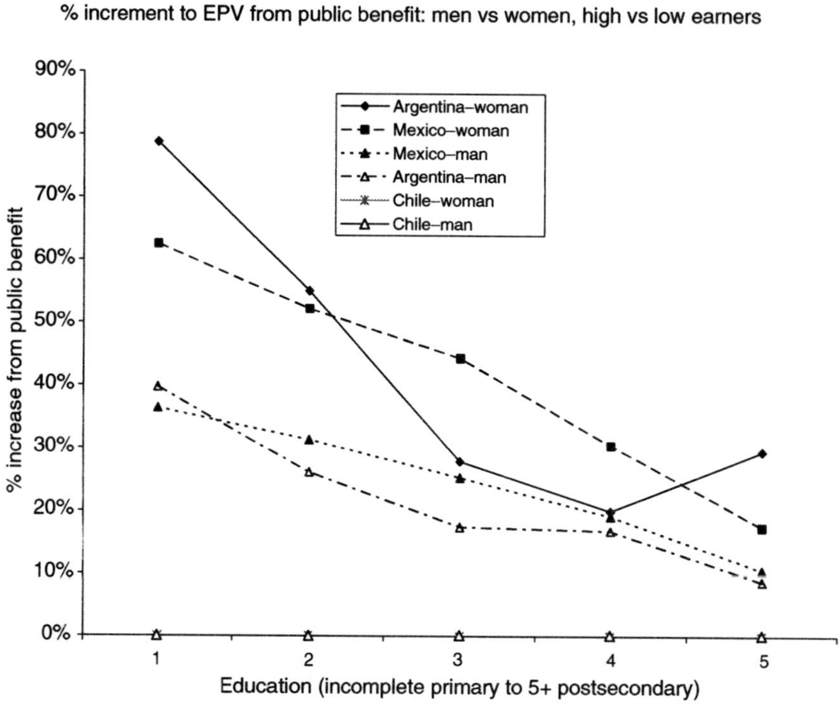

Figure 4-3. Women and low earners get largest % increment to EPV from public benefit. *Note*: EPV = expected present value.

public benefits, ten-year women the smallest. In Argentina, a substantial benefit and net subsidy go to women who work only ten years. A high implicit tax rate must be imposed on high-earning men and full-career women to finance these benefits. Even without taking account of these taxes, the ratio of benefits received by a full-career or an average woman relative to a ten-year woman is much higher in Mexico than in Argentina. The lower payoff in Argentina may discourage women from market work. In contrast, for Chile the minimal size of the public benefit means that the higher work incentive of the private annuity dominates (Figure 4-6).

Women's Benefits Relative to Men Before and After Reform

Because of uncertainty regarding future benefit levels under the old insolvent systems, we cannot compare the absolute dollar values of the benefits women would have received under the old systems to those under the new.

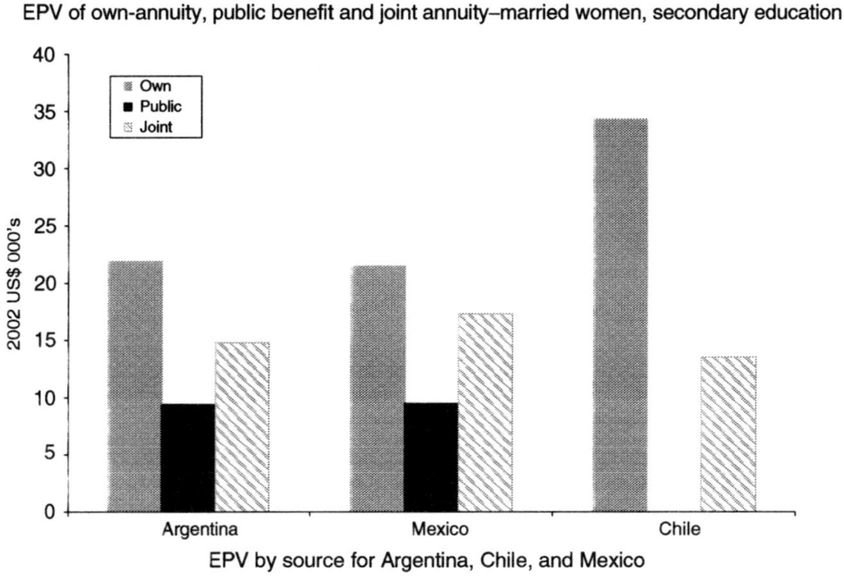

Figure 4-4. Joint annuity adds more than public benefit to EPV of average woman. *Note*: EPV = expected present value.

However, we can compare the female/male ratios of benefits before and after reform, under the assumption that the counterfactual would have had the same distributional effects as the original system (see the section on methodology above). We therefore ask: (*a*) Did the gender gap in pensions get larger or smaller in the process of the reform?, and (*b*) which subgroups of women (and men) gained or lost the most? We find that, in general, the gender ratio is projected to improve because of the reform, and the greatest relative gains will be received by low-earning married women (and single men). Full-career women gained more than did ten-year women in Chile and Mexico, consistent with their emphasis on work incentives, but ten-year women gained more in Argentina (Figures 4-7a, 4-7b, and 4-7c).

A Priori Expectations about the New versus the Old Systems

The old systems provided DB according to a formula that depended on wages and years of contributions. In general, the formula gave generous benefits to workers who contributed for only ten years and then withdrew from the labor market; these workers were disproportionately women.[12] Married women got a widow's benefit that was 50 percent of their husband's pension in Chile, 75 percent in Argentina, and 90 percent in Mexico.

TABLE 4-4 Present Value of Lifetime Annuity, Joint Annuity, and Public Benefit (r = 5% during Accumulation, 3.5% Discount Rate after Retirement, Real Wage Growth = 2%; in 2002 US$ (1,000s))

Education	*1*	*2*	*3*	*4*	*5*
Chile					
Average man					
Individual annuity	$32.4	$46.9	$69.9	$97.4	$224.4
Cost of joint annuity (if married)	−5.6	−8.2	−12.2	−16.9	−39.0
Average woman					
Own-annuity	$13.9	$19.4	$34.3	$56.5	$104.0
MPG (if price-indexed)	3.1	0	0	0	0
MPG (if wage-indexed)	18.5	14.6	4.3	0	0
Joint annuity received (if married)	6.3	9.1	13.5	18.8	43.3
% incr. from MPG (price-indexed)	22	0	0	0	0
% incr. from MPG (wage-indexed)	133	75	13	0	0
% incr. from joint annuity	45	47	39	33	42
Full-career woman					
Own-annuity	$23.6	$31.8	$51.5	$70.8	$121.7
% incr. from joint annuity	27	28	26	27	36
10-year woman					
Own-annuity	$8.3	$9.9	$12.9	$20.5	$32.8
% incr. from joint annuity	75	92	105	92	132
Argentina					
Average man					
Individual annuity	$27.7	$42.2	$63.2	$65.5	$126.9
Flat	11.0	11.0	11.0	11.0	11.0
Cost of joint annuity (if married)	−5.8	−8.9	−13.3	−13.8	−26.7
% incr. from flat	40	26	17	17	9
Average woman					
Own-annuity	$7.7	$11.0	$21.9	$30.5	$59.7
Flat	6.1	6.1	6.1	6.1	17.6
Widow's flat	3.3	3.3	3.3	3.3	3.3
Joint annuity received (if married)	6.5	9.9	14.8	15.3	29.6
% incr. from flat	79	55	28	20	29
% incr. from widow's flat	42	29	15	11	5
% incr. from joint annuity	84	89	68	50	50
FC woman					
Own annuity	$18.2	$25.1	$40.9	$42.8	$74.4
Flat	13.0	13.0	13.0	13.0	13.0
% incr. from flat	71	52	32	30	17

TABLE 4-4 (*Continued*)

Education	*1*	*2*	*3*	*4*	*5*
% incr. from widow's flat	18	13	8	8	4
% incr. from joint annuity	36	39	36	36	40
10-year woman					
Own-annuity	$5.3	$8.0	$10.2	$12.5	$21.0
Flat	6.1	6.1	6.1	6.1	6.1
% incr. from flat	120	81	63	51	31
% incr. from widow's flat	64	43	34	28	16
% incr. From joint ann.	128	131	153	130	149
Mexico					
Average man					
Individual annuity, no SQ	$46.2	$53.7	$66.1	$83.3	$142.5
SQ	16.8	16.8	16.7	16.0	15.0
Cost of joint annuity (if married)	−11.9	−13.3	−15.6	−18.7	−29.7
% increase from SQ	36	31	25	19	11
Average woman					
Own-annuity if no SQ	$13.6	$16.2	$21.5	$34.8	$71.1
SQ to own-account	8.5	8.5	9.5	10.6	12.3
Joint annuity (if married)	13.2	14.7	17.3	20.7	32.9
% incr. from SQ	62	52	44	30	17
% incr. from joint annuity	97	91	80	60	46
Full-career woman					
Own-annuity if no SQ	$28.3	$35.2	$43.1	$63.3	$97.5
SQ	16.8	16.8	16.7	16.0	15.0
% incr. from SQ	59	48	39	25	15
% incr. from joint annuity	46	42	40	33	34
10-year woman					
Own-annuity if no SQ	$8.2	$9	$10.7	$15.1	$21.8
SQ	6.1	6.0	6.0	6.1	6.1
% incr. from SQ	74	67	56	41	28
% incr. from joint annuity	160	164	162	137	151
Rewards for work in 3 countries: Benefits to full-career/10-year woman					
Public benefit + own-annuity (percentage)					
Chile	283	322	401	346	371
Argentina	231	236	287	267	294
Mexico	315	346	357	374	403
Public benefit (percentage)					
Chile[a]					
Argentina	174	174	174	174	174
Mexico	275	278	277	262	245

(*cont.*)

TABLE 4-4 (*Continued*)

Education	*1*	*2*	*3*	*4*	*5*
Public benefit: Average/10-year woman (percentage)					
Chile[a]					
Argentina	100	100	100	100	223
Mexico	140	140	158	173	202

Source: Calculations by authors. See text and James, Edwards, and Wong (forthcoming) for fuller discussion of data and methodology.

Notes: For educational categories see Table 4-1a. Married full-career and 10-year women get the same joint annuity and other widow's benefits as do average women, but these benefits constitute different percentages of their own-annuity.

[a] Full-career and 10-year women in Chile do not get any public benefit. Only the woman with an average work history in the lowest wage category gets a public benefit, if it is price-indexed. A larger group gets it if it is wage-indexed.

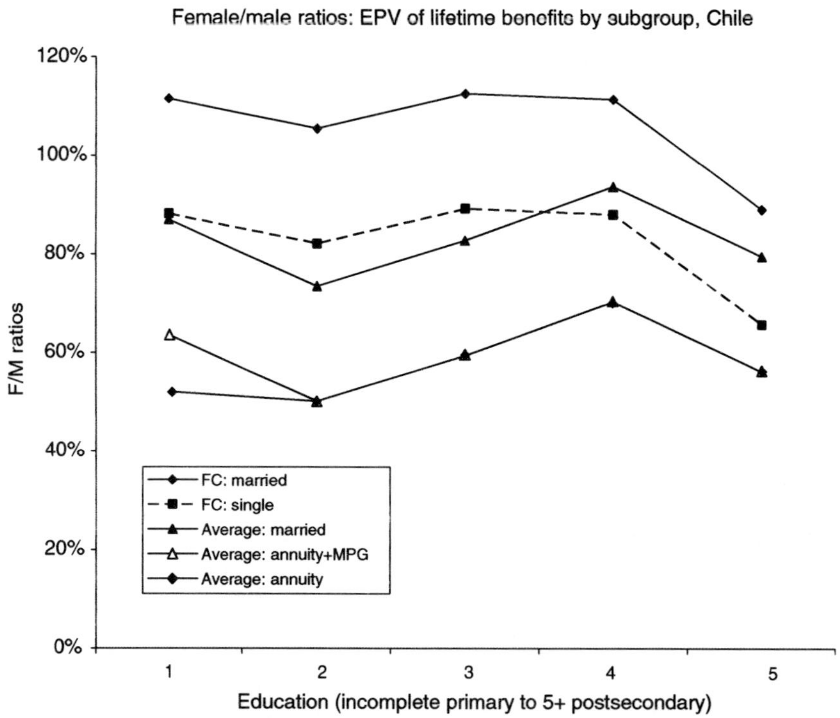

Figure 4-5a. EPV of full-career married women exceeds that of men in Chile. *Note*: EPV = expected present value.

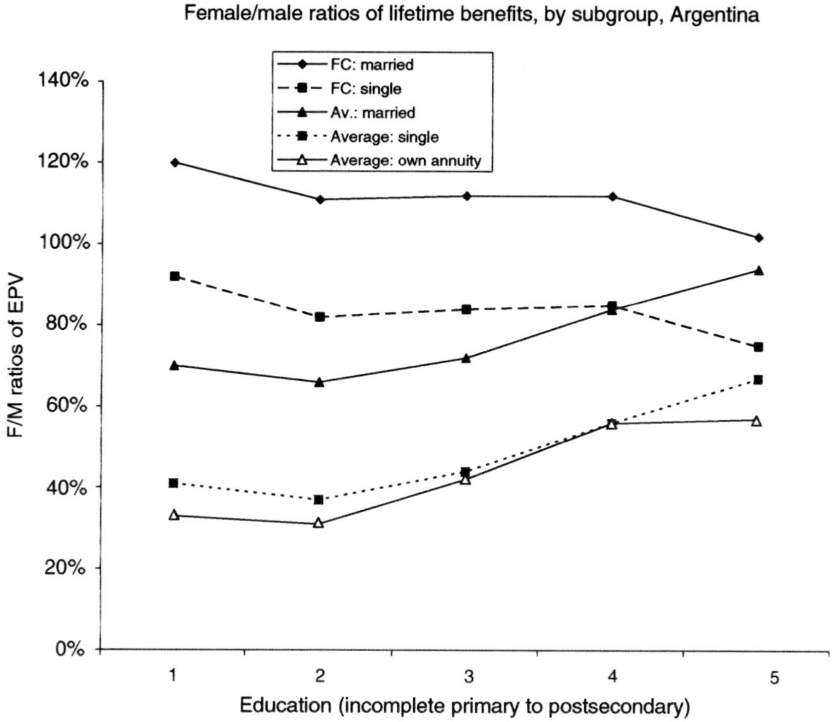

Figure 4-5b. EPV of full-career married women exceeds that of men in Argentina. *Note*: EPV = expected present value.

Implicitly, unisex tables were used. Women could retire five years earlier than men with no actuarial penalty in Chile and Argentina. In all three countries, a minimum pension protected low-earning women who satisfied the eligibility requirements.

Contrary to these provisions that favored women, the old systems based their benefits on the wage earned during the last few working years, which favored men. Because of inflation and real wage growth, a woman who worked at ages 20–30, before childbearing, would find her pension based on wages that would appear to be very low compared with prevailing wages at her retirement at ages 60–65. Moreover, this formula for the pensionable wage base favored workers with steep age–earnings profiles, who tended to be highly educated men. By contrast, in the new system contributions made in early adulthood add more to present value of lifetime benefits than contributions made in the final years because of compound interest that far exceeds the growth rate of prices or wages.

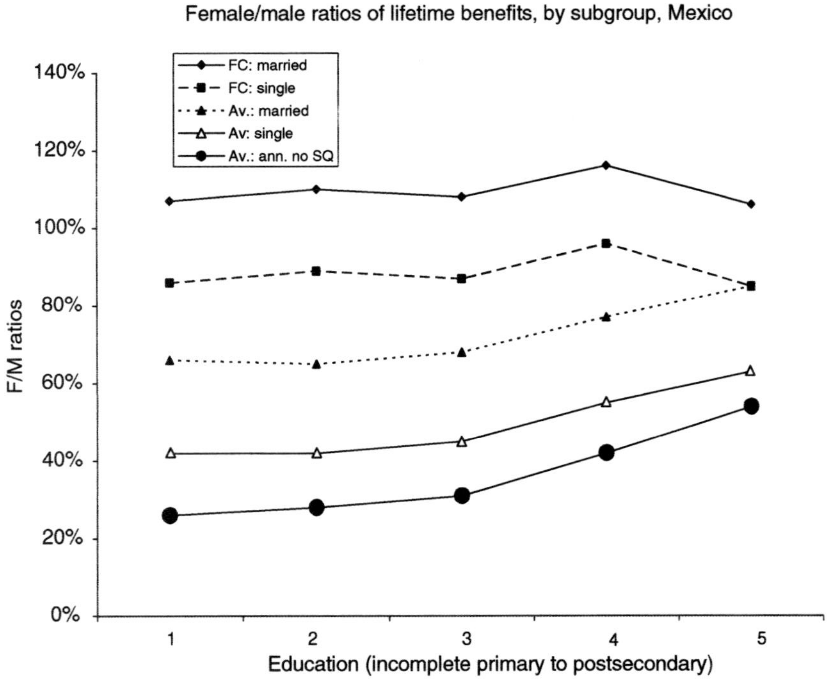

Figure 4-5c. EPV of full-career married women exceeds that of men in Mexico. *Note*: EPV = expected present value.

In the old systems in Chile and Argentina, women usually had to give up their own pension to get the widow's pension, so women who worked much of their lives in the labor market got little or no incremental benefit. In the new systems, women keep their own benefit as well as the requisite joint annuity. Further, as we have seen, the new public benefits are tilted toward low earners, who are predominantly women. Thus there are pushes and pulls in both directions a priori, so the impact of the reforms on gender ratios is an empirical question, which we shall explore.

It is also worth noting that pensions in the old system often were not indexed for inflation, yet inflation was high in these countries, devaluing the benefit. This especially hurt women, who live longer and therefore experience greater price increases. In contrast, annuities in the new system in Chile are price-indexed; Mexico plans to index them also. Public benefits in these countries are also indexed for inflation or higher. We abstract from inflation because of its uneven nature and the unpredictable ad hoc responses that were made by the old systems, which biases our results against the new systems.[13]

TABLE 4-5 Female/Male Ratios of Expected Present Value of Lifetime Benefits in New vs Old Systems (in Percentages)

Education	*1*	*2*	*3*	*4*	*5*
Chile					
Old system					
Av.: own pension	78	63	100	99	75
Av.: own + widow's	78	67	100	99	76
FC: own pension	82	72	94	68	70
FC: own + widow's	82	72	94	68	70
10 yr: own + widow's	78	58	54	60	45
New system					
Av.: own-annuity	52	50	59	70	56
Av.: own + MPG	64	50	59	70	56
Av.: own + MPG + joint	87	73	83	94	79
FC: own-annuity	88	82	89	88	66
FC: own + joint	112	105	113	111	89
10 yr: own + joint	55	49	46	49	41
Argentina					
Old system					
Av.: own pension	21	13	33	55	60
Av.: own + widow's	40	30	47	64	68
FC: own pension	76	50	48	68	62
FC: own + widow's	80	57	55	69	65
10 yr: own + widow's	40	30	27	31	30
New system					
Average woman: own-annuity	33	31	42	56	57
Average woman: own + flat	41	37	44	56	67
Average woman: own + flat + joint	70	66	72	84	94
FC: own + flat	92	82	84	85	75
FC: own + flat + joint	120	111	112	112	102
10 yr: own + flat + joint	63	60	55	57	52
Mexico					
Old system					
Average woman: own pension	39	33	29	33	59
Average woman: own + widow's	77	71	68	72	97
FC: own pension	70	60	63	73	91
FC: own + widow's	108	99	102	112	130
10 yr: own + widow's	69	57	52	46	44
New system					
Average woman: own annuity	26	28	31	42	54
Average woman: own incl. SQ	42	42	45	55	63
Average woman: own + SQ + joint	66	65	68	77	85
FC: own incl. SQ	86	89	87	96	85
FC: own + SQ + joint	107	110	108	116	106
10-year: own + SQ + joint	51	50	48	50	45

Source: Calculations by authors. See text and James, Edwards, and Wong (forthcoming) for fuller discussion of data and methodology.

Notes: The denominator is married man in same educational category. For ratios with own-annuity, this applies to men and women. For ratios with public benefit, this also applies to men and women. See text for methodology and see Table 4-1a for educational categories.

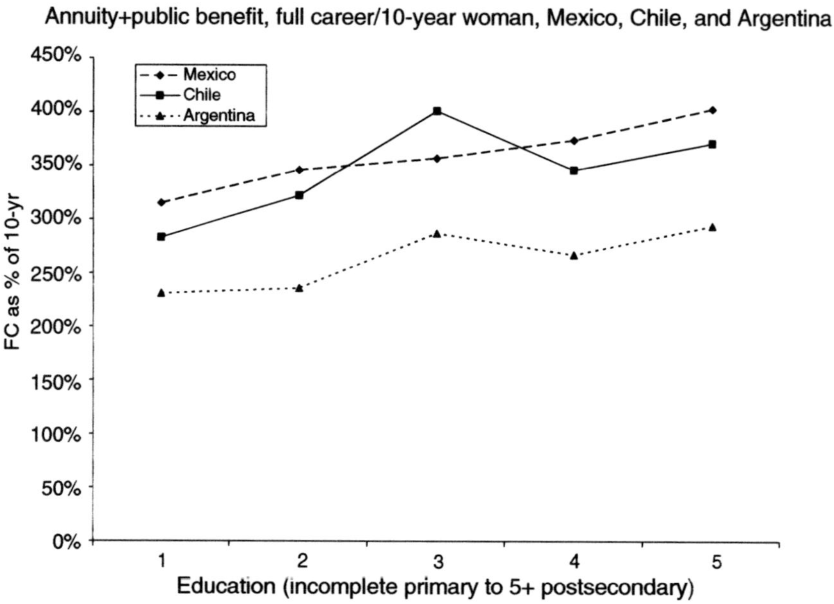

Figure 4-6. Full-career woman gets lower payoff for extra work (relative to 10-year women) in Argentina than in Mexico or Chile.

Results: Gender Ratios under the New and Old Systems

We now compare the ratios of lifetime benefits under the old and new systems for men and women with the same education. We find that (*a*) female/male ratios generally fall postreform when only the own-annuity is taken into account; (*b*) in Argentina and Mexico they rise modestly postreform when both the public and private benefits are included (this is the situation for single women with average work histories); (*c*) in all three countries gender ratios are much higher when benefits from the joint annuity are added and, of course, they are higher for full-career women; so (*d*) this brings the postreform relative position of average married women and full-career women, whether married or single, above that in the old system. These changes after the reform are due to the targeting of transfers to low earners, the fact that women do not have to give up their own pensions to receive the widow's benefit, and the heavier weight placed by the new system on early contributions due to compound interest (Table 4-5). For example, in Argentina the female/male ratio of lifetime pension for a single woman with an average work history and a secondary school education is projected to rise from 42 percent based on her own pension in the new system, to 44 percent including the flat benefit, to 72 percent if she marries, and to 112 percent if she works full career, compared with 33, 47, and 55 percent, respectively, for her single, average, married, and full-career married counterparts in the old system.

Which Subgroups Benefited (or Lost) the Most?

To further analyze which subgroups benefited the most from the reform, we calculate the ratio of postreform/pre-reform lifetime benefits for various marital, educational, and labor market groups. As noted above, we focus on relative changes because we do not know what the absolute benefit would have been under the counterfactual. Additionally, we wish to see how the relative positions of different subgroups of men changed. Therefore, instead of comparing women with men of the same education, we analyze the postreform changes for subgroups of each gender, relative to changes for married men in the top education category. That is, we calculate the postreform/pre-reform ratio for each subgroup and then divide (normalize) by the ratio for married male workers in the top educational group (see Table 4-6 and Figures 4-7a, 4-7b, and 4-7c). A ratio above 100 percent indicates that the given subgroup has gained more (or lost less) than did married males with the highest education. As expected, the biggest relative gainers were:

- low earners (as proxied by low educational category) of both genders, but especially women, who are the lowest earners in each category and therefore benefit disproportionately from the public benefit;
- married women (in Chile and Argentina)—because they can now keep their own annuity plus the joint annuity, whereas previously they had to give up one or the other;
- full-career women (in Chile and Mexico)—because they gain most from the actuarially fair private annuity; and
- single men—because they no longer have to subsidize the widow's benefit that was financed from the common pool in the old systems.

In all three countries, workers in the two lowest educational groups gain relative to those in the two highest groups. Married women and single men generally gain relative to married men. In Chile and Argentina, married women gain more than do single women (but vice versa in Mexico, because of the generous widow's benefit in the old system). In Chile and Mexico, full-career women gain the most from the reform—and over time this may induce more women to participate in the labor market full career. In Chile, the relative position of ten-year women actually falls. In Argentina, however, average and ten-year women register the largest relative gains because of that country's flat benefit for retirees with only ten years of work.

TABLE 4-6 Expected Present Values of Postreform/Pre-reform Lifetime Benefits (in Percentages) (Relative to Ratio for Married Men in Top Educational Group) (r = 5% during Accumulation, 3.5% during Annuity Stage, Real Wage Growth = 2%)

Education	*1*	*2*	*3*	*4*	*5*
Chile					
Average man					
Married man	123	117	117	94	100
Single man	148	141	142	114	121
Women					
Average woman: own + MPG	99	92	69	67	74
Average woman: own + MPG + joint	136	128	97	89	105
Full-career woman: own-annuity	133	134	112	122	94
Full-career woman: own + joint annuity	168	172	141	154	128
10-year woman: own + joint annuity	85	98	99	77	91
Argentina					
Average man					
Married man	188	130	94	111	100
Single man	219	154	112	132	121
Women					
Average woman: own annuity + flat	373	366	128	114	112
Average woman: own + flat + joint	325	281	144	143	137
Full-career woman: own + flat	228	216	167	140	123
Full-career woman: own + flat + joint	278	251	188	178	155
10 year woman: own+flat+joint	294	252	186	204	173
Mexico					
Average man					
Married man	181	150	122	89	100
Single man	219	181	147	107	120
Women					
Average woman: own incl. SQ	199	195	187	146	108
Average woman: own incl. SQ + joint	154	138	122	96	88
Full-career woman: own incl. SQ	225	221	169	116	94
Full-career woman: own + SQ + joint	180	166	130	92	82
10-year woman: own incl. SQ + joint	134	130	114	95	103

Source: Calculations by authors. See text and James, Edwards, and Wong (forthcoming) for fuller discussion of data and methodology.

Notes: Includes lifetime benefits from own-annuity, public pillar, and joint annuity (for married). Each cell i shows (PVnew/PVold)i/(PVnew/PVold)k where (PVnew/PVold) = ratio of the present value of lifetime benefits in the new versus old systems for group i. This is normalized by the ratio for reference group k, where k = married men in the highest educational category. If the number in a cell is >100%, this means the category gained more than top married men. For educational categories see Table 4-1a, and for methodology see text.

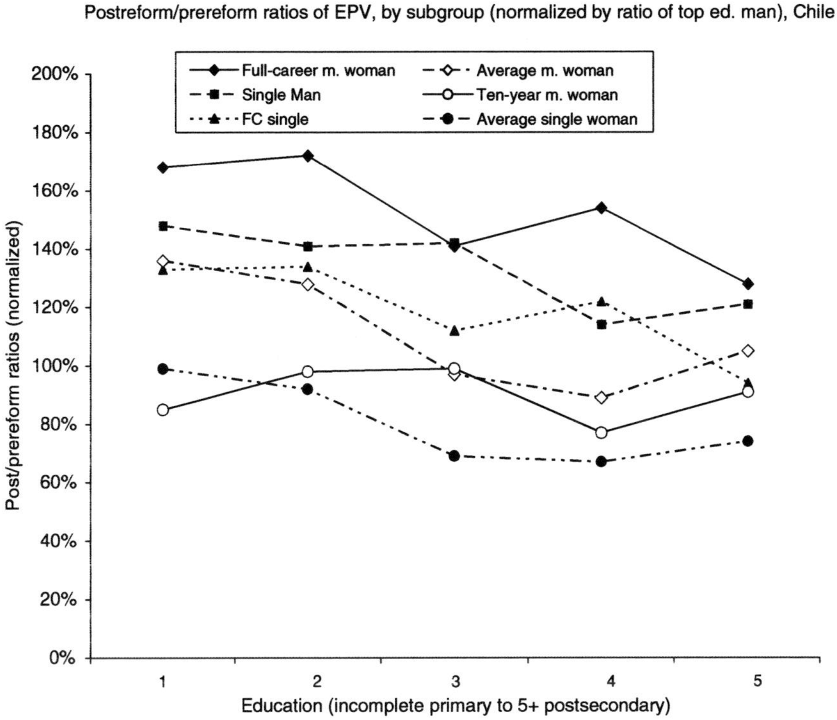

Figure 4-7a. Low-earning full-career married women and single men are biggest relative gainers from the reform in Chile. *Note*: EPV = expected present value.

Single Women

Given the importance of the joint annuity, how do single women fare? This question is important because an increasing proportion of women are divorced or never married. Divorce became legal in Chile in 2004, and the proportion of divorced women doubled in Mexico over the past three decades. Cohabitation is not uncommon among low-educated groups in Latin America, and many children are born out of wedlock to parents in informal arrangements. Single women are a heterogeneous group, including those who were divorced, widowed, and never married, whose behavior may vary. Construction of synthetic work histories of single women, broken down into subgroups when possible, indicates that full-career women without joint annuity or widow's benefit are a reasonably good proxy for never-married women (James, Edwards, and Wong, forthcoming).

In the new systems in all three countries, lifetime pensions of full-career single women are lower than those of men, because of their smaller wages

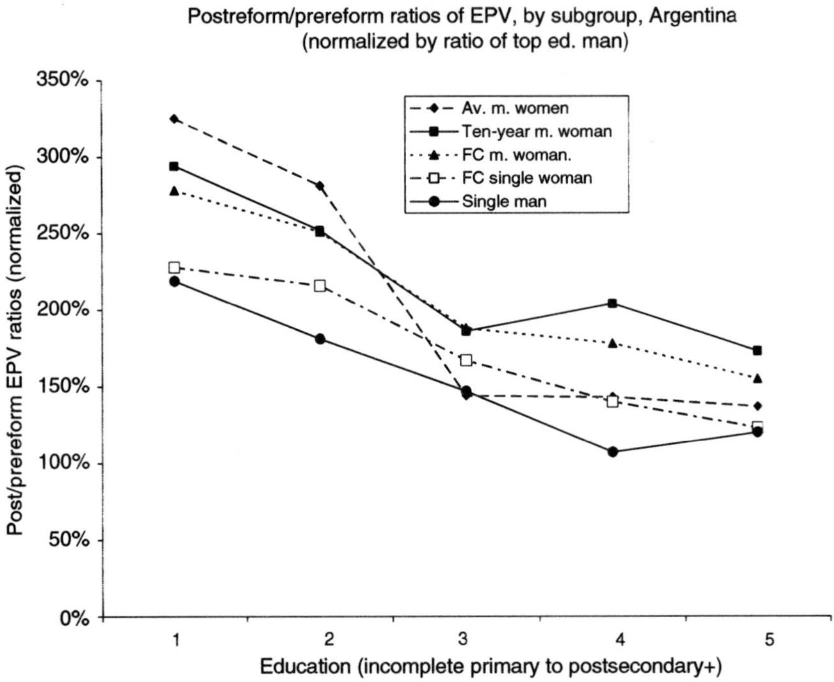

Figure 4-7b. Low-earning average and 10-year married women gained most of all (Argentina). *Note*: EPV = expected present value.

and greater longevity, or of full-career married women, because they do not get the joint annuity. In Argentina and Mexico, the pension income of single full-career women rises postreform compared to single or married men, because of the relatively generous public benefit that flattens total benefits. In contrast, in Chile, where they are unlikely to collect an equalizing public benefit, their position falls relative to single men but rises relative to married men (Table 4-6 and Figures 4-7a, 4-7b, and 4-7c). Concerns about the situation of single women could be addressed through measures such as (*a*) the use of unisex mortality tables in pricing annuities (redistributing from men in general to women in general), (*b*) partial wage-indexation of public benefits for the very old (redistributing to those who live longer), or (*c*) equalization of women's retirement age with that of men (requiring them to work as long as men to raise their old-age consumption). Basically, the pensions of single women are likely to approach those of men only when their wages and work experience approach those of men.

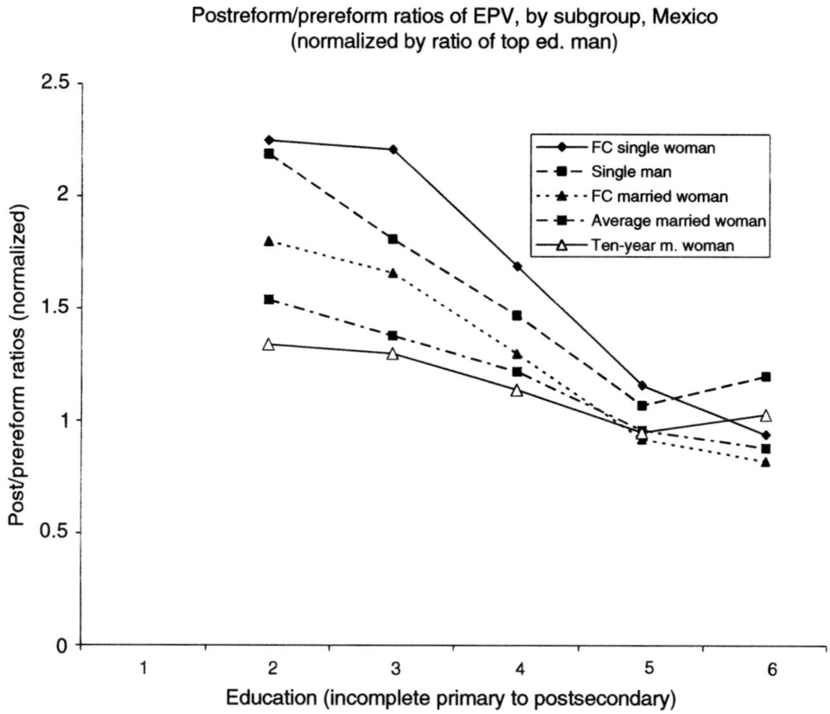

Figure 4-7c. Low-earning FC single women and single men are biggest relative gainers from the reform in Mexico. *Note*: EPV = expected present value.

Implications for Social Security Reform in Other Countries

To sum up, the empirical investigations show that (*a*) women's own-annuities are lower than those of men in multipillar pension schemes, as they would be in any scheme tying benefits closely to contributions; but (*b*) women are recipients of net public transfers and private intrahousehold transfers through joint pensions required in the new systems. Consequently, (*c*) women have gained more than men from the reforms; the lifetime gender ratio has improved (these ratios would improve still more if the retirement age for men and women were equalized). Finally, (*d*) work incentives are stronger in Chile and Mexico, where full-career women gain the most, while Argentina affords greater protection for women with limited labor market participation.

Individual account systems can improve relative outcomes for women and have done so in Latin America. However, the gains to women are not inevitable. The gender impact largely depends on the detailed design features of these reforms. The favorable outcomes we have described for Latin-American women contrast with those in the transition economies of Eastern and Central Europe, where preliminary investigations suggest that women lost relative to men because of the removal of privileges they had in the old system, maintenance of an earlier retirement age, absence of a targeted public pillar, the weakening of survivor's benefits, and the failure to require joint annuities (Castel and Fox 2001; Woycicka 2001). In Sweden, too, women's position deteriorated for many of the same reasons (Stahlberg, Kruse, and Sunden 2006*a*, 2006*b*). Other countries contemplating such reforms, and countries trying to improve traditional DB systems, can draw a number of lessons on how to improve gender outcomes.

1. *A safety net and minimum pension are especially important for women.* Because of women's lower lifetime earnings, a redistributive public benefit is particularly important. Chile's MPG, Mexico's SQ, and Argentina's flat benefit are projected to improve women's lifetime pensions substantially, narrowing the gender gap. Two dangers are (*a*) rules that largely exclude women (such as Mexico's twenty-four-year requirement for the MPG), and (*b*) rules that discourage their participation in the formal labor market (such as the high marginal tax rate for low earners who have just met the twenty-year eligibility rule in Chile). The MPG and Argentina's flat benefit could be redesigned to increase with years worked, thereby providing positive work incentives. Mexico's SQ already does this.

2. *The public benefit should be at least partially wage-indexed for successive cohorts.* It is essential that the public benefit rise at least as fast as prices so its purchasing power does not fall over the lifetime of the retiree, a trend particularly harmful to women, who live longer than men. Most reformed Latin-American systems price-index the public benefit. However, price-indexing may not be enough to equalize benefits for men and women in the long run. The simulations for Chile showed that as wages grow, a price-indexed MPG would set a floor for very old women and future cohorts far below the pensions of men and the average standard of living. In practice, Chile's MPG has increased with wages and is likely to keep women's retirement income rising on par with the average standard of living. A wage-indexed MPG is costlier, however, and produces larger work disincentives. The Swiss system uses a compromise: it indexes its benefit half to wages and half to prices. Policymakers and citizens will have to evaluate this tradeoff between saving money versus maintaining the relevance of the safety net over time.[14]

3. *Annuitization and inflation insurance for annuities are important for women.* Annuitization, which provides a guaranteed income for life, is especially important for women in view of their greater longevity. Although it is

automatically achieved by a DB system, it could also be built into an individual account system. Latin-American workers can either purchase an annuity or take gradual withdrawals; lump-sum withdrawals are not allowed unless the person's pension exceeds a high threshold. However, if the person lives longer than expected, the gradual withdrawal may become very small as voluntary savings are used up. This problem can be prevented by mandatory annuitization, at least up to a threshold well above the poverty line.

Inflation insurance is important for the income from the individual account, just as for the public benefit. In Latin America, during the accumulation stage account, balances grow with the rate of interest, which is generally greater than the inflation rate. During the payout stage, annuities in Chile are price-indexed; Mexico plans to do the same. Chile facilitates price-indexing by the prevalence of indexed bonds and other financial instruments in which insurance companies can invest. The paucity of indexed instruments in many other countries will make price-indexing more difficult and costly.

4. *Joint pensions should be required in the payout stage.* Women often work fewer years as part of an informal family contract in which the husband agrees to support the wife in exchange for the time she spends caring for the family. In Latin America this contract is enforced even after the husband's death by requiring that all workers purchase survivor's insurance before retirement and joint pensions on retirement[15]—an important requirement to build into any individual account system. In contrast, when spousal and widow's benefits are financed from the common pool, as in DB systems, single men and women are penalized, since they must pay into the pool even though they are not eligible for this benefit.[16] An added bonus of joint annuities is that they defuse the contentious unisex issue; in the case of joint annuities, payouts for men and women are largely invariant to the choice of unisex versus gender-specific tables. The systems we are analyzing do not contain detailed mechanisms for how to handle accumulations and joint annuities in the case of divorce. These rights clearly need to be defined, with account-splitting a logical solution when marriages dissolve.

5. *Widow's benefits should not penalize working women.* The treatment of widow's benefits in DB systems often penalizes working women. In the old Chilean and Argentine schemes, and in many other countries, working women must choose between their own or the widow's benefit—they cannot get both. Thus, women who work in the market for much of their lives pay substantial taxes with little or no incremental benefit. On the contrary, in the new Latin-American systems the widow keeps both her own and the joint annuity, because her husband has financed the latter. Market work by the wife is rewarded and widows are protected, without imposing an

additional burden on the public treasury. Women's right to keep their own-annuity in addition to the joint annuity is a major reason for the narrowed gender gap in the new systems.

6. *Equalizing retirement ages for men and women and providing work incentives will substantially narrow the gender gap.* Part of the reason for the lower own-annuities of women in Chile and Argentina is that women's retirement age is five years earlier than men's retirement age—also common in other countries. Under reasonable assumptions about rates of return, women's annuities would go up by 50 percent if they retired five years later (they earn interest in the meantime and the annuity covers fewer years). This scenario would substantially narrow the gender gap in pensions without requiring public or household transfers and would ensure that lifetime retirement savings are allocated to old age instead of young old age. This is especially important for single women, who will not receive a boost to their incomes from the joint annuity. The postponed access to retirement saving may encourage additional work by older women, and will therefore increase the country's productive capacity. For the same reason, as noted above, it is important to build work incentives into the public benefit, both in traditional and in new multipillar systems.[17]

7. *Which women should benefit from redistributions?* Among low earners, each country must decide whether it wishes to target those who have chosen to work fewer years versus those whose productive capacity is low so they can only earn low wage rates. Many countries are very conflicted on this issue. As we have seen, Chile, Argentina, and Mexico have made different decisions about which groups of women should be subsidized and, in doing so, are encouraging different behaviors. In particular, their rewards for women who engage in market versus home work differ.

Mexico's SQ is a flat payment per day worked, so is strongly promarket work. It redistributes most to those who work a lot in the market, although at low wage rates. Argentina, on the other hand, subsidizes women who stay at home with a flat benefit that they receive so long as they participated in the labor market for ten years. This redistribution gives older women a subsidized income even if they had the educational capacity to work and earn high wages but chose not to do so. Chile is ambivalent on this issue. Its MPG redistributes to women with low earnings—but only if they have worked in the market for at least twenty years. Other countries solve this problem by treating years spent caring for children as part of working time. Along similar lines, husbands could be required to contribute to the individual accounts of their spouses who work in the home, through the income tax system. This would reduce the need for a public subsidy.

It may be interesting to see how the current US system compares with Latin America in its choice between subsidizing low wages versus low work, homework versus market work. In the USA, a higher rate of return is provided to those with low lifetime earnings, providing they have worked for at least ten years. (This tends to be offset by above-average mortality among low earners.) The US formula does not distinguish between people who have worked a little at high wage rates and those who have worked a lot at low rates. Studies have shown that often low earnings result from low years of work rather than low wage rates (Coronado, Fullerton, and Glass 1999, 2000; Gustman and Steinmeier 2000).

Caveats and Gaps

This chapter has identified a number of issues and gaps that have yet to be addressed, such as price versus wage indexation of the public benefit, the retirement age differential between men and women, and the retirement income problem faced by single women, divorced women, and women cohabiting without formal marriage. On a more fundamental level, this chapter has dealt with women who are in or who have husbands in the formal labor market and the contributory social security system. It does not address the large group of rural women in low-income countries who do not meet these criteria and who may have little income or savings when they become old. If the family system does not work for these women, a noncontributory program of some sort is needed to keep them out of poverty. How such a program should be structured and how it relates to the contributory scheme is a complex topic that goes beyond the purview of this chapter.

Every system works in practice somewhat differently from what was initially written on paper, partly due to unexpected circumstances that require system modification and partly due to behavioral responses to system incentives. This outcome was very true of the Latin-American systems in the past and will certainly be true of the new systems. For example, it is well known that the labor force participation rates of women are increasing, so younger female cohorts will have higher relative pensions than older cohorts. The new systems themselves may accelerate this process. The Argentine reform has already been modified several times and is likely to be modified again in the coming years as economic conditions change. Similarly, the political decision to raise the MPG in Chile on par with wages rather than prices means that it is much more pervasive than was initially envisaged. Finally, recent research has found that most workers retire earlier than the 'normal' age and contribute to the system for only part of their working lives (Berstein, Larrain, and Pino 2005; Edwards and James 2005; James, Martinez, and Iglesias 2006). This directly reduces their accumulations, pensions, and eligibility for the public benefit.

Each of these changes is likely to alter the gender gap in pensions as well as the redistributive and equalizing role of public benefits. We cannot really know how the system *has worked*, as distinct from how it *is projected to work*, until after many workers have retired and data on their behavior and incomes become available. In the meantime, we can examine how the systems that were put in place originally would work and, most important, which design features produce these results. These positive findings will in turn teach us how to create newer systems that are most likely to give us the gender effects that we normatively prefer.

Notes

[1] In the USA, 60% of people older than 65 years and 72% of those older than 85 years are women, and this disparity has increased over time. The poverty rate of women older than 65 years is 15%, compared with 7% for men older than 65 years. The poverty rate for women older than 85 years is 20%, and for divorced, separated, or never-married elderly women, it is 27% (see Shirley and Spiegler 1998; Street and Wilmoth 2001). Poverty rates for the elderly are more difficult to measure in developing countries, where older people are likely to live with their grown-up children in extended family arrangements. Moreover, we do not know how the total consumption of the household is distributed.

[2] For similar reasons, women are likely to serve as caregivers for their husbands, but then outlive their spouses and need formal caregivers themselves. Thus, costs of provisions for long-term care are especially important for women. However, this issue goes beyond the scope of this chapter.

[3] In all three countries fees as percentage of assets were higher initially than they are now due to fixed costs and rising assets. Lower fees produce higher pensions but leave gender ratios unchanged, since both men and women are charged the same proportion of their contributions or assets.

[4] In Argentina the new system has been under re-examination because of the fiscal crisis and political pressures to increase benefits. The contribution rate, for example, has been temporarily reduced and a new minimum pension that is about 45% of the average taxable wage has been introduced. Moreover, individuals are now permitted to claim credits for periods of self-employment on their date of retirement, simply in exchange for taking a 20% reduction in benefits in lieu of prior contributions. About half of all current retirees receive the minimum benefit (personal communication with Rafael Rofman, World Bank, April 2005). Women are recipients disproportionately (but note that most of these pensions are based on the old system, since the new system has been in effect only for ten years). The old system also changed frequently, was not always implemented as written, and several regimes coexisted. We base our analysis and discussion on the new system that was put in place in 1994 and the old system as written, for the main regime, shortly before the reform.

[5] Actually, the worker can choose to apply this contribution toward a public DB or a private DC plan similar to the Chilean model. As of 2001, over 80% of all affiliates were in the private DC rather than the public DB, which is why this chapter focuses on the private DC option.

[6] INFONAVIT historically provided a negative real return, but the hope of the reformers was that this would eventually change. In our simulations we assume a 0 real return.

[7] The Chile estimates are based on CASEN 94, a nationally representative household survey. Our estimates are based on the urban sample—approximately 100,000 individuals aged 16 years or older. The Argentine data are based on the microdata set of the Encuesta Nacional de Gastos de los Hogares (ENGH) for 1996–7, a nationally representative household survey from urban areas. The sample contains 103,858 individuals, of whom 69,895 were aged 16 years or older. The Mexican data come from the 1997 Mexican National Employment Survey (ENE-97) completed by the Instituto Nacional de Estadística, Geografía e Informática (INEGI), or the Mexican Statistical Bureau. The sample contains information on 119,405 individuals aged 12 years or older. We use the subsample corresponding to more urban areas (communities of 100,000 people or more), which is about 78% of the sample. For more details on data-sets, potential data problems, and construction of tables, see James, Edwards, and Wong (2003*a*, 2003*b*, and forthcoming).

[8] In the USA and Europe, where portfolio choice might be greater, it has sometimes been argued that women are more conservative investors than men—e.g. see Jianakoplos and Bernasek (1998), Bajtelsmit, Bernasek, and Jianakoplos (1999), Bernasek and Shwiff (2001). For surveys of this literature, see US GAO (1997) and Burnes and Schulz (2000). The restrictions on portfolios in Latin America during the period of our study preclude this possibility. However, in 2002 Chile introduced portfolio choice, and other countries are following suit, so the problem may also arise in Latin America.

[9] Our analysis concentrates throughout on the benefit rather than the cost side. We do not know the future cost of the public pillar, its intergenerational burden, or its gender incidence, either in the old or new systems. Net redistributions from public benefits (transfers received minus taxes implicitly paid to finance them) are discussed in James, Edwards, and Wong (2003*a*, 2003*b*, and forthcoming), based on the simplifying assumptions that each cohort covers its own bill and, within each cohort, the tax burden is distributed proportionally to earnings, as proxied by the present value of lifetime own-annuities.

[10] Labor informality in Latin America leads many workers, especially women, to contribute for less than half of their adult lives, so they fail to meet the twenty-year requirement. Chile also offers a noncontributory social assistance program called pensiones asistenciales, or PASIS, funded out of general revenues, which pays about 50% of the MPG. PASIS is designed to keep out of poverty those elderly not eligible for contributory benefits. The vast majority of its recipients are women living in rural areas.

[11] Many men, however, do not contribute when they work, leading to the problem of low density of contributions. The government apparently is unable to enforce the contribution requirement effectively. Consequently, retirees will have low pensions

and may demand that the government bail them out. How to handle this problem is a pressing issue today in most Latin-American countries.

[12] Several subsystems coexisted in Chile and Argentina, but a common formula paid 50% of pensionable salary for the first 10 years of work plus 1% per year thereafter. In Mexico, the old system paid a proportion of the base salary for the first ten years plus an increment for every year over ten. The proportion of the base varied negatively with wages, ranging from 13% for high earners to 80% for low earners. The increment for additional years varied positively with wages, ranging from 0.56 to 2.45% per year (see James, Edwards, and Wong 2003*a*, 2003*b*, and forthcoming for details).

[13] Note that the old systems sometimes indexed the minimum benefits for inflation but did not index higher benefits. In this case, many people received the minimum pension during inflationary periods. This produced high gender ratios but at very low absolute pension levels.

[14] The US social security system now price-indexes the benefit once the individual has retired, but wage-indexes the first pension received so that successive cohorts start out with pensions that have gone up with wage growth. Some policymakers have proposed full price indexation, so that the real benefit will be frozen in today's value. Critics point out that this will lead the benefit to eventually become much smaller relative to the average wage and the average standard of living in society. One compromise would wage-index for the bottom half while price-indexing for the upper half (progressive indexation), which would lead eventually to a flat benefit. Another compromise would index the entire public benefit half to wages and half to prices, as in Switzerland (or to longevity increases, which is roughly equivalent).

[15] In Chile wives do not have to purchase joint pensions to cover their husbands.

[16] In the USA, a spouse older than 65 years receives 50% of her husband's benefit, even if she has not worked and contributed. After he dies she gets 100% of his benefit, which means that married couples receive larger benefits than (and are subsidized by) singles with the same total earnings, and couples with one wage-earner get larger benefits than (and are subsidized by) couples in which both husband and wife work, with the same total earnings. Furthermore, the nonworking wife in a single-earner family gets a larger benefit than the wife in a dual-earner family with the same total family income. For examples, see Shirley and Spiegler (1998).

[17] This could also be built into traditional DB systems by reducing the benefits of husbands on an actuarially fair basis to finance the survivor's benefits of their wives. Widows could then keep their own benefit in addition to the survivor's benefit, thereby improving their own as well as the treasury's well-being.

References

Arenas de Mesa, Alberto, David Bravo, Jere R. Behrman, Olivia S. Mitchell, and Petra E. Todd (2008). 'The Chilean Pension Reform Turns 25: Lessons from the Social Protection Survey', this volume.

Asociación Internacional de Organismos Supervisores de Fondos de Pensiones (AIOS) (2005). *Boletin Estadistico.* Santiago: Chile.

Bajtelsmit, Vickie, Alexandra Bernasek, and Nancy Jianakoplos (1999). 'Gender Differences in Defined Contribution Pension Decisions', *Financial Services Review,* 8(1): 1–10.

Bernasek, Alexandra and Stephanie Shwiff (2001). 'Gender, Risk and Retirement', *Journal of Economic Issues,* 35(2): 345–56.

Bernheim, Douglas, Lorenzo Forni, Jagadeesh Gokhale, and Lawrence Kotlikoff (2001). 'Mismatch between Life Insurance Holdings and Financial Vulnerabilities—Evidence from the Health and Retirement Survey', draft paper.

Berstein, Solange, Guillermo Larrain, and Francisco Pino (2005). 'Coverage, Density and Pensions in Chile: Projections for the Next 30 Years', *Superintendencia of Pension Fund Administrators.* Santiago: Chile.

Burnes, Kathy and James Schulz (2000). *Older Women and Private Pensions in the United States.* Waltham, MA: National Center on Women and Aging, Brandeis University.

Castel, Paulette and Louise Fox (2001). 'Gender Dimensions of Pension Reform in the Former Soviet Union', in R. Holzmann and J. Stiglitz (eds.), *New Ideas about Old Age Security.* Washington, DC: World Bank.

Coronado, Julia, Don Fullerton and Thomas Glass (1999). 'Distributional Impacts of Proposed Changes to the Social Security System', in J. Poterba (ed.), *Tax Policy and the Economy,* 13.

—— —— —— (2000). 'The Progressivity of Social Security', NBER Working Paper W7520. Cambridge, MA: National Bureau of Economic Research.

Edwards, Alejandra Cox (2000*a*). 'Pension Projections for Chilean Men and Women: Estimates from Social Security Contributions' (translated to Spanish as 'El Futuro de las Pensiones en Chile'), *Estudios Publicos* No. 79. Winter, 2000 CEP (Centro de Estudios Públicos), Santiago, Chile.

—— (2000*b*). 'A Close Look at the Living Standards of Chilean Elderly Men and Women', manuscript.

—— (2001*a*). 'Social Security Reform and Women's Pensions', Policy Research Report on Gender and Development, Working Paper Series No. 17. Washington, DC: World Bank.

—— (2001*b*). 'Gender Inequities in the Pension and Social Protection Systems in the Region', paper presented in conjunction with annual meeting of Board of Governors of Inter-America Development Bank and Inter-American Investment Corp., Santiago, Chile, March 17.

—— (2001*c*). 'A Close Look at the Living Standards of Argentinean Elderly Men and Women', Photocopy, Urban Institute, Washington, DC.

—— (2002). 'Gender-Differentiated Effects of Social Security Reform: The Case of Chile', *The World Bank Economic Review,* 16(3).

—— and Estelle James (2005). 'Do Individual Accounts Postpone Retirement? Evidence from Chile', presented at NBER Summer Institute on Aging.

Ginn, Jay, Debra Street, and Sara Arber (eds.) (2001). Women, Work and Pensions. Buckingham, UK: Open University Press.

Gustman, Alan and Thomas L. Steinmeier (2000). 'How Effective is Redistribution under the Social Security Benefit Formula?', NBER Working Paper W7597. Cambridge, MA: National Bureau of Economic Research.

James, Estelle and Dimitri Vittas (2001). 'Annuities Markets in Comparative Perspective: Do Consumers Get Their Money's Worth?', in Private Pensions Systems: Administrative Costs and Reforms. Paris: OECD.

—— and Xue Song (2001). *Annuities Markets Around the World: Money's Worth and Risk Intermediation*, CeRP Working Paper 16/01. Turin, Italy: Center for Research on Pensions and Welfare Policies.

—— Gary Ferrier, James Smalhout, and Dimitri Vittas (2000). 'Mutual Funds and Institutional Investments: What Is the Most Efficient Way to Set Up Individual Accounts in a Social Security System?', in John Shoven (ed.), *Administrative Costs and Social Security Privatization.* Chicago, IL: University of Chicago Press, pp. 77–136.

—— James Smalhout, and Dimitri Vittas (2001). 'Administrative Costs and the Organization of Individual Account Systems: A Comparative Perspective', in R. Holzmann and J. Stiglitz (eds.), *New Ideas about Old Age Security.* Washington, DC: World Bank.

—— Alejandra Cox Edwards, and Rebeca Wong (2003*a*). 'The Gender Impact of Pension Reform: A Cross-Country Analysis', World Bank Discussion Paper. Washington, DC: World Bank.

—— —— —— (2003*b*). 'The Gender Impact of Pension Reform', *Journal of Pension Economics and Finance*, 2(2).

—— —— —— (forthcoming). *The Gender Impact of Social Security Reform.* Chicago: University of Chicago Press.

—— Guillermo Martinez, and Augusto Iglesias (2006). 'The Payout Stage in Chile: Who Annuitizes and Why?', *Journal of Pension Economics and Finance*, 5(2): 121–54.

Jianakoplos, Nancy and Alexandra Bernasek (1998). 'Are Women More Risk Averse?', Economic Inquiry, 36(4): 620–30.

Organisation for Economic Cooperation and Development (OECD) (2003). 'The Effects of Partial Careers on Pension Entitlements', Working Paper. Paris: OECD.

Parker, Susan and Rebeca Wong (2001). 'Welfare of Male and Female Elderly in Mexico: A Comparison', in *The Economics of Gender in Mexico: Work, Family, State, and Market.* Washington, DC: World Bank.

Rofman, Rafael (2005). Personal communication with the author, April.

—— (2008). 'The Pension System in Argentina', this volume.

Shirley, Ekaterina and Peter Spiegler (1998). 'The Benefits of Social Security Privatization for Women', SSP (12). Washington, DC: Cato Institute.

Sinha, Tapen and Maria de los Angeles Yañez (2008). 'A Decade of Government-Mandated Privately Run Pensions in Mexico: What Have We Learned?', this volume.

Stahlberg, Ann-Charlotte, Agneta Kruse, and Annika Sunden (2006*a*). 'Pension Design and Gender: Analyses of Developed and Developing Countries', in Neil Gilbert (ed.), *Gender and Social Security Reform—What's Fair for Women?* New Brunswick, NJ and London: Transaction.

—— Marcela Cohen Birman, Agneta Kruse, and Annika Sunden (2006*b*). 'Pension Reforms and Gender: The Case of Sweden', in Neil Gilbert (ed.), *Gender and Social Security Reform—What's Fair for Women?* New Brunswick, NJ and London: Transaction.

Street, Debra and Janet Wilmoth (2001). 'Social Insecurity? Women and Pensions in the United States', in Jay Ginn, Debra Street, and Sara Arber (eds.), *Women, Work and Pensions.* Buckingham, UK: Open University Press.

US General Accounting Office (GAO) (1997). *Social Security Reform: Implications for Women's Retirement Income,* GAO/HEHS-98–42. Washington, DC.

Wong, Rebeca and Susan Parker (2001). 'Social Security Reform in Mexico: A Gender Perspective', paper presented at the Population Association of America Meetings, Washington, DC, 2001, and at Interamerican Conference on Social Security, Fortaleza, Brazil, March 2001.

Woycicka, Irene (ed.) (2001). 'Gender Impact of Social Security Reform in Central and Eastern Europe', photocopy. Warsaw: Gdansk Institute for Market Economics.

Chapter 5

Pension Reform and Gender Inequality

Michelle Dion

This chapter examines an effect of pension reform that was largely unanticipated, or at least seldom explicitly considered, when many pension reforms were being adopted throughout Latin America: the effects of privatization on women's welfare.[1] Though this issue was largely absent in early reform debates, academic researchers and international organizations—including the United Nations (UN) Economic Commission on Latin America and the Caribbean (ECLAC), the International Labour Organisation (ILO), and even the World Bank—began to consider it in the early 2000s.[2] Although the literature is increasingly recognizing that pension policy design produces different distributional outcomes according to gender, it often disagrees in its evaluation on whether these outcomes are generally negative, positive, or neutral for the welfare of women. These disagreements have come about because some analysts view publicly mandated pension systems as serving an insurance function, though often not explicitly, while others view them as serving a redistributive function. From these different perspectives derive different criteria to evaluate gendered outcomes of pension privatization, which explains why assessments of the gender effects of pension privatization differ.

This chapter has three objectives regarding the gendered outcomes of structural pension reform in Latin America. First, it provides a brief overview of the sources of gender inequalities and discusses elements of pension policy affecting gendered welfare. Second, it explains and critiques the insurance-based criteria for evaluating the gender effects of pension reform. These criteria, often employed by economists, emphasize lifetime benefits, actuarial fairness, or consumption outcomes. Third, it offers an alternative set of criteria for evaluating gender outcomes based on three dimensions: women's ability to claim social citizenship rights, gender stratification, and the distribution of welfare responsibility among the market, state, and family. These criteria are consistent with a sociological understanding of public pension systems as welfare or redistributive state policy.

The author thanks Christina Ewig, Evelyne Huber, Stephen J. Kay, Milko Matijascic, Jenny Pribble, Tapen Sinha, and John Williamson for comments and suggestions, and she accepts responsibility for any of the chapter's remaining shortcomings.

Finally, it compares interpretations of the gendered effects of pension reform in Latin America based on insurance and distributive assumptions to illustrate why disagreements in the literature persist.

Labor Market and Pension Policy as Sources of Gender Inequalities

Labor market differences and pension policies often *both* contribute to gender differences in access to and generosity of pension benefits (Bertranou 2006; Mesa-Lago 2006; James, Edwards, and Wong 2008). In Latin America, women's participation in the labor market often differs from that of men in four ways that have important effects on their ability to earn pension rights and benefits comparable to those of men.

1. Despite increasing rates of women's employment throughout the region, women still tend to have lower economic activity rates than do men (see Table 5-1). This difference can be attributed to women's reproductive and caring responsibilities and has an important impact on the accumulation of contributions required to receive either a statutory minimum pension or pension benefits comparable to those of men.
2. When women do enter the labor force, they often experience higher levels of unemployment than men (Giménez 2005: 61–2; see also Table 5-1). Higher unemployment levels also lead to lower contribution rates to publicly mandated pension systems.
3. Labor markets in Latin America tend to be segmented by gender, and women are more likely to be concentrated in low-productivity, or informal and low-quality, jobs (see Table 5-1). Consequently, they are much less likely to have social insurance coverage or to make regular contributions to voluntary public social insurance schemes. Women's segmentation in the labor force also contributes to lower average wages for women compared to men.
4. Women's wages at all ages and levels of education are lower than men's, a situation reflecting both the segmentation of women's employment and wage discrimination (see Table 5-1 and Sinha and de los Angeles Yañez 2008).

Together, these differences in women's labor market participation patterns lead to lower contribution densities and benefits in any kind of pension system, including publicly mandated pension systems for women as compared to men.

Given these differences in the labor market for men and women, pension policies can either translate or mitigate these labor market inequalities into

TABLE 5-1 Gender Inequalities in the Labor Market (1989–2004)

	Economically Active Population (EAP) Participation Rates in Urban Areas			*Open Unemployment Rates in Urban Areas*			*Urban Population Employed in Low Productivity Sectors (%)*			*Year*	*Earned Income Ratio*[a]	*Wage Ratio*[b]
	Year	*Men*	*Women*	*Year*	*Men*	*Women*		*Men*	*Women*		*Female/ Male*	*Female/ Male*
Argentina (Buenos Aires)	1990	76	38	1990	5.7	6.4	1990	42.2	48.0	1990	65	76
	2004	78	52	2004	11.9	15.8	2004	39.4	41.1	2004	61	68
Bolivia	1989	73	47	1990	9.5	9.1	1989	48.8	71.5	1989	59	60
	2002	77	57	2003	5.2	7.9	2002	58.5	76.6	2002	61	77
Brazil	1990	82	45	1990	4.8	3.9	1990	44.7	56.8	1990	56	65
	2003	79	55	2003	9.0	13.8	2003	40.7	51.1	2003	66	87
Chile	1990	72	35	1990	8.1	9.7	1990	33.8	47.5	1990	61	66
	2003	73	45	2003	8.5	12.4	2003	27.8	38.0	2003	64	83
Colombia	1991	81	48	1990	6.7	13.0	1991	—	—	1991	68	77
	2002	79	57	2003	14.8	20.0	2002	—	—	2002	77	99
Costa Rica	1990	78	39	1990	4.9	6.2	1990	35.1	40.1	1990	72	74
	2004	78	45	2004	5.7	8.1	2004	36.7	42.4	2002	75	85
Dominican Republic	1992	86	53	1990	11.3	31.5	1997	47.5	46.0	1997	75	90
	2004	79	56	2004	12.6	30.5	2004	49.6	45.9	2002	68	89
El Salvador	1990	80	51	1990	10.0	9.7	1990	45.9	67.9	1995	63	79
	2004	74	51	2004	8.8	3.8	2004	47.8	62.5	2001	73	100

Mexico	1989	77	33	1990	3.4	3.1	1996	41.7	47.6	1989	55	73
	2004	80	47	2004	4.7	3.1	2004	42.2	50.7	2004	63	78
Peru	1997	83	62	1997	8.1	13.8	1997	53.7	69.3	1997	60	73
	2003	74	54	2003	7.3	6.2	2003	58.1	72.5	2003	61	78
Uruguay	1990	75	44	1990	7.3	11.1	1990	34.8	46.1	1990	45	64
	2004	71	49	2004	10.2	16.6	2004	41.6	50.3	2002	82	71

Source: ECLAC (2006*b*: Tables 17, 21.1, 21.2, 22, 27).

[a] Income differential among the entire employed population, calculated as the quotient of average female income and average male income, multiplied by 100.

[b] Income differential among wage or salary earners, calculated as the quotient of average female income and average male income, multiplied by 100.

differences in pension welfare. Four aspects of public pension policy play important roles in determining women's access to and quality of pensions (Bertranou 2006; Mesa-Lago 2006).

1. Because women on average earn less than men do in the labor market, they more often earn the minimum pensions guaranteed by the public pension system. Where reforms have increased the number of years of contributions to be eligible for the minimum pension, such reforms are more likely to affect women, who less often meet the minimum contributions necessary to qualify for the minimum pension.
2. The way in which the pension benefit is calculated can have important effects on women's versus men's pensions. If benefits are calculated over lifetime contributions, as they are in DC systems, the system is likely to compound the labor market inequalities experienced by women. In contrast, women's benefits are more likely to be more comparable, though still probably less, to those of men under DB plans that use either average wages or wages during a particular period to calculate the pension benefit. Likewise, a more generous minimum pension can also mitigate gender inequalities.
3. The use of gender-specific actuarial, or life tables accentuates gender inequalities in pension benefits because women tend to live longer than men. When gender-specific life tables are used, a man and woman with similar contribution densities, wages, and retirement ages will receive different pension benefits because it is assumed that the woman's benefits will be distributed over a longer period due to her higher life expectancy.
4. Earlier permissible retirement ages also tend to result in smaller pensions for women in DC pension systems.

Though the design of pension policy can mitigate the gender inequalities created by the labor market, analysts disagree on whether pension policy is the appropriate tool for addressing labor market inequalities. Those that emphasize the insurance functions of public pension policy tend to be skeptical of using policy to promote gender equality, while those that view pensions as having a redistributive social function emphasize the necessity of designing policy to mitigate market inequalities. Because each of these perspectives includes different assumptions about the role of pension policy, it is no surprise that disagreements persist regarding whether pension privatization in Latin America has improved or worsened women's old-age welfare. The next section explains the insurance approach to pensions and argues that though the insurance approach is often couched in language of 'fairness', such claims are based on a misplaced emphasis on efficiency and are actually unfair to women.

Pensions as Insurance: The Use of Lifetime Benefits, Actuarial Fairness, and Consumption Criteria

Some of the recent literature on structural pension reform and gender (including James, Edwards, and Wong 2008) has been written by economists who approach the question of the effects of pension privatization on women's welfare in Latin America using economic or insurance criteria that are presented as value-neutral but that actually prioritize efficiency over equity. The two most common criteria from an insurance approach used to evaluate the gender effects of structural reform emphasize either lifetime benefits and actuarial fairness or comparable consumption during old age for men and women due to intrafamily transfers.

Lifetime Benefits and Actuarial Fairness

Some economists, particularly those working with the World Bank, use lifetime benefits as their preferred metric to evaluate the actuarial fairness of pensions. Lifetime benefits are the average accumulated benefits of a retiree between retirement and death, and pensions are actuarially fair to the extent that contributions are closely linked to risks and therefore to the cost of benefits. Actuarial fairness is used to evaluate pensions because pension designs that do not use all available information to estimate risks and closely link contributions to benefits can result in keeping those with shorter longevity from participating in pension programs, leaving only the 'bad risks' (those with greater longevity) insured. When pensions are not actuarially fair, resources are inefficiently allocated because when some individuals contribute more than they receive in benefits, they cannot use those resources for other productive purposes. This emphasis on the insurance function and efficiency of public pension systems and the importance of comparing lifetime benefits is apparent in the World Bank's *Averting the Old Age Crisis* (1994). For instance, the book argues that a system that privileges insurance and saving over redistribution has advantages, such as reducing evasion, promoting employment, and promoting efficiency (1994: 76). It also argues that many DB pension systems, though progressive in the structure of their monthly replacement rates, are actually regressive because the rich tend to outlive the poor (WB 1994: 10).[3] Redistribution, according to the *Averting the Old Age Crisis* model, should only be administered through minimum safety net pensions for the elderly poor.

Regarding gender, economists regularly use lifetime benefits to measure the actuarial fairness of pensions between men and women. Because women tend to live longer than men, if monthly benefits for men and women are equal, then women will have larger lifetime benefits. Some argue, therefore, that when contributions and benefits are not closely linked, women will take advantage of the disparity and contribute as little as possible, and men will cease to participate because the system is *actuarially* unfair (Schwarz 2006).[4] If women, on average, live longer than men, then to be fair their contributions to the pension system beyond those for the minimum pension should be comparable to the cost of their greater longevity (Schokkaert and Van Parijs 2003*a*: 257–8).

Recent studies also use comparisons of women's and men's lifetime benefits to assess the gender impacts of pension privatization in Latin America (James, Edwards, and Wong 2003, 2008). For instance, James, Edwards, and Wong (2008) find that though female-to-male lifetime benefits fall for single women and men, female-to-male lifetime benefit ratios improve when the redistributive pillar or provisions, such as flat-rate or minimum-guaranteed pensions, are included (in Argentina and Mexico) and when survivor's pensions are included (in Argentina, Mexico, and Chile). Under certain circumstances, women may receive lifetime benefits that exceed those of men, according to the authors' simulations. That is, the generosity of women's lifetime benefits is partly because of their average longevity, not because they enjoy a comparable level of welfare to men. In this way, the study authors can present a more positive interpretation of the gender effects of pension reform in Latin America compared to comparisons based on the gender disparities in monthly benefits.

Though the use of lifetime benefits and actuarial fairness is often invoked in the use of technical, presumably value-neutral criteria for evaluating pensions, the use of these criteria to evaluate pension reforms prioritizes efficiency over equity. Perhaps more problematic is that using lifetime benefits, and thus implicitly actuarial fairness, to evaluate the gender effects of pension reform can be used to hide discriminatory practices. Indeed, the use of gender-specific actuarial tables for the calculation of pension benefits is not allowed in the USA precisely because the Supreme Court ruled that they violated the Civil Rights Act 1964 and the Equal Employment Opportunity Act 1972 in *Los Angeles Department of Water and Power v Manhart* in 1978. The basis of this decision was an argument that it was unfair to discriminate against an individual of a group based on the characteristic of the group (Simon 1988). That is, although women generally live longer than men, it would be unfair to discriminate against those women who do not.[5] This theme is a recurring one in the literature criticizing the use of lifetime benefits or actuarial fairness to evaluate gender and pension reform (Fultz and Steinhibler 2003; Ginn 2004: 7). By using lifetime benefits to compare the pensions of women and men, some analysts distort the distributional effects of pension reform in a way that minimizes the harm done to women's welfare and equal rights.

Others argue that though women may have greater longevity, sex is hardly the only, or even best, predictor of risk. It is unfair for women to be punished for an immutable group characteristic like their greater longevity when other predictors of risk are routinely ignored (Simon 1988; Fultz and Steinhibler 2003; Myles 2003: 267; Ginn 2004: 7). For instance, race may be a useful predictor of longevity but to use it to calculate pension benefits would be considered discriminatory. Further, many of the best predictors of risk are class-related or behavioral, rather than immutable, and continue to be ignored, including income, occupation, education, smoking, weight, regular exercise, and so on. Fultz and Steinhibler (2003) most clearly make this point when they argue that even in privatized systems, publicly mandated pension systems serve the public function of risk pooling and therefore pooling should occur across *all* risks, including those associated with gender.

In addition to gender-based discrimination through the use of lifetime benefit or actuarial fairness criteria, several authors provide compelling reasons why women *should* be entitled to higher lifetime benefits than men. For instance, in heterosexual couples, women who outlive their partners may not only have to care for their ailing partners but also then lack such care themselves at the ends of their own lives or have to get it from the state or market. In such cases, it is unclear that quantity of life is an advantage if the quality of the longer life is poor (Ginn 2004). In such circumstances, men are not just subsidizing the income of women but compensating them for either caring responsibilities or the burden of living longer.

The most compelling argument against using lifetime benefits and actuarial fairness to evaluate the gender effects of pension reform rests on the logic that such practices reinforce discrimination against a group (women) unable to change the characteristic on which the discrimination is based. This was the logic of the *Manhart* decision in the USA and recent directives in the European Union that reject the use of gender-specific actuarial tables as gender discrimination. If policy in advanced industrialized democracies rejects the use of actuarial tools as being discriminatory against women, lifetime benefits and actuarial fairness—similarly biased criteria that accept discriminatory practices on technical grounds—should not be used to evaluate the gender fairness of pension reform. As Simon explains, 'The point is that practices, such as the one in *Manhart* that treat the gender difference as unproblematic, make it more difficult for the uprooting of the habituated gender assumptions to unfold. This, and not hidden prejudice, makes the actuarial use of gender for insurance purposes unacceptable' (1988: 796). In other words, using lifetime benefits to evaluate gender outcomes only serves to perpetuate and legitimize discriminatory practices in public pension policy.

Survivor's Benefits, IntraFamily Transfers, and Consumption

Averting the Old Age Crisis does a fair job of highlighting the special needs of elderly women, including widows, who are most likely to be poor and dependent on family members for support in old age. Despite a balanced discussion of the poor treatment of widows in rural India and the risks of relying on informal support networks for women's old-age welfare, the report emphasizes formalizing intrafamily transfers by splitting contribution credits and providing survivor's pensions rather than promoting policies to ensure women's entitlement to their own benefits. The book's principal recommendations for protecting women's old-age welfare include a universal minimum pension without regard to employment, splitting of contributions of married couples, mandatory survivor benefits, and additional benefits for the very old (WB 1994: 252–3). The first of these recommendations would do the most to reduce gender inequalities. Unfortunately, some of these recommendations were not uniformly or consistently implemented in many Latin-American pension reforms.

Despite apparent concern for the gender effects of structural pension reform in *Averting the Old Age Crisis*, recent evaluations of the gender effects of Latin-American pension reform sponsored by the Bank downplay the negative effects by focusing on informal and formal intrafamily transfers. For example, Parker and Wong (2001) find that elderly men and women in Mexico tend to have similar levels of consumption, despite the fact that fewer women have access to their own pensions. Because elderly women received income support from their family relationships, they conclude that the reformed system does not necessarily fail them. Others emphasize formal intrafamily transfers through the requirement that husbands purchase joint annuities with survivor's benefits (James, Edwards, and Wong 2003, 2008). According to such defenders of structural pension reforms, intrafamily transfers and transfers due to public benefit pillars support the claims that women have gained more from the reforms than men have (James, Edwards, and Wong 2008). In fact, access to own pensions for women has declined and the inequality of monthly benefits and family dependence has increased.

Unfortunately, reliance on intrafamily transfers for women's old-age welfare also entails certain costs if considered from the point of view of gender-egalitarian values. Such transfers reinforce male breadwinner norms, especially when restrictions are placed on the ability of women to provide comparable survivor benefits to their husbands, as in some Latin-American countries. Further, such benefits 'reproduce personal relationships of power and dependence among family members', a situation that helps maintain the traditional division of labor (Leitner 2001: 103). When women derive their rights to pension benefits primarily from their roles as mothers or wives, their dependency diminishes their worth and equality (Sen 1984; Marco 2002; Ginn 2004). In addition, by reinforcing male breadwinner norms, widow's pensions provide little reward to married women who enter the formal labor market.

Perhaps more problematic is that an emphasis on widow's pensions ignores the reality of changing family structures in Latin America. Over the past few decades, marriage rates in many Latin-American countries have declined, especially among lower-income families (see Table 5-2). In the context of serial monogamy or unmarried partnerships, survivor's pensions are outdated tools for ensuring women's welfare in old age (Schokkaert and Van Parijs 2003*b*: 278; Ginn 2004: 5). Though some reformed pension systems in Latin America allow unmarried heterosexual partners to claim survivor's benefits, these women must often provide proof of cohabitation and the mutual parentage of their children. For example, in most reformed systems, women can claim survivor's benefits if they can prove they had a child with the pensioner. When there are no children, women may have to prove economic dependence on or cohabitation with the pensioner for a minimum number of years, ranging from two years, as in Colombia and Costa Rica, to five years, as in Argentina and Mexico (Giménez 2004: 127–30). For low-income women, for whom cohabitation has historically been and continues to be more common, such requirements are likely to limit their ability to receive survivor's benefits. Divorce and single-female-headed households have also become more common throughout Latin America (see Table 5-2). Divorced women who have expected widow's pension benefits may be denied such benefits if their former partners remarry. For these reasons, *Averting the Old Age Crisis* (1994) recommends splitting pension contributions and credits between husband and wife at divorce, though few reformed pension systems in Latin America adequately protect women's share of pension rights. Consequently, many of the reformed systems, by relying on survivor's pensions to provide for women's welfare, are likely to leave growing numbers of women unprotected and dependent on social assistance in old age.

Insuring Individuals or Families?

Insurance approaches to evaluating pension reform tend to emphasize either individual lifetime benefits and actuarial fairness or intrafamily transfers to ensure against risks. These two positions are inconsistent in their assumptions about the appropriate unit of analysis or comparison—individuals or the family. On the one hand, actuarial fairness requires that individual benefits and incentives be efficient and closely link contributions to benefits. On the other hand, intrafamily transfers through survivor's

TABLE 5-2 Family Structure and Marriage and Divorce Rates in Latin America (1990–2004)

	Year	*One-Person Household* [a]	*Single-Parent Nuclear W/ Male Head* [a]	*Single-Parent Nuclear W/ Female Head* [a]	*% of One-Person Households*			*% of One-Parent Nuclear, Headed by*		*Marriage Rates (per 1000 of Population)*		*Divorce Rates (per 1000 of Population)*	
					Year	*Men*	*Women*	*Men*	*Women*	*Year*	*Rate*	*Year*	*Rate*
Argentina	1990	12.5	1.2	6.4	1990	31.4	68.6	15.9	84.1	1996	4.2		
(Buenos Aires)	2002	15.3	2.4	8.5	2004	36.4	63.6	16.3	93.7	2002	3.2		
Bolivia	2002	8.7	1.8	10.5	2002	52.6	47.4	14.8	85.2				
Brazil	1990	7.9	1.2	8.4	1990	44.1	55.9	12.4	87.6	1996	4.6	1996	0.6
	2002	9.8	1.3	10.2	2003	46.6	53.4	10.8	89.2	2002		2002	
Chile	1990	6.5	1.2	7.7	1990	42.9	57.1	13.2	86.8	1996	5.8	1996	0.43
	2000	7.9	1.3	7.3	2003	44.8	55.2	12.1	87.9	2003	3.6	1998	0.42
Colombia	1991	4.8	1	9.6									
	2002	8.3	1.5	10.7	2004	55.4	44.6	12.3	87.7				
Costa Rica	1990	5	1	9.5	1990	44.6	55.4	9.8	90.2	1996	6.9	1997	1.26
	2002	6.8	1.1	11.7	2004	53.7	46.3	6.8	93.2	2003	6	1998	2.04
Dominican					1992	54.5	45.5	16.5	83.5	1998	3.5	1996	0.29
Republic	2002	9.4	1.5	11.3	2004	58.3	41.7	16.7	83.3	2001	2.8	2001	0.96
El Salvador	1995	6.1	1.2	10.2	1990	56.4	43.6	15.1	84.9	1996	4.7	1996	0.46
	2001	7.8	1.4	11.6	2004	56.5	43.5	9.9	90.1	2003	3.8	2003	0.64
Mexico	1989	4.6	1.2	6.4	1989	49.4	50.6	16.1	83.9	1996	7.2	1996	0.42
	2002	6.5	1.5	9.4	2004	46.4	53.6	12.4	87.6	2003	5.6	2003	0.62
Peru					1997	64.0	36.0	18.3	81.7	1997	3.2		
	2001	7.6	2.1	8	2003	60.1	39.9	15.2	84.8				
Uruguay	1990	13.9	1.3	7.2	1990	29.4	70.6	15.0	85.0	1996	5.4	1996	2.03
	2002	17.7	1.6	8.6	2004	35.3	64.7	15.5	84.5	2003	4.3	2003	4.24

Sources: ECLAC (2005, Table IV.1), ECLAC (2006*c*, Table 1.1.14), and UN (2000, 2003, Tables 23 and 25).
[a] % of total households.

pensions provide little incentive for women to contribute to their own pensions. The position is problematic because individual fairness is used to justify policies that hurt women's rights, and then the negative effects of these policies are assumed to be ameliorated by policies that expect women to receive benefits from family members rather than from individual entitlements.

Pensions as Redistributive Welfare Policy: Alternative Criteria for Assessing Gender Impacts

Though economists tend to emphasize the insurance function of public pension policy, sociologists and political scientists evaluate policy outcomes from a different perspective, one that prioritizes the distributional consequences of different public policies instead of economic efficiency. Recent research from this perspective suggests that most welfare policies can be usefully compared along three dimensions: social citizenship, stratification, and the role of family, market, and state in the provision of welfare (Esping-Anderson 1990). Further, the gender impacts of welfare policy can be evaluated using gendered, or gender-sensitive, versions of these dimensions (Orloff 1993; O'Connor, Orloff, and Shaver 1999). This section focuses on how these gendered dimensions can be adapted to evaluate the gender impact of pension reform in Latin America, arguing that these criteria provide a superior metric for such evaluations.[6]

Social Citizenship

Marshall (1950) explains the extension of citizenship rights in modern society as a process concurrent with industrialization that led to the granting of first civil, then political, and, finally, social rights to citizens of the modern nation-state. The replacement of poor relief with modern social safety nets, including pensions, reflects the development of individual social citizenship rights. In practice, social citizenship rights in a pension system can be measured according to the extent that they provide benefits to enable retired persons to live independently and maintain a socially acceptable standard of living, and that the right to a pension is based on citizenship rather than employment.[7] Most of the pension reforms and privatizations in Latin America have followed the World Bank model to varying degrees by shifting the bulk of pension provision from DB to DC models, and critiques of these pension reforms often focus on the tightening of the relationship between contributions and benefits, which they say erodes social citizenship rights (Giménez 2005: 45–6).

The gender effects of policy can be evaluated according to the extent to which reforms disproportionately affect women's abilities to claim pension benefits as a right of social citizenship. Policies that promote women's social citizenship 'guarantee women access to paid employment and services that enable them to balance home and work responsibilities' (Orloff 1993: 317). Preschool or daycare, home-help for elderly family members, and gender-neutral parental leave are examples of such policies (Orloff 1993; O'Connor 1996; Esping-Andersen 1999). For pensions to be gender-neutral with regard to social citizenship, the minimum contributions to receive benefits or a minimum pension should not disproportionately disadvantage women, and women should not be concentrated among the recipients of poor relief or assistance pensions, a situation that implies a weaker claim to citizenship rights (Leitner 2001: 104–5; Marco 2002). Women should be able to claim pensions as a matter of right rather than on the basis of their roles as wives and mothers (Orloff 1993: 315; Giménez 2005: 46). The effect of many of the Latin-American pension reforms since the 1990s has been to erode women's social citizenship rights by increasing barriers to pensions.

Many reforms in Latin America increased the minimum contributions necessary to receive minimum guaranteed pensions, which is likely to deny disproportionately women their social citizenship rights. For example, Mexico increased contribution requirements from 10 to 25 years; the Dominican Republic went from 15 to 25 or 30 years; Chile and Argentina went from 10 years to 20 and 30, respectively (see Table 5-3). Given women's lower workforce participation rates and concentration in informal and low-productivity sectors without social insurance coverage, these increases in the contribution requirements disproportionately prevent them from claiming pension rights. According to simulated women's workforce participation in Argentina, Chile, and Mexico, women's lifetime contributions are likely to range from 17 to 36 years across the three countries (James, Edwards, and Wong n.d.). In all three countries, only ten years of contributions were needed under the old system to receive pension benefits, and the simulated contributions would have been sufficient for women to enjoy pension benefits of their own. In Chile, nearly all women are expected to have lifetime contributions that guarantee a minimum pension because the contribution requirement was raised only to 20 years. In Mexico, however, the contribution requirement was raised to 25 years, which puts it just out of range for most women, who tend to work 19–24 years. Only the most educated Mexican women are expected to work long enough to receive the guaranteed minimum pension.[8] In Argentina, the new requirement of 30 years of contributions to receive the flat pension benefit effectively excludes all but highly educated women, according to simulated contribution estimates. In contrast, simulated men in all three countries were likely to contribute at least thirty-five years, and often longer, across all educational groups (James, Edwards, and Wong n.d.).

Because many of the reformed systems are too young to provide firm evidence for evaluating the gender effects of reform, research must rely on labor market data often collected prior to the reforms and simulations based on such data. This is particularly problematic since pension reforms were expected to provide incentives for formal sector employment and contributions that cannot yet be evaluated.

On the one hand, reform advocates argue that the higher contribution requirements for minimum pensions are likely to provide incentives for women to work and contribute longer, enabling them to earn their own pensions in greater numbers. They also say that reforms often eliminated the rules that provided disincentives for married women to seek formal (as opposed to informal) sector employment, such as the provision in Mexico that now allows women to provide social insurance benefits for an unemployed husband. Therefore, even though women are unlikely to earn their own minimum pension benefits if their work patterns remain unchanged, according to reform advocates, the pension reforms may create sufficient incentives for women to change their work habits to bring them in line with the requirements for a minimum or flat pension.

On the other hand, trends in women's labor market participation and preliminary evidence from Chile, which has the oldest reformed system in the region, suggest that estimates of women's pensions on the basis of simulated work experiences are overly optimistic. For instance, James, Edwards, and Wong (2008, n.d.) do not have actual contribution densities for men and women who work. For their simulations, they assume that when women are working, they are also contributing to social security, though women's employment patterns in the region suggest that a good proportion of women, especially at lower levels of education, are likely to be concentrated in the informal sector without social security coverage. This means that the authors have probably overestimated the accumulation of contributions for women, especially those with less education.[9] Furthermore, evidence from Chile demonstrates that women are less likely to be affiliated to the pension system, continue to have lower contribution density rates than men, and are more likely in surveys to overestimate their contributions than men. Women continue to represent over 70 percent of the population not affiliated to the social security system in Chile (Bravo et al. 2006).[10] According to estimates based on self-reported and actual contributions by men and women to the privatized pension system in Chile, women's self-reported mean months of contributions is only 73 percent of that of men, and women's actual mean number of months of contributions is 70 percent of that of men (based on the table 'Contribution Patterns to the Chilean Retirement System by Sex, Age, and Education', in Arenas de

TABLE 5-3 Requirements for Contributory and Noncontributory Minimum Pension Benefits

	Chile	*Peru*	*Colombia*	*Argentina*	*Uruguay*	*Mexico*	*Bolivia*	*El Salvador*	*Costa Rica*	*Dominican Republic*	*Brazil*
Contributory public pension system											
Year of reform (implemented)	1981	1992–93	1994	1994	1996	1995 (1997)	1997	1998	1995–2000	2001 (2003)	1998, 2003
Type of reform	Substitutive	Parallel	Parallel	Mixed	Mixed	Substitutive	Substitutive	Substitutive	Mixed	Substitutive	Parametric
Requirements for minimum or basic contributory pension											
Age—men	65	65	60	65	60	65	n/a	65	62/65	60/65	65/none
Age—women	60	65	55	60	60	65	n/a	60	60/65	60/65	60/none
Years of contributions	20	20	20	30	35	25	n/a	25 years	39/20 years	30/25	12/35 for men 12/30 for women
Noncontributory pensions											
Social assistance pensions	Yes	No	No	Yes	Yes	No	Yes	No	Yes	Yes	Yes
Year of reform	1981			1993	1995		1993		1995	—	1974
Age for eligibility	70			70	70		65		65	—	70
Means tested or universal	Means tested			Means tested	Means tested		Universal		Means tested	—	Means tested

Sources: Author's elaboration based on Holzmann and Hinz (2005), Tables 7.2 and 7.3, and AIOS (2003).

Notes: Peru: minimum pensions only for those born before 1945.

Colombia: age and contribution requirements gradually increase to 62 years for men, 57 years for women, and 26 years of contribution by 2015.

Argentina: reduced old-age benefit for those aged 70 years and older with 10 years of contributions at 70% of flat universal benefit.

Uruguay: reduced old-age benefit for those aged 70 and 15 years of contributions.

Mexico: a noncontributory old-age benefit has been implemented in the federal district only.

Bolivia: no minimum age if funds purchase annuity with 70% replacement rate. At age 65 years, can retire if funds sufficient to buy 70% replacement rate of national minimum wage.

Mesa et al. 2008). This is consistent with recent estimates that indicate that the average man's contribution density in Chile is 60 percent, compared to only 43 percent for women (Bravo et al. 2006). By age 40, working women will have contributed less than half as many years as working men (Arenas de Mesa et al. 2008).

This evidence suggests that pension reform alone does not provide enough incentive for women to seek formal sector employment to receive pension benefits. Further, women's self-reported contribution rates tend to exceed their actual contributions more than men's self-reported rates (Arenas de Mesa et al. 2008). This means that it is likely that simulations based on household surveys (e.g. those by James, Edwards, and Wong 2008) overestimate the contributions that women are making to their pension funds and therefore provide overly optimistic characterizations of women's access to pension benefits in the reformed systems. Though reformed pension rules may create incentives for women to change their labor market participation to secure their access to benefits, evidence from Chile suggests that women's labor force participation combined with reformed pension rules will continue to prevent many women from earning their own guaranteed minimum or flat-rate pensions in many reformed systems in Latin America. Despite the incentives created by the pension system, women may still face structural barriers to formal labor market participation. To the extent that women are less able than men to claim their own pension benefits due to the new contribution requirements, women's social citizenship rights are jeopardized.

Pension reform supporters also claim that women's welfare is protected by public pillars or noncontributory social assistance and survivor's pensions (James, Edwards, and Wong 2008). Several countries with reformed pension systems have implemented noncontributory social assistance pensions or reduced benefit contributory pensions for the very old (see Table 5-3). In terms of social citizenship, universal, noncontributory pensions would provide the most complete social citizenship rights and gender equality. In the Southern Cone, reduced benefits at age 70 were adopted for workers who either have contributed fewer years than the regular retirement benefit or meet a means test. Given their work histories and longevity, women are likely to be concentrated among the beneficiaries of these social assistance pensions (Bertranou 2003). However, when the benefit levels of noncontributory or social assistance pensions do not meet basic needs or are significantly less than the minimum pensions of workers, noncontributory pensions are more consistent with poor relief and do not reflect full social citizenship rights. That is, if the benefits of such pensions are significantly lower than other minimum guaranteed pensions for workers, the higher concentration of women among recipients of social assistance pensions implies that women are not entitled to full citizenship rights and equates women, due to labor market segmentation and discrimination or their caring responsibilities, with needy groups otherwise unable to provide for their own welfare.

Supporters of structural pension reform also emphasize that married women will benefit from new requirements for joint annuities and survivor's pensions that were adopted with many reforms (James, Edwards, and Wong 2008). From a social citizenship rights perspective, conditioning women's pension benefits on their dependency or family roles erodes their citizenship rights to a pension as autonomous citizens (Leitner 2001; Giménez 2005). Though women may be entitled to social assistance or survivor's pensions in reformed pension systems, the benefits of those pensions may be insufficient to ensure that women are able to maintain a decent standard of living or a standard of living consistent with full social citizenship. In many reformed systems, social assistance pensions are less than the minimum pension of wage earners or may not be sufficient to maintain a household above the poverty line.

Policies to promote women's full social citizenship with regard to pensions can address the differences in labor market participation between women and men or compensate women for their caring responsibilities. Labor market policies could include those that support women's employment (such as daycare services) or counteract wage discrimination and labor market segmentation faced by women. Such policies are likely to require long-term investments and be of limited immediate effect. Pension policies likely to have more immediate effect on women's social citizenship include adjusting contribution requirements for minimum pensions to be within reach of the majority of women, protecting women's access to partner's pensions through pension contribution splitting, and providing women with credits and contributions for their caring responsibilities. Women's access to the minimum-guaranteed or flat-rate pensions is very sensitive to the number of years of contributions required, which is illustrated by the contrast of Chile's twenty-year, Argentina's thirty-year, and Mexico's twenty-five-year requirements (James, Edwards, and Wong n.d.). Working women will be much more likely to meet Chile's minimum requirement of twenty years than those in either Argentina or Mexico. For the financial soundness of the pension systems, contribution requirements must be increased, but the increases can be done such that they are less likely to disproportionately hurt women by taking into account existing patterns of women's workforce participation.

Women's rights can also be protected by ensuring that women who have not worked outside the home receive credit for their partner's contributions should the union dissolve (Schokkaert and Van Parijs 2003*b*). For example, recent reforms to marriage law in Chile have not provided protection for divorced women, who may lose their survivor's benefits should their former spouse remarry. Finally, women's caring responsibilities can be acknowledged by providing contributions (or at least credits toward minimum contribution requirements) to women's individual accounts. Examples of such credits are common in Latin America. In Uruguay, a 1920s law guaranteed a mother's right to a pension after working in the labor market only ten years. In Brazil, women automatically receive five years of credit toward requirements to receive a pension. Such credits are not uncommon in European social security systems and would help ensure that women are able to claim their own minimum guaranteed pensions (Leitner 2001; Ginn 2004).

Gender Inequality and Stratification

Stratification refers to the extent that welfare regimes eliminate, perpetuate, or create inequalities in society. Though social policies may redistribute income, they can also potentially stratify social groups in terms of status and rights (Esping-Andersen 1990: 56–8). For instance, regimes with several occupationally distinct public pension or health insurance systems reinforce the existing hierarchy among different occupational groups. In Latin America, social insurance systems are highly stratified, especially due to the existence of separate and more generous social insurance systems for public sector employees and the military. Pension privatization exacerbates existing stratification when public sector employee, military, or police schemes are exempted from reform, as in most Latin-American countries. Since most of the pension reforms in the 1990s shifted DB to DC funding, the new pension systems perpetuate stratification or inequalities in the labor market. Though postreform pension systems often have some mechanism for redistribution to support low-income pensioners, the amount of redistribution is often limited.

Social insurance rules can also affect gender stratification, with the potential to either mitigate or exaggerate existing gender inequalities in the labor market (O'Connor, Orloff, and Shaver 1999: 31–2). As explained above, women's labor market participation differs from that of men in Latin America because women participate at lower rates, are more likely to be unemployed or segmented in low-productivity or informal sectors, and face wage discrimination (see Table 5-1). To evaluate gender-based stratification after pension reform, the differences between women and men's old-age welfare should be compared following the reform. Gender-stratifying pension policy will compound the inequalities between men and women produced by the labor market. In this case, monthly rather than lifetime benefits are the appropriate comparison because the value of monthly benefits determines differences in consumption, standard of living, and economic independence.

Based on various estimates of the ratio of women's to men's monthly benefits, structural pension reforms implementing DC pillars are likely to increase gender stratification in old age. For example, according to simulations by James, Edwards, and Wong (n.d., Table 7.1), ratios of women's to men's monthly own-pension benefits including minimum guaranteed pensions or flat-rate benefits are 0.21–0.54 in Argentina, Mexico, and Chile. The most equitable own-monthly pension benefits are in most cases concentrated among the most highly educated women. According to simulations by Rofman and Grushka (2003: 44), the difference between the replacement rates of monthly benefits of single women and men grew substantially after Argentina's reform. At the same time, married men who are required to buy a joint annuity benefited very little from the reform, are not much better off than single women, and are much worse off than single men. Alternative simulations for Chile provide slightly more optimistic estimates of the ratio of single women's monthly benefits to those of men, especially if women are assumed to prolong their work (Arenas de Mesa and Gana Cornejo 2003). Depending on the assumptions of the simulations for replacement rates under the reformed DC systems, gender ratios for monthly benefits can vary greatly. In almost all simulations, however, women's own-monthly pension benefits are less than those of men with comparable education and contribution histories.[11] Further, these gender differences are often greater than those that occurred under the unreformed systems.

The disparity between men's and women's monthly benefits is not only due to labor market inequalities but is also compounded by particular aspects of reformed pension policies. In general, the largest source of benefit difference derives from the calculation of benefits over the entire contribution life of the worker (one of the key features of DC reforms), which does little to ameliorate labor market inequalities. This explains why differences in labor market participation, rather than actuarial tables and retirement ages, is the largest source of the difference in women's and men's monthly pension benefits (Wong and Parker 2001). An alternative to the gender stratification common with reforms using DC individual accounts is the contrasting case of Brazil, which tightened the link between contributions and benefits in its 1998 reform (see Matijascic and Kay 2008). Despite this tighter link, Brazil's new system is likely to yield less gender stratification than DC-reformed systems. Brazil gives women credit for five years of contributions toward time of service pension requirements, and their pension benefits are 94–103 percent of those of men at comparable levels of income, age, and work history, according to simulations (Rocha da Silva and Schwarzer 2003: 127). Though the tightening of the contributions and benefits link tends to increase gender inequality regardless of whether DC individual accounts or notional defined accounts are used, the simulated results for Brazil suggest that reforms implementing notional defined accounts may be less gender-stratifying than DC reforms.[12] Though Brazil's pension system still faces many challenges (Matijascic and Kay 2008), its reform provides an example of an alternative model that may prove less gender-stratifying than DC reforms.[13]

Apart from the shift to defined contributions, many pension reforms in Latin America allow either earlier retirement ages for women or the use of gender-specific actuarial tables in the pricing of annuities, both of which contribute to the lower monthly pension benefits of women. In all the countries that enacted structural pension reforms—except for Peru, the Dominican Republic, Mexico, and Uruguay—women have the right to retire up to five years earlier than men. When women do retire earlier, they lose up to five years of additional contributions, which would entitle them to higher pension benefits (assuming they have enough contributions to qualify for at least the minimum-guaranteed or flat-rate benefits). The effect of earlier retirement for women will result in greater gender stratification if women regularly retire early. For example, the ratios of monthly benefits of women with average work histories to average men in Chile are estimated to increase by 15–20 percentage points if women retire at age 65 years rather than 60 years, and ratios of women's to men's monthly benefits improve 9–16 percentage points if women in Argentina delay retirement to age 65 years (James, Edwards, and Wong 2008).

In addition to different retirement ages, the use of gender-specific actuarial tables to price annuities is allowed throughout Latin America. The real effect of gender-specific actuarial tables on the equality of monthly benefits is probably smaller than the inequalities created by the labor market or retirement ages. According to simulations for Mexico, using unisex actuarial tables to price annuities reduced gender stratification less than improving women's wages (Wong and Parker 2001). For Argentine men and women with equal funds accumulated in their individual accounts, the annuity of a single woman would be about 86 percent that of a single man, and the annuity of a married woman would be almost 106 percent that of a married man due to the use of gender-specific life tables (Rofman and Grushka 2003: 47; see also James, Edwards, and Wong n.d., Table 4.9). In Chile the use of unisex life tables would tend to increase women's pension replacement rates by about 6 percent and reduce those of men by about 7 percent (Arenas de Mesa and Gana Cornejo 2003: 202; James, Edwards, and Wong n.d., Table 3.9). However, the recent government reform proposal suggests that the issue of unisex life tables requires further study due to its complexity (Consejo 2006). Despite the modest improvement in gender stratification to be expected from the use of unisex life tables for the pricing of annuities, a case for using unisex tables can be made based on the argument that to do otherwise would be gender discrimination (Simon 1988; see above section on actuarial fairness).

State policy can also try to address the sources of labor market inequality or use pension policy to redress gender stratification. Though addressing labor market inequalities would have the greatest effect, change in the labor market is likely to be complicated and slow moving. Instead, governments can implement relatively minor changes to reduce some of the gender stratification currently exacerbated by the reformed pension systems. First, policymakers can increase the likelihood that women will be entitled to their own minimum or flat-rate pension instead of survivor's or social assistance pensions using the recommendations discussed at the end of the section on social citizenship rights. Second, they can require that the pricing of annuities be made using unisex actuarial tables, which is the standard in many advanced industrialized democracies. Finally, they can increase women's retirement age to that of men to encourage women to stay in the workforce longer to earn a minimum pension. However, increasing the retirement age to encourage longer workforce participation has the added risk of further eroding women's social citizenship rights, a tradeoff likely to be addressed differently according to prevalent patterns of women's workforce participation and social security contribution in each country. In some cases, it may be possible to increase women's retirement wage if at the same time minimum contributions are adjusted downward for both men and women (or women are given caring credits) to ensure that more women are likely to meet the minimum requirement.

Welfare Role of the State, Market, and Family

Social insurance policies also distribute the responsibility for risk pooling and welfare among the market, state, and family. Market failures and risks can be covered by private insurance, state insurance, or family networks. Any state policy that shifts the provision of services from families to the state is parallel to the shift of responsibility from the market to the state (Orloff 1993: 313–14). In the case of structural pension reform, the creation of privately administered individual accounts with DC benefits represents a shift from the state to the market. Not only are individual retirement accounts and annuities privately administered, but pension benefits are also determined according to the market performance of the pension funds. In countries where the state guarantees and funds a minimum pension for workers whose retirement savings will not finance the minimum pension, the state is still providing some protection from market failure. Likewise, noncontributory social assistance pensions, where they have been implemented, add an additional layer of state protection.

Overall, most pension reforms have shifted some risk back to workers by requiring them to rely on the market to generate their pension savings while only providing a minimal safety net to protect from market failures. Because a shift back toward the market will leave some individuals exposed to the risk of market failure, it is likely that families will also have to increase their support for elderly family members when both the market and state fail to guarantee sufficient income support. That is, when more workers retire with only the minimum pension or a social assistance pension, they are likely to depend more heavily on their families to make up the gap between their pension support and welfare needs. Because women tend to be the primary caregivers in most families, shifts of the welfare burden onto families is likely to increase their work disproportionately. One consequence of this shift that has been little explored is the effect it is likely to have on the ability of families, especially among the poor, both to provide support for elderly family members and to invest sufficiently in the welfare and human capital of younger family members. It would be a perverse outcome indeed if families encouraged children to leave school to earn enough to support elderly relatives.

In addition, many reformed systems also shift responsibility for welfare from the state to families by increasing the role of family relationships for the provision of women's welfare through survivor's pensions. Many reforms were at least implicitly based on the nuclear family model (Marco 2002). The reliance on survivor's pensions to provide for women's welfare has already been discussed with regard to women's social citizenship and gender stratification. With regard to the distribution of welfare responsibility among the market, state, and family, it is worth questioning again the appropriateness of increasing the role of families at a time when family structures and responsibilities are in flux (see Table 5-2). Given the rise in informal family arrangements, divorce, serial monogamy, and female-headed households, attempts to formalize intrafamily contracts through pension legislation seem misplaced. Pension legislation should not be used to create incentives (or intrafamily dependency) on one particular family model.

Responsibility for old-age welfare in these reformed systems has implicitly or explicitly shifted from the state to the family. The implicit shift occurs because of the emphasis on the market and the likelihood that response to market failures will now be the responsibility of families. The explicit shift is the emphasis on survivor's pensions for women's welfare. As with the other dimensions of gendered welfare outcomes, pension policy cannot address all inequalities created by the market, but it can seek to protect individuals in old age from market and family failures. To this end, pension reforms should ensure that minimum pensions and social assistance pension amounts are sufficient to mitigate the dependence of the elderly on their families. This is important because dependence on families with scarce resources may create shortages for investment in younger family members. Further, pension reforms should not rely on nor try to formalize a traditional breadwinner family model that is becoming less common throughout the region. Instead, benefits, particularly for women, should be individualized and protected regardless of marriage. Finally, in the absence of policies that ensure women's rights to claim individual pension benefits, legal provisions should be adopted and enforced to protect women's claims to pension credits or contributions in the event of divorce or separation. This is an important concept that was included in *Averting the Old Age Crisis* but was seldom implemented in practice. Such legal protections are now being considered as part of the reform debate in Chile (Consejo 2006).

How Do Reformed Pensions Fare Using Distributional Criteria?

Whereas the gender impact of pension reform appears positive when evaluated using insurance and efficiency criteria, a distributional welfare perspective suggests that such assessments are overly optimistic. Through the lens of the distributive outcomes, many pension reforms seem to have a negative gender impact because they decrease social citizenship rights for women, increase gender stratification in benefits, and increase the burden on families. Rather than mitigate gender inequalities in the labor market, many pension reforms seem to reproduce or even amplify inequalities. Though some aspects of reforms were intended to provide incentives for women's labor market participation and independence (such as provisions for providing benefits to husbands), other aspects of reforms are likely to reinforce women's gender roles as wives and mothers and increase women's dependence on such roles for their welfare (such as survivor's pensions). This implies a dual system whereby the basis for men's pensions is social insurance and women's pensions is charity, social assistance, or family dependence (Marco 2002).

The use of these gendered dimensions of welfare to evaluate pension reform in Latin America is also a useful means to estimate how pension reforms are changing the models of welfare in the region. The three dimensions of welfare regimes used above to evaluate the gender impacts of pension reform (social citizenship, stratification, and role of the state) can also be used to distinguish among three ideal types of welfare regimes common in advanced industrialized democracies: liberal, conservative, and social democratic (Esping-Anderson 1990, 1999).[14] In Latin America, welfare policy has approximated in its design the conservative ideal type, though with significantly lower levels of coverage in many countries (Filgueira and Filgueira 2002; Barrientos 2005). Characteristics common to conservative regimes are high levels of stratification and inequalities of social citizenship rights, especially according to occupation; an emphasis on providing a minimum safety net consistent with Christian democracy; and reinforcement of traditional family and gender roles. In many cases, Latin-American pension reforms strengthened characteristics of conservative welfare regimes, such as women's dependence (Giménez 2005: 52). Other aspects of the reforms, in particular the role of the market in providing pension benefits, are consistent with liberal welfare regimes, moving the overall regime type toward a conservative–liberal hybrid.

Conclusion

This chapter has explained that the source of disagreements in the literature regarding the gendered effects of pension reform in Latin America stems from the differences in the criteria used and related normative assumptions regarding the function of public pension policy. It argues against the use of insurance-based criteria, such as actuarial fairness and the use of intrafamily transfers, to evaluate the gendered outcomes of pension reform on the basis that these criteria reinforce gender inequality and perpetuate discriminatory practices against women. It also argues that when viewed as redistributive welfare policy, reforms to public pension systems, such as those adopted throughout Latin America in the 1990s, often disenfranchise women from their social citizenship, aggravate gender inequalities, and reinforce traditional family roles for women.

Though addressing labor market and intrafamily inequalities through labor market or family policy would be difficult and uncertain, some straightforward reforms could mitigate the negative effects of both the market and current policies. For instance, the contribution requirements for the minimum guaranteed or flat benefit pensions in privatized systems could be adjusted to be closer to the actual workforce participation patterns of average women at all levels of education. In most cases, the adjusted contribution requirements would still be much higher than in the unreformed systems. Of course, such a reform would have important financial consequences, especially when the majority of pensioners are expected to receive state-subsidized minimum pensions in privatized systems. With proper studies, however, it should be possible to adjust the requirements to be within reach of most working women to provide them with incentives to work a few years longer but without being so far out of their reach as to be a disincentive to participate in the newly reformed public pension system altogether. Reforms could also better compensate women for their caring responsibilities. Contribution or credit splitting within couples would at least give women whose primary responsibilities are in the home their own independent claim to pension benefits without increasing dependence. Further, contributions to their individual accounts or at least credits toward minimum contribution requirements could be given to women for their caring responsibilities. Finally, eliminating the use of gender-specific life tables and equalizing retirement ages between men and women could also improve women's pensions in the reformed systems.

Since most pension reforms in Latin America were motivated by macroeconomic rather than distributional concerns (Madrid 2003), it is not surprising that the gendered effects of privatization were not explicitly considered. The recent interest in gendered effects is likely to move such considerations onto the agenda as some countries begin to consider re-reform. If the recent report of the Presidential Advisory Board on Social Security (Consejo 2006), commissioned by Chilean President Michelle Bachelet, is indicative of a new trend in the region, not only are future pension reforms of privatized pension systems likely, but also gender will be a new concern during those reform discussions.

Notes

[1] Other assessments regarding the lack of gender considerations during the reform process can be found in Marco (2002), Arenas de Mesa and Gana Cornejo (2003), Bertranou (2003), Bonadona (2004), Marco (2004*b*), and Dion (2006).

[2] Some early published research on gender consequences of the Chilean reform includes Arenas de Mesa and Montecinos (1999) and the gender effects of privatization in general (Sinha 2000). Since then, the World Bank (Edwards 2001; Parker and Wong 2001; James, Edwards, and Wong 2003, 2008), the ILO (Bertranou 2001; Bertranou and Arenas de Mesa 2003), the UN ECLAC (Marco 2004*a*), and the International Social Security Association (Gilbert 2006) have all published studies of the gender effects of pension privatization.

[3] See also Rune (2003) for a discussion of the normative assumptions of the World Bank's pension reform model in *Averting the Old Age Crisis*.

[4] This argument assumes, however, that for actuarial fairness to be determined, men will have to complete information about not only their contributions and benefits, but also those of women.

[5] In the USA, for example, the longevity of women overlaps with that of men more than 80% of the time; less than 20% of women are likely to live longer than men (Christiansen 1983).

[6] These gendered dimensions are consistent with many prior studies of the effects of pension reform on women's welfare in Latin America. This analysis simply places pensions more explicitly within theoretical debates on gender and welfare.

[7] In the language of Esping-Anderson's model of welfare regimes, this dimension is *de-comodification* (1990, 1999: 43).

[8] Often, pension reform advocates point out that the reforms are better for women because even if they do not earn the minimum or flat guaranteed pension, they can at least withdraw their accumulated contributions. However, this point is irrelevant if we recall that under the previous system nearly all women who worked would contribute enough to meet the minimum contribution requirements for a minimum pension (ECLAC 2006*a*).

[9] According to data on the contribution densities of men and women enrolled in the social security system, women have marginally higher contribution rates or a higher percentage of weeks or months during which regular contributions are made. However, this is because a higher proportion of women work only in the informal sector and never formally enroll in the system. In contrast, men are more likely to move in and out of the formal sector and thus are likelier to be enrolled in the social security system even when they work in the informal sector later. These data should not be construed to imply that women contribute at rates similar to men.

[10] It would be preferable to compare the proportions of the female and male EAP that are affiliated to the social security system, but the summary of Chile's Social Protection Survey (Bravo et al. 2006) does not provide this information.

[11] Arenas de Mesa and Gana Cornejo (2003: 191) summarize the results of several different simulations of replacement rates in the Chilean system. The comparison illustrates the sensitivity of simulated results to model assumptions regarding labor market participation and economic growth and investment return rates.

[12] Simulations by Rocha da Silva and Schwarzer (2003) also suggest that the ratio of women's benefits to those of men have improved at all levels of income, age, and work history.

[13] In this sense, the Brazilian case may serve to test counterfactual hypotheses regarding gender and pension privatization.

[14] Some have argued for the inclusion of additional regime types (e.g. see Huber and Stephens 2001), but those alternatives are not discussed here.

References

Arenas de Mesa and Pamela Gana Cornejo (2003). 'Protección Social, Pensiones y Género en Chile', in Fabio M. Bertranou and Alberto Arenas de Mesa (eds.), *Protección Social, Pensiones, y Género en Argentina, Brasil, y Chile.* Santiago: Oficina Internacional del Trabajo, pp. 137–225.

—— and Verónica Montecinos (Fall 1999). 'The Privatization of Social Security and Women's Welfare: Gender Effects of the Chilean Reform', *Latin American Research Review*, 34: 7–37.

—— Alberto, David Bravo, Jere R. Behrman, Olivia S. Mitchell, and Petra E. Todd (2008). 'The Chilean Pension Reform Turns 25: Lessons from the Social Protection Survey', this volume.

Asociación Internacional de Organismos de Supervisión de Fondos de Pensiones (AIOS) (2003). *La capitalización individual en los sistemas provisionales de*

América latina (December), http://www.safjp.gov.ar/NR/rdonlyres/B6936AF1-2969-49C5-9044-81D0506A75CF/30/Libro_aios.pdf, accessed October 16, 2006.

Barrientos, Armando (2005). 'Latin America: Towards a Liberal-Informal Welfare Regime', in Ian Gough and Geof Wood (eds.), *Insecurity and Welfare Regimes in Asia, Africa, and Latin America: Social Policy in Development Contexts.* Cambridge: Cambridge University Press, pp. 121–68.

Bertranou, Fabio M. (2001). 'Pension Reform and Gender Gaps in Latin America: What are the Policy Options?', *World Development,* 29(5): 911–23.

—— (2003). 'Protección Social, Pensiones, y Género', in Fabio M. Bertranou and Alberto Arenas de Mesa (eds.), *Protección Social, Pensiones, y Género en Argentina, Brasil, y Chile.* Santiago: Oficina Internacional del Trabajo, pp. 13–30.

—— (2006). 'Pensions and Gender in Latin America: Where Do We Stand in the Southern Cone?', in Neil Gilbert (ed.), *Gender and Social Security Reform: What's Fair for Women?* New Brunswick, NJ: Transaction, pp. 81–108.

—— and Alberto Arenas de Mesa (eds.) (2003). *Protección Social, Pensiones, y Género en Argentina, Brasil, y Chile.* Santiago: Oficina Internacional del Trabajo.

Bonadona, Alberto (2004). 'Género y sistemas de pensiones en Bolivia', in Flavia Marco (ed.), *Los sistemas de pensiones en América Latina: Un análisis de género.* Santiago, Chile: UN ECLAC, pp. 153–78.

Bravo, David, Jere Behrman, Olivia Mitchell, and Petra Todd (2006). *Encuesta de protección social 2004: Presentación general y principales resultados.* Santiago, Chile: Subsecretaría de Previsión Social.

Christiansen, Hanne D. (December 1983). 'Equality and Equilibrium: Weaknesses of the Overlap Argument for Unisex Pension Plans', *The Journal of Risk and Insurance,* (50)4: 670–80.

Consejo Asesor Presidencial para la Reforma Provisional (2006). *Informe Final: El derecho a una vida digna en la vejez, hacia un contrato social con la previsión en Chile. Santiago, Chile,* http://www.consejoreformaprevisional.cl/view/informe.asp, accessed October 19, 2006.

Dion, Michelle (2006). 'Women's Welfare and Social Security Privatization in Mexico', *Social Politics,* 13(3): 400–26.

Economic Commission on Latin America and the Caribbean (ECLAC) (2005). *Social Panorama 2004.* Santiago, Chile: ECLAC.

—— (2006*a*). *Shaping the Future of Social Protection: Access, Financing and Solidarity.* Santiago, Chile: ECLAC.

—— (2006*b*). *Social Panorama 2005.* Santiago, Chile: ECLAC.

—— (2006*c*). *Statistical Yearbook 2005.* Santiago, Chile: ECLAC.

Edwards, Alejandra (February 2001). 'Social Security Reform and Women's Pensions', World Bank Gender and Development Working Paper, series no. 17.

Esping-Andersen, Gosta (1990). *Three Worlds of Welfare Capitalism.* Oxford: Oxford University Press.

—— (1999). *Social Foundations of Postindustrial Economies.* Oxford: Oxford University Press.

Filgueira, Carlos H. and Fernando Filgueira (2002). 'Models of Welfare and Models of Capitalism: The Limits of Transferability', in Evelyne Huber (ed.), *Models of Capitalism: Lessons for Latin America.* University Park: Pennsylvania State University Press, pp. 127–58.

Fultz, Elaine and Silke Steinhibler (2003). 'The Gender Dimensions of Social Security Reform in the Czech Republic, Hungary, and Poland', in Elaine Fultz, Markus Ruck, and Silke Steinhilber (eds.), *The Gender Dimensions of Social Security Reform in Central and Eastern Europe: Case Studies of the Czech Republic, Hungary and Poland.* Budapest: ILO Subregional Office for Central and Eastern Europe, pp. 13–41.

Gilbert, Neil (ed.) (2006). *Gender and Social Security Reform: What's Fair for Women?* New Brunswick, NJ: Transaction.

Giménez, Daniel M. (2004). 'Género, Previsión y Ciudanía Social', in Flavia Marco (ed.), *Los sistemas de pensiones en América Latina: Un análisis de género.* Santiago, Chile: UN ECLAC, pp. 99–152.

—— (2005). 'Gender, pensions and social citizenship in Latin America', *Serie Mujer y Desarrollo 46.* Santiago, Chile: Women and Development Unit, ECLAC, January.

Ginn, Jay (2004). 'Actuarial Fairness or Social Justice? A Gender Perspective on Redistribution in Pension Systems', Working Paper 37/04, Center for Research on Pensions and Welfare Policies, University of Turin.

Holzmann, Robert and Richard Hinz (2005). *Old-Age Income Support in the 21st Century An International Perspective on Pension Systems and Reform.* Washington, DC: World Bank.

Huber, Evelyne and John D. Stephens (2001). *Development and Crisis of the Welfare State.* Chicago, IL: Chicago University Press.

James, Estelle, Alejandra Cox Edwards, and Rebeca Wong (July 2003). 'The Gender Impact of Pension Reform', *Journal of Pension Economics and Finance.*

—— —— —— (2008). 'The Gender Impact of Social Security Reform in Latin America', this volume.

—— —— —— (n.d.) *The Gender Impact of Pension Reform: And Which Policies Shape This Impact,* unpublished book manuscript, http://www.estellejames.com/downloads/gender-book.pdf, accessed October 17, 2006.

Leitner, Sigrid (2001). 'Sex and Gender Discrimination within EU Pension Systems', *Journal of European Social Policy,* 11(2): 99–115.

Madrid, Raul (2003). *Retiring the State: The Politics of Pension Privatization in Latin America and Beyond.* Stanford, CA: Stanford University Press.

Marco, Flavio (2002). 'Factores jurídicos, demográficos y laborales que determinan diferencias de género en el sistema de pensiones. Los casos de Argentina y Chile', Proyecto Impacto de género de las reformas de pensiones en América Latina. Santiago, Chile: Comisión Económica para América Latina y el Caribe (CEPAL), Unidad Mujer y Desarrollo.

—— (ed.) (2004*a*). *Los sistemas de pensiones en América Latina: Un análisis de género.* Santiago, Chile: ECLAC.

—— (2004*b*). 'Rasgos generales de los sistemas provisionales de capitalización individual y de sus contextos laborales y demográficos', in Flavia Marco (ed.), *Los sistemas de pensiones en América Latina: Un análisis de género.* Santiago, Chile: UN ECLAC, pp. 31–60.

Marshall, T. H. (1950). *Citizenship and Social Class and Other Essays.* Cambridge: Cambridge University Press.

Matijascic, Milko and Stephen J. Kay (2008). 'Pensions in Brazil: Reaching the Limits of Parametric Reform in Latin America', this volume.

Mesa-Lago, Carmelo (July 2006). 'Private and Public Pension Systems Compared: An Evaluation of the Latin American Experience', *Review of Political Economy*, 18(3): 317–34.

Myles, John (2003). 'What Justice Requires: Pension Reform in Ageing Societies', *Journal of European Social Policy*, 13(3): 264–9.

O'Connor, Julia S. (Summer 1996). 'From Women in the Welfare State to Gendering Welfare State Regimes', *Current Sociology*, 44: 1–124.

—— Ann Shola Orloff, and Sheila Shaver (1999). *States, Markets, Families: Gender, Liberalism and Social Policy in Australia, Canada, Great Britain and the United States.* Cambridge: Cambridge University Press.

Orloff, Ann Shola (June 1993). 'Gender and the Social Rights of Citizenship: The Comparative Analysis of Gender Relations and Welfare States', *American Sociological Review*, 58: 303–28.

Parker, Susan W. and Rebeca Wong (2001). 'Welfare of Male and Female Elderly in Mexico: A Comparison', in Elizabeth G. Katz and Maria C Correira (eds.), *The Economics of Gender in Mexico: Work, Family, State and Market.* Washington, DC: World Bank, pp. 249–90.

Rocha da Silva, Enid and Helmut Schwarzer (2003). 'Protección social, jubilaciones, pensiones y género en Brasil', in Fabio M. Bertranou and Alberto Arenas de Mesa (eds.), *Protección Social, Pensiones, y Género en Argentina, Brasil, y Chile.* Santiago, Chile: Oficina Internacional del Trabajo, pp. 65–136.

Rofman, Rafael and Carlos Grushka (2003). 'Protección social, jubilaciones, pensiones y género en Argentina', in Fabio M. Bertranou and Alberto Arenas de Mesa (eds.), *Protección Social, Pensiones, y Género en Argentina, Brasil, y Chile.* Santiago, Chile: Oficina Internacional del Trabajo, pp. 31–62.

Rune, Ervik (2003). 'Global Normative Standards for National Solutions for Pension Provision: The World Bank, ILO, Norway and South Africa in Comparative Perspective', Working Paper 8, Stein Rokkan Centre for Social Studies, Bergen University Research Foundation, April.

Schokkaert, Erik and Philippe Van Parijs (2003*a*). 'Social Justice and the Reform of Europe's Pension Systems', *Journal of European Social Policy*, 13(3): 245–63.

—— —— (2003*b*). 'Just Pensions: Reply to Myles, Oksanen and Fornero', *Journal of European Social Policy*, 13(3): 276–9.

Schwarz, Anita M. (2006). 'Pension System Reforms', Social Protection Discussion Paper No. 0608. Washington, DC: World Bank, September.

Sen, Amartya (1984). *Resources, Values, and Development.* Cambridge, MA: Harvard University Press.

Simon, Jonathan (1988). 'The Ideological Effects of Actuarial Practices', *Law & Society Review*, 22(4): 771–800.

Sinha, Tapen (2000). *Pension Reform in Latin America and Its Lessons for International Policy Makers.* Norwell, MA: Kluwer.

—— and Maria de Los Angeles Yañez (2008). 'A Decade of Government-Mandated Privately Run Pensions in Mexico: What Have We Learned?', this volume.

United Nations (UN) (2000). *Demographic Yearbook 2000.* New York: United Nations.
—— (2003). *Demographic Yearbook 2003.* New York: United Nations.
Wong, Rebeca and Susan W. Parker (April 2001). 'Social Security Reform in Mexico: A Gender Perspective', unpublished manuscript.
World Bank (WB) (1994). *Averting the Old Age Crisis: Policies to Protect the Old and Promote Growth.* New York: Oxford University Press.

Chapter 6

Reflections on Pension Reform in the Americas: From 'Averting the Old-Age Crisis' to 'Keeping the Promise of Old-Age Security' and Beyond

Estelle James, Truman Packard, and Robert Holzmann

On 'Averting the Old-Age Crisis'

Estelle James

If you are fortunate enough to write something that people actually read, you may find that the message you think you are sending and the message readers receive are quite different. What you have written becomes part of the public domain and you cannot control how it is interpreted and used after that. Twelve years after *Averting the Old Age Crisis* was released (WB 1994), and after much controversy about its recommendations, I would like to dispel some of the myths about what *Averting the Old Age Crisis* said, what it did not say, and what it all means.

The basic message of *Averting the Old Age Crisis* and the reasons behind the message still hold. In fact, many more people accept this message today than when the book was published in 1994; it seems almost self-evident and uncontroversial now. In essence, the book says that old-age security plans should have two mandatory parts. One component is responsible for handling workers' savings, resulting in income smoothing over their lifetimes. This part should be funded, with the funds privately managed, and would usually be a DC system. The second component has a redistributive and poverty-prevention objective, transferring lifetime income from high earners to lifetime low earners who cannot save enough in prime age to support themselves in old age. This part would be PAYGO or tax-financed and publicly managed, and would usually define the benefit in such a way as to set a floor on old-age income. This division of responsibility provides fiscal sustainability and national savings that result from shifting away from a complete reliance on PAYGO as populations age, as well as a labor market advantage by establishing a close link between contributions and benefits, for the consumption-smoothing objective. It also addresses the empirical evidence that governments are not very efficient at allocating a country's capital and that the private sector has no motivation to provide a safety net to keep people out of poverty.

Aside from stating these fundamental principles, *Averting the Old Age Crisis* does not provide a precise blueprint for how countries should set up their systems. Rather, it provides several options about how the public and private pillars (the funded and tax-financed pillars) *could* be organized. It was up to each country's policymakers to determine which variation to implement. Although many have accused the book of directing policymakers to copy Chile's plan, those who have read *Averting the Old Age Crisis* know that this is not the case.

Many countries have adopted multipillar systems over the years that have passed since the publication of *Averting the Old Age Crisis*. Their experiences have clarified some implementation issues. A sequel to *Averting the Old Age Crisis* would concentrate on these issues, particularly low coverage, high administrative costs and fees, payout issues, and pitfalls in financing the transition. I address these issues below.

Low Coverage and Low Density of Contributions

The private pillar, which manages workers' retirement savings, is based on contributions. Retirees eventually get a benefit based on their contributions. Much of the discussion in Latin America today concerns the low coverage rate or low density of contributions in the new privatized systems. While many people belong to the system, they do not contribute much over their lifetimes, which will result in low pensions. However, this situation is not surprising, occurring as it does in low- and middle-income countries. *Averting the Old Age Crisis* shows the close correlation between coverage rate and the state of a country's development. Although the old-age schemes are mandatory—many people, due to myopia, do not voluntarily postpone their consumption sufficiently—it is difficult to enforce in low- and middle-income countries because self-employment and small firms dominate, the informal sector is large, women are less likely to be educated and work in the market, and the government's capacity is limited. This is true whether the contributory system is old or new, DC or DB.

To some extent, the family system provides old-age support in these countries. However, if the family system is failing and the government cannot enforce contributions, greater coverage in the mandatory formal system can be achieved through the public pillar and must be financed out of general government revenues. That is, coverage must be part of a noncontributory plan. Of course, for many of the same reasons these countries experience difficulties enforcing their mandatory contribution systems, they also have limited capacity to collect taxes. Policymakers must therefore carefully analyze the desirability of greater coverage through general revenues. Another reason for financing old-age programs through earmarked contributions rather than general taxes is that people may be more willing to contribute incremental amounts that they will eventually get back as benefits. Thus, difficult trade-offs with other public goods and services are avoided. If government cannot collect these earmarked contributions, then general revenue finance is the only way to go and the difficult trade-offs are unavoidable.

Each country's government must address these policy questions. Should resources be shifted from other public services toward old-age pensions? Should the government attempt to raise taxes—and will it be able to do so? Whose taxes should be raised and whose services cut? If we are looking at pensions only, it would seem that more benefits and greater coverage are always preferable. However, if we are looking at the economic priorities of the country as a whole, as we must, then the right policy is much more country-specific and difficult to determine. If the elderly are especially poor and no better way to get them out of poverty is feasible, then the argument for a universal, tax-financed public benefit is compelling. However, in many countries poverty is not concentrated among the elderly. In many countries, young families with children may be poorer, and key public goods such as education and health services underfunded. In these cases, a universal, tax-financed old-age program may not be a top priority.

Averting the Old Age Crisis is agnostic on the question of whether the redistributive public benefit should be for contributors only and financed out of payroll taxes or universal and financed out of general revenues. It is also neutral on whether the benefit should take the form of an MPG, a means-tested benefit for all, or a flat benefit. The book is agnostic because the authors believed that each option had pros and cons and that the answer, therefore, would depend on a country's individual conditions and priorities. However, a sequel to *Averting the Old Age Crisis* would go into greater detail on the criteria for choice. I address some of these criteria below.

The MPG is the cheapest way to protect contributors and to set a floor on their retirement income. It is also very easy to administer because only the pension needs to be evaluated. Means-tested benefits are similar to MPGs; however, they consider all income and sometimes assets. Rather than covering only contributors, these means-tested benefits cover the entire elderly population, so they achieve greater coverage than does the MPG. In principle, they are better targeted toward the poor than are flat pensions (discussed later), and can therefore be much cheaper. In the real world, however, some of these advantages are lost by high transaction costs, inaccurate targeting, or bribery. One study calculated that 30 percent of all expenditures on means-tested programs for the elderly in India were lost due to bribery (Palacios and Sluchynsky 2006). Means tests are particularly difficult to apply in developing countries, where many old people live with their extended families. Whose income counts, and who gets the benefits? Which equivalence scales should be used? Perhaps most important, means tests reduce incentives to save, work, and contribute.

In contrast, a flat benefit that is paid to every person once he or she passes a residence and age test is easier to administer, less subject to corruption, and less distortionary than a means-tested benefit—a big advantage in low-income countries. The big disadvantage is that a uniform payment to every old person can cost a lot of money and government must consider whether that money should be spent in some other way. It could give that money to young families, or to children who attend schools, or to health clinics in rural areas, and so on. Even worse, the flat benefit may appear to be cheap when the country is poor and has a young population, which might lead a government to promise a generous pension. However, twenty years later, when the population has begun to age, the flat benefit has become much costlier. So if a flat pension is adopted, it is important to include with it an exit strategy. One way to keep costs low and under control as populations age is to set a high age of eligibility, such as 70 years, and index it to life expectancy, so the eligible age gradually rises as longevity increases. Another way is to claw benefits back from high earners through the income tax system, so the proportion of old people who retain the benefit falls as national per capita income rises.

Administrative Costs and Fees

High administrative costs and fees is another significant issue in Latin America. *Averting the Old Age Crisis* discusses this issue, but not in great detail, perhaps because competition was expected to do the job. However, as the mandatory funded pillars have evolved in Latin America and elsewhere, high costs and fees have been observed. Many of these costs arose in the early stages, with start-up expenses—putting technology in place, beginning a collection and recordkeeping system, covering the fixed cost per account, and paying marketing expenses to gain the new clientele. Because assets were small and start-up costs high, costs as percent of assets were also high initially, and most, though not all, were passed on to worker-investors in the form of high fees. As assets have grown, however, costs as a percent of assets have fallen dramatically. For example, in the Chilean system, which has been operating for more than twenty-five years, costs are now under 1 percent of assets (whether measured on a current-year basis or a lifetime equivalent fee basis)—considerably less than the mutual fund or 401(k) industry in the USA.

The question we must address is whether the current situation is good or bad. Compared with voluntary retail plans such as those in the USA, Chile's record is good. However, when we compare Chile's pension system with large, institutional pension funds, we find that its costs are high and should be lower. Moreover, fees are much higher than costs. In many Latin-American countries, the rate of return on equity of the AFPs (Administradoras de Fondos de Pensiones, or pension fund managers) is 30–60 percent, and even higher by some estimates. In a mandatory scheme this rate is unacceptable. If we believed that worker-investors have a high price-elasticity of demand, we could rely on them to exert downward pressures on price and upward pressures on efficiency. However, evidence in financial markets suggests that small investors are not price-elastic. Indeed, they may not even be aware of the price that they pay, responding instead to marketing, which raises costs and fees. What, then, should be done?

We do not yet have the full answer to this question, but it appears that a good starting point is the recognition that scale economies are greater for the account management function—which includes collections, record-keeping, and communications—than for the investment function. This situation calls for an unbundling of these two functions, because their optimum degree of concentration differs. Account management could be largely centralized (in one or a small number of firms), through a public agency, a private clearinghouse, or a competitive bidding process. Centralization allows scale economies to be realized, facilitates account transfers, and enables a low-cost method for allocating investments.

Once account management is centralized and separate, asset managers need not even know the identities or amounts associated with each client; they simply get an aggregate sum of money to invest, through the account manager, following the allocation choices of its affiliates. Such 'blind' allocations should reduce the ability of asset managers to market, thereby reducing their marketing costs. Two alternative methods could be used for selecting the allowable asset managers: competitive bidding, to provide a choice of a limited number of investment firms, or open entry, with added measures to assure low costs. Well-known examples of systems that use the competitive bidding approach are the Bolivian pension system, which has the lowest fees in Latin America, and the Thrift Saving Plan for federal civil servants in the USA, which operates at the lowest cost of any pension fund in the world: six basis points. Examples of systems that use open entry with added measures to keep fees low are Sweden's, which effectively imposes price controls, and Mexico's, which assigns new entrants to low-cost pension funds and restricts the ability of existing affiliates to move toward high-cost pension funds. Sweden's costs are low, but most countries could not be counted on to use price controls effectively in the long run. It is too early to determine how successful Mexico will be. For countries like Mexico that rely to some extent on market competition to keep prices down, the question of how to present fee information to elicit an elastic response from workers is an important one that needs to be explored. Behavioral economics has taught us that it matters how information is presented; we need greater experimentation.

Payouts

When the authors wrote *Averting the Old Age Crisis,* they did not pay much attention to the payout stage, because that stage was years away. Nor did countries starting their multipillar systems pay much attention to payouts, for the same reason. However, it is now time to put these arrangements in place, because they do require considerable advance planning, including constructing accurate mortality tables for annuities. Policymakers have to determine whether to require annuitization, in order to ensure lifelong income, or to offer other options. Given a choice, would retirees purchase annuities, which provide longevity insurance, and will insurance companies offer credible annuities with a high money's-worth ratio? In the event retirees do not, what would be the government's contingent liability? In addition, policymakers will have to establish the allowable retirement age and decide whether to permit early retirement. They also have to establish risk categories, including whether to require gender-specific or unisex mortality tables. Should price-indexed annuities be required to maintain real values over the retiree's lifetime? Should joint annuities be required to protect spouses? Above all, policymakers have to formulate the regulations that will produce the outcomes they seek.

The experience of Chile's pension system, which has been in place long enough to have many retirees, indicates that if retiree choice is very limited, many people will purchase annuities, and insurance companies then develop to meet the demand. (Two-thirds of Chile's retirees under the new system have purchased annuities.) Competition is effective in producing a high money's-worth ratio, perhaps because payouts for a given premium are easily compared, and having many indexed instruments in which insurance companies can invest enables them to offer price-indexed annuities at relatively low costs. Furthermore, joint annuities substantially increase wives' lifetime retirement income, almost to that of men. Insurance companies will use gender-specific tables unless they are prohibited. Even if they are prohibited, insurance companies will likely look for proxies for gender. In addition, workers will start taking out their money at the earliest feasible age, possibly running out of money if the age is too low. Above all, a well-constructed regulatory regime is essential.

Pitfalls in Financing the Transition

With respect to transition costs, we must ask if they are higher than was expected and how countries should cover them. When funded pillars were adopted, workers were often given a choice of switching. For a couple of reasons, policymakers estimated very conservatively how many workers would switch. First, it is better to guess low and be pleasantly surprised. Second, guessing low produces low transition costs, making it politically easier to sell the idea of the conversion. In almost every case, more workers than expected switched, so transition costs were higher.

Such an outcome is not an insurmountable problem. Indeed, this consequence should be good for these systems in the long run. The absence of a plan for covering the transition costs is more of a problem since it is very difficult to devise politically acceptable ways to finance the transition. Covering transition costs requires either cutting benefits and services or increasing taxes, at least for the short and medium term. It could mean relying on debt finance to cover costs. Chile was able to accumulate a budgetary surplus to cover transition costs, but it did this under Pinochet, when Chile was hardly a democracy. In contrast, relying on debt as the primary means to finance the transition is problematic for two reasons. First, the government must pay high debt service, and the increased debt negates the object of increasing national saving. Second, government dissaving offsets private saving, canceling out any positive saving effect. If I were at the Bank today overseeing a country implementing such a reform, I would put pressure on the government to devise a realistic way to finance the transition without creating a huge increase in its explicit debt.

Conclusion

Partially funded multipillar systems have the great advantage over PAYGO single-pillar systems because they are fiscally sustainable without the governments having to impose large tax increases as populations age. They also have the advantage over centrally controlled funded systems because they are less subject to politically motivated capital allocations, and so yield a more efficient use of retirement savings. However, multipillar systems pose such implementation problems as low coverage or low density of contributions, high administrative costs, failure to provide lifelong income protection, and debt-financed transitions. In general, life consists of choosing the problems you wish to confront; you choose some because they are less serious and more tractable than others.

Because many countries have undergone pension reform in the years since the publication of *Averting the Old Age Crisis*, we have a clearer grasp today of some of the implementation problems inherent in multipillar systems. In the preceding paragraphs, I have outlined some potential solutions to these problems. The empirical experience of these countries that have adopted new systems can teach us what works well, what does not work, and what issues remain for future analysis.

The Economic Rationale for the Multipillar Model: Distinctions That Matter and Those That Do Not

Truman Packard

In the preceding section, Estelle James refers to points that she would like to make if she were to cowrite a sequel to *Averting the Old Age Crisis* (WB 1994). I have often felt that *Keeping the Promise of Social Security in Latin America* (Gill, Packard, and Yermo 2004) is that sequel. In fact, the first working title that Indermit Gill, Juan Yermo, and I came up with for the book was *A Crisis Not Yet Averted.* However, we thought that title might make it even more difficult to get the draft through the internal review process of the World Bank, so we went with the less controversial *Keeping the Promise of Social Security in Latin America* instead.

In this section, I summarize some of the issues raised in *Keeping the Promise of Social Security in Latin America* and underline the most important points for pension policymakers. In particular, I address the issues of low coverage and the expected outcome of pension reforms. In many ways, what I address in this section appears very similar to what Estelle James writes in the previous section.

Is an objective of pension reform to increase coverage, as the authors of *Averting the Old Age Crisis* noted? We frequently came back to this question during the review process of *Keeping the Promise of Social Security in Latin America.* In trying to answer it, I can empathize very much with Estelle James and the main authors of *Averting the Old Age Crisis* because several misperceptions about *Keeping the Promise of Social Security in Latin America* have arisen, often from those who have not actually read the book. The authors of *Averting the Old Age Crisis* did *not* say that private individual retirement accounts will solve all problems. Likewise, the authors of *Keeping the Promise of Social Security in Latin America* did not say that individual accounts were a big waste of time, nor that countries should replace pension fund managers with universal pensions.

I question whether *Averting the Old Age Crisis* actually claimed that pension reforms would increase coverage. However, rightly or wrongly and somewhat opportunistically, the proponents of the pension reforms enacted in Latin-American countries sugarcoated the difficult measures that were pushed through with the promise of gains in coverage through an expected improvement in workers' incentives to participate in the new pension systems, and they backed these promises with *Averting the Old*

Age Crisis and other World Bank publications. Thus, while it might be comforting for the proponents of reform and even many of us at the World Bank to seek recourse from critics in what *Averting the Old Age Crisis* actually says on the matter, given the low coverage of pension systems in Latin America, clearly people in the region expected much more from pension reform. Whatever the book actually says, it is a matter of record that reform proponents fueled these expectations with frequent and sometimes embellished references to a perceived and exaggerated orthodoxy in pension policymaking, most visibly represented in *Averting the Old Age Crisis.*

In an attempt to clarify the most important points made in *Keeping the Promise of Social Security in Latin America,* I would like to point to a part of the book that, in my opinion, is its most distinguishing feature but which does not get much attention from the people who have commented on it: the conceptual microeconomic framework of insurance and savings in Chapter 6 (borrowed from Ehrlich and Becker 1972).

In terms of actual policy recommendations, much of what the book says is similar to what is said in *Averting the Old Age Crisis.* However, *how* the authors came to these conclusions is very different, and it is precisely this difference that is critically important for readers to understand. By applying a microeconomic framework of insurance and savings, we were able to focus rigorously on the primary policy objectives of old-age income security: ensuring efficient consumption smoothing and preventing poverty in old age. By using a classical insurance approach, we arrived at two very powerful conclusions. First, as populations age and old age becomes more widespread, mechanisms that pool this risk are strained and individual savings become a more efficient way to cover the loss of earnings-ability and to achieve consumption smoothing. Second, as economies develop and households get richer, and if poverty among the elderly is relatively less frequent than poverty among other groups because of this development, then risk pooling is the most appropriate instrument to cover poverty in old age. Put more simply, as countries get richer, publicly offered risk-pooling mechanisms to cover the relatively rare risk of poverty in old age grow in importance.

In this way, we arrived at a set of policy conclusions that look a lot like some of the conclusions made in *Averting the Old Age Crisis,* but the path we took to get there is very different and is critical to our arguments. Critics might ask, if we arrived at a similar place, does it really matter how we got there? Is it overly academic to insist that applying an economic rationale makes a difference? I would argue that *how* we arrived at our recommendations does matter, and that insisting on working through the economic rationale for policy recommendations makes a difference to real-world reform outcomes.

By anchoring our arguments in a microeconomic model and focusing on the primary objectives of pension policy, we were able to identify what the fundamental distinctions that frame the pension policy debate should really be. From a microeconomic perspective, the fundamental distinction is not PAYGO financing versus prefunding, nor is it public versus private management. The real fundamental distinction is between instruments that *define benefits* (a form of risk pooling) versus those that *define contributions* (essentially, individual savings). By arriving at this fundamental distinction through the application of an economic model, we could afford to be much more agnostic in our book about second-order issues and features of pension reforms that have provoked very heated debates or that have led to sometimes unrelenting policy positions.

The distinctions of PAYGO financing versus prefunding, public versus private management, and mandatory versus voluntary participation (a dimension of pension policy not really touched on in *Averting the Old Age Crisis*, but one which we explore extensively in *Keeping the Promise of Social Security in Latin America*) are essentially secondary. These are clearly important issues in pension policy. However, they are distinctions on which one can afford to be agnostic if one accepts the fundamental principles of defining benefits (risk pooling) to cover the risk of poverty in old age, and defining contributions (individual savings) to cover the loss of earnings-ability. Thus, in *Keeping the Promise of Social Security in Latin America* we are able to press for individualization and individual savings accounts to achieve better consumption smoothing without having to rely on arguments of government failure (although there are plenty of examples of this in Latin America's history), nor on an overly naive view of what private markets can achieve. We do not need these arguments in order to recommend measures that look, in many ways, very similar to those of *Averting the Old Age Crisis*. However, having a strong economic rationale to examine policies allowed us to be agnostic about and see the merits of pension reforms in the 1990s that did not take the traditional Latin-American path, including those that implemented individualization through notional defined contribution (NDC) accounts and took other similar measures, such as Brazil's 'social security factor' that incorporated some NDC features.

The danger of not having an underlying microeconomic rationale for the same policy prescriptions is that without such a rationale, reform proponents prescribe the multipillar approach without any guidance as to the relative weights that each pillar should have. Without guidance, policymakers can assign, and have assigned, the weights of the pillars arbitrarily and sometimes in the pursuit of secondary objectives, to the detriment of poverty prevention and consumption smoothing.

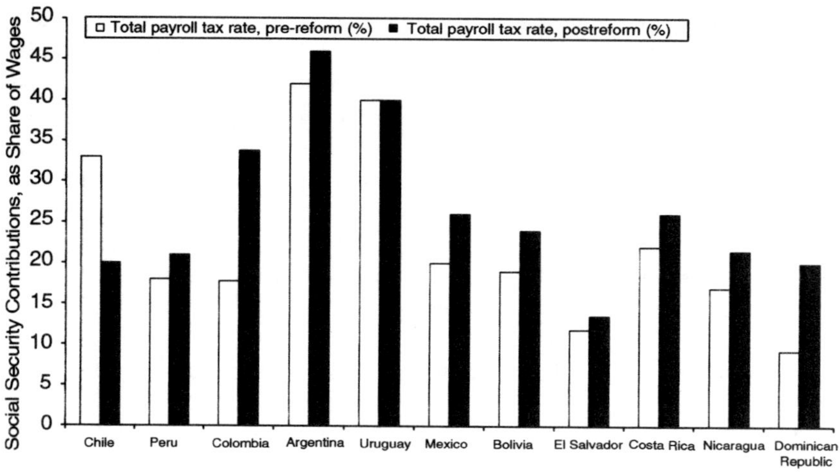

Figure 6-1. Payroll taxes for national pension systems (pre- and post-pension reforms).

To illustrate this danger, I would like to take a point from the perceived pension orthodoxy of the 1990s—namely, that *the introduction of individual retirement accounts leads to capital market development*. This assertion was just one of several widely accepted justifications for many of the reforms that took place in Latin America. However, in order for this development to take place, a very large injection of cash into the new individual accounts is necessary. Without guidance in weighting the private-savings pillar relative to the poverty-prevention public pillar, a policymaker pursuing the objective of capital market development might set the contribution rate—or the share of earnings that are subject to the mandatory contributions—very high, or at least higher than he or she otherwise would if the only objective were to achieve efficient consumption smoothing. Indeed, among Latin America's pension reforms, only in Chile and Uruguay did the mandatory contribution rate, collected as a payroll tax, actually fall (see Figure 6-1). Across Latin America today, the share of earnings subject to mandatory pension contributions is much greater than in OECD countries. In Chile, where it is lowest, the share of earnings subject to mandatory contributions is about twice that of most OECD countries. In Peru, there is no ceiling on the portion of earnings subject to the mandate (see Figure 6-2). Thus, paradoxically, even where pension systems were seemingly 'privatized', the impact of government on household savings and insurance decisions actually increased with pension reform. Among lower-income households, where credit is scarce, such large savings mandates can deter participation, exacerbating the coverage problem.

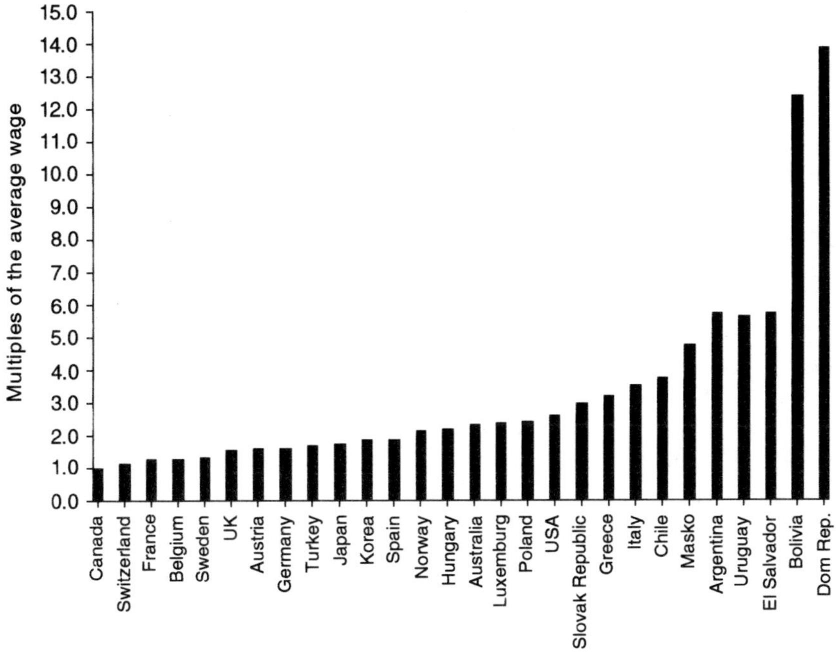

Figure 6-2. Earnings subject to mandatory contributions, as multiples of the average wage.

In contrast, by working through a microeconomic model, we are able to show that the multiple pillars of old-age income security are not distributed equally in economic space. Additionally, the weights that should be assigned to each pillar will vary from country to country and, indeed, in the same country over time, as certain economic fundamentals change. These fundamentals include (*a*) the generosity of the pre-reform defined benefits and thus household expectations of what a publicly mandated pension system should deliver, (*b*) the availability of financial instruments for households to take up on a voluntary basis to complement or act as an alternative to the mandatory system, and (*c*) governments' institutional capacity not only to target minimum pension benefits accurately to the poorest, but also to regulate the provision of mandated services by strong private actors in the financial sector. The conclusion that the relative weights of the pillars of old-age income security will vary from country to country, and even in the same country over time, has clear implications for the design of pension reform in a region as diverse as Latin America, with countries as different in level of development and regulatory capacity as Nicaragua and Chile. From our perspective, one size *cannot* fit all.

In *Keeping the Promise of Social Security in Latin America,* we argue that the fundamental distinction that policymakers should keep in mind is between risk-pooling to cover poverty in old age and individual savings to achieve efficient consumption smoothing. To use the widely accepted lexicon of pension policy, the differences that really matter are between 'pillar zero' and 'pillar three'. The economic distance between pillars zero and one and between pillars two and three is too small to justify a huge amount of debate and expense in political capital.

So, *is* low coverage a problem? The answer is clearly yes. But what is the real nature of this problem? There are two problematic groups for pension policymakers: the 'poor noncontributors' and the 'nonpoor noncontributors'. A basic targeted flat benefit financed with general revenues responds rather conclusively to the needs of the first group and, at the same time, establishes a good form of 'poverty insurance' (in the real insurance sense of covering only those who suffer the 'bad state' of old-age poverty) for the rest of the population.

For the nonpoor noncontributors, the real coverage problem is actually a policy dilemma. In fact, it is a dilemma (one of three) raised in the first few pages of *Averting the Old Age Crisis*: 'If mandatory schemes are needed because of shortsighted workers, how can these same workers be counted on to make wise investment decisions?' (WB 1994: 203). In other words, *Averting the Old Age Crisis* questions whether people will achieve consumption smoothing efficiently if left to their own devices. The authors of *Keeping the Promise of Social Security in Latin America* pose a similar question, with a twist: 'Once a fiscally sustainable poverty-prevention pension is securely in place, what is the appropriate level of state-mandated consumption smoothing?'

In *Keeping the Promise of Social Security in Latin America,* we chose to be skeptical about government mandates to pursue the consumption-smoothing objective of pension policy. We chose to believe more in people's rationality and somewhat less in their myopia. However, that skepticism for mandates does not mean that we advocate a repeal of the mandate to save privately, either immediately or totally over time. It does mean, however, that where mandates do exist, policymakers must scrutinize them for their demand-side and supply-side effects. In doing so, policymakers simultaneously grapple with the issues of low coverage and high system costs. How much saving is mandated is really an issue of coverage because a large savings mandate may dissuade people from participating in the system at all. On the supply side, it is an issue affecting costs. A large mandate managed by the private financial sector in countries where governments have little regulatory capacity can lead to the kind of competition problems and industry concentration that we have seen in Latin America's private pension systems, as well as to higher prices than households would pay in truly competitive markets.

Conclusion

In sum, *Keeping the Promise of Social Security in Latin America* expressed strong support for the forward steps Latin-American policymakers have taken to reform their pension systems. However, the magnitude of their achievements cannot be cause for complacency, as a growing number of workers and their households require better protection than social security systems currently offer.

Pension Systems and Reform: The World Bank's Evolving Conceptual and Operational Framework

Robert Holzmann

The past decade has brought increased recognition of the importance of pension systems to the economic stability of nations and the security of their aging populations. Populations are aging and, in developing countries, the traditional systems for support of the elderly are being eroded by migration, urbanization, and other factors that break down extended families. At the same time, pension systems, where they exist, are proving limited and increasingly costly.

A Framework for Pension Reform

The framework for analyzing pension systems and their reform should be based on some core principles and the capacity to achieve a flexible and context-specific set of social and economic outcomes. It should not narrowly prescribe the structure, implementing institutions, or operations of a system. On a practical level, the application of such a standard requires the articulation of goals and criteria against which a proposed reform can be evaluated.

Goals of a Pension System and Reform

The primary goals of a pension system should be to provide adequate, affordable, sustainable, and robust retirement income, while seeking to implement welfare-improving schemes in a manner appropriate to the individual country.

An *adequate* system is one that provides benefits to the full breadth of the population that are sufficient to prevent old-age poverty on a country-specific absolute level, in addition to providing a reliable means to smooth lifetime consumption for the vast majority of the population. An *affordable* system is within the financing capacity of individuals and the society, and does not unduly displace other social or economic imperatives or have untenable fiscal consequences. A *sustainable* system is financially sound and can be maintained over a foreseeable horizon under a broad set of reasonable assumptions. Finally, a *robust* system has the capacity to withstand major shocks, including those coming from economic, demographic, and political volatility.

The design of a pension system or its reform must explicitly recognize that pension benefits are claims against future economic output. To fulfill their primary goals, pension systems must contribute to future economic output. Reforms should, therefore, be designed and implemented in a manner that supports growth and development and diminishes possible distortions in capital and labor markets. This requires the inclusion of secondary developmental goals, which seek to create positive developmental outcomes by minimizing the potential negative impacts that pension systems may have on labor markets and macroeconomic stability while leveraging positive impacts through increased national saving and financial market development.

Review and Extension of the Original Concept of Pension Reform

The evolution of the general perspective and the World Bank's perspective on pension reform over the past decade reflects the extensive experience with reform in countries and an ongoing dialogue with academics and partner organizations, as well as intensive discussion and evaluation within the World Bank of pension reforms worldwide. As a result, the original concept of a specific three-pillar structure—(*a*) a mandated, unfunded, and publicly managed DB system; (*b*) a mandated, funded, and privately managed DC scheme; and (*c*) voluntary retirement savings—has been extended to include two additional pillars: (*d*) a basic ('zero') pillar to deal more explicitly with the poverty objective, and (*e*) a nonfinancial ('fourth') pillar to include the broader context of social policy, such as family support, access to health care, and housing.

The past decade of experience, while contributing considerable depth to the understanding of the nuances and challenges of pension reform, has reinforced the need in nearly every circumstance to move away from a single-pillar design. Experience has demonstrated that the multipillar design is better able to deal with the multiple objectives of pension systems—most importantly poverty reduction and income smoothing—and to address more effectively the kinds of economic, political, and demographic risks facing any pension system. The proposed multipillar design is much more flexible and better addresses the main target groups in the population. Advance funding is still considered important, but the limits of such funding in some circumstances are also seen much more sharply. The main motivation for the Bank to support pension reform has not changed. Instead it has been strengthened by the past decade of experience: most simple pension systems do not deliver on their social objectives, they create significant distortions in the operation of market economies, and they are not financially sustainable when faced with an aging population.

The extensive experience in implementing pension reforms in a range of settings since the early 1990s has motivated a review and refining of the framework in terms of the appropriate objectives and path of a reform effort. From the World Bank's perspective, the evolution of thinking and policy on pensions is characterized by five main additions.

A better understanding of reform needs and measures. A better understanding includes: first, assessing the need for reform beyond fiscal pressure and demographic challenges to address issues such as socioeconomic changes and the risks as well as opportunities from globalization; second, understanding the limits and other consequences of mandating participation in pension systems, particularly for low-income groups, for which risks other than old age may be more immediate and much stronger; and, finally, reassessing the continued importance, but also the limitations, of prefunding for dealing with population aging in recognition of the importance of associated behavioral changes, including enhanced labor supply and later retirement.

The extension of the reform model beyond the three-pillar structure. The reform model should encompass explicitly as many as five pillars and move beyond the conventional concentration on the first and second pillars. Experience with low-income countries has brought into focus the need for a basic, or zero (noncontributory), pillar distinguished from the first pillar in its primary focus on poverty alleviation to extend old-age security to all the elderly. Experience in low- to middle-income countries has heightened awareness of the importance of the design and implementation of the third, voluntary pillar, which can effectively supplement the basic elements of a pension system to provide reasonable replacement rates for higher-income groups, while constraining the fiscal costs of the basic components. Last, but not least, is recognition of the importance of a fourth pillar for retirement consumption that consists of a mixture of access to informal support (such as family support), other formal social programs (such as health care), and other individual financial and nonfinancial assets (such as home ownership) and the need to incorporate their existence or absence explicitly into the design of the pension system and old-age security.

An appreciation of the diversity of effective approaches. This diversity includes the number of pillars, the appropriate balance among the various pillars, and the way in which each pillar is formulated in response to particular circumstances or needs. Some pension systems function effectively with only a zero pillar (in the form of a universal social pension) and a third pillar of voluntary savings. In some countries, the introduction of a mandatory second pillar is required to gain popular acceptance for a reform of the first pillar, while the political economy of other countries makes a reformed (first-pillar) public system in conjunction with voluntary schemes the only realistic alternative.

A better understanding of the importance of initial conditions. A good understanding of initial conditions is important in establishing the potential for and limitations within which reforms are feasible. There is now greater awareness of the extent to which the inherited pension system as well as the economic, institutional, financial, and political environment of a country dictate the options available for reform. This is particularly important in establishing the pace and scope of a viable reform.

A strong interest in, and support of, country-led features in pension design and implementation that are often innovative. These features include (*a*) a nonfinancial or NDC system as an approach to reforming or implementing an unfunded first pillar (Holzmann and Palmer 2006); (*b*) use of a single clearing house and other approaches to reduce costs for funded and privately managed pillars; (*c*) the transformation of severance payments into combined unemployment and retirement-benefit savings accounts; and (*d*) public prefunding under an improved governance structure, as introduced in a number of high-income countries. While each of these features is promising, they depend on close attention to country circumstances and require close monitoring and evaluation, as transferability to other countries cannot be assumed.

Three Key Concepts in Considering Pension Reform

Although the essential policy formulation explicitly recognizes country-specific conditions and leads to implementation of the multipillar model in a variety of ways, from the World Bank's perspective three key concepts should be considered.

First, all pension systems should, in principle, have elements that provide basic income security and poverty alleviation across the full breadth of the income distribution. Fiscal conditions permitting, this suggests that each country should have provisions for a basic pillar, which ensures that people with low lifetime incomes or who participate only marginally in the formal economy are provided with basic protection in old age. This may take the form of a social assistance program, a small means-tested social pension, or a universal demogrant available at higher ages (e.g. age 70 years and older). Whether this is feasible will depend on the prevalence of other vulnerable groups, availability of budgetary resources, and design of the complementary elements of the pension system, as will the specific form, level, eligibility, and disbursement of benefits.

Second, if the conditions are right, prefunding for future pension commitments is advantageous for both economic and political reasons and may, in principle, be undertaken for any pillar. Economically, prefunding requires the commitment of resources in the current period to improve the future budget constraints of government and the resources to support retirees; it usually contributes to economic growth and development. Politically, prefunding may better guarantee the capacity of society to fulfill pension commitments because it ensures that pension liabilities are backed by assets protected by legal property rights, regardless of whether the funding is through government debt or other types of assets. The decision to prefund, however, requires careful consideration of benefits and costs, as net benefits are not automatically assured and political manipulation can make prefunding illusory. This decision also requires a close look at the implementation capacity of a country.

Third, in countries where prefunding promises to be beneficial, a mandated and fully funded second pillar provides a useful benchmark (but not a blueprint) against which the design of any reform should be evaluated. As a benchmark, it serves as a reference point for the policy discussion and a means to evaluate crucial questions about welfare improvement and the capacity to finance the transition from PAYGO to funded regimes. The efficiency and equity of alternative approaches to retirement savings, such as a significant reliance on voluntary individual or occupational systems, should be evaluated in relation to this benchmark.

Design and Implementation Issues

Through its pension reform activities in client countries and the work of other institutions and analysts, the World Bank has developed a clear understanding of good and best practices—of what works and what does not—in an increasing number of design and implementation areas. In a variety of other areas, however, open issues remain, and the search for good solutions continues. These open areas range from design issues of the various pillars and their relative weight to issues of financial sustainability, administration, implementation, and political economy, and to lessons from multipillar pension reforms in the world's regions.

Readiness of the Financial Market and Regulatory and Supervisory Issues

The introduction of mandated funded pension pillars has given rise to considerable debate inside and outside the World Bank, and it will take many more years before a clear consensus is reached. This section addresses three major issues that have arisen: (*a*) Can funded pensions be introduced in a rudimentary financial market environment, and if so, what are the minimum conditions? (*b*) What are the good or best regulatory practices that typical client countries should follow? (*c*) What are the good or best supervisory practices to be followed?

Readiness, Minimum Conditions, and Synergies

Not all countries are ready to introduce a funded pillar, and those that are not, should not do so. Nevertheless, the introduction of a funded pillar does not need perfect conditions, with all financial products available from the very beginning, since the pillar is introduced gradually and creates synergies for moving toward improved financial markets. Hence, minimum conditions need to be satisfied, and these can be highlighted when discussing three types of countries and their financial market readiness (Impavido, Musalem, and Vittas 2002).

There are three main types of financial markets: (*a*) those that are incomplete but the segments that operate are sound, are associated with high per capita income, have a credible macroeconomic policy framework, and have open capital accounts (but domestic and international financial instruments are not perfect substitutes); (*b*) those that are incomplete and the segments that operate are predominantly unsound, are associated with low per capita income, have a long history of macroeconomic policy imbalances, and have closed capital accounts; and (*c*) those that have an intermediate position between the two.

Countries with incomplete but sound financial systems that have relatively high per capita income, credible macroeconomic policies, and free capital movements offer the best case for funded pension and annuity systems. This is true for several reasons. First, (voluntary) funded pension and annuity products are luxury financial services. They are demanded at high rather than low per capita income (i.e. at high per capita income, the time preference or discount rate is lower, which increases the valuation of purchasing coverage for future contingencies, and family ties are weaker, which reduces self-insurance within the family). Second, credible macroeconomic policy provides an enabling environment for the development of long-term financial instruments (e.g. pension savings and annuities). Third, even under incomplete financial markets (e.g. embryonic capital markets), but where sound banks are operating, they provide a vehicle for channeling long-term savings into long-term loans to borrowers (government, enterprises, and individuals). Finally, open capital accounts do not constrain pension funds from investing in the local market.

The second type of country—those with chronic macroeconomic imbalances and other limitations—provide little room for the development of funded pensions and annuities. Longterm savings instruments cannot prosper in a macroeconomic environment with high and volatile inflation, and pensions and annuities are not affordable at low per capita income. Furthermore, the financial systems of these countries are essentially limited to the banking sector, which is usually weak. Although it would be possible to invest abroad, these countries, by having weak domestic financial institutions, should have closed capital accounts. Hence, before trying to develop these instruments, the authorities should focus on establishing a credible long-term macroeconomic framework and strengthening prudential regulation and supervision of banks. These two conditions are necessary for the successful development of funded pensions and annuities.

In the third and intermediary category of financial systems, there are a variety of cases. There are countries with a credible macroeconomic policy, a relatively sound banking system, and an open capital account. However, they may have very incomplete financial markets (underdeveloped securities markets, insurance, pensions, and mortgages) and relatively low per capita income. These countries have the preconditions for developing funded pensions and annuities, although their relatively low per capita income imposes a barrier to the scale of the market. Initially, the portfolios of these funds would be composed primarily of government bonds and banks' long-term certificates of deposit. In addition, they could have small fractions in shares, foreign securities, and possibly leasing companies. As financial markets develop, investment regulations should allow more diversified portfolios by allowing higher investments in shares, foreign securities, corporate bonds, and asset-backed securities and small investments in venture capital companies.

These countries will obtain the benefits from the development of funded pensions and annuities. Gains from financial sector development will initially be concentrated in development of the government bond market and long-term lending through banks. In a second stage, benefits will come from development of the corporate bond market and asset-backed securities. In a later stage, they will come from the stock market. The development of funded pensions and annuities will encourage financial market innovation through development of the fund management industry and improved financial regulations, including stronger minority shareholder rights, transparency, and corporate governance. They will also provide competition to the banking system and foster efficiency and innovation in financial markets.

In summary, instead of a full-fledged financial system with a full array of efficient institutions and financial instruments, the following minimum conditions are needed for the successful introduction of a funded pillar (Vittas 2000): (*a*) the presence of a solid core of sound banks and insurance companies; (*b*) a long-term commitment by government to pursue sound macroeconomic policies; and (*c*) a long-term commitment to financial sector reform through the establishment of a sound regulatory and supervisory framework for pensions and insurance products and providers.

References

Ehrlich, Isaac and Gary Becker (1972). 'Market Insurance, Self Insurance and Self Protection', *Journal of Political Economy*, 80: 623–48.

Gill, Indermit, Truman Packard, and Juan Yermo (2005). *Keeping the Promise of Social Security in Latin America.* Stanford, CA: Stanford University Press.

Holzmann, Robert and Edward Palmer (2006). *Pension Reform: Issues and Prospect for Non-Financial Defined Contribution (NDC) Schemes.* Washington, DC: World Bank.

Impavido, Gregorio, Alberto R. Musalem, and Dimitri Vittas (2002). 'Contractual Savings in Countries with a Small Financial System', in James Hanson, Patrick Honohan, and Giovanni Majnoni (eds.), *Globalization and Financial Systems in Small Developing Countries.* Washington, DC: World Bank.

Palacios, Robert and Oleksiy Sluchynsky (2006). 'The Role of Social Pensions', Pension Reform Primer Working Paper Series, Washington, DC: World Bank.

Vittas, Dimitri (2000). 'Pension Reform and Capital Market Development: "Feasibility" and "Impact" Preconditions', Policy Research Working Paper 2414, Development Research Group, Finance, Washington, DC: World Bank.

World Bank (WB) (1994). *Averting the Old-Age Crisis: Policies to Protect the Old and Promote Growth.* Washington, DC: World Bank.

Chapter 7

Bounded Rationality in Latin-American Pension Reform

Kurt Weyland

From the late 1980s onward, a stunning wave of social security privatization began to sweep across Latin America. Nine countries—Argentina, Bolivia, Colombia, Costa Rica, the Dominican Republic, El Salvador, Mexico, Peru, and Uruguay—have implemented private pension systems inspired by the Chilean precedent. Three more nations—Ecuador, Nicaragua, and Venezuela—have passed reform laws but have stalled in their implementation (excellent analyses in Madrid 2003; Müller 2003; Brooks n.d.).

Were these momentous changes, with enormous economic, social, and political consequences for the adopting countries, the product of rational choices, as the advocates of social security privatization assume? Did governments make reform decisions in careful and systematic ways? Did they process the relevant information thoroughly, evaluate dispassionately the costs and benefits of the Chilean model, and assess its applicability to the specific circumstances of their own nation? Thus, did decision-making on social security privatization approximate the standards of comprehensive rationality?

Based on field research in Bolivia, Brazil, Costa Rica, El Salvador, and Peru, this chapter argues that many decisions on emulating the Chilean model did not follow the procedures of full, 'economic' rationality, but were profoundly shaped by the inferential shortcuts of *bounded* rationality. Instead of proactively scanning the international environment for the relevant information, experts and policymakers mostly reacted to information about an outstanding foreign model—Chilean-style privatization—that happened to be particularly available to them. And rather than conducting systematic, balanced, cost–benefit analyses of this innovation, many of them were overly impressed by the initial success of Chile's private pension funds and used associative reasoning in depicting social security privatization as the main cause for the dramatic increase in domestic savings and productive investment and the resulting growth boom experienced by this Southern Cone country. Furthermore, instead of thoroughly adapting the Chilean import to their own country's requirements, decision-makers in a number of countries stayed strikingly close to the original; typically of boundedly rational decision-makers, they preferred imitation over innovation and redesign. Thus, these pension reformers did not apply the principles of comprehensive rationality, but displayed the three principal shortcuts documented by cognitive psychologists in innumerable experiments and field studies, namely the heuristics of *availability*, *representativeness*, and *anchoring*.[1]

The *availability* heuristic shapes memory recall and, as its basis, attention. This cognitive shortcut gives particularly vivid, drastic, and striking information a disproportionate impact that can distort judgments of frequency and significance. For instance, people tend to overestimate the risks of a plane crash compared to the dangers of car driving. Especially after a dramatic incident such as 9/11, many individuals were reluctant to fly, preferring long trips on busy highways and exposing themselves to the objectively greater risks of accidents (see in general Kahneman, Slovic, and Tversky 1982: chs. 1, 11–14, 33; Gilovich, Griffin, and Kahneman 2002: chs. 3–5). In this vein, Chile's bold model of radical pension privatization, transmitted by Chilean experts and consultants through personal contacts, captured the attention of decision-makers in Latin America and, in a logically problematic fashion, crowded out alternative sources of relevant information. As the Chilean blueprint monopolized the agenda, other innovations—such as the NDC scheme developed in Europe (Cichon 1999)—had great difficulty entering decision-makers' radar screen. Therefore, Latin America's pension reform debate during the 1990s focused singlemindedly on the pros and cons of the Chilean model.

The *representativeness* heuristic induces people to base judgments on logically irrelevant similarities. Accordingly, they overestimate the significance of patterns that appear in small samples and mistake short-term trends as proof of structural tendencies. They also resort to associative reasoning and attribute the characteristics of parts to wholes, and vice versa; thus, they see the components of successful systems as inherently good (Kahneman, Slovic, and Tversky 1982: chs. 1–6; Gilovich, Griffin, and Kahneman 2002: chs. 1–2). Applying this shortcut, many Latin-American experts and decision-makers inferred from the initially stellar rates of return of Chile's private pension funds that the new model was inherently superior to the old PAYGO system. They held privatization responsible for the rise in domestic savings and investment in Chile, which fueled sustained growth from 1985 onward.

Finally, the heuristic of *anchoring* induces people to base their judgments on any given clue, even a logically arbitrary hint. Although they adjust their inferences in light of additional information and experiences, they diverge from their starting point much less than full rationality would require. Like an anchor, it continues to tie down their judgments. For instance, people estimate that the product of 8 × 7 × 6 × 5 × 4 × 3 × 2 × 1 is much larger than 1 × 2 × 3 × 4 × 5 × 6 × 7 × 8 (see in general Gilovich, Griffin, and Kahneman 2002: chs. 6–8). Accordingly, pension reformers in many Latin-American countries tried to follow the Chilean model closely; the initial projects were often copied from Chile. While political considerations and pressures in later stages of the decision-making process led to more or less profound changes in several nations, these modifications mostly affected the administration or range of applicability of pension privatization, rather than reshaping the core of the new scheme, namely the institution of private pension funds in the obligatory social security system. Since boundedly rational decision-makers shy away from the computational effort of a thorough restructuring, the new social security systems of many Latin-American countries retain great similarities to the Chilean original. Ironically, this is true especially in countries such as Bolivia and El Salvador, whose limited formal labor market and underdeveloped capital market differ most starkly from Chile's. Although it was unclear whether these countries fulfilled the preconditions for instituting a private pension system (cf. WB IEG 2006: 19–29), and although full rationality would therefore have advised caution, these countries demonstrated particular zeal in importing the Chilean model.

In fact, intensive field research on the decision-making process reveals that rationality was especially bounded in those countries that followed the Chilean model most closely, namely Bolivia, El Salvador, and Peru. Given their relative scarcity of domestic technical expertise, those nations relied most heavily on advice from Chilean consultants, who eagerly promoted their own innovation. Moreover, the institutional and political weakness of the established pension agencies in these countries meant that their pension reform teams were dominated by economic generalists who lacked training and experience in the specific issue area; social security experts were marginalized in the reform process. Since the pivotal decision-makers had little prior knowledge of social security,[2] they faced particularly great uncertainty in assessing a bold, unprecedented innovation such as Chilean pension privatization, which had a comparatively short track record and unclear economic and social effects. To cope with this uncertainty, they relied especially heavily on cognitive shortcuts. Since they lacked established connections to alternative sources of knowledge (such as that available from the ILO), they based their judgments primarily on the information that happened to be available, provided by the missionary efforts of Chilean consultants and, from the early 1990s onward, the promotional activities of the World Bank (see especially WB 1994).

The institutional weakness of the state, particularly in Bolivia, El Salvador, and Peru, and especially in the social policy arena (e.g. Morón and Sanborn 2004; interview with Flores 2002), further reinforced the propensity to resort to cognitive shortcuts. Personnel turnover in the upper echelons is very high, not only at the ministerial level (cf. Corrales 2002), but also in lower-ranking policymaking and even technical positions. As a result, incoming decision-makers have a short time horizon; if they want to leave any mark and make a difference during their precarious tenure, they must launch projects quickly. Institutional weakness thus precludes a wide-ranging, proactive scanning of the international environment for relevant experiences and a systematic, careful assessment of their promise. Instead, the ticking clock compels decision-makers—and the technical personnel from whom they commission background studies and draft projects—to use expedient means to process information and design reform plans as fast as possible. Time constraints foreclose compliance with the demanding standards of comprehensive rationality and force hard-pressed decision-makers to apply cognitive shortcuts, especially the heuristics of availability, representativeness, and anchoring.

In short, those countries imitated the Chilean model most fully whose decision-making procedures diverged most starkly from the standards of comprehensive rationality. There is a clear correlation: the tighter the bounds of rationality, the more faithful the emulation of the Chilean original. Countries with lower technical capacity relied much more heavily on Chilean consultants, who sought to replicate their own innovation in other settings. By contrast, countries with a deeper pool of expertise—such as Costa Rica and Brazil—considered a wider range of evidence, undertook more careful cost–benefit analyses, and adapted structural pension reform more thoroughly to their own needs. As a result, they diverged much more clearly from the Chilean model than did Bolivia, El Salvador, and Peru.

As the correlation between decision-making processes and reform choices suggests, Chilean-style pension privatization spread in Latin America due to bounded rather than comprehensive rationality. Cognitive shortcuts that facilitate information processing but can cause significant distortions and biases strongly affected the diffusion of this policy innovation. However, the bounds of rationality were more or less tight, depending on the technical capacity and pool of expertise that different countries commanded. Thus, divergences from comprehensive rationality prevailed in all nations but were particularly severe in less developed countries than in more advanced nations with a longstanding tradition of welfare state development.

The present chapter substantiates these arguments through an analysis of the decision-making process in Bolivia, Brazil, Costa Rica, El Salvador, and Peru. The next section analyzes the need for social security reforms in Latin America during the 1990s. The subsequent three sections examine the operation of the three cognitive heuristics mentioned earlier. The final section draws conclusions from the investigation.

Demand and Supply Factors in the Initiation of Structural Pension Reform

Both comprehensive and bounded rationality arguments assume that decision-making proceeds in a goal-oriented fashion. Actors pursue fairly clear, fixed interests, in light of which they assess their environment and identify problems. To address these difficulties, they assess the promise of potential solutions. But the two approaches diverge on how decision-makers conduct these assessments. Advocates of rational choice, who apply comprehensive rationality assumptions to political analysis, assume that actors pursue their interests optimally: they analyze problems thoroughly, evaluate all possible solutions systematically, and adopt the option that has the greatest ratio of benefits over costs. Thus, where full rationality prevails, subjectivity plays no role; the objective needs raised by a problem trigger the best possible solution (Tsebelis 1990: ch. 2).

By contrast, bounded rationality arguments claim that information processing is limited by human reliance on cognitive shortcuts. Decision-makers consider only the information that—partly for arbitrary reasons—is available to them, and they evaluate it in unsystematic, distorted ways. Therefore, objective problems as such do not bring forth solutions; instead, cognitive and ideational factors influence decision processes and outputs as crucial intervening factors. They serve as filters that keep some options off decision-makers' radar screens and highlight some aspects of costs and benefits while de-emphasizing others. Due to these distortions and biases, the solutions adopted are often not the best possible means for attaining decision-makers' own interests (Jones 1999; Bendor 2003).

Deviations from full rationality are evident in the initiation of social security privatization in Latin America. Certainly, these reform efforts did respond to clear problems that had accumulated over the years and reached serious proportions in a number of countries and crisis levels in some. Above all, actuarial disequilibria and financial deficits had come to plague many social security systems, creating a need for determined remedies (Mesa-Lago 1989). But privatization was not necessarily the best possible response. In fact, the tremendous transition cost of this drastic change was bound to exacerbate fiscal problems for many years to come (cf. Matijascic and Kay 2006: 8–9). Relief lay far in the future, outside the attention span that political leaders subject to electoral constraints could afford to apply. Given the steep discount rates arising from democratic competition, a reform that was certain to cause significantly more financial costs than benefits in the short and medium term does not automatically look like the best possible option for fully rational decision-makers, especially politically calculating chief executives. By demonstrating the limited cognitive availability of reform options, bounded rationality arguments can better account for the zeal with which many Latin-American governments pursued pension privatization.

Latin-American pension systems certainly suffered from difficulties that called for significant change. As experts of various ideological stripes emphasized, the region's pension schemes were on the 'ascent to bankruptcy' (Mesa-Lago 1989). In particular, rapid population aging undermined the actuarial and financial sustainability of established PAYGO systems. This problem had reached crisis levels in the mature social security systems of the Southern Cone. Unable to pay retirement benefits, Argentina, for instance, had to declare pension emergencies. Other nations faced less dire straits, but the need for fiscal subsidies was on the increase, or financial equilibrium depended on illegitimate expedients, such as the dramatic compression of real pension values through accelerating inflation. Even countries such as El Salvador, with young populations and recently created pension systems, saw problems looming on the horizon (Mesa-Lago, Córdova, and López 1994).

Undeniably, there was a need for change. The pension reform efforts of the 1990s responded to real problems. They did not result from symbolic fashions or the spread of new international norms but were triggered by clear, objective, widely perceived difficulties. This demand factor played an important role in setting in motion the wave of social security privatization.

However, the problem did not determine the solution. The actuarial and financial disequilibria afflicting the existing systems did not require full-scale privatization. Objective needs as such did not bring forth the reforms of the 1990s. In addition to these demand factors, supply factors played an independent role. The particular availability of the Chilean model of pension privatization in Latin America and the corresponding neglect of other reform options, such as the NDC scheme being developed in Europe, were also decisive. Because boundedly rational decision-makers did not proactively search for and process all the relevant information, but became captivated by a policy blueprint that happened to be especially available to them, cognitive and ideational factors deeply shaped Latin-American pension reform. The objective situation clearly did not determine outcomes; instead, subjective factors, namely the mental schemes and strategies for processing uncertain information that cognitive psychologists analyze, significantly affected the decision-making process.

The Special Availability of the Chilean Privatization Model

The relevance of Chilean-style privatization for the problems facing their social security systems became obvious to decision-makers in many

Latin-American countries not through a wide-ranging, systematic, proactive search, but through personal encounters with Chilean consultants promoting their own innovation. While experts and policymakers throughout Latin America had undoubtedly heard about Chile's radical departure from regional pension traditions, the significance of this blueprint for the difficulties confronting their own nations only 'clicked' because of face-to-face contacts. It suddenly dawned on them that Chile's bold experiment might offer the solution for which they had groped for years. The unease caused by mounting difficulties quickly gave way to the promise that the Chilean model could offer a way out.

In Bolivia, for instance, the pension privatization project had an unplanned origin. As Helga Salinas, then budget director of the finance ministry and later leader of the first reform team, reports, she had for a while searched for ways to stem the increasing fiscal drain caused by the social security system. The solution suddenly appeared when she attended a conference, organized by Bolivia's business peak association, which featured as a keynote speaker José Piñera, the father of Chile's privatization. His charismatic promotion of the Chilean model made things 'click' for Salinas: she came to see full-scale privatization as a definitive solution for the worsening difficulties plaguing Bolivia (interview with Salinas 2002; similar interview with Bonadona 2002). Thus, a personal encounter, the particularly vivid presentation of a bold, novel blueprint, and the subsequent intense contact with Piñera and other Chilean consultants impressed a new idea on the policy agenda of Bolivian decision-makers. The solution that they had searched for in vain ended up falling into their lap.

Similarly, El Salvador's established social security schemes faced increasing administrative and financial difficulties by the early 1990s. A loan from the Inter-American Development Bank (IDB) funded a reform project designed to make moderate changes inside the established PAYGO system. However, a Chilean consultant who was hired to offer advice for this limited purpose went beyond his narrow mandate and made the privatization model cognitively available. As this bold innovation attracted the attention of Salvadoran decision-makers, the reform project unexpectedly took a completely new turn, shifting from the elaboration of parametric modifications to a profound paradigmatic change (interviews with Ramírez 2004; Tamayo 2004; Proceso de Implementación n.d.).

Peru's pension privatization project emerged in a similarly serendipitous way. In the run-up to the 1990 presidential election, Chilean consultants advised market-oriented candidate Mario Vargas Llosa and helped his aides draw up a comprehensive program of profound market reforms that included a revamping of the social security system. When the populist Alberto Fujimori defeated Vargas Llosa, the new president unexpectedly adopted an orthodox adjustment plan along the lines proposed by his opponent. In this context, a congressional deputy from Vargas Llosa's coalition, Mario Roggero, submitted the privatization project to Congress and lobbied the executive to embrace it. He even invited José Piñera, who in a lengthy conversation persuaded President Fujimori of the benefit of drastic reform (Roggero 1993: 88–92, 101–3; interview with De los Heros 2002). Economy Minister Carlos Boloña, a free-market enthusiast, then took charge of the project and pushed it through the decision-making process in 1991–2. Accordingly, personal contacts with Chilean experts played a crucial role in the advance of social security privatization in Peru.

These personal encounters, through which the bold, novel Chilean model made a striking, vivid impression on crucial decision-makers and so became particularly available, were facilitated by geographic proximity and historic and cultural affinities. By following these bonds of similarity, the availability heuristic bridged gulfs of socioeconomic difference; Bolivia, El Salvador, and Peru had far smaller formal labor markets and less developed capital markets than did Chile. From a fully rational perspective, it was far from clear that the Southern Cone country's innovation constituted a promising model for these relatively undeveloped nations to emulate. However, the special availability of Chilean-style privatization pushed these rational, functional considerations into the background and drew decision-makers' attention to considering this drastic change.

Geography and longstanding historical connections helped to make the Chilean model especially available in Bolivia and Peru. Interestingly, leading decision-makers in far-away El Salvador also perceived a special affinity with Chile, which prompted a wide range of learning efforts (CINDE 1994). As a former finance minister reported (interview with Daboub 2004), El Salvador has long seen itself as 'the Chile of Central America'—dynamic, world-open, and ready to face the challenges of global competition. In fact, the country has enacted the market reform program more faithfully than any of its neighbors. One reason was the threat from the revolutionary left that the governments of the 1980s faced and that triggered a market-oriented response—as in Chile during the 1970s and 1980s. These perceived affinities made Salvadoran government officials especially receptive to inspiration from Chile.

For these reasons, which are arbitrary in functional, rational terms, Chile's experience with privatization was especially available to decision-makers in Bolivia, El Salvador, and Peru. In fact, this outstanding experiment attracted so much attention that other important reform experiences remained in the background. As Chile's blueprint turned into the obligatory point of reference for friends and foes of pension privatization, Bolivian, Peruvian, and Salvadoran decision-makers showed surprisingly little interest in the reform projects pursued in Colombia, Argentina, and other Latin-American countries. While Chile may have commanded the best technical knowledge on social security privatization, Argentina and Colombia could offer interesting lessons on the politics of enacting this reform under democracy. On the political regime dimension, Bolivia, El Salvador, and even Peru were certainly more similar to those nations than to Chile, which had imposed pension privatization under a brutal dictatorship. In general, fully rational actors would find it beneficial to study a variety of reform variants and options.

However, boundedly rational decision-makers followed the availability heuristic, concentrated their attention on a singular outstanding model, and neglected other information sources. Accordingly, members of the Bolivian, Peruvian, and Salvadoran reform teams uniformly report that they had little if any systematic contact with the Argentine and Colombian experts designing reform projects at the same time (e.g. interviews with Gottret 2002; Grandi 2002; Guevara 2002; Pantoja 2002; Vargas 2002). This omission is especially striking in the case of Bolivia, which had in the late 1980s hired Walter Schulthess, the leader of the Argentine team in the early 1990s, for a consulting job on social security. Although Bolivia had this personal contact with Argentina, the Bolivian team took its inspiration almost exclusively from Chile once the agenda had shifted to radical change.

Moreover, the availability heuristic focused Latin-American decision-makers' attention on the most outstanding experiment conducted in their home region, making them overlook important experiments on other continents. As the intraregional reform wave gathered steam in the mid-1990s, European countries designed a hybrid between full-scale privatization and the PAYGO system. Like the Chilean model, this NDC scheme tied pension benefits firmly to accumulated contributions, which were assigned to individuals in a virtual account. However, it financed benefit payments not out of these accumulated funds but out of current workers' social security taxes, as does the PAYGO system and avoided the enormous fiscal transition cost caused by full-scale privatization. From a rational perspective, this novel option certainly deserved study, but it did not enter the radar screen of Bolivian and Salvadoran decision-makers.[3] Under the spell of the availability heuristic, they focused their attention on an intraregional innovation and neglected the NDC scheme, as did their counterparts in most of Latin America (Brooks and Weaver 2005). In this way, bounded rationality limited information processing.

In sum, boundedly rational decision-makers in Bolivia, El Salvador, and Peru did not conduct a wideranging, proactive search for relevant information, but were captivated by a singularly bold experiment that became uniquely available through personal contacts with Chilean experts. These face-to-face encounters made information about the Chilean model particularly vivid and impressed upon decision-makers that this blueprint could serve as a solution for their problems. Consequently, the significance and relevance of the Chilean precedent 'clicked'. Unplanned contacts then opened the door for an intense, longstanding import of information. In fact, the Bolivian and Salvadoran reform teams relied very heavily on Chilean consultants in elaborating privatization projects, and their Peruvian counterparts also learned a great deal from Chile (interviews with Bonadona 2002; Du Bois 2002; Galindo 2002; Gottret 2002; León 2002; Pantoja 2002; Romero 2002; Salinas 2002; Vargas 2002; Ramírez 2004; Solórzano 2004; Tamayo 2004).

Initially, this focus on Chile also prevailed in Brazil and Costa Rica. One of the first privatization proposals advanced in Brazil—elaborated by academic and government-linked experts for a free-market think tank financed by business—explicitly took its inspiration from Chile (IL 1991). Many government officials and pension specialists also saw the Chilean model as an obligatory point of reference (interview with Leite 1990). Even social-democratic Costa Rica sent a high-ranking delegation of governmental experts on a study mission to Chile in 1989. Representing economic agencies and the main social policy institution, this group assessed the strengths and weaknesses of the new private system (Comisión Técnica de Pensiones 1990). Availability accordingly guided a wide range of countries to pay special attention to the Chilean model.

Brazil and Costa Rica, however, commanded a much deeper pool of social security expertise than did Bolivia, El Salvador, and Peru. Their long-established welfare states had attracted well-qualified cadres that formed cohesive professional corps and enhanced the strength of the main institutions administering the pension system. These institutions in turn controlled voluminous fiscal resources and enjoyed considerable political power. Despite looming financial problems, the Brazilian and Costa Rican pension systems were not confronting urgent, acute fiscal crises. Due to this satisfactory performance, social security specialists retained a great deal of influence and were not displaced by economic generalists, as in Bolivia, El Salvador, and Peru, where the weakness of established institutions or severe financial problems led to a takeover by novices.

Longstanding specialists were less easily swayed by cognitive shortcuts such as the availability heuristic than were newcomers, the economic generalists. Thorough training and years of experience gave these experts a stock of knowledge and access to alternative sources of information. Consequently, they did not rely only on the ideas made available by Chile's promoters of pension privatization. Their background knowledge limited the impact of cognitive heuristics on their information processing and judgments.

Therefore, while the information made available by Chilean experts or study trips to Chile elicited considerable interest in Brazil and Costa Rica, and while it stimulated drastic reform proposals and privatization efforts, it did not launch those countries on the same trajectory of change as in Bolivia, El Salvador, and Peru. The Chilean model certainly was an obligatory point of reference for discussions in Brazil and Costa Rica, but did not dominate the reform debate as much as in the other nations, nor monopolize the attention of experts and decision-makers, despite its availability. Brazil and Costa Rica's greater pool of specialized expertise reduced the impact of the availability heuristic.

Rather, Brazilian and Costa Rican pension reformers had and sought access to alternative sources of information and inspiration. They considered a wider range of reform options than their Bolivian, Peruvian, and Salvadoran counterparts, who remained fixated on the Chilean model. For instance, the ILO representative in Costa Rica helped the country's first change team establish contact with the main architect of the Uruguayan reform, a mixed public/private system that conformed much more to the social-democratic values prevailing in Costa Rica than the radical, free-market Chilean blueprint (interviews with Rodríguez 2004; Bonilla 2005). Similarly, Brazilian pension experts—even those who were advocates of a drastic transformation—examined a range of foreign experiences. In the early 1990s, when the pension reform debate heated up, the Social Security Ministry in cooperation with the UN Economic Commission for Latin America organized an international seminar that studied a variety of foreign models (MPS 1993–4). Thus, links to international organizations other than the World Bank, which from the early 1990s onward forcefully promoted the Chilean model, helped Brazilian and Costa Rican decision-makers broaden their view beyond the highly available intraregional model that enthralled the reform teams of other countries.

However, even in Brazil and Costa Rica the availability heuristic confined decision-makers' attention mostly to reform experiences inside their home region. European innovations such as the NDC scheme remained off their radar screen. Only after privatization efforts hit an insurmountable barrier in Brazil in the late 1990s did the World Bank make this innovation available to pension specialists, who quickly 'fell' for it, adapted it to local needs, and obtained congressional approval for this modified version (Pinheiro 2004).

In conclusion, the availability heuristic turned Chile's radical pension privatization into an outstanding reference point for reformers across Latin America. This cognitive shortcut operated with special force in those countries with limited pools of domestic expertise and technical capabilities, as Bolivia, El Salvador, and Peru, where rationality was tightly bounded and where the focus on Chile was disproportionately strong. The more decision-making deviated from the standards of comprehensive rationality, the more Chilean-style reform served as the predominant source of inspiration.

Efforts to emulate the Chilean model were a product of bounded rather than full rationality.

Overestimating the Promise of the Chilean Privatization Model

Once Chile's radical reform had become cognitively available as a potential solution to the pension problems plaguing Latin-American countries, specialists sought to assess its performance and promise. They did not try to emulate this foreign innovation simply for reasons of symbolic or normative legitimacy, but assessed its promise as a means for resolving difficulties they had identified as threats to their interests. Rather than falling prey to international fads and fashions, they proceeded in a goal-oriented way, as any minimally rational actor would do. They based their emulation decisions on indications that the Chilean model was yielding positive results and therefore held the promise of producing benefits for their own countries.

However, in assessing the payoffs of Chile's radical privatization, many reformers, especially in Bolivia, El Salvador, and Peru, did not conduct comprehensive, systematic cost–benefit analyses. Rather, they applied the representativeness heuristic, basing their judgments in a logically problematic way on the overinterpretation of similarities and other forms of associative reasoning. Recall that with representativeness, people extrapolate short trends and take them as evidence of lasting tendencies, thus drawing excessively firm conclusions from small samples. Similarly, they attribute the qualities of whole systems to their constituent parts, and vice versa. In all these ways, they jump to conclusions by overestimating the significance of similarities ('representativeness'; see in general Kahneman, Slovic, and Tversky 1982: chs. 1–6; Gilovich, Griffin, and Kahneman 2002: chs. 1–2).

Accordingly, most members of the Bolivian, Peruvian, and Salvadoran change teams and many advocates of pension privatization in Brazil and Costa Rica were impressed by the high rates of return that Chile's private pension funds initially achieved. Bolivia's former national pension secretary invoked the annual average yield on investments (not including administrative fees) of 14 percent attained in Chile until the mid-1990s—only to add that in subsequent years this performance had deteriorated significantly (interview with Peña Rueda 2002; similarly, Exposición de Motivos 1993: 1, and interviews with De los Heros 2002; Du Bois 2002; Tamayo 2004). Many pension reformers thus resorted to the representativeness heuristic in interpreting Chile's high returns in the 1980s as evidence for the inherent superiority of the private pension scheme. Based on this initial stretch of experience—a small sample—they inferred the quality of the whole system. As a result, Chile's innovation quickly gained an aura of success and stimulated a rationally unjustified level of enthusiasm.

These sanguine assessments paid insufficient attention to two important issues. First, they underestimated the volatility of these initial rates of return and did not consider the possibility that chance factors may have boosted them. They did not take into account regression toward the mean. Because high success can result in part from nonsystemic factors that are subject to change, it tends to be followed by much more mediocre performance. In fact, after reaching 13.81 percent on average from 1981 to 1994, the rates of return of Chile's private pension funds amounted to only 6.37 percent from 1994 to 2003 (computed from SAFP 2004).

Second, privatization advocates extolling the rates of return did not consider the cost caused by the high fees that private pension fund administrators charged their affiliates. Considering this 'bite' by calculating returns over total contributions, not over the net deposits in affiliates' individual retirement accounts, yields significantly less impressive figures. 'In Chile [for instance] the return on capital between July 1981 and April 2000 was 11.1 percent, but once commissions are factored in, lower-income earners received a 7.34 percent return, and higher-income earners received a 7.69 percent real average return' (Kay and Kritzer 2001: 48). A comprehensive, fully rational assessment of the investment performance of private pension funds would have suggested more sober findings. The representativeness heuristic gave pension privatization a halo of success that does not withstand closer scrutiny.

A similar boundedly rational shortcut associated pension privatization with Chile's macroeconomic success from the mid-1980s onward. At the time that private pension fund administrators accumulated rapidly growing resources, Chile's savings rate rose significantly, productive investments increased, and economic growth accelerated to 6–7 percent per year for more than a decade. Based on this temporal coincidence, many observers jumped to conclusions, postulating a causal connection. Although the World Bank (1994: 92, 209, 307–10) expressed caution, Latin-American pension privatization supporters advertised this change as a crucial means for stimulating domestic savings, investment, and development (interviews with Mercado 1994: 10, 15–16; Ramírez 1994: 102–3; Comisión para la Reforma 1996: 22; Bonadona 1998: 69–70, 91; Bonadona 2002; De los Heros 2002; Du Bois 2002; Peñaranda 2002; Vargas 2002; Solórzano 2004). An associative inference from whole to part that is typical of the representativeness heuristic reinforced the aura of success attached to the Chilean model.

Interestingly, however, the savings argument has not withstood rigorous empirical examination; statistical investigations have yielded inconclusive results (Samwick 2000; Escobar and Nina 2004: ii, 17; interview with Martínez Orellana 2004). Even the World Bank, which had forcefully advocated pension privatization in the 1990s, soon backed away from this claim. Remarkably, its chief economist, Joseph Stiglitz, in 1999 disqualified many promises invoked by the Bank as 'myths' that could not withstand rational scrutiny in light of experience (Orszag and Stiglitz 1999). Prominently among these myths figured the claims that 'individual accounts raise national saving' and that 'rates of return are higher under individual accounts' (Orszag and Stiglitz 1999: 8). The initial enthusiasm was eventually unveiled as a product of problematic inferences, such as the representativeness heuristic (see recently WB IEG 2006: 35 and *passim*).

Despite its lack of a firm basis, however, the savings argument crucially boosted political support for drastic pension reform because it attributed broad macroeconomic benefits to this change. As a result, a social sector that had for decades been the domain of specialists suddenly acquired major significance for economic generalists. While since the late 1970s, finance ministry officials had begun to worry about the actuarial disequilibria and financial deficits plaguing many Latin-American social security systems, now a wide range of economic generalists took a strong interest in pension reform. The privatization of the retirement system seemed to hold the key to putting the region, which had suffered a 'lost decade' of austerity and stagnation during the 1980s, back on an accelerated growth path. In depicting structural pension reform as a crucial instrument for high-salience development goals, the domestic savings argument broadened the range of actors that became involved in the issue area. Economic generalists started to push very hard for privatization and tried to overcome passive or active resistance from established pension experts and bureaucrats, who sought to defend the existing PAYGO system.

Above all, this unproven inference made the emulation of the Chilean model appealing to chief executives, who often lacked strong ideological commitment to market reform. As presidents hesitated to incur the political costs and risks of drastic institutional change, the macroeconomic benefits predicted by the representativeness heuristic proved decisive for tipping the balance. In Peru, for instance, President Fujimori was skeptical about the introduction of market principles into the social sectors, but the promise that social security privatization would fuel economic development finally clinched his support (interviews with De los Heros 2002; Du Bois 2002; Peñaranda 2002). Therefore, a judgment derived via the representativeness heuristic that lacked a firm scientific basis was crucial for importing the Chilean model to Peru, as with a number of other Latin-American countries.

While this associative inference attracted support from economic generalists and political leaders, it did not automatically carry the day. Out of conviction and interest, established social security specialists and bureaucrats, together with societal interest groups such as trade unions, criticized the performance and promise of the Chilean model. Whereas privatization advocates extolled the presumed economic benefits of structural change, the critics pointed to the social deficits of this novel blueprint and the exorbitant fiscal transition costs that its adoption would entail. They stressed the limited population coverage of the private pension system, the social exclusion perpetuated by the lack of redistribution, and the gender inequality produced by a strictly contributive scheme. They also highlighted the fiscal problems caused by the channeling of pension contributions into private accounts—an issue that privatization advocates sought to downplay as the short-term cost required for long-term benefits.

Cognitive factors played an important role in the resolution of these debates. By associating privatization with great macroeconomic benefits, the representativeness heuristic motivated officials of powerful economic ministries to participate in pension policy, changing the very constellation of political actors in the issue area. Moreover, the postulated connection to increased savings, investment, and growth made structural pension reform especially appealing to the presidents of these countries. But the outcome of the reform debate also depended on political–institutional factors, especially the strength of the economic ministries in intrastate bargaining and the chief executive's clout in the legislative arena.

Where social security agencies suffered from financial deficits, administrative problems, and political weakness, they could not resist sustained pressure from the economic ministries, which are among the most powerful agencies of contemporary Latin-American states. For these reasons, privatization advocates defeated opponents inside the state in Bolivia, El Salvador, and Peru. In Brazil and Costa Rica, by contrast, existing welfare schemes had attained a reasonably good performance and were not suffering from severe financial difficulties, and the agencies administering them commanded considerable expertise, bureaucratic institutionalization, and political strength. As a result, they managed to hold their own against the economic ministries, which determinedly promoted pension privatization in both countries and actually launched several reform efforts in Brazil (interviews with Carvalho 1992; Moraes 2003; Aguilar 2004). When the Brazilian Social Security Ministry lost out in intrastate conflicts, it could count on opposition to radical change in Congress, opposition that some of its officials helped to stimulate and mobilize (interviews with Carvalho 1992; Gabriel 1992). Disagreements inside the state spilled over into the legislative arena.

The president's clout with Congress obviously affected the prospects of pension privatization throughout Latin America (Madrid 2003: 56–8). In contrast to Chile, where a brutal dictatorship imposed the reform, functioning democracies required parliamentary approval for this major institutional change—giving the many opponents among party politicians and societal interest groups access to decision-making. To counter the promises of fiscal and macroeconomic benefits that economic generalists derived from the representativeness heuristic, opponents invoked the social limitations of the private social security system and defended sectors that would lose from privatization.

In Brazil and Costa Rica, Congress has considerable autonomy and clout; presidents cannot push their projects through Parliament. The consensual decision-making style institutionalized in Central America's model democracy privileges negotiation and compromise and precludes dramatic transformations such as radical social security privatization (Jiménez 2000). The firm commitment of most party politicians, congressional deputies, and many state officials to social-democratic values also limited the depth of market-oriented reform (interviews with Aguilar and Durán 1996: 138, 140–1; Rodríguez 1996: 1, 6–9; Aguilar 2004; Carrillo 2004; Céspedes 2004; Durán 2004; Jiménez 2004; Rodríguez 2004). In Brazil, entrenched statist convictions prevented free-market ideas from gaining ideological hegemony (interview with Bornhausen 2003), and the prevalence of clientelism made many congressional deputies reluctant to pass market reforms, which threatened to diminish their access to patronage. Moreover, pronounced party fragmentation made it difficult for chief executives to win solid support for their projects, especially constitutional amendments, which were required for enacting pension privatization because the 1988 charter gave many details of the existing social security system constitutional protection. For these political–institutional reasons, the advocacy of market-oriented social security reform, motivated by the enthusiastic assessments of the Chilean model derived via the representativeness heuristic, found only limited support in Brazil and Costa Rica. As a result, Costa Rica adopted a very moderate mixed public/private system, whereas Brazil rejected privatization and reformed the existing PAYGO scheme (Pinheiro 2004).

In Bolivia and El Salvador, by contrast, the presidents managed to assemble a more stable legislative coalition that guaranteed them majority support. Their own parties held a larger share of congressional seats than in Brazil, and they found reliable allies. Also, the more adversarial nature of party politics in both countries allowed these majorities to push through their will against the opposition. In fact, the governments eventually rammed privatization bills through Congress; their supporters closed ranks and marginalized the opposition. In a more autocratic fashion, Peru's Fujimori took advantage of the closing of Congress after his self-coup of April 1992 to impose drastic social security reform by decree-law. Thus, the political predominance of these countries' presidents allowed the reform projects inspired by the representativeness heuristic to go forward. Due to favorable political–institutional conditions, cognitive shortcuts managed to shape decision outputs in Bolivia, El Salvador, and Peru.

Anchoring and the Imitation of the Chilean Model

Countries that decided to adopt Chilean-style pension privatization often copied much of the original blueprint and introduced only limited modifications to meet their own specific needs. Paradoxically, less developed nations with particularly small formal labor markets and underdeveloped capital markets remained especially faithful to the original. Although the Chilean model did not seem to fit their socioeconomic structures,[4] they followed this precedent closely. The heuristic of anchoring, which induces decision-makers to base their judgments on given clues, helps account for this paradox. To save computational effort, boundedly rational decision-makers typically preferred imitation over innovation; they did not rethink or consider redesigning the foreign model, as comprehensive rationality would require.

Given the limitations of domestic technical capacity, this tendency to imitate the Chilean model prevailed especially in Bolivia, El Salvador, and Peru. Leading reform team members in all three countries stressed that they had largely copied Chile: 'We took 90 percent [of the new system] directly from Chile' (interview with Du Bois 2002;[5] similar interviews with Bonadona 2002; Galindo 2002; Gottret 2002; León 2002; Pantoja 2002; Romero 2002; Salinas 2002; Vargas 2002; Ramírez 2004; Solórzano 2004; Tamayo 2004).

Imitation prevailed, especially in the early stages of the privatization project, conducted by technical experts. The heuristic of anchoring induced economic generalists to stay very close to the Chilean model and rely heavily on Chilean consultants. Indeed, José Piñera and his associates designed the outlines of the Bolivian and Salvadoran reform proposals, elaborated many specific rules and regulations (e.g. on the supervision of private pension funds), and conducted the initial simulations of fiscal transition costs (Price Waterhouse 1993: bibliography; Proceso de Implementación n.d.). Although Peru drew up its reform with more autonomy, it imitated the Chilean system in many aspects and brought in specialists from its southern neighbor to help at crucial steps. Consequently, the draft bills that technical reform teams presented to the political leadership were very similar to the Chilean blueprint.

Political calculations and requirements prompted some modifications, however. As numerous psychological experiments show, the heuristic of anchoring ties down people's judgments and limits departures from initial clues, but by no means does it preclude such departures. Rather, it leaves some room for adjustments (Epley and Gilovich 2002), and so political considerations led to adaptations of the Chilean model. Nonetheless, anchoring confined these modifications mostly to rules stipulating the privatization scheme's range of application while keeping its core intact: Bolivia, El Salvador, and Peru created privately managed individual retirement accounts in the obligatory pension system. They all emulated the central features of the Chilean blueprint.

To make the new system of social protection more equitable, counter criticism of the exclusionary nature of 'neoliberal' privatization, and boost his future electoral fortunes, Bolivian president Gonzalo Sánchez de Lozada (1993–7) insisted on complementing pension privatization with a novel scheme of basic, universalistic old-age support. His government created a 'solidarity bond' (Bono de Solidaridad, or BONOSOL) that guaranteed every citizen older than 65 years an annual payment of US$248 (Graham 1998: 151–67; Müller 2004). Similarly, Costa Rica and Argentina maintained the established public social security system to guarantee all affiliates a basic level of income support (actually quite generous in Costa Rica); the new private pension funds offered additional benefits or replaced only part of the old PAYGO system (Demarco 2004). In these cases, the principles of the Chilean model governed only a segment of affiliates' social security contributions. Nevertheless, while these modifications restricted the range of the private pension system, anchoring safeguarded its core.

Likewise, Peru's Fujimori instituted a parallel scheme, giving affiliates a choice between the old PAYGO system and the new private pension funds. In this way, he sought to preserve the established social security institute, which was making great strides in overcoming its administrative and financial problems and therefore had greater political clout than its counterparts in Bolivia and El Salvador (Ausejo 1995). Although this political decision drew ferocious criticism from market-oriented government officials and their Chilean advisors, it was actually more faithful to the maxim of freedom of choice and was framed in these terms by its advocates (Roggero 1993). In some sense, this deviation from the Chilean model was 'more Catholic than the Pope'.

By contrast, Bolivia temporarily suspended the principle of free competition in its new private pension system due to the exceptionally small size of its formal labor market. Since there were few affiliates, admitting numerous pension fund companies threatened to preclude economies of scale and further increase the administrative costs of the new scheme. In fact, Bolivians' low per capita incomes made the reform team concerned about the high fees that pension fund companies in fully competitive markets such as Chile charged. Even Chilean consultants stressed that a large share of these fees paid for expensive marketing campaigns with which companies tried to steal away affiliates from their competitors (Claro y Asociados 1994: 6–8; see also Vittas and Iglesias 1992: 5, 9, 22–4, 35). Due to governmental regulations, different companies had similar investment portfolios and rates of return; therefore, competition focused not on financial performance but on peripheral aspects, such as glossy promotional materials and the good looks of sales agents.

Effectively, competition was not fulfilling its economic rationale by guaranteeing consumers greater financial benefits, and its costs—high administrative fees—ate up a good part of affiliates' contributions. For the first five years of the new system, the Bolivian government therefore allowed only two private pension fund companies to enter and made each responsible for half the population (Guérard and Kelly 1997: 103–23; Mercado 1998: 152, 168). While this temporary suspension of free competition deviated from free-market principles, Chilean consultants 'authorized' it as a necessary step towards making privatization feasible in an exceptionally small market.

Importing the Chilean model with few modifications and confining these adjustments mostly to peripheral aspects relieved the cognitive and computational burden on decision-makers who had limited expertise in social security. Enacting a major institutional change such as pension privatization constitutes a monumental task. Copying a foreign blueprint and relying heavily on external advice greatly facilitates this task for boundedly rational policymakers. To save information-processing effort, the Bolivian, Peruvian, and Salvadoran reform teams followed the Chilean original very closely. Applying the heuristic of anchoring, they introduced only those alterations that crucial political considerations or pressing technical needs seemed to require. And these modifications affected mostly peripheral aspects such as the range of application of pension privatization—they left the core of the Chilean model untouched, namely the institution of privately managed individual retirement accounts in the obligatory social security system. Due to the heuristic of anchoring, the wave of diffusion that swept across Latin America therefore produced a good deal of convergence. As countries of diverse characteristics imitated the basic outlines of the Chilean model, similarity spread amid diversity.

Like the other cognitive shortcuts, anchoring had most force in countries that lacked strong domestic expertise in social security. Where the crises of established pension institutions allowed economic generalists to dominate decision-making, copying from the Chilean original was especially pronounced. By contrast, the higher the level of specialized domestic knowledge and the political clout of established pension agencies, the greater and more significant were the modifications that Latin-American countries introduced. Accordingly, Costa Rica, with its longstanding experience in social protection, its wealth of domestic expertise, and its powerful welfare state institutions, adopted a privatization scheme that differed greatly from Chile's. It ended up not relying much on advice from the originating country but rather seeking out other sources of inspiration more in line with its firm commitment to social-democratic values.

Initially, Costa Rican pension reformers followed the availability heuristic and commissioned a reform plan from a leading administrator of Chile's private pension system, namely the head of the pension superintendency, Julio Bustamante. However, this proposal was strikingly similar to the free-market Chilean scheme (Bustamante 1995: 20, 23) and diverged starkly from the norms of social solidarity and broad citizen coverage that Costa Rica's consensual political culture held in high esteem and that the existing pension agency was determined to defend. The Costa Rican team therefore rejected Bustamante's proposal out of hand and looked instead for a reform model that conformed more closely to national preferences (interviews with Durán 2004; Valverde 2004). Through the intermediation of the ILO, the team consulted Rodolfo Saldain, the main architect of Uruguay's moderate, mixed system, which maintained an important public pillar and combined it with a private scheme (interviews with Rodríguez 2004; Bonilla 2005). Indeed, Saldain made a crucial contribution in helping to design the outline of the Costa Rican reform plan: private pension funds became compensation mechanisms for the gradual reduction of income replacement rates in the public scheme that increasing actuarial and financial pressures seemed to require. Thus, as PAYGO benefit levels gradually fell, the accumulation of individual retirement funds in privately managed accounts would fill the gap. This slow substitution would remain limited; however, the public scheme would continue to guarantee a high level of social protection for all affiliates (Saldain 1996; interviews with Aguilar 2004; Carrillo 2004; Durán 2004; Rodríguez 2004; Bonilla 2005; Saldain 2006). In fact, a crucial part of the Costa Rican reform was a concerted effort to increase the rate of affiliation, which has stagnated in most privatized pension systems. Consequently, from early on, the moderate Costa Rican plan diverged clearly from the radical Chilean precedent.

Political pressures during the lengthy process of concertation and negotiation that the proposal underwent in Costa Rica's consensual political system produced further changes. Above all, state and societal providers—not only private companies—were allowed to administer individual retirement accounts. In fact, a state institution became the default option for affiliates who did not select a pension fund administrator. Consequently, more than 80 percent of affiliates are vested in public institutions (Martínez Franzoni and Mesa-Lago 2003: 27). Costa Rica's new social security system thus differs greatly from the Chilean original. Due to the country's impressive level of technical expertise, the heuristic of anchoring did not hold much sway.

Conclusion

The spread of pension privatization in Latin America resulted more from bounded than from comprehensive rationality. Cognitive shortcuts shaped decision-making and its outputs. The *availability* heuristic induced most social security specialists, economic generalists, and policymakers to pay disproportionate attention to the Chilean model of radical restructuring while neglecting other promising reform experiences inside the region and beyond. The *representativeness* heuristic suggested to economic generalists, in particular, the inherent superiority of the private scheme over the PAYGO system due to its high rates of return and the macroeconomic benefits associated with it. The heuristic of *anchoring* led decision-makers to prefer imitation over innovation and redesign, especially in less developed countries. Therefore, Bolivia, El Salvador, and Peru followed the Chilean original very closely and confined modifications to specific, mostly peripheral aspects.

Cognitive heuristics had special force and impact in countries with limited domestic expertise, as in Bolivia, El Salvador, and Peru. Since those nations had a small pool of social security specialists, they were strongly influenced by external inputs. Moreover, the institutional weakness of established pension agencies and the serious actuarial disequilibria or financial problems plaguing them allowed economic generalists to push aside social security specialists and dominate reform teams. Without specialized training and longstanding expertise in the issue area, these novices were especially prone to using cognitive shortcuts to make sense of abundant yet uncertain information about a highly complex subject matter. As a result, they were strongly drawn to the Chilean model and relied heavily on advice from Chilean consultants, though they lacked the background to crosscheck this advice and the network and connections to gain access to other sources of inspiration.

The absence in these countries of Weberian bureaucracies—that is, firmly institutionalized public agencies staffed by well trained, meritocratically recruited, and hierarchically supervised experts (see in general Rauch and Evans 2000)—reinforced the reliance on cognitive shortcuts. High personnel turnover led appointees to initiate reforms quickly to have any chance of success. A systematic proactive search for relevant international experiences and a thorough analysis of their costs and benefits were out of the question. Instead, time constraints forced political decision-makers and their technical advisors to use such shortcuts as availability and representativeness to identify and assess external sources of inspiration. This institutional factor helped bounded rationality prevail over comprehensive rationality.

By contrast, Brazil and especially Costa Rica had more solid bureaucratic institutions and a strong pool of domestic social security expertise. Appointees therefore did not face high time pressures and could draw on specialized knowledge to assess the inferences suggested by cognitive shortcuts. Certainly, the heuristics of availability and representativeness played a role, as is evident in Costa Rica's commissioning of its first pension reform plan from a Chilean consultant and the repeated advocacy of privatization projects by Brazil's economic ministries. But these heuristics did not carry the day because established pension specialists had access to alternative sources of knowledge that allowed them to criticize the inferences derived from cognitive heuristics. Moreover, their social security institutions commanded a good deal of political clout, which they used to defend the public PAYGO scheme. For these reasons, Brazil refused to institute Chilean-style privatization and Costa Rica adopted a profoundly modified version of the original model.

In summary, the more strongly experts and policymakers deviated from the norms of comprehensive rationality and relied on the cognitive shortcuts of bounded rationality, the more closely did they follow the Chilean model of radical pension privatization. To a considerable extent, the dramatic spread of this bold blueprint thus resulted from suboptimal information processing and rash conclusions, and was not fully rational.

Notes

[1] The present chapter draws heavily on material and arguments advanced in my book manuscript, Bounded Rationality and Policy Diffusion: Social Sector Reform in Latin America (2007), but develops these arguments in a new fashion.

[2] A number of pension reform team members, especially in Bolivia, El Salvador, and Peru, and even in Costa Rica, told me in interviews that they lacked professional training or administrative background in social security when they started to elaborate pension reforms.

[3] Peru privatized its pension system in 1992–3, before Sweden enacted an NDC scheme.

[4] For instance, the small size of the formal labor market keeps effective social security coverage in countries such as Bolivia and El Salvador particularly low. Since many workers move back and forth between the formal and informal sectors, they fail to accumulate substantial individual retirement accounts with which they could accrue pensions of reasonable value. Even in Chile, only '40 percent of workers affiliated with the private pension system are likely to accumulate sufficient funds for a benefit above the minimum pension' (Matijascic and Kay 2006: 8). In Bolivia and El Salvador, this percentage is much lower, leaving many workers excluded from

social insurance benefits in old age (cf. Borzutzky 2002: 228; Holzmann and Hinz 2005: 11, 81, 95–8).

[5] Du Bois was one of two interviewees who argued that their country would have privatized its pension system even without the Chilean precedent because this reform was part of the broader neoliberal program. It is interesting to note, however, that the connection of pension privatization to other market reforms was not very tight. Peru, for instance, enacted this change within two years of drastic orthodox adjustment, whereas in Bolivia more than eleven years passed (and in Costa Rica approximately eighteen years).

References

Aguilar, Róger (2004). Author interview with Director Actuarial y de Planificación Económica, Caja Costarricense de Seguro Social. San José, June 16.

—— and Fabio Durán (September 1996). 'La Reforma del Sistema Nacional de Pensiones de Costa Rica,' *Seguridad Social*, 202: 135–49.

Ausejo, Flavio (1995). 'La Reforma del Instituto Peruano de Seguridad Social', in Augusto Alvarez Rodrich and Gabriel Ortiz de Cevallos (eds.), *Implementación de Políticas Públicas en el Perú*. Lima: Editorial Apoyo, pp. 133–44.

Bendor, Jonathan (2003). 'Herbert A. Simon: Political Scientist', *Annual Review of Political Science*, 6: 433–71.

Bonadona, Alberto (1998). *Marco Regulador, Privatización y Reforma de Pensiones*. La Paz: Ediciones ABC.

—— (2002). Author interview with core member of pension reform team (1991–7). La Paz, August 9.

Bonilla, Alejandro (2005). Author's telephone interview with chief, Studies and Operations Branch, International Social Security Association. Geneva, January 25.

Bornhausen, Roberto Konder (2003). Author interview with former president of Federação Brasileira de Bancos and of Instituto Liberal. São Paulo, July 17.

Borzutzky, Silvia (2002). *Vital Connections: Politics, Social Security, and Inequality in Chile*. Notre Dame, IN: University of Notre Dame Press.

Brooks, Sarah (n.d.). 'Social Protection and the Market: The Making of Latin American Pension Reform', book manuscript, Department of Political Science, Ohio State University.

—— and Kent Weaver (2005). *Lashed to the Mast? The Politics of Notional Defined Contribution Pension Reforms*. Chestnut Hill, MA: Center for Retirement Research, Boston College.

Bustamante, Julio (1995). 'Agenda para el Desarrollo de una Propuesta de Reforma del Sistema Nacional de Pensiones', manuscript. San José.

Carrillo, Ubaldo (2004). Author interview with Director de Pensiones, Gerencia de Pensiones, Caja Costarricense de Seguro Social. San José, June 23.

Carvalho, Celecino de (1992). Author interview with Diretor de Previdência Social, Ministério da Previdência Social. Brasília, June 22.

Centro Internacional para el Desarrollo Económico (CINDE) (1994). *Soluciones Descentralizadas/Privadas a Problemas Públicos*. San Salvador: CINDE.

Céspedes, Víctor Hugo (2004). Author interview with Asesor de la Presidencia Ejecutiva, Caja Costarricense de Seguro Social. San José, June 24.

Cichon, Michael (October 1999). 'Notional Defined-Contribution Schemes', *International Social Security Review*, 52(4): 87–105.

Claro y Asociados (1994). *Comentarios al Anteproyecto de Ley del Sistema de Fondos de Pensiones de Capitalización Individual.* Santiago, Chile: Claro y Asociados.

Comisión para la Reforma al Sistema de Pensiones (1996). Propuesta de Reforma al Actual Sistema de Pensiones. San Salvador: Comisión para la Reforma.

Comisión Técnica de Pensiones (1990). *Sistema de Pensiones en Chile: Informe de la Visita Efectuada a Chile.* San José: Caja Costarricense de Seguro Social.

Corrales, Javier (July 2002). 'Cuánto Duran los Ministros de Educación en América Latina?', *Formas & Reformas de la Educación: Serie Políticas*, 4(12): 1–4.

Daboub, Juan José (2004). Author interview with former finance minister. San Salvador, July 9.

De los Heros, Alfonso (2002). Author interview with former labor minister (1991–92). Lima, July 8.

Demarco, Gustavo (2004). 'The Argentine Pension System Reform and International Lessons', in Kurt Weyland (ed.), *Learning from Foreign Models in Latin American Policy Reform.* Washington, DC: Woodrow Wilson Center Press, pp. 81–109.

Du Bois, Fritz (2002). Author interview with former adviser to Economy Ministers Carlos Boloña (1991–92) and Jorge Camet (1993–97). Lima, July 2.

Durán, Fabio (2004). Author interview with former Director Actuarial y de Planificación Económica, Caja Costarricense de Seguro Social. San José, June 25.

Epley, Nicholas and Thomas Gilovich (2002). 'Putting Adjustment Back in the Anchoring and Adjustment Heuristic', in Thomas Gilovich, Dale Griffin, and Daniel Kahneman (eds.), *Heuristics and Biases.* Cambridge: Cambridge University Press, pp. 139–49.

Escobar, Federico and Osvaldo Nina (2004). *Pension Reform in Bolivia*, Study no. GI-E6. La Paz: Grupo Integral.

Exposición de Motivos y Proyecto de Ley de Pensiones (1993). 'Sistema Previsional de Capitalización Individual', manuscript. La Paz.

Flores, Hugo (2002). Author interview with Task Manager for Health, Inter-American Development Bank. La Paz, August 12.

Gabriel, Almir (1992). Author interview with federal senator (PSDB-PA). Brasília, June 17.

Galindo, Mario (2002). Author interview with former official of Ministerio de Finanzas and Vice-Ministro de Microempresa. La Paz, August 2.

Gilovich, Thomas, Dale Griffin, and Daniel Kahneman (eds.) (2002). *Heuristics and Biases: The Psychology of Intuitive Judgment.* Cambridge: Cambridge University Press.

Gottret, Pablo (2002). Author interview with Superintendente de Pensiones, Valores y Seguros and ex-director of World Bank pension reform project. La Paz, July 30.

Graham, Carol (1998). *Private Markets for Public Goods: Raising the Stakes in Economic Reform.* Washington, DC: Brookings Institution.

Grandi, Evelyn (2002). Author interview with former Subsecretaria Nacional de Pensiones (1995–97). La Paz, August 2.

Guérard, Yves and Martha Kelly (1997). 'Bolivia's Pension Reform', in *The Deepening of Market Based Reform: Bolivia's Capitalization Program*. Washington, DC: Woodrow Wilson Center, Latin American Program, Working Paper No. 231, pp. 81–131.

Guevara, Carlos (2002). Author interview with former member of pension reform team (1993–96). La Paz, July 31.

Holzmann, Robert and Richard Hinz (2005). *Old Age Income Support in the 21st Century*. Washington, DC: World Bank.

Instituto Liberal (IL) (1991). Previdência Social no Brasil: Uma Proposta de Reforma. Rio de Janeiro: IL.

Jiménez, Ronulfo (2000). 'El Proceso de la Aprobación de la Ley de Protección al Trabajador', in Ronulfo Jiménez (ed.), *Los Retos Políticos de la Reforma Económica en Costa Rica*. San José: Academia de Centroamérica, pp. 247–72.

—— (2004). Author interview with Director, Consejo Económico, Presidencia de la República, and former leader of pension reform project (1998–2000). San José, June 17.

Jones, Bryan (1999). 'Bounded Rationality', *Annual Review of Political Science*, 2: 297–321.

Kahneman, Daniel, Paul Slovic, and Amos Tversky (eds.) (1982). *Judgment under Uncertainty: Heuristics and Biases*. Cambridge: Cambridge University Press.

Kay, Stephen and Barbara Kritzer (2001). 'Social Security in Latin America', *Economic Review* (Federal Reserve Bank of Atlanta), 86(1) (first quarter): 41–52.

Leite, Celso Barroso (1990). Author interview with former Secretário de Previdência Social, Ministério da Previdência e Assistência Social. Rio de Janeiro, March 19.

León, Alberto (2002). Author interview with pension reform team member and Gerente General, Asociación de Administradoras Privadas de Fondos de Pensiones. Lima, July 2.

Madrid, Raúl (2003). *Retiring the State: Pension Privatization in Latin America and Beyond*. Stanford, CA: Stanford University Press.

Martínez Franzoni, Juliana and Carmelo Mesa-Lago (2003). *Las Reformas Inconclusas: Pensiones y Salud en Costa Rica*. San José: Friedrich Ebert Stiftung.

Martínez Orellana, Orlando (2004). Author interview with former Central Bank official and pension reform consultant. San Salvador, July 6.

Matijascic, Milko and Stephen Kay (2006). 'Social Security at the Crossroads: Toward Effective Pension Reform in Latin America', *International Social Security Review*, 59: 1 (January): 3–26.

Mercado, Marcelo (1994). 'La Transformación del Sistema de Pensiones en Bolivia', Presentation at Corporación de Investigación, Estudio y Desarrollo de la Seguridad Social (CIEDESS). Santiago, Chile.

—— (1998). 'La Reforma del Sistema de Pensiones de la Seguridad Social', in Juan Carlos Chávez Corrales (ed.), *Las Reformas Estructurales en Bolivia*. La Paz: Fundación Milenio, pp. 125–80.

Mesa-Lago, Carmelo (1989). *Ascent to Bankruptcy: Financing Social Security in Latin America.* Pittsburgh: University of Pittsburgh Press.

—— Ricardo Córdova, and Carlos López (1994). *El Salvador: Diagnóstico y Propuesta de Reforma de la Seguridad Social.* San Salvador: Centro Internacional para el Desarrollo Económico.

Ministério da Previdência Social (MPS) (1993–4). *A Previdência Social e a Revisão Constitucional,* 7 vols. Brasília: MPS/Comissão Econômica para América Latina e Caribe (CEPAL).

Moraes, Marcelo Viana Estevão de (2003). Author interview with former Secretário de Previdência Social, Ministério da Previdência e Assistência Social. Brasília, August 4.

Morón, Eduardo and Cynthia Sanborn (2004). 'The Pitfalls of Policymaking in Peru: Actors, Institutions and Rules of the Game', Lima: Universidad del Pacífico, Centro de Investigación, http://www.iadb.org/res/index.cfm? fuseaction=LaResNetwork.ProjectSearch&st_id=82&final_draft=yes August.

Müller, Katharina (2003). *Privatising Old-Age Security: Latin America and Eastern Europe Compared.* Cheltenham, UK: Edward Elgar.

—— (2004). 'Non-Contributory Pensions in Latin America: Bolivia's BONOSOL', paper for XXV International Congress, Latin American Studies Association, Las Vegas, October 7–9.

Orszag, Peter and Joseph Stiglitz (1999). 'Rethinking Pension Reform: Ten Myths about Social Security Systems', paper for 'New Ideas about Old Age Security' conference, World Bank, Washington, DC, September 14–15.

Pantoja, Isabel (2002). Author interview with former member of pension reform team. La Paz: July 31.

Peña Rueda, Alfonso (2002). Author interview with former Secretario Nacional de Pensiones (1995–97). La Paz, July 24.

Peñaranda, César (2002). Author interview with former Jefe de Asesores, Ministerio de Economía y Finanzas. Lima, July 12.

Pinheiro, Vinícius (2004). 'The Politics of Social Security Reform in Brazil', in Kurt Weyland (ed.), *Learning from Foreign Models in Latin American Policy Reform.* Washington, DC: Woodrow Wilson Center Press, pp. 110–38.

Price Waterhouse (1993). *Proyecto de Reforma del Sistema Previsional Boliviano: Proyecciones Financieras del Sistema Vigente de Seguridad Social y del Sistema de Capitalización Individual.* Unpublished, January 27.

Proceso de Implementación de la Reforma al Sistema de Pensiones de El Salvador (n.d.). Unpublished.

Ramírez, Víctor (1994). 'El Sistema de Pensiones de El Salvador', in *Soluciones Descentralizadas/Privadas a Problemas Públicos.* San Salvador: Centro Internacional para el Desarrollo Económico (CINDE), pp. 92–103.

—— (2004). Author interview with Intendente del Sistema de Pensiones Público and leading reform team member. San Salvador, July 8.

Rauch, James and Peter Evans (January 2000). 'Bureaucratic Structure and Bureaucratic Performance in Less Developed Countries', *Journal of Public Economics,* 75(1): 49–71.

Rodríguez, Adolfo (1996). 'Ventajas, Peligros y Desafíos de la Reforma de Pensiones en Costa Rica', Unpublished. San José.

______ (2004). Author interview with Superintendente General de Valores and former Secretario Técnico, Programa Reforma Integral de Pensiones (1995–98). San José, June 21.

Roggero, Mario (1993). *Escoja Usted.* Lima: n.p.

Romero, Alfredo (2002). Author interview with former leader of pension reform team (1992). Lima, July 17.

Saldain, Rodolfo (1996). 'Sistema Nacional de Pensiones—Costa Rica: Principios y Objetivos', Unpublished. San José.

—— (2006). Author interview with former consultant to Costa Rica's pension reform team (1996–97). Montevideo: May 8.

Salinas, Helga (2002). Author interview with former budget director, Ministerio de Finanzas. La Paz, July 26.

Samwick, Andrew (May 2000). 'Is Pension Reform Conducive to Higher Saving?', *Review of Economics and Statistics*, 82(2): 264–72.

Solórzano, Ruth del Castillo de (2004). Author interview with leading pension reform team member and Directora Ejecutiva, Asociación Salvadoreña de Administradoras de Fondos de Pensiones. San Salvador, July 7.

Superintendencia de Administradoras de Fondos de Pensiones (SAFP) (2004). *Rentabilidad Real Anual del Fondo de Pensiones.* Santiago, Chile: SAFP, www.safp.cl/inf_estadistica/index.html, accessed May 12, 2004.

Tamayo, Sergio (2004). Author interview with pension reform team member and Asesor, Intendencia del Sistema de Pensiones Público. San Salvador, July 6.

Tsebelis, George (1990). *Nested Games: Rational Choice in Comparative Politics.* Berkeley, CA: University of California Press.

Valverde, Jorge (2004). Author interview with Jefe del Departamento de Pensiones, Gerencia de Pensiones, Caja Costarricense de Seguro Social. San José, June 30.

Vargas, Teresa (2002). Author interview with former core member of pension reform team and Directora de Prestaciones, Intendencia de Pensiones. La Paz, July 31.

Vittas, Dimitri and Augusto Iglesias (1992). *The Rationale and Performance of Personal Pension Plans in Chile.* Washington, DC: World Bank.

Weyland, Kurt (2007). *Bounded Rationality and Policy Diffusion: Social Sector Reform in Latin America.* Princeton, NJ: Princeton University Press.

World Bank (WB) (1994). *Averting the Old Age Crisis.* Washington, DC: Oxford University Press.

—— and Independent Evaluation Group (IEG) (2006). *Pension Reform and the Development of Pension Systems.* Washington, DC: World Bank.

Part II

Country Studies

Chapter 8

Perspectives from the President's Commission on Social Security Reform

John F. Cogan and Olivia S. Mitchell

Social Security faces a severe financial problem. In about fifteen years, the program will begin to experience permanent annual cash deficits, when annual benefit payments will exceed the amount collected in payroll tax revenues. By 2041, according to the Social Security Trustees 2002 Report, the Social Security trust fund is projected to be insolvent, meaning that the program will be legally unable to pay scheduled benefits. One way of expressing the financial shortfall is to compute the present value of the difference between system outlays and revenues over a 75-year horizon, which is currently equal to a permanent and immediate tax rate increase of 1.86 percent of payroll, or equivalent to $3.2 trillion in present value. If the policy of PAYGO financing is continued for the next 25 years, a 50 percent payroll tax increase will be required at that time to pay scheduled benefits.

Social Security's bleak financial outlook is not its only significant problem. For current workers, system benefits represent very low returns on payroll tax contributions. The inflation-adjusted return is 1–2 percent for workers earning an average wage, less than 3 percent for low-income retirees and negative for some higher earners and dual-worker couples. Moreover, Social Security fails to provide adequate protection against poverty. For example, 1 in every 4 divorced, separated, or never-married women older than 65 years lived in poverty in 1999. Those in the bottom half of the American earnings distribution, including a larger segment of the African-American and Hispanic population, lack a pool of private savings to support them in old age, and Social Security has no minimum poverty line benefit. Finally, there is ample evidence that the system induces workers to save less and retire early, so that the program's structure creates potentially

This chapter previously appeared in the *Journal of Economic Perspectives* 17(2) Spring 2003: 149–72. Reprinted by permission.

The authors thank Sarah Anderson, Charles Blahous, Jeffrey Brown, Rich Burkhauser, David Koitz, Kent Smetters, and Sylvester Schieber for comments on an earlier draft. Timothy Taylor offered very useful editorial suggestions. Opinions remain those of the authors and are not necessarily those of others on the President's Commission to Strengthen Social Security, the Bush administration, or of the institutions with which the authors are affiliated.

substantial capital and labor market inefficiencies (Congressional Budget Office 1998; Gruber and Wise 2002).

In 2001 President George W. Bush appointed the President's Commission to Strengthen Social Security, with sixteen members drawn equally from both major political parties. As members, we were charged to provide the president with recommendations to modernize the Social Security system, restore its fiscal soundness, and develop a workable system of personal retirement accounts as part of a newly structured program.[1] In this chapter, we offer our own perspectives on Social Security reform, drawn from service on the President's Commission. We begin with a discussion of the use of personal retirement accounts as a method of prefunding the Social Security system. The Commission to Strengthen Social Security developed three reform scenarios that incorporate personal retirement accounts as a central element in a modernized system of old-age security. Here, we focus on one reform plan in particular, one that promises an enhanced and more reliable safety net while also providing workers the opportunity to invest in personal accounts with diversified investment choice and potentially lower risk. Reforms of this sort can, we believe, help put Social Security on a self-financing basis for the first time in over a quarter of a century.

Perspectives on Funding and Personal Accounts

If Social Security reform is to reduce the tax burden imposed on future generations while maintaining adequate benefit levels, the system must move toward a prefunded program (Feldstein 1996). Moving from what is mainly a PAYGO unfunded transfer program to a funded Social Security program might be accomplished in several ways. The federal government might invest surplus Social Security funds directly in capital markets. The federal government could use surplus funds to pay down the publicly held debt. Or the government must permit individuals to carry out the prefunding in the form of personal investment accounts.

Centralized Government Investment of Social Security Surpluses

In 1998, Alan Greenspan testified before Congress that government investment of Social Security surpluses in stocks and bonds would have 'very far-reaching potential dangers for a free American economy and a free American society'. Similar concerns were held by the Senate and the president. In 1999 the Senate rejected—with a 99–0 vote—a proposal to allow the government to invest the Social Security surpluses in the capital market. In his 2001 charge to the Commission, President Bush ruled out allowing the federal government to invest Social Security in corporate assets.

Commissioners' views were no different. Members worried that surpluses would be used for 'socially targeted' investments, rather than for diversified capital market holdings. Moreover, if the federal government were to become a major corporate shareholder, commissioners worried that it would vote its shares in ways that would serve political or social objectives at the expense of Social Security returns and the economy's overall performance. Shoven (2001) offered testimony about the costly impact of the California State employee pension fund trustees' decision to divest the fund of tobacco stocks. Schwarz (2001) testified about her analysis of government investment in other countries, where she found that most countries in which the government invested pension funds had very poor experiences. At worst, government-invested pension funds lost money during the 1990s; at best, they earned bank-level rates of return. Her pessimistic conclusion was that 'experience with publicly managed funds has been disastrous'.

Financial considerations aside, a program of government investment would also mean that the government, rather than workers and retirees, would own and dispose of the accumulated retirement assets. Commissioners felt that personal ownership of retirement assets would give some workers an incentive to save more, while adoption of a DC structure would mitigate the program's adverse incentives to retire earlier.

Using Surpluses to Pay Down the Publicly Held Debt

To avoid the perils of government investment in private firms, the government might alternatively use Social Security trust fund revenues to pay down the publicly held debt. In contrast, adopting a personal account system financed by payroll taxes would mean that future annual Social Security surpluses would not be available for reducing the federal debt held by the public. The latter issue did not overly worry commissioners, as most were skeptical of the federal government's ability to sustain a policy of using Social Security surpluses to pay down the federal debt. This skepticism stemmed from our reading of Social Security's extensive legislative history (for historical background, see Weaver 1982; Cogan 1998; Schieber and Shoven 1999). From Social Security's founding in the mid-1930s through the mid-1990s, each time surpluses occurred—as a result of policy design, a wartime economy, or a peacetime period of noninflationary economic growth—the congressional response was to raise benefits or liberalize eligibility.

The process began with the original Social Security Act 1935 under the auspices of President Franklin Roosevelt. His initial plan was to amass substantial surpluses during the program's early years, which were to be used to reduce federal debt held by the public. The reduction in other federal debt and the interest savings were to be credited to the Social Security program through a reserve account. Later, when Social Security was forecasted to incur deficits, the reserve account would be drawn down to finance benefit payments. The plan hit difficulties almost immediately. By the end of the 1930s, the Social Security system's reserve policy collapsed under dual pressure from those who sought to liberalize benefits and from those who feared that surpluses might lead to higher federal spending on programs other than Social Security. In 1939, Congress dissipated the surplus by raising benefits, issuing the first benefit checks a year earlier than originally planned and granting eligibility to survivors and spouses.

During the 1940s, the wartime economy again produced large Social Security surpluses. By 1950, the accumulated surpluses were sufficient to finance the next ten years of benefit payments. Again, pressure mounted to spend the surplus, and Congress responded. In each election year during the 1950s, Congress raised benefits or expanded eligibility. By the end of the decade, the surplus had been spent. By the 1960s, strong economic growth had produced Social Security surpluses. For a third time, federal government's response was the same. Congress boosted benefits a total of seven times over the nine-year period from 1965 to 1973. These benefit increases totaled 83 percent, and along with a poorly performing economy, they brought Social Security to the brink of insolvency by the mid-1970s.

Since then, Congress has not significantly raised Social Security benefits in real terms. However, deficits plagued the program until the mid-1980s, and system's surpluses over the next decade were modest in size. Not until 1992 did the surpluses accumulate to one year's worth of benefit payouts. Then in 1994, facing deficits in the disability program that threatened payments to currently disabled workers, Congress enacted legislation to divert funds from the Social Security old-age program to pay for the Disability Insurance program. Formally, this was accomplished by reducing the Old-Age and Survivors Insurance tax rate and boosting the Disability Insurance tax rate by equal amounts. This tax diversion, which continues today at a rate of $25 billion per year, will total about $160 billion by the end of this fiscal year.

Commissioners also found little reason to believe that Social Security surpluses remaining after the legislative actions just described were used to reduce the debt substantially. In our view, it was more credible that Social Security surpluses produced an increase in federal spending on non-Social Security programs and tax reductions, a viewpoint that is widespread among economists. For instance, at a 1989 American Enterprise Institute conference on Social Security, conference participants Alan Blinder, Barry Bosworth, James Buchanan, William Nordhaus, James Poterba, John Shoven, and Carolyn Weaver all expressed the view that previous Congresses had spent Social Security surpluses (Weaver 1990). Similar conclusions were reached by Aaron, Bosworth, and Burtless (1989) and earlier by Munnell and Blais (1984). There is little hard research evidence on this point, though the only systematic economic analysis of the issue, by Crain and Marlow (1990), found statistical support for the conclusion that Social Security surpluses led to more non-Social Security spending. In view of the persistent tendency of past Congresses to spend Social Security surpluses, the Commission concluded that it seemed imprudent to assume that future Congresses would behave differently.

This conclusion was reinforced by budgetary actions that occurred during the Commission's deliberations in 2001. A combination of recession, appropriations increases, and a tax cut transformed anticipated federal budget surpluses into deficits. Surplus Social Security revenues were once again being used to finance federal spending other than on the retirement system. Many commissioners felt that individually owned personal accounts would more strongly insulate workers' Social Security taxes from political pressures and thereby improve the chances of prefunding. Though future Congresses may never be completely precluded from using a share of workers' accounts for purposes other than retirement, individual ownership, in our view, would make it more difficult.

The Meaning of the Trust Fund

When describing Social Security's financial problems, the Commission focused on the program's future cash flow shortfalls, rather than on trust fund accounting. An examination of Social Security cash flows recognizes that, as a practical matter of government finance, Congress will be required to take some budgetary action when the Social Security system begins to incur annual cash flow deficits and when the general fund will need to repay what it has borrowed from the Social Security trust fund. At that point, the federal government will have to raise additional revenues by taxing or borrowing, cutting Social Security benefits, or freeing up revenue by cutting other government programs.

The practical meaning of the trust fund, as opposed to cash flow shortfalls, depends on how Social Security affects the rest of the federal budget. If Social Security surpluses are used to reduce other federal debt, the trust fund balance represents a governmental asset, the value of which equals the amount of debt reduction and associated interest savings. However, if Social Security surpluses are used to finance more non-Social Security spending or tax reductions, then the trust fund balance does not represent a governmental asset. Instead, it is more accurately viewed as a political claim on future general fund revenues that will have to compete with other budgetary claims.

This distinction also means that focusing on the trust fund can give a misleading assessment of how personal accounts affect federal finances. Under standard budgeting practice, the trust fund balance is treated as a governmental asset regardless of whether the surplus revenues are used to reduce the publicly held debt. Hence, diverting a share of Social Security payroll taxes into personal accounts appears to drain the trust fund's assets and to reduce investment returns credited to these trust fund assets. However, if Social Security surpluses are not used to reduce the federal debt but instead are spent on current consumption, then they are not a governmental asset to be drained, and there are no investment returns to be reduced by personal accounts.

The trust fund's use of a 75-year time horizon also produces a misleading assessment of the impact of personal accounts, even if future trust fund surpluses were used for debt reduction. Payroll-tax-financed personal accounts reduce the trust fund's net income during the early years of the policy, but in later years, the trust fund's net income rises as personal account annuities offset Social Security liabilities. Using a fixed time horizon truncates the years of net income gain and thereby produces a downwardly biased estimate of how personal accounts enhance Social Security solvency.

To see this, consider a plan under which workers could divert 2 percentage points of their payroll tax rate into personal accounts. Assume that those who opt for personal accounts are required to forgo in traditional Social Security benefits the diverted contributions plus a 3 percent real rate of return on these contributions. Under the assumptions used by the Social Security Trustees, the 3 percent real return is precisely what the trust fund would have earned on these funds, so the policy would seem financially neutral for the trust fund in perpetuity. Yet, if a 75-year horizon were used to assess the policy, the long-run actuarial imbalance would rise from its current level of −1.86 percent of payroll to −2.46 percent, a 32-percent increase. Clearly, the bias created by using a fixed 75-year time horizon is not trivial.

This problem can be easily avoided by extending the accounting time horizon to perpetuity. Alternatively, many economists have proposed to use 'generational accounting' to track Social Security and other long-term fiscal liabilities not currently tracked on budget.[2] Adopting a longer-term perspective would remove the budget's current bias against prefunding implicit long-term liabilities and give policymakers an essential tool for making and justifying more informed long-term decisions.

Prefunding necessarily implies increasing current saving, which we have argued is not readily accomplished via a governmental trust fund. Indeed, we believe that focusing on trust fund accounting can itself be misleading and certainly does not enhance the prospects for maintaining fiscal solvency in the long run. For this reason, and in keeping with the president's charge, the Commission proposed several alternative structures for funded personal retirement accounts.

A Two-Tiered System

Most commissioners did not contemplate permitting workers to invest their entire payroll taxes in private securities, believing that this idea would be too radical a departure from the current program. Furthermore, President Bush's charge to the Commission proposed that personal accounts should augment Social Security, rather than replace it. Consequently, commissioners concurred that a reformed Social Security system should have two interrelated tiers.

An advantage of such an approach is that it allows building on the existing retirement system. A modified traditional Social Security program serves as Tier I and would provide an enhanced safety net. Its benefit structure would be altered in several ways, discussed below, to improve its role as a backstop against old-age poverty. Personal retirement accounts in Tier II would offer an investment-based component, enhancing individuals' opportunity to build financial wealth as a source of retirement income.

The concept of a two-tiered program has been the subject of considerable prior academic research, and it is regarded as a mainstream idea today in policy circles. The essential elements of a two-tiered US program were presented to the Greenspan Commission two decades ago (Boskin 1982). Since then, numerous proposals embodying a two-tier structure have been developed by economists and policymakers (e.g. see Weaver 1990; Gramlich 1996; Feldstein and Samwick 1998; Moynihan 1998; Schieber and Shoven 1999; Koitz 2001). Elected officials are also familiar with the real-world example of the Thrift Saving Plan, which is a retirement program adopted fifteen years ago for federal civilian (and later military) personnel. A wide range of two-tiered plans has been discussed in Congress. Additionally, a two-tiered approach has been successfully implemented in a number of countries, including England, Australia, and, most recently, Sweden. A two-tiered approach not only serves as a mechanism for prefunding through private accounts, but it also has other advantages. For instance, a two-tiered approach gives the Social Security program a greater degree of transparency. Since its inception, Social Security has balanced the tension between social adequacy and individual equity. Social adequacy seeks to ensure that retirees attain a certain standard of living in old age, which requires income transfers from high-earner to low-earner workers over their lifetimes. Individual equity, on the other hand, seeks to ensure that each worker's contributions are closely linked to his or her retirement benefits.

The current program's complexity is the result of years of legislative efforts to meet these competing goals with a single benefit formula. This complexity has produced many inequities and anomalous redistribution patterns, and it yields a surprisingly low level of lifetime income redistribution (Coronado, Fullerton, and Glass 2000; Gustman and Steinmeier 2000; Liebman 2001). Creating two separate tiers under Social Security, each with its own goal, would improve the overall program's transparency and equity. Thus, in each of the Commission's plans, social adequacy became the principal objective of Tier I, while individual equity became the main objective of Tier II. This greater transparency would enable policymakers to make more informed choices about appropriate benefit and tax levels, and it should also enable plan participants to make better savings and retirement decisions.

An additional policy rationale for a two-tiered system is that it may entail less political and economic risk than a single-tiered program (Shoven 2001). Despite considerable confusion on this point among public policy officials, the news media, and the public at large, traditional Social Security benefits are not 'guaranteed'. As the Social Security Administration indicates (http://www.ssa.gov/history/nestor.html):

> There has been a temptation throughout the program's history for some people to suppose that their FICA [Federal Insurance Contributions Act] payroll taxes entitle them to a benefit in a legal, contractual sense. That is to say, if a person makes FICA contributions over a number of years, Congress cannot, according to this reasoning, change the rules in such a way that deprives a contributor of a promised future benefit.... Congress clearly had no such limitation in mind when crafting the law.... Like all federal entitlement programs, Congress can change the rules regarding eligibility—and it has done so many times over the years. The rules can be made more generous, or they can be made more restrictive. Benefits which are granted at one time can be withdrawn....

Furthermore, the US Supreme Court ruled in *Flemming* v. *Nestor* (63 US 603 [1960]) that workers and beneficiaries have no legal ownership over their benefits, even after a lifetime of paying taxes into the system. The payment of scheduled benefits under the Social Security system remains contingent on the hope that politicians elected 20–30 years from now will decide to generate the revenue needed to pay benefits scheduled under present law, given the constraints and choices they face at that future date.

History shows that Congress has previously altered scheduled Social Security benefits a number of times, and in some instances, the benefit changes have been quite substantial. For instance, Congress passed legislation that reduced the growth of scheduled benefits in 1977, 1983, and 1993. The 1977 amendments reduced benefits by 19 percent from their promised levels for workers who were aged 62 years in 1980 and by 30 percent for workers aged 54 years in 1980 (Commission on the Social Security 'Notch' Issue 1994: 78). Looking ahead, commissioners felt that the political risk of achieving a given level of retirement income is substantial, since the system faces even larger shortfalls as a result of the program's worsening financing problems.

There is also economic risk stemming from the linkage between benefit promises and national average earnings. Given an individual worker's lifetime wage profile, variations in national average earnings due to changes in productivity produce variations in individuals' Social Security benefits.[3] Social Security's benefit formula, in effect, spreads 'productivity' risk across cohorts, imparting additional uncertainty regarding eventual benefits paid under the current system.

Achieving a given level of retirement income through investment-based individual accounts is, of course, also subject to uncertainty due to capital market volatility. But commissioners believed that this risk would be better managed with a Tier I level of benefits in place, paired with the opportunity to diversify investments via a personal account in Tier II.

Changes in First-Tier Benefits: From Wage Indexing to Price Indexing

Personal accounts alone will not put the Social Security program on a sound financial basis. Meeting President Bush's charge to restore the program's fiscal soundness required additional steps to reduce the growth of future liabilities. In assessing its options, the Commission undertook a review of current and past policy for determining Social Security benefits and its implications for future costs.[4] In particular, this research investigated current benefit promises and the role of wage versus price indexing in the benefit formula.

Under current law, initial retirement benefits are indexed to wages, and after retirement, they are price indexed. When calculating initial Social Security benefits, a worker's average indexed monthly earnings are computed by indexing that worker's highest thirty-five years of earnings to the average growth in national earnings. Next, initial monthly benefits are derived from the worker's average monthly earnings, a formula also indexed to average earnings.[5] The main rationale for wage indexing is to ensure that initial benefits for each cohort of retirees replace a specified portion (the 'replacement rate') of that cohort's pre-retirement pay. Under current rules, a worker who earns median wages over an entire career receives an expected initial benefit worth roughly 40 percent of the median wage at retirement. After the initial level of benefits is in place, subsequent benefit payments are linked to the Consumer Price Index, not the rate of wage increase. Wage indexing has been part of the Social Security program for less than half of its history. From the program's inception in 1935 until 1975, neither workers' wage histories nor benefits for currently retired workers were indexed to wage growth or inflation rates. Rather, when deciding to grant a benefit increase, Congress balanced the social adequacy of benefit levels against the resources available to finance an increase. In doing so, Congress focused mainly on preserving the purchasing power of benefits, while paying little attention to wage replacement rates (Hsiao 1979). For example, the current 40 percent replacement rate policy was established in a 1977 law, but as late as 1970, the replacement rate for a worker with median wages was only 34 percent (Committee on Ways and Means 2000).

Wage indexing means that the purchasing power of Social Security benefits will likely rise from one retirement cohort to the next, as increases in worker productivity cause wages to grow faster than prices. The intermediate assumptions of the Social Security Trustees project that real wages will grow at a 1.3 percent average annual rate during the next decade and at a 1 percent annual rate thereafter (Social Security Board of Trustees 2001: 84). Under this assumption, a 'typical' worker aged 45 years in 2001 who earns the average Social Security taxable wage every year and retires at age 65 years is slated to receive a monthly payment 20 percent higher in real terms than the benefit paid to an average worker retiring in 2001. Similarly, scheduled benefits for today's teenagers are scheduled to be 60 percent higher than benefits paid to a typical worker retiring in 2001.[6]

Wage indexing has been controversial from the time it was first proposed. Both the report of the 1975 Consultant Panel on Social Security and the minority report of the Advisory Council on Social Security (1979: 233–4) issued strong objections to the policy on equity and cost grounds.[7] Their equity concerns can be illustrated with a simple example. Consider two workers whose retirement ages are five years apart and who have identical earnings at each point in their life cycles. These workers will receive different inflation-adjusted Social Security benefits even though they have contributed identical amounts to Social Security, solely because the general level of real wages rises over time. Similarly, both the Consultant Panel and the Advisory Panel expressed concerns that wage indexing would threaten Social Security's financial solvency. The Consultant Panel on Social Security (1976: 6) warned that financing a wage-indexed system would ultimately require an eventual 50–80 percent increase in the payroll tax rate. History has justified their concerns: since wage indexing was adopted, the Social Security Trustees have reported that the program has been financially insolvent in twenty-three of their last twenty-five annual reports. By contrast, actuarial calculations performed for our Commission showed that if the real purchasing power of initial benefits paid to future retirees were maintained at the level provided to today's retirees—that is, adjusted for prices rather than for wages—future benefits could be paid without any increase in the payroll tax rate. While a wage replacement policy might have been a worthy Social Security program goal at an earlier historical period, our view is that this goal's importance has diminished as per capita incomes have risen and other retirement savings vehicles, such as IRAs and 401(k) plans, have become more widely available. Wage replacement may be viewed as a desirable goal of a comprehensive pension policy, without needing to be the principal and overriding objective of Tier I of a revamped Social Security program. Our reforms would allow future Congresses to increase the real initial level of Social Security benefits, if it were feasible to do so, after considering and balancing the competing needs of programs to enhance security, health care, and retirement well-being.

An Illustrative Reform Plan

The Commission sketched three reform plans in its final report. Here we focus on one of them, known as Model 2, to illustrate key points. That approach would replace wage indexing with a policy under which initial benefits would grow from one retirement cohort to the next at the rate of growth of prices. Therefore, workers in successive retirement cohorts with identical real wages would automatically receive the same real monthly benefits. This policy would be implemented in 2009, so that no beneficiary currently older than 55 years would see any change in benefits. As a result, inflation-adjusted benefits received by future retirees would be slightly higher than those received by workers who retired in 2001. For workers currently younger than 55 years, initial benefits would grow 1 percent per year more slowly than under current law.

Price indexing initial benefits is a very powerful reform: our calculations indicate that it would produce long-term savings sufficient to put Social Security back on a sound actuarial footing. As noted earlier, the Social Security system now confronts a long-run actuarial deficit of 1.86 percent of payroll (if the shortfall were smoothly assessed over a 75-year calculation window). In other words, an immediate and permanent tax increase of 1.86 percent of payroll would close the actuarial gap, assuming the surpluses would be saved and not spent. Moving to price indexing would reduce Social Security's long-term liabilities by 2.07 percent of payroll over the same period, thereby creating an actuarial surplus of 0.2 percent of payroll over the 75-year horizon. Commissioners proposed that the resulting surplus, the present value of which amounts to about $300 billion, could be allocated to raising inflation-adjusted benefits to low-wage workers and widows of deceased low-wage workers.

Some might think that price indexing would be difficult to implement, since politicians might be unwilling to reduce the replacement rate. We disagree, on the grounds that Congress has, in the past, reduced replacement rates on several occasions. For instance, the 1977 Social Security amendments reduced replacement rates by 30 percent for workers aged 54 years and younger in 1980. The 1983 amendments, by raising the 'normal' retirement age, will cut replacement rates by 14 percent when they are fully phased in. The 1993 amendments, by taxing Social Security benefits, reduced replacement rates by 7 percent for some middle-income retirees and by as much as 20 percent for high-income retirees. We also emphasize that, under Commission plans, retirement income from both tiers of the new Social Security program would provide benefits for low- and middle-income workers that are at least as high as they are at present, and for many, benefits would be much higher.

Tier II: Personal Retirement Accounts

President Bush's charge to the Commission called for plans that would allow workers a choice to invest part of their payroll taxes in a voluntary personal retirement account, as part of a reform that improved the Social Security system's long-term fiscal status and in a way that did not increase payroll taxes nor permanently divert general revenues. This charge had several policy implications for the structure of Tier II accounts.

First, these voluntary accounts would need to be structured, so participants would find them potentially attractive. The plans should offer participants some investment choice while they would still be relatively inexpensive to operate. Keeping fees low implied that the accounts should be made as large as possible quickly, competition among fund managers should be encouraged, and investment choices should be limited to hold down management fees. Second, these accounts would have to be at least partially financed by permitting workers to redirect a portion of their payroll taxes into these accounts. Third, participants who elected to contribute less payroll tax to the traditional system should receive lower Tier I Social Security benefits, though, of course, they would receive their Tier II personal account benefits, as well. Fourth, the personal retirement accounts should be targeted at lower-paid workers, both to maintain system progressivity and because this segment of the labor force is least well served by corporate pensions and tends to have the lowest saving rates.

Designing Personal Accounts

To illustrate how the policy objectives were weighed in practice, it is useful to focus again on the Commission's Model 2. Under this plan, all workers younger than 55 years would be permitted to redirect 4 percentage points of their payroll taxes voluntarily into their personal accounts, up to a $1,000 cap. This cap would be indexed to wage growth. The personal account would enable a young worker earning $25,000 annually to anticipate building a retirement account worth over $150,000 in retirement wealth (in 2001 dollars). While all persons currently younger than 55 years could participate in and benefit from personal accounts, we anticipated that lower-wage workers would benefit the most, since they are least likely to have company-sponsored pensions at present.

Under this plan, workers who opt for a personal account would be required to forgo a portion of their traditional Social Security benefit. The Commission recommended that the amount foregone depend on the amount of payroll taxes the worker elected to divert to personal accounts instead of basing the amount on the size of the personal account annuity at retirement. Under Model 2, for instance, the amount foregone equals the worker's contributions plus a 2 percent real rate of return. Consequently, a worker who expected personal account investments to yield a real return higher than 2 percent would anticipate being better off opting for the personal account. Because workers who opt for personal accounts expect to receive the full amount of each dollar of investment returns above the 2 percent threshold, the policy does not distort incentives for saving. The Commission considered, but did not adopt, an alternative that would condition first-tier benefits on the actual amount that workers had accumulated in their personal accounts at retirement. This approach, called a 'clawback', suffers from the drawback that it reduces the marginal return on savings and, therefore, distorts savings decisions. The Commission's offset policy also has the desirable feature that it minimizes possible adverse impacts of personal accounts on Social Security's progressivity. High-wage workers will forgo a larger share of their traditional benefits than will low-wage workers for each dollar of personal account contributions.[8]

Administrative Considerations

Substantial discussion focused on the design of an administrative plan for personal retirement accounts (for discussion of administrative design issues, see Mitchell 1998; Shipman 1999; Shoven 2000; Feldstein and Liebman 2002). Ultimately, the Commission proposed starting with a centralized approach, similar to the federal Thrift Saving Plan that today covers civil servants and military employees. Under this format, a single central governing board would collect contributions, manage records and, via a competitive process, select private-sector managers who would invest participant assets. In addition, recordkeeping and benefit payments would be handled by the governing board or would be outsourced. This proposal strikes a balance between the scale economy benefits from centralization of recordkeeping versus the attractiveness of enhanced competition. The Commission proposed that after a few years, plan participants would be permitted to move their investments from the centralized system into a more decentralized one with licensed, private money managers. This two-phased approach should avoid the need to regulate fund loads or charges, since a combination of competition and information provided by the central fund administrator was anticipated to drive down fees and charges.

Investment Options in the Personal Accounts

When analyzing the investment options offered under a system of personal retirement accounts, the Commission proposed to offer investors a limited choice of indexed portfolios, including a Government Securities Investment fund that held mainly short-term US Treasury securities; a Fixed Income Index Investment fund that tracks a US bond market index; a Common Stock Index Investment fund tracking the Standard & Poor's 500 Index of large-company stock; a Small Capitalization Stock Index Investment fund that tracks the Wilshire 4500 stock index; and an International Stock Index Investment fund that holds corporate assets located in Australia, Europe, and the Far East. In addition, the Commission recommended that one investment option include Government Treasury Inflation-Protected Securities. Those who later elect to move their accounts to private management would gain some additional choices, but they would still have to invest in low-cost diversified accounts. In all cases, the accounts would be required to invest in a broad range of corporations across all major commercial sectors. Further, the amount of the fund invested in any particular corporation could not significantly exceed the market value of that corporation, relative to other firms in the fund.

Recent economic research also suggests the high value of offering participants a portfolio balanced between stocks and bonds, should workers and retirees fail to indicate how to allocate their personal retirement accounts (Benartzi and Thaler 2001; Choi et al. 2002; Mitchell and Utkus 2002). We therefore proposed that investors should be permitted to change the investment allocations in their personal retirement accounts annually. This provision would offer some flexibility, yet it would also encourage participants to think of their investments as 'long-term savings' rather than short-term funds.

The Key Role of Actuarial Assumptions

In keeping with past practice of having serious proposals thoroughly vetted, the financial impact of all the Commission's reform plans was scored by the Office of the Chief Actuary at the Social Security Administration. This office provided the actuarial assumptions used in cost and benefit projections developed under advice from the Social Security Board of Trustees. Since the actuarial assumptions used by Social Security are well known and easily available at http://www.ssa.gov, we offer a sense of some key magnitudes rather than providing detail. In all cases, the projections assume a real expected future return on stocks of 6.5 percent per year. Corporate and Treasury bonds are assumed to deliver a real rate of return of 3.5 and 3.0 percent, respectively. The actuary's projections further assume that a typical participant holds a balanced fund, with half of the assets in a broadly diversified equity portfolio and half in a similarly diversified bond portfolio. The administrative costs of private retirement accounts are assumed to total 30 basis points (0.3% of the account balance).

Commissioners regarded these assumptions as conservative. The US government's Thrift Saving Plan, for example, operates with administrative costs of only 8 basis points. Also, under the assumed rates of return and portfolio composition, the expected real return net of expenses for a 50/50 stock/bond portfolio is 4.6 percent, a return lower than that used in many academic and policy studies.

Access to Funds

Commissioners thought hard about whether to permit pre-retirement access to the funds in personal retirement accounts. On the one hand, all agreed that retirement funds should be earmarked for old age, implying that workers should not be permitted to consume the assets if it would leave them dependent on government's antipoverty programs during retirement. On the other hand, a clear appeal of personal retirement accounts is that they grant workers ownership over their own assets. This latter view was of particular concern for groups anticipating below-average life expectancies, such as African-Americans, the ill, and the lifetime poor. Ultimately, the Commission concurred that personal account funds would have to be preserved until retirement. Pre-retirement stringencies should not be the cause of individuals facing even greater stringencies during retirement. This philosophy is in keeping with current Social Security policy, since benefits now cannot be accessed prior to retirement nor used as collateral for a loan.

Commission members also felt strongly that retirees should have a range of possibilities for making withdrawals from their personal accounts. Drawing on economic studies of annuity markets (Brown et al. 2001), our models proposed that account distributions could take the form of an annuity or periodic withdrawals, similar to the current 401(k) system. The Commission recommended that a portion of funds above a minimum threshold would be accessible as a lump-sum distribution. The threshold amount would be designed so that the yearly income received from an individual's Social Security benefit plus the joint annuity (if married) would protect either spouse from falling below the poverty line during retirement. Remaining assets could be bequeathed at death. Because lower-income households have shorter life expectancies, the bequest option adds to the Social Security system's progressivity and would offer better protection to widows than would today's Social Security rules. In the case of divorce, personal retirement account assets accumulated during marriage would be divided between divorcing partners. This step would enhance protection of former spouses as compared to today's Social Security rules that do not provide benefits to former spouses from marriages lasting under ten years.[9]

Another topic of debate pertained to how participants might invest their personal retirement account assets after retirement and whether they might be encouraged to switch to more conservative investments at some given age. The main results assumed that a typical individual would hold personal retirement funds in a 50/50 balanced stock and bond fund during both the accumulation and decumulation periods (with the assumed return mentioned above of 4.6% after inflation). After any lump-sum distributions, Tier II benefits would be received in the form of a variable annuity, depending on the returns received in the underlying investment portfolio. For those preferring greater certainty, and because the current Social Security system pays benefits entirely as an inflation-indexed annuity, commissioners also proposed permitting inflation-indexed annuities during the retirement phase.[10] Brown, Mitchell, and Poterba (2000) show that under plausible assumptions about risk-aversion, retirees already receiving a real annuity under the traditional Social Security system would prefer a Tier II of variable annuities with a higher return rather than more real annuities.

In this context, it is worth noting that only about one-quarter of total Social Security assets would be held in stocks by those opting for personal accounts, including both Tier I traditional system and Tier II personal retirement accounts.

Benefits under the Reformed System

When comparing benefits under the current system and the several alternatives proposed, the issue arose as to whether one should adjust personal account annuities for financial risk. After discussion, commissioners concluded that the best approach was to present all annuities in terms of their expected values and to also discuss the risks of each annuity in a qualitative manner. With this thought in mind, we summarize the reform plans

TABLE 8-1 Projected Monthly Social Security Benefits under Alternative Scenarios; Projected to 2052, under Model 2 Structure (in Constant 2001 dollars)

I. Lifetime Low-Wage Earner	
Today's benefit	637
Projected Benefit with Personal Account	
Low yield	867
Medium yield	1,050
High yield	1,090
Current program payable	713
Scheduled benefit	—
II. *Lifetime Medium-Wage Earner*	
Today's benefit	1,052
Projected Benefit with Personal Account	
Low yield	1,204
Medium yield	1,525
High yield	1,595
Current program payable	1,179
Schedule benefit	—
III. *Lifetime Maximum-Wage Earner*	
Today's benefit	1,366
Projected benefit with personal account	
Low yield	1,565
Medium yield	1,907
High yield	1,983
Current program payable	1,557
Scheduled benefit	2,151

Source: CSSS Final Report (2001).
Note: These categories, developed by the Social Security actuaries, are specified (in 2001 dollars) such that a lifetime 'low' earner would have averaged approximately $15,900 per year, whereas the medium earner averaged $35,300 per annum, and the high earner $56,400.

by referring to expected projected retiree benefits under the alternative reform proposals.

Results are summarized in Table 8-1, where anticipated outcomes are illustrated for 'low', 'average', and 'high' earners under different policy scenarios (in 2001 dollars). These categories, developed by the Social Security actuaries, were specified such that a low earner in 2001 received a lifetime average of approximately $16,000, whereas a medium earner averaged about $35,300 per year and a high earner $56,400 per year. Results in Table 8-1 depict benefits received at Social Security's normal retirement age currently and in 2052, since the latter represents benefits anticipated by a worker covered by the new system over an entire work life.

In Table 8-1, the first row of each panel labeled 'Today's benefit' indicates today's benefit payments delivered to a worker at each lifetime earnings level. The next 3 rows depict benefits anticipated under a Model 2 reform for workers who elected personal accounts, allowing for alternative investment portfolios. The inflation-adjusted medium return is 4.6 percent, while the lower yield is based on an assumed real return of 2.7 percent, and the high yield plan assumes a real return of 4.92 percent (Commission to Strengthen Social Security 2001*b*: 18–19). To illustrate the comparisons, a lifetime low-wage worker retiring today receives benefits worth $637 per month. This is well below benefit payouts projected for a low-wage employee opting for personal accounts, which would amount to $870–$1,100 per month. The row labeled 'Current Program Payable' illustrates that benefits of only $713 could be financed with currently legislated tax rates. We note that reformed system benefits for low and medium earners exceed current and payable future benefits. The final row, titled 'Scheduled Benefits', refers to the benefits payable if taxes were raised to cover projected shortfalls. For the low earner, a scheduled (but not currently affordable) benefit of $986 is below the Commission's Model 2 payout, assuming a medium portfolio yield.

A key lesson from Table 8-1 is that all workers who opt for personal accounts under Model 2 can expect retirement benefits at least as high as, and in some cases much larger than, today's benefits adjusted for inflation. Most would also anticipate payments higher than those the system can afford to pay in the future under current law, and even conservative low earners would receive higher benefits than the current program promises. The gains relative to benefits the current system can afford to pay are more modest, however. This illustrates the point that while Model 2's personal accounts can be expected to raise retirement income received from the Social Security system (combining Tier I and Tier II), rates of return would not be anticipated to be substantially higher.

Inasmuch as the system is progressive, the pattern of benefits paid will vary by earnings levels, as we have shown. Under Model 2, today's teenager planning to retire in 2052 with a lifetime of medium earnings could expect Social Security payments 42 percent larger than today's benefits. Results are even better for low earners, since the increment would be even larger than 65 percent in real terms, compared to today's retiree. High-wage workers would also anticipate a benefit increase, but the percentage increment is lower, at 40 percent, in keeping with the progressive intent of the reform. The greater progressivity results from the fact that personal retirement accounts are initially capped at $1,000, so low-wage workers earning $25,000 or less can redirect 4 percentage points of their payroll taxes, but workers earning above $25,000 could redirect only a smaller percentage. Additionally, as was noted above, improved protections are provided against poverty, so benefit levels paid to all low-wage workers would be raised the most.

In summary, under Model 2, Tier I benefits would deliver higher replacement rates to low earners than can be financed under current law, and absolute benefits would increase for all under the first pillar. Tier II offers investors the option of doing better on the whole, as compared to the current system, and even conservative low- and medium-earning workers would expect to do better than what can be afforded with current tax financing.

Impact on Federal Government Finances

Measuring the impact of proposed Social Security reforms on the federal government's finances is not straightforward when moving to a funded system. One reason is that neither the annual federal budget nor the ten-year projections currently recognize the existence of long-term Social Security liabilities, since these liabilities arise outside the ten-year window traditionally used in policy projections. Nevertheless, failure to recognize this debt can create the false appearance among policymakers that there is little fiscal benefit from moving a primarily PAYGO system to a funded system that reduces long-term Social Security liabilities. A related problem is that traditional tools for measuring the impact of reform, such as the long-term actuarial balance, are ill-suited to capturing the full financial benefit of moving to a funded system.

Perhaps the best place to see this is by taking a qualitative look at the impact of particular reforms on Social Security finances. Figure 8-1 indicates the impact of Model 2 on Social Security's financial shortfall over the next seventy-five years. These estimates assume two-thirds participation rates in the personal retirement accounts (results for alternative participation results appear in Commission's report). As Figure 8-1 shows, under current law, Social Security is expected to run cash surpluses until 2016, after which point, annual deficits become a permanent and growing problem. Annual deficits as a percentage of taxable wages are expected to rise to nearly 2 percent by 2020, 4 percent by 2030, and over 6 percent by 2075, the last year of Social Security's actuarial horizon. Under Model 2, the annual deficit begins a few years sooner, in 2010. It then grows more slowly, reaches its maximum at 4 percent of payroll in 2030 and shrinks thereafter. Surpluses are first achieved in 2059 and continue to rise thereafter. Consequently, the reform proposal ultimately replaces current law's permanent and rising deficits with rising surpluses. By the end of the

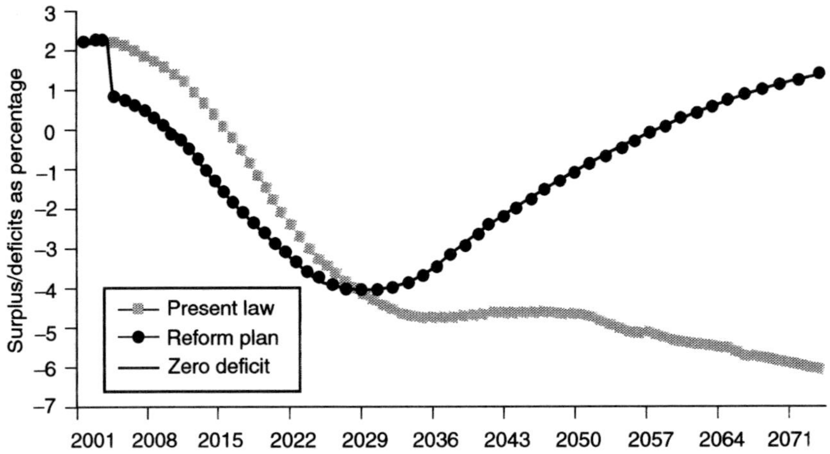

Figure 8-1. Impact of proposed reform (Model 2) on Social Security. (*Source*: CSSS Final Report 2001.)

75-year actuarial horizon, the surpluses are expected to reach 1.4 percent of payroll.

Perhaps the most interesting question for policymakers is how to quantify the improvement in Social Security's finances from the reform proposal. One useful summary statistic is the reduction in the amount of additional government revenues required to finance promised benefit payments. Yet even this seemingly straightforward statistic is subject to measurement problems, because the Social Security actuaries assume a fixed seventy-five-year time horizon. This truncates the returns that accrue in the form of lower traditional Social Security liabilities for persons who opt for personal accounts. According to calculations performed for the Commission, the present value of the reduced revenue requirements under Model 2 is excluded because the fixed time horizon totals about $1 trillion.

Keeping in mind this measurement problem, Table 8-2 compares the change in governmental revenue required under Model 2 with the traditional measure of Social Security's financial shortfall under current law. The traditional measure is the present value of the difference between Social Security's outgo and its income over the seventy-five-year actuarial horizon, less the balance in the fund at the beginning of the time period. This measure, when expressed as a percentage of taxable payroll over the same time horizon, is called the actuarial balance. In 2001 the actuarial balance was 21.86 percent, or if measured in present discounted value terms, the trustees estimated the shortfall as $3.2 trillion.

TABLE 8-2 Impact of Social Security Reform on Government's Revenue Requirement

	Current Law *Revenue Required* *($PV Trillions)*	*Reform Model 2*	
		Change in Revenue Required ($PV Trillions)	*% Reduction*
Traditional measure Congress 'saves' all surpluses	$3.2	–$2.0	63%
Alternative 2 Congress spent past surpluses, but 'saves' future surpluses	$4.1	–$2.0	49%
Alternative 3 Congress 'spends' all surpluses	$5.1	–$2.3	45%

Source: Author's computations, CSSS Final Report (2001).

When the Social Security actuaries examined Model 2, they calculated both the reduction in Social Security surpluses during years in which Social Security runs surpluses and the change in deficits during years in which Social Security incurs deficits. The present value of this change is $2.0 trillion; in other words, Model 2 costs 63 percent less as compared to the government's revenue shortfalls under scheduled benefits and current tax law. This set of estimates implicitly assumes that past Social Security surpluses were 'saved'—that is, they were used to reduce the national debt and, hence, are available to finance future deficits. The inclusion of future surpluses in the traditional measure implicitly assumes that future surpluses will be similarly used and, hence, will be available to finance future deficits. Nevertheless, as we have argued above, Congress has previously used Social Security surpluses to finance consumption related to spending increases and tax reductions, rather than for debt reduction. A similar pattern could reasonably be expected for the future.

Table 8-2 also indicates that moving to a funded system inevitably requires an investment, which may be viewed as the net additional general revenue requirement associated with the proposed reform. For Model 2, from 2005 to 2009, additional resources are needed to ensure that promised benefits can be paid and personal accounts can be funded. In dollar terms, transition financing requirements for Model 2 would initially be comparatively small ($4 billion in 2010) and they would grow to a maximum of just over $73 billion in 2016 (measured in 2001 dollars).

Thereafter, the amount of new cash requirements for the reformed system would diminish. Starting in 2029, the new system would require less general revenue than the old one on a permanent basis. Thus, Model 2 requires $0.9 trillion, or about half of 1 percent of GDP in present value terms, between now and 2029. The Commission concluded that such an amount would not pose major economic problems, though it could possibly raise political concerns. Of course, putting the program on a long-term sustainable footing has some obvious rationale as well.

Conclusions

Commissioners concurred that the evidence is clear: Social Security reform is both economically necessary and socially imperative, and the sooner reforms are implemented, the better. If nothing is done to reform the system, low earners will be particularly vulnerable to benefit cuts, and all workers as well as retirees will confront substantial economic insecurity in old age. The Commission's proposed reforms would also put Social Security on a self-financing basis for the first time in over a quarter of a century, consistent with its founder Franklin Roosevelt's vision. Our work shows that personal retirement accounts can play an important role in a reformed, financially sustainable, and more progressive Social Security system. We also anticipate that many workers would elect personal accounts when they are presented with a clear statement of the substantial political risks facing the current Social Security system.

Notes

[1] The reports, hearings and proceedings of the President's Commission to Save Social Security (2001), along with other background information, can be found at <http://www.csss.gov>. The Commission was cochaired by Senators Daniel Patrick Moynihan and Richard Parsons, who is chairman and chief executive officer of AOL/Time Warner. Along with the two of us, the other twelve members were Leanne Abdnor, former executive director of the Alliance for Worker Retirement Security; Sam Beard, founder and president of Economic Security 2000; Bill Frenzel, former US Representative; Estelle James, consultant with the World Bank; Robert Johnson, CEO of Black Entertainment Television; Gwendolyn King, former Commissioner of Social Security; Gerry Parsky, former Assistant Secretary of the Treasury; Tim Penny, former US Representative; Robert Pozen, at the time vice chairman of Fidelity Investments; Mario Rodriguez, Hispanic Business Roundtable; Thomas Saving, current Social Security Public Trustee; and Fidel Vargas, vice president of Reliant Equity Investors. The staff members of the Commission also included two economists, Jeffrey Brown and Kent Smetters.

[2] The generational accounting approach was developed by Auerbach, Gokhale, and Kotlikoff (1991). See also the Symposium on Generational Accounting in the Winter 1994 issue of this journal (Auerbach, Gokhale, and Kotlikoff 1994; Haveman 1994).

[3] An underappreciated point is that the Social Security program's current benefit formula could subject low-wage workers to greater economic risk than high-wage workers. This outcome arises because for a low-wage worker, an additional dollar of lifetime annual earnings adds 90 cents to Social Security benefits, while for a high-wage worker, each additional dollar adds only 15 cents to benefits. For this reason, fluctuations in lifetime pay and/or the national average wage could produce larger variations at the lower end of the pay distribution. Empirical research to evaluate the sensitivity of various earnings profiles to this type of variability would be useful.

[4] This review was conducted by a subgroup of commissioners known as the 'Fiscal Subgroup', headed by Cochairman Richard Parsons. It included the Commission's four economists (the two authors of this chapter, along with Thomas Saving and Estelle James) as well as Lea Abdnor, Gerald Parsky, Tim Penny, and Robert Pozen.

[5] Specifically, in 2001, a single worker who retired at the normal retirement age received benefits worth 90% of the first $561 of monthly average indexed monthly earnings (AIME); 32% of each additional dollar of AIME up to $3,381; and 15% of each additional dollar of AIME thereafter. These bend points, or the dollar amounts that define the ranges over which percentage replacement rates are applied, are indexed to the growth in average earnings of all workers covered by Social Security.

[6] These calculations include the fact that Social Security's normal retirement age is scheduled to rise to 67 years in 23 years. In the above examples, both typical workers will pay an early retirement penalty of about 7% for retiring at age 65 years.

[7] The 1979 Consultant Panel was chaired by economist William Hsiao, and members included James Hickman, Ernest Moorhead, and economist Peter Diamond. The minority views in the 1979 Advisory Council are those of Henry Aaron and Gardner Ackley.

[8] This outcome results from the fact that the offset is proportional to earnings, while traditional benefits rise less than proportionately with earnings. The Commission also considered an alternative approach in which the percentage of Social Security benefits a worker would be required to forgo would depend on the percentage of payroll taxes the worker diverted to his personal account. Under such an approach, a worker who diverted 20% of his payroll taxes to personal accounts would forgo, say, 20% of his benefits. This approach was rejected because it would create a greater incentive for high-wage workers to opt for personal accounts than it would for low-wage workers, and it would not preserve as much of Social Security's progressivity as the Commission's preferred approaches.

[9] All the Commission's reform plans recognize the historical relationship between Disability Insurance benefits and Old-Age and Survivors Insurance finances benefits. Today, the Primary Insurance Amount benefit formula is a common one, and the programs' finances are affected in similar ways by demographic changes. Hence, Disability Insurance program outlays are projected to rise by 45% as a percentage

of payroll over the next 15 years, and Disability Insurance costs will exceed Disability Insurance tax revenue starting in 2009. The Commission acknowledged that a reformed Social Security system must take into account the fact that planned retirement is a very different life event from an unplanned onset of disability. Personal retirement accounts are partially intended to replace the finances benefit component in Social Security. Disability Insurance beneficiaries with abbreviated work histories might have relatively low-account balances. Some may argue that this justifies isolating the Disability Insurance finances benefit structure from any changes that would affect Old-Age and Survivor's Insurance finances benefits, but testimony provided to the Commission indicated that many Disability Insurance beneficiaries sought to maintain a parallel structure for both Disability Insurance and Old-Age and Survivor's Insurance. We recommended further research to determine the optimal approach to balancing these adequacy and equity concerns in the Disability Insurance system. For an introductory survey of disability programs in this journal, see Burkhauser and Daly (2002).

[10] Another controversial question had to do with the financial and economic costs and benefits of providing guaranteed investments in the context of personal retirement accounts. Even the inflation-indexed annuities would only be guaranteed to rise with inflation—not guaranteed in their real return. The Commission elected not to propose such guarantees, instead calling for more research on the likely structure of such investment options. For relevant research on pension guarantees, useful starting points include Bodie and Merton (1993), Bodie (2001), Feldstein and Ranguelova (2000), Lachance and Mitchell (2002), and Smetters (2002).

References

Aaron, Henry J., Barry Bosworth, and Gary Burtless (1989). *Can America Afford to Grow Old?* Washington, DC: Brookings Institution.

Advisory Council on Social Security (1979). 'Report of the 1979 Advisory Council on Social Security', Committee on Ways and Means, House of Representatives, 96th Congress, 1st Session, December 7.

—— (1997). Report of the 1994–1996 Advisory Council on Social Security, Volume I: *Findings and Recommendations.* Washington, DC: Advisory Council on Social Security.

Auerbach, Alan, Jagadeesh Gokhale, and Lawrence Kotlikoff (1991). 'Generational Accounts: A Meaningful Alternative to Deficit Accounting', in D. Bradford (ed.), *Tax Policy and the Economy 5.* Cambridge, MA: MIT Press, pp. 55–110.

—— —— and Laurence J. Kotlikoff (Winter 1994). 'Generational Accounting: A Meaningful Way to Evaluate Fiscal Policy', *Journal of Economic Perspectives,* 8(1): 73–94.

Benartzi, Shlomo and Richard Thaler (2001). 'Naïve Diversification Strategies in Retirement Savings Plans', *American Economic Review,* 91(1): 79–98.

Bodie, Zvi (2001). 'Financial Engineering and Social Security Reform', in J. Campbell and M. Feldstein (eds.), *Risk Aspects of Social Security Reform.* Chicago, IL: University of Chicago Press, ch. 8.

—— and R. Merton (1993). 'Pension Benefit Guarantees in the United States: A Functional Analysis', in R. Schmitt (ed.), *The Future of Pensions in the United States*. Philadelphia, PA: University of Pennsylvania Press, pp. 194–234.

Boskin, Michael J. (1982). 'Alternative Social Security Reform Proposals', Paper presented to the National Commission of Social Security Reform, August 20.

Brown, Jeffrey R., Olivia S. Mitchell, and James M. Poterba (2000). 'The Role of Real Annuities and Indexed Bonds in an Individual Accounts Retirement Program', in John Y. Campbell and Martin Feldstein (eds.), *Risk Aspects of Investment-Based Social Security Reform*. Chicago, IL: University of Chicago Press, pp. 321–60.

—— —— James Poterba, and Mark Warshawsky (2001). *The Role of Annuity Markets in Financing Retirement*. Cambridge, MA: MIT Press.

Burkhauser, Richard V. and Mary C. Daly (Winter 2002). 'Policy Watch: US Disability Policy in a Changing Environment', *Journal of Economic Perspectives*, 16(1): 213–24.

Choi, James et al. (2002). 'Finances Contribution Pensions: Plan Rules, Participant Decisions and the Path of Least Resistance', in James Poterba (ed.), *Tax Policy and the Economy*, vol. 16. Cambridge, MA: MIT Press, pp. 67–113.

Cogan, John (1998). 'The Congressional Response to Social Security Surpluses, 1935–1994', *Part of Essays in Public Policy*. Stanford, CA: Hoover Institution, no. 92.

Commission on the Social Security 'Notch' Issue (1994). 'Final Report on the Social Security "Notch" Issue'. Washington, DC, December 31.

Commission to Strengthen Social Security (CSSS) (August 2001a). 'Interim Report', Washington, DC.

—— (December 2001b). 'Strengthening Social Security and Creating Personal Wealth for all Americans', Final Report, Washington, DC.

Committee on Ways and Means, US House of Representatives (October 2000). *2000 Green Book*. Washington, DC: US Government Printing Office.

Congressional Budget Office (July 1998). 'Social Security and Private Saving: A Review of the Empirical Evidence', Report.

Consultant Panel on Social Security (August 1976). 'Report of the Consultant Panel on Social Security', *Joint Committee Report*, 94th Congress, 2nd Session.

Coronado, Julia Lynn, Don Fullerton, and Thomas Glass (February 2000). 'The Progressivity of Social Security', NBER Working Paper.

Crain, Mark W. and Michael L. Marlow (1990). 'The Causal Relationship between Social Security and the Federal Budget', in Carolyn Weaver (ed.), *Social Security's Looming Surpluses: Prospects and Implications*. Washington, DC: AEI Press, pp. 119–34.

Feldstein, Martin S. (May 1996). 'The Missing Piece in Policy Analysis: Social Security Reform', *American Economic Review*, 86(2): 1–14.

—— —— (2002). *The Distributional Aspects of Social Security and Social Security Reform*. Chicago, IL: University of Chicago Press.

—— and Elena Ranguelova (August 2000). 'Accumulated Pension Collars: A Market Approach to Reducing the Risk of Investment-Based Social Security Reform', NBER Working Paper No. 7861.

—— and Andrew A. Samwick (1998). 'Potential Effects of Two Percent Personal Retirement Accounts', *Tax Notes*, May 4: 615–20.

Gramlich, Edward M. (1996). 'Different Approaches for Dealing with Social Security', *Journal of Economic Perspectives*, 10(3): 55–66.

Gruber, Jonathan and David Wise (December 2002). 'Social Security Programs and Retirement Around the World: Micro Estimation', NBER Working Paper.

Gustman, Alan L. and Thomas L. Steinmeier (March 2000). 'How Effective is Redistribution under the Social Security Benefit Formula?', NBER Working Paper.

Haveman, Robert (1994). 'Should Generational Accounts Replace Public Budgets and Deficits?', *Journal of Economic Perspectives*, 8(1): 95–111.

Hsiao, William (1979). 'An Optimal Indexing Method for Social Security', in Colin D. Campbell (ed.), *Financing Social Security*. Washington, DC: American Enterprise Institute.

Koitz, David (2001). *Seeking Middle Ground on Social Security Reform*. Stanford, CA: Hoover Institution Press.

Lachance, Marie-Eve and Olivia S. Mitchell (2002). 'Understanding Individual Retirement Guarantees', NBER Working Paper.

Liebman, Jeffrey B. (2001). 'Redistribution in the Current US Social Security Program', NBER Working Paper.

Mitchell, Olivia (1998). 'Administrative Costs of Public and Private Pension Plans', in Martin Feldstein (ed.), *Privatizing Social Security*. Chicago, IL: University of Chicago Press, pp. 403–56.

—— and Steve Utkus (2002). 'Company Stock and Retirement Plan Diversification', NBER Working Paper.

Moynihan, Daniel Patrick (1998). 'Social Security Saved!', Address to the Institute of Politics: Spring Exercise on Social Security Reform, John F. Kennedy School of Government, Harvard University, March 16.

Munnell, Alicia and Lynn Blais (1984). 'Do We Want Large Social Security Surpluses?', *New England Economic Review*, September/October: 5–21.

President's Commission to Strengthen Social Security (December 2001). *Strengthening Social Security and Creating Personal Wealth for All Americans*. Washington, DC: US Government Printing Office.

Schieber, Sylvester J. and John B. Shoven (1999). *The Real Deal: The History and Future of Social Security*. New Haven, CT and London: Yale University Press.

Schwarz, Anita (2001). 'International Experience with Private Retirement Accounts', Testimony before the President's Commission to Strengthen Social Security, September 6.

Shipman, William (1999). 'Administrative Challenges Confronting Social Security Reform', Testimony before the House Budget Committee Task Force on Social Security, April 27.

Shoven, John B. (ed.) (2000). *Administrative Aspects of Investment-Based Social Security Reform*. Chicago, IL: University of Chicago Press.

—— (2001). 'Implementing a Two-Tier Social Security Program', Testimony to the President's Commission to Strengthen Social Security, September 6.

Smetters, Kent (March 2002). 'Controlling the Cost of Minimum Benefit Guarantees in Public Pension Conversions', *Journal of Pension Economics and Finance*, 1(1): 9–33.

Social Security Board of Trustees (March 2001). 'The 2001 Annual Report of the Board of Trustees of the Federal Old-Age and Survivors Insurance and Disability Insurance Trust Funds', Washington, DC: US Government Printing Office.

Weaver, Carolyn L. (1982). 'The Crisis in Social Security', Duke University Policy Studies Working Paper.

—— (ed.) (1990). *Social Security's Looming Surpluses: Prospects and Implications*. Washington, DC: AEI Press.

Chapter 9

Reforms to Canadian Social Security, 1996–7

Robert L. Brown

The Canadian Social Security System

The Canadian social security system underwent a series of reforms in 1996–7. These changes were minor and could be viewed as only 'tweaks' to the existing system. Proof of this is the ability to describe the Canadian social security system at a general level and not to differentiate whether the description refers to the system before or after the 1996–7 reforms.[1]

Government-sponsored retirement income security in Canada comes in three tiers. First, there is Old Age Security (OAS), which is the grandfather of Canadian retirement income security, having first been legislated in 1927. Benefits had been increased on an ad hoc basis over the history of the plan and are now indexed to inflation. At first, benefits were not paid until aged 70 years. Now, all persons in Canada aged 65 years or older who are citizens or legal residents may qualify for either a full or partial OAS pension. In general, those with 40 years of residence after age 18 are eligible for a full pension. Those with fewer than 40 years may receive a partial pension on a prorated basis (t/40), provided they have at least 10 years' residence. OAS benefits are paid out of general tax revenues and are taxable income. The maximum OAS monthly pension as of January 2006 was $484.63,[2] or $5,815.56 per year (at a time when average annual earnings were about $35,000). The benefit is fully indexed to the consumer price index, with benefit increases taking place quarterly. The importance of OAS in the total income-security package has declined over the past few decades. In 1967, OAS benefits equaled about 21 percent of the average wage. They are now closer to 16 percent.

Before 1989, OAS was universal for those aged 65 years and older, subject only to residence requirements (it was paid on a demogrant basis). No income or asset tests were applied. In 1985, the federal government, debating the merits of the continued universality of OAS benefits, proposed to partially de-index the OAS, adjusting only for cost-of-living increases in excess of 3 percent per annum. At the time the legislation was proposed, the rate of inflation had been close to 9.5 percent for the previous decade, so the intent was to bring about a partial benefit reduction. However, inflation in Canada over the past decade has been consistent at around 2 percent per annum, which means the proposed change would have resulted in no benefit increases at all. Regardless, this provision was abandoned in the face of strong opposition from senior citizens groups.

In 1989, however, the government introduced measures to 'claw back' the OAS benefit from recipients with a net income of $51,765 ($62,144 in 2006) a year. Seniors have to pay back their OAS benefits at a rate of 15 cents for every dollar that net income exceeds $62,144. Seniors with net incomes of $100,914 or more get no OAS pension. This legislation marked the end of the long-standing principle of universality of the OAS. For a while, the clawback incomes ($62,144 and $100,914) were not fully indexed but were adjusted to the rate of inflation less than 3 percent. As a result, more and more Canadians faced the clawback each year. Since 2000, the clawback thresholds have been fully indexed to inflation. This clawback of benefits from the wealthy changed OAS from a demogrant benefit to a welfare benefit similar to the Guaranteed Income Supplement (GIS), explained next.[3]

The second tier of Canadian social security is the GIS. Technically, GIS is a part of the OAS system. It was introduced to the Canadian scheme in 1966 at the time of the inception of the Canada/Quebec Pension Plans (C/QPP, described below). When the C/QPP was introduced, there was a ten-year transition period before retirees could collect a full C/QPP retirement benefit. The GIS was added to OAS as a temporary measure to cover this ten-year transition, providing income-tested benefits for those with no or low C/QPP benefits. However, this 'temporary' add-on is still with us (it is, in fact, expanded) and remains an essential element of the government income security system.

When the GIS was introduced, it provided, in combination with the OAS pension, an income guarantee to single pensioners equal to about 25 percent of the average wage. A pensioner couple was guaranteed an income equal to about half of the average wage. In 1975, the Spouse's Allowance (SA) was added. It is payable to OAS/GIS pensioners' spouses as well as widows and widowers, aged 60–64 years, on an income-tested level. These households are thus guaranteed a minimum income equivalent to that of a GIS pensioner couple.

As of January 2006, the maximum monthly GIS single-person benefit was $593.97, or $7,127.64 a year (at a time when average annual earnings were about $35,000). For a single pensioner, the maximum GIS is reduced by $1 for each $2 of income (other than OAS). For a married couple with both spouses receiving the basic OAS pension, the maximum monthly supplement of each pensioner is reduced by $1 for every $4 of the combined monthly income (other than OAS). For a single pensioner, the GIS stops being paid when income reaches $34,368.

There is no asset test associated with the GIS, only an income test, which is based on the individual's income tax return from the previous year and is virtually automatic. Citizens do not appear to be stigmatized by the GIS income test. GIS benefits are indexed quarterly to inflation and paid out of general tax revenues; no contributions are required. GIS benefits are nontaxable, although those eligible for GIS would probably not pay much tax anyway. Nearly 80 percent of all single GIS recipients are women (National Council of Welfare 1996*a*: 7).

GIS benefit levels have been increased several times since its inception (over and above the automatic cost-of-living increases), and GIS is now a significant part of the retirement income security system in Canada. However, as income from the C/QPP and private pensions has grown, the proportion of seniors receiving GIS has fallen.

The third tier of retirement income benefits come from the C/QPP. These plans are virtually identical and the description of the CPP that follows will generally be true for the QPP as well, with differences noted.[4] Workers have full mobility of 'pension credits' and can move seamlessly between the two plans. The QPP has been somewhat more progressive than the CPP over the years, probably because the QPP is easier to amend. For example, the QPP introduced flexible retirement between ages 60 and 70 years (details follow) well before the CPP did.

The C/QPP, first introduced in 1966, are contributory, DB plans. Full benefits were first paid in 1976 (thus requiring only ten years of participation vs today's forty years). While their main benefit is retirement income (70% of cash flow), the plan also pays benefits for disability and death, plus children's, orphans', and survivors' benefits. With 9.9 percent contributions, the C/QPP have operating surpluses (discussed in more detail below).[5]

Contributions to the C/QPP total 9.9 percent of earnings between the year's basic exemption (YBE, equal to $3,500 constant) and the year's maximum pensionable earnings (YMPE, equal to $42,100 in 2006), which was originally meant to approximate the average wage and is indexed to the average wage. Contributions are a compulsory 9.9 percent and are shared equally by employers and employees; self-employed make the full contribution. In all cases, the C/QPP contributions receive a tax credit. That is, they are tax deductible but at a defined constant marginal income tax rate applied to all earners. In the CPP, anyone who is retired with CPP retirement benefits does not contribute even if they are earning income, which has not been the case for the QPP since 1998.

The retirement benefit equals 25 percent of a worker's career-average earnings, but with earnings credits indexed to the average wage (more details about this formula are given below). To get this benefit, a worker must have forty years of contributions to the C/QPP. Technically, the formula uses the best 85 percent of years of wages between ages 18 and 65 years.[6] Any years where no contributions are made—years of no labor-force participation or years of earnings below $3,500—are entered as 'zeros', until 40 years are credited. Years before 1966 are not counted, which affects only those now aged 58 years or older. For those who retire early, the formula uses 85 percent of age-of-retirement minus 18, which actually creates a slight subsidy and incentive for early retirement. Special 'dropout' years are allowed for years of disability and of child rearing that qualify so long as the years of earnings are ultimately not under ten.

The maximum C/QPP retirement benefit in 2006 was $844.58 per month, or a maximum of $10,135 a year, at a time when average annual earnings were about $35,000. Benefits, which are taxable income, are indexed to the cost-of-living, with annual increases. The benefit is paid as a joint-and-60 percent-survivor benefit. Benefits are paid to those eligible no matter where they reside. There is no income or asset test for the receipt of C/QPP benefits.

The full benefit is payable at age 65. However, the plans allow flexible retirement between ages 60 and 70 years. For both early and late retirement, there is a permanent adjustment in benefits equal to 0.5 percent per month. That is, someone retiring at age 60 years would get 70 percent of a full benefit, while someone retiring at age 70 years would get 130 percent. Years of earnings after age 65 years can be substituted for lower earnings years prior to age 65 years. Between ages 60 and 65 years, the 0.5 percent adjustment is close to being actuarially neutral, but after age 65 years, the 0.5 percent adjustment creates a disincentive to stay in the labor force. Retirement prior to age 65 years requires proof of no labor-force attachment at the time of application, though one can then return to the labor force with no loss of benefits.

Recent actuarial valuations of the CPP show that the plan is viable for a seventy-five-year time horizon. Because of less favorable demographics, including lower fertility and immigration, recent QPP actuarial valuations show that, while the QPP is healthy in the short term, there may be a need for future contribution rate increases or benefit decreases. The Y2004 administrative expense ratio for the CPP was 1.6 percent and for the QPP it was 1.2 percent (of one year's expenditures).

In total, these systems are highly progressive. For the very poor, income/replacement ratios at retirement exceed 200 percent. For someone consistently earning the average wage, the replacement ratio from government-sponsored systems totals about 40 percent. For the very well-to-do with large private savings or pensions, the only government-sponsored income they would receive is the C/QPP. C/QPP retirement benefits equal 25 percent of career-average earnings (indexed to wages) but stop at the average wage. As noted above, the maximum C/QPP retirement benefit in 2006 was $844.58 per month, or $10,135 a year. Thus, as one moves into higher-income brackets, these C/QPP retirement benefits produce ever lower replacement ratios. GIS and OAS income is also subject to clawback and OAS and C/QPP income is fully taxable when taken. Consequently, this means that there is a huge gap in retirement income security for wealthy Canadians that must be filled with private savings or employer-sponsored private pension plans.

In this regard, the government provides some strong tax incentives to save for retirement. Contributions to retirement savings vehicles are mostly tax deductible for the contributor (whether it is the worker or the employer). Investment income accrues tax free. However, when retirement income is taken, it is taxable in full. In other words, the Canadian retirement savings tax policy treats retirement savings like deferred income.

The limits placed on private saving for retirement have not increased as rapidly as inflation or wages and so are not as liberal as they were when first legislated. Canadians can save up to 18 percent of their wages, to a maximum of $18,000, if participating in a DC scheme or in an individual account (called a 'registered retirement savings plan'). These limits are on total contributions, worker plus employer. If a DB scheme is used, then the limits are stated as being an annual accrual no larger than 2 percent of wages, with a maximum benefit accrual of $2,000 per annum. The DC factors are thus nine times that of the DB factors, because, when the legislation was passed in the mid-1980s, an average annuity factor at age 65 years was approximately equal to 9, which made the two options virtually equivalent. The dollar limits above are now indexed to wage growth.

Why Did Social Security Reforms Take Place in 1996–7?

The economic and political climate in 1996 paved the way for reform. In the early 1990s, Canadian governments (both federal and provincial) were running deficits, with the federal deficit peaking in 1993 at $40 billion. By 1996–7, federal debt totaled $563 billion, up 50 percent since 1990, or 69 percent of the GDP. Thirty-five percent of federal revenue was being spent on interest on the debt, 36 percent of which was held in foreign hands (Brown 1999: 12). In addition, because both Britain and the USA had lowered personal income tax rates and corporate tax rates, there was pressure on the Canadian government to follow suit. At that time, Canada ranked first among the G-7 nations in terms of direct taxes on individuals (Canadian Institute of Actuaries 1995: 20). Thus, the federal

TABLE 9-1 Life Expectancy in Canada (1931–96)

Year	*At Birth*		*At Age 65*		*At Age 75*	
	Male	*Female*	*Male*	*Female*	*Male*	*Female*
1931	60.0	62.1	13.0	13.7	7.6	8.0
1951	66.3	70.8	13.3	15.0	7.9	8.7
1971	69.3	76.4	13.7	17.5	8.5	10.6
1996	75.4	81.2	16.0	19.9	9.7	12.4

Source: Statistics Canada Life Tables (several years).

government was under extreme pressure to decrease spending. One of the main methods of trimming the federal budget was to decrease the cash flow to, and cost sharing with, the provincial governments. This was particularly evident in health-care delivery (a provincial responsibility cost shared with the federal government).

The second reason for the 1996–7 reforms was the growing public concern about the aging of the Canadian population. In 1996 Canada was still a relatively young population, with only 1 person in 8 being aged 65 years or older. However, Canada had a very strong 'baby-boom/baby-bust' phenomenon. Because of the rapidly shifting demographics, the ratio of elderly dependents was forecast to rise to one in four by 2036 (Denton, Feaver, and Spencer 1996: 28–30). Overall, Canada was expected to have one of the fastest rising old-age dependency ratios in the period from 1996 to 2036 of any developed nation (Brown 1999: 10). At the same time, Canada was experiencing rapid increases in life expectancy, in common with most Western industrialized nations (see Table 9-1).

The government was concerned about the expected rise in costs of social security that this population ageing would create. In particular, the government presented expected costs for OAS/GIS in total, as shown in Table 9-2.

The final reasons for the timing of the reforms were actuarial in nature. The C/QPP were created in 1966. For the early cohorts of workers, contributions to the plans totaled 3.6 percent of contributory wages between the YBE and the YMPE, split equally between the employer and the employee

TABLE 9-2 Projected Net (After Taxes) Costs of OAS/GIS ($B)

1996	*2001*	*2011*	*2030*
20.8	24.7	34.4	77.3

Source: Government of Canada (1996*b*: 34).

TABLE 9-3 Long-Term Economic Assumptions

	1960s Environment	*1990s Environment*
Senior dependency ratio (aged 65/20–64)	0.33	0.40
Annual increase in real wages (%)	2	1
Real interest rate (%)	2	4
Cost of social security if PAYGO (%)	11.0	14.5
Cost of social security if fully funded (%)	16.5	7.2

(the self-employed paid the full 3.6%). This contribution rate schedule remained unchanged until the mid-1980s. Even with this low contribution rate, the C/QPP plans were able to build up reserve funds equal to two-years' expenditures. However, by the mid-1980s, the reserve funds were being depleted and were destined for exhaustion by 2016. Further, C/QPP actuarial reports indicated that contribution rates would have to rise to 14.2 percent of contributory wages if no changes were made to the plan (OSFI 1995). At first, the government reacted solely by making gradual ad hoc increases in the contribution rate. By 1997, the combined contribution rate was 6 percent, split between worker and employer.

A report from the Canadian Institute of Actuaries (1996), showing why PAYGO funding was no longer advantageous, proposed that the C/QPP move to 'smarter' funding. The report argued that both economic and demographic variables had changed since the implementation of the C/QPP in 1966. Table 9-3 contains data provided by the actuaries in support of a change in the funding philosophy.[7] The cost data are for a plan providing a 40 percent replacement rate for someone consistently earning the average wage (fully indexed) or the total of OAS plus C/QPP benefits.

Those familiar with the financing of social security systems will note that in the 1960s, the dependency ratio and the annual increase in real wages favored PAYGO funding with real interest rates at 2 percent per annum. However, by the 1990s, the shift in all three variables created a strong bias toward a more fully funded system.

1996–7 Reforms

Why the Seniors Benefit Failed

In its budget speech of March 6, 1996, the government announced the most fundamental amendments to social security in Canada since the introduction of the C/QPP in 1966. It proposed that in 2001 a new Seniors Benefit would replace OAS and GIS. The government said that this action was necessary to make this part of the social security system sustainable in the long term.

Under the proposed Seniors Benefit, those elderly receiving the GIS would receive $120 more per year. In fact, under the proposed amendments, 75 percent of seniors would have received the same or higher benefits; 16 percent would have received lower benefits; and 9 percent would have received no benefits at all (National Council of Welfare 1996*b*: 17). The new benefit would be nontaxable income and fully indexed to inflation.

The clawback of the Seniors Benefit would have been based on the combined income of spouses—as is the case for GIS. (In contrast, the OAS clawback is based on individual income.) The proposed benefit had two levels of clawback. As personal income rose from $0 to $12,520, the Seniors Benefit was to be reduced by 50 cents per dollar of such income. Then the clawback was zero until personal income reached the level of $25,921, at which point a new 20 percent clawback took hold. This system would have resulted in no benefit being paid once individual income reached $51,721 or family income reached $77,521 (vs $84,484 for an individual and $168,968 for a couple under the existing OAS/GIS system). All these levels would be indexed, in full, to inflation.

Under the proposed system, the federal government expected to see projected savings of $0.2 billion in 2001, $2.1 billion in 2011, and $8.2 billion in 2030 (which is 10.7% of the program cost) (Canada 1996*b*: 34). Voters reacted negatively, or at least apathetically, to what appeared to be very small- and very long-deferred savings in exchange for losing the extremely popular OAS/GIS system.

Analysts of the proposed system criticized the high marginal tax rates that resulted. If the marginal clawback and marginal income taxes were added together, then some seniors would lose 78 cents of every dollar of private income they had after age 65 years. It was argued that these rates would create a significant disincentive to save for retirement.[8]

Another flaw in the Seniors Benefit that led to its being abandoned was that the clawback was based on family income, not individual income, as under OAS. Thus, older women who had never participated in the paid labor force would no longer have any retirement income in their own right. They would lose that aspect of economic autonomy in their spousal relationship and in their community of women who have not been employed. This factor was an important one in the death of the Seniors Benefit proposal and a flaw that the government appeared to have underestimated.

The 1997 Reform of the Canada/Quebec Pension Plans (C/QPP)

On February 14, 1997, the minister of finance announced that the government had an agreement with the provinces to amend the CPP. Similar amendments were to be made to the QPP. In introducing the reforms to the Canadian public, the government used arguments of affordability and sustainability as their theme: 'The changes will ensure that the CPP is affordable to future generations and can be sustained in the face of an ageing population, increasing longevity, and the retirement of the baby boom generation' (Canada 1997: 6).

Reforming the CPP is not easy, and radical reforms are unlikely. Under the constitution of Canada, pensions are a provincial responsibility. Changes to the CPP can take place only with the support of two-thirds of the provinces with two-thirds of the total Canadian population (including Quebec).

The 1997 reforms to the C/QPP should be categorized as tweaks to the existing system as opposed to major reforms. In particular, the government made a point of stressing to Canadians that many important aspects of the CPP were not to be changed:

- All retired CPP pensioners or anyone older than 65 years as of December 31, 1997 would not be affected by the proposed changes. Anyone currently receiving CPP disability benefits, survivor benefits, or combined benefits would also not be affected.
- All benefits under the CPP would remain fully indexed to inflation.
- The ages of retirement—early, normal, or late—would remain unchanged.

However, several amendments were announced that decreased the benefits to be paid in the future (by about 9.3% in total), increased the level of funding, and increased the rate of return on any reserve funds.

The first change took place in the area of disability income benefits, enhancing differences between the CPP, and QPP. Between 1966 and 1986, disability income benefits paid by the CPP and the QPP had run very much in parallel. However, starting in 1986, CPP disability income benefits rose sharply relative to those paid by the QPP. In fact, the CPP actuary projected that if these benefits continued at their elevated level, the CPP would exhaust its reserve funds by 2016 (OSFI 1995). In 1985 disability benefits represented 13 percent of all CPP expenditures. By 1995, these benefits had grown to 19.7 percent of overall costs (OSFI 1995). This increase, by itself, would add 1.5 percentage points to the long-term costs of the CPP (Canada 1996*a*: 24).

No one should have been surprised by this increase, however, as the government had liberalized the requirements for these benefits on more than one occasion. In 1987 the length of contributory service required to qualify for disability benefits was shortened (the QPP rules were not changed). Also in 1987, the disability benefit was increased, making it equivalent to the QPP benefits. In 1992 the government lifted the time limit on late applications. This change opened the program to many workers who previously had been denied benefits. There was also a campaign to make workers and employers more aware of these changes and CPP disability benefits in general.

Another reason for the growing difference between the CPP and QPP in this benefit category was a change in the adjudication of disability. The CPP introduced some nonmedical factors, including an individual's ability to find work, but rescinded the inclusion of these factors in September 1995. The CPP also recognized several 'new' causes of disability not recognized by the QPP, such as stress, chronic fatigue, and environmental hypersensitivities; the QPP continued to use a more physical case-base for disability. In addition, in the past when workers had to have profound physical disabilities to qualify for the CPP benefits, there was little follow-up to reassess claims for continued disability. The auditor general estimated that this inaction was costing the CPP $65 million a year in overpayments (Ford 1996: 88). The CPP administration responded by implementing a program of reassessment in May 1993, which helped to decrease continuing disability claims.

The only actual legislated amendment to the CPP disability income benefits in the 1997 reforms was the increase of the contribution period for eligibility. Instead of requiring contributions in only two of the past three years, the amendment required contributions in four of the past six years. All other changes affected the adjudication guidelines. The change in the eligibility requirement and the more intense review of existing files have brought the CPP disability expenses back into balance with those experienced by the QPP.

Another change, designed to reduce benefits, was made in the method used to determine retirement pensions and other earnings-related benefits, such as survivor's benefits. Prior to the amendments, these benefits were determined based on the contributor's average career earnings updated to the average of the YMPE in the past three years before calculation. This formula was changed to the average of the YMPE in the past five years before calculation, a change that made the C/QPP more like the average pension in the private sector. More private-sector pensions base retirement benefits on a final five-year formula than on a final three-year formula.

The next benefit change was the value of the CPP death benefit. Before amendment, this benefit was equal to 6 months of retirement benefits, to a maximum of 10 percent of the YMPE. In 1997, the YMPE was $35,800, so the maximum death benefit then was $3,580. However, the 1997 reforms set a new maximum of $2,500, which does not adjust to inflation.

A more subtle change was made in the way contributions to the C/QPP are made. Before amendment, workers contributed only on wages between the YBE and the YMPE; the YBE was equal to 10 percent of the YMPE. In 1997 the YMPE was $35,800, so the YBE was $3,500 (rounded down). Under the reforms, the YBE was then frozen at $3,500. This adjustment is actually an important feature of the C/QPP (and somewhat ingenious), which makes the plans more progressive. Consider a worker who earns $30,000 in a given year. That worker contributes only on earnings between $3,500 and $30,000 (a maximum of $26,500). However, the worker earns benefits on the full $30,000 for that year. More importantly, someone who earns $3,600 contributes on a base of $100 (and the employer matches this small contribution), but accrues benefits on $3,600. For those earning less than $3,500, no benefit accrual occurs in that year. Over time, the progressiveness of the frozen YBE will erode due to inflation. It is highly doubtful, however, that more than a handful of Canadians ever understood or appreciated this reality. In addition, more Canadians now earn years of benefit accruals.

This amendment also made the C/QPP more like contributory private pension plans—the majority of private pension plans in Canada require employee contributions—since with private plans, workers contribute on all of their earnings.

It should be noted that while the official C/QPP contribution rate today is 9.9 percent, because of the YBE, no one actually contributes 9.9 percent of their entire C/QPP base earnings. To make a fair comparison to a private pension plan, this needs to be understood. With the 2006 YMPE being $42,100, maximum worker/employer contributions are $1,910.70. For a self-employed person, the maximum contribution is $3,821.40.

The 1997 CPP reforms also introduced an automatic stabilizing principle. The CPP is supposed to continue in existence, with the benefits described previously, financed by a 9.9 percent contribution rate. If the CPP actuary shows that the present benefits are not sustainable at the 9.9 percent contribution rate, then two things happen. First, the contribution rate moves half of the distance to the necessary long-term contribution rate as determined by the CPP actuary. At the same time, benefits are de-indexed to bring them slowly down in value until the new (slightly higher) contribution rate is in balance with the new (slightly lower) benefit structure. Thus, sustainability is guaranteed and is achieved by (equal) adjustments to both benefits and contributions.

The final amendment to the C/QPP was the rapid ramping up of contributions with a resultant rapid increase in the reserve funds. In the early existence of the C/QPP, the reserve funds held were equal to about two years' worth of total expenditures. Contribution rates were increased linearly to 9.9 percent in total by 2003 (from 6% in 1997). These extra contributions, over what would have been needed on a PAYGO basis, will create reserve funds equal to five years of expenditures. Stated another way, by 2017 CPP assets will equal 20 percent of its liabilities (i.e. it will be 20% funded).

Until 1997, the CPP reserve funds were lent to the provincial governments, who paid federal long-term bond rates on this debt. The new reserve funds are invested by the independent Canada Pension Plan Investment Board (CPPIB). As an aside, the QPP reserve funds had always been invested widely in private-sector assets by the Caisse de depot et placement du Quebec. The CPPIB can invest in a highly diversified portfolio with the objective of achieving higher rates of return than under the pre-reform provincial-bond arrangement. The CPPIB is subject to broadly the same investment rules as other pension funds in the private sector.

The Canada Pension Plan Investment Board

The CPPIB began operations in April 1998, with a mandate to invest in the best interests of CPP contributors and beneficiaries and to maximize long-term returns without undue risk of loss. The benchmark used to evaluate their investment outcomes is the achievement of real returns, after inflation, that exceed the return on a portfolio of government real-return bonds nine years out of ten.

By December 2005, the CPP portfolio had grown to $92.5 billion, and the CPPIB expects to be managing $200 billion by 2016. The rate of return in fiscal year 2004–5 was 8.5 percent, versus 17.6 percent the previous year. Over the five-year period, 2000–4 inclusive, the CPP reserve fund earned a real (inflation-adjusted) rate of return of 4.48 percent. The last CPP actuarial report shows that the CPP was more than solvent over a 75-year horizon assuming investment returns of 4.1 percent real, as one of more than a dozen variables.

As of December 31, 2005, 56.6 percent of the CPP assets were publicly traded stocks; 29.7 percent were government bonds (a legacy from the previous fund investments); 8.4 percent were real-return assets; 4.3 percent were private equity; and 1.0 percent were cash and money market securities. Going forward the CPPIB intends to diversify the portfolio more broadly by increasing the holdings in real estate, infrastructure, and other real-return assets.

Based on the latest CPP actuarial report (OSFI 2004), CPP contributions are expected to exceed benefits until 2022, providing a sixteen-year period before any portion of the investment income is needed to help pay CPP benefits.

The CPPIB and the government have worked very hard to guarantee that the CPPIB will remain independent from political pressure and to provide strong evidence of ethical governance. To date, the CPPIB has been well received by the public.

Conclusion

The C/QPP reforms of 1997 can be viewed as tweaks to the system as opposed to massive change. Most of the amendments were subtle and not fully understood by the average Canadian citizen. These reforms were made without apparent opposition, which is somewhat surprising given that contribution rates were raised from 6 to 9.9 percent over a short 6-year period.

The failure of the Seniors Benefit in 1996 and the causes of its demise are an interesting study. The failure was political, not actuarial. The government failed to understand how popular the OAS was and how emotional the response would be to proposed reforms given the very small- and long-deferred savings that were projected to result.

The Canadian social security system today provides Canadians with a high level of income security while leaving ample room for individual savings and investments (see Brown and Prus 2004). The reforms of 1997 have meant that the CPP now rests on a healthy foundation. Indeed, the latest CPP actuarial report shows that this system is sustainable for at least the next seventy-five years.[9] In summary, there seems to be wide acceptance of Canada's current social security system among Canadian voters.

Notes

[1] For an excellent summary of the 1996–7 reforms, see Belánd and Myles (2005).

[2] Unless otherwise indicated, monetary units are Canadian dollars.

[3] For information about the OAS, go to www.sdc.gc.ca/en/gateways/nav/top_nav/program/isp.shtml

[4] For information on the Canada Pension Plan, go to www.sdc.gc.ca/asp/gateway.asp?hr=en/isp/cpp/cpptoc.shtml&hs=cpr. For information on the Quebec Pension Plan, go to www.rrq.gouv.qc.ca/en/

[5] For full information on all of these benefits, go to http://www.sdc.gc.ca/en/isp/pub/factsheets/rates.shtml

[6] Note that 0.85(65-18) is 40 years.

[7] To read the CPP actuarial reports, go to www.osfi-bsif.gc.ca/osfi/index_e.aspx?DetailID=499. To read the QPP actuarial reports, go to www.rrq.gouv.qc.ca/en/programmes/regime_rentes/analyse_actuarielle_sommaire.htm

[8] For more information on the impact of clawbacks on labor force participation, retirement saving, and decisions to retire, see Baker (2002), Baker, Gruber, and Milligan (2003*a*, 2003*b*), Shillington (2003), Milligan (2005), and Mintz et al. (2005).

[9] The QPP is not as healthy because of higher dependency ratios expected in the future in that province.

References

Baker, M. (2002). 'The Retirement Behavior of Married Couples: Evidence from the Spouse's Allowance', *Journal of Human Resources*, 37(1): 1–34.

—— J. Gruber and K. Milligan (2003*a*). 'The Retirement Incentive Effects of Canada's Income Security Programs', *Canadian Journal of Economics*, 36(2): 261–90.

—— (2003*b*). 'Simulating the Response to Reform of Canada's Income Security System', NBER Working Paper 9455. Cambridge, MA: National Bureau of Economic Research.

Belánd, D. and J. Myles (2005). 'Stasis Amidst Change: Canadian Pension Reform in an Age of Retrenchment', in G. Bonoli and T. Shinkawa (eds.), *Ageing and Pension Reform Around the World: Evidence from Eleven Countries*. Chelthenam, UK: Edward Elgar.

Brown, R. L. (1999). *Economic Security for an Aging Canadian Population*, Society of Actuaries Monograph M-RS99–2.

—— and S. G. Prus (October 2004). 'Social Transfers and Income Inequality in Old Age: A Multinational Perspective', *North American Actuarial Journal*, 8(4).

Canada, Government of (February 1996*a*). *An Information Paper for Consultations on the Canada Pension Plan*. Ottawa: Department of Finance.

—— (March 1996*b*). *The Seniors Benefit: Securing the Future*. Ottawa: Department of Supply and Services.

—— (1997). *Securing the Canada Pension Plan: Agreement on Proposed Changes to the CPP*. Ottawa: Human Resources Development Canada.

Canadian Institute of Actuaries (1995). *Troubled Tomorrows: The Report of The Canadian Institute of Actuaries Task Force on Retirement Savings*. Ottawa.

—— (May 1996). *Report of the Task Force on the Future of Canada/Quebec Pension Plans*. Ottawa.

Denton, F. T., C. H. Feaver, and B. G. Spencer (June 1996). 'The Future Population of Canada and Its Age Distribution', IESOP Research Paper No. 3, Program for Research on the Independence and Economic Security of the Older Population. Hamilton, McMaster University.

Ford, D. A. (1996). 'Canada Pension Plan Disability' in *Experts' Forum on Canada Pension Plan Reform*, Caledon Institute of Social Policy, May 1, 1996. Ottawa: Renouf.

Milligan, K. (October 2005). 'Making it Pay to Work: Improving the Work Incentives in Canada's Public Pension System', *C. D. Howe Institute Commentary*, 218.

Mintz, J., D. Chen, Y. Guillemette, and F. Poschmann (September 2005). 'The 2005 Tax Competitiveness Report: Unleashing the Canadian Tiger', C. D. Howe Institute Commentary 216.

National Council of Welfare (1996*a*). *A Pension Primer*, Catalogue no. H68–23/1996E. Ottawa: Minister of Supply and Services.

National Council of Welfare (1996*b*). *A Guide to the Proposed Seniors Benefit.* Ottawa: Minister of Supply and Services.

Office of the Superintendent of Financial Institutions (OSFI) (1995). 'Canada Pension Plan: Fifteenth Actuarial Report as at December 31, 1993', Ottawa.

—— (2004). 'Canada Pension Plan: Twenty-First Actuarial Report as at December 31, 2003', Ottawa.

Shillington, R. (April 2003). 'New Poverty Traps: Means-Testing and Modest-Income Seniors', *C. D. Howe Institute Backgrounder,* 65.

Statistics Canada (several years). *Life Tables, Canada and the Provinces.* Ottawa: Ministry of Industry, Science and Technology.

Chapter 10

A Decade of Government-Mandated Privately Run Pensions in Mexico: What Have We Learned?

Tapen Sinha and Maria de los Angeles Yañez

In 1942 social security became compulsory in Mexico. Administered by the Instituto Mexicano del Seguro Social (IMSS) and known as Seguro de Invalidez, Vejez, Cesancía en Edad Avanzada y Muerte (IVCM, or Disability, Old Age, and Death Security), the program covered the following risks for all workers in the formal sector: accidents at work and sickness caused by work; maternity and sickness unrelated to work; life insurance and incapacity; and old-age pension (at the age of 60).

On July 1, 1997, a new privatized pension plan—called the Seguro de Retiro, Cesantía en Edad Avanzada y Vejez (RCV, or Retirement and Old Age Insurance)—took effect, replacing the old system for new entrants to the labor market. Also introduced was a separate component, the Seguros de Invalidez y Vida (IV, or Life and Disability Insurance). Under the new system, the old IVCM PAYGO system was abandoned. Workers entering the labor force after July 1, 1997 had to join the new plan (about one million workers enter the labor force every year). Workers who were already in the labor market can choose between the old and new plans at retirement.

The reforms were instituted with the purported purpose of rescuing the old system from fiscal unsustainability (IMSS 1995). The IMSS claimed that

We thank the Instituto Tecnológico Autónomo de México (ITAM) and the Asociación Mexicana de Cultura (AC) for their generous support of our research. Much of the information reported in this chapter come from the Comisión Nacional del Sistema de Ahorro para el Retiro (CONSAR), the government pension regulatory agency. We are grateful to them for sharing this information. Discussions with various colleagues were useful. In particular, conversations with Olivia Mitchell, Andras Uthoff, Estelle James, and Roberto Bonilla were illuminating, as were discussions with participants of various forums where some of these results were presented. In particular, participants of the conference organized by the Mexican Congress, the conference organized by the National Actuarial Association in Mexico (CONAC), and the conference of the Society of Actuaries made valuable comments. We thank Nancy Condon and Stephen J. Kay for meticulously editing this document and for making a series of very useful comments. However, we alone are responsible for the opinions expressed herein. These do not necessarily represent the views of the institutions with which we are affiliated.

by 2003 the system would produce deficits. Unfortunately, the assumptions behind the model used for these projections were never fully disclosed. This muddled and hurried reform has given birth to a new system in which many affiliates may end up with very little in their accounts, and the government may have to bail them out by paying the minimum pension. This chapter shows that the transition costs could be high, and that management fees have taken a big bite out of retirees' savings (about 20% of their benefits).

This chapter first provides a short description of the new system with special attention to the *cuota social*, or social quota, and the housing subaccount. It then discusses the coverage issue in the context of the government's claim that higher coverage would be an important advantage of the new system. It then looks at the market structure of the pension funds in Mexico and investment portfolios, and tackles the cost structure of running the funds, transition costs, and cost of the payout phase, noting the inequality between men and women in terms of the pension payout in the future. Finally, it reviews the conditions that will lead low-income affiliates to fall back on the minimum pension guaranteed by the reform.

Contribution Rates Under the Old and New Systems

Under the old system, total contributions were 8.5 percent of base salary, with a tripartite split among employers (5.95%), employees (2.125%), and the government (0.425%). There was an additional payment of 2 percent of base salary into the Sistema Para el Retiro (SAR, or the retirement account). The maximum included in the base salary was equal to ten times the minimum wage.

The IV has a premium of 2.5 percent of wage, of which the employer pays 1.75 percent, the worker pays 0.625 percent, and the government pays 0.125 percent. Since the 1997 reform, the government has contributed an additional amount independent of the wage of the person. Called the cuota social, this additional amount is set at 5.5 percent of the minimum salary in the Federal District of Mexico. For workers earning one minimum wage or less, the social quota is enormously important: it is equivalent to 90 percent of the minimum wage. Even for affiliates earning 3 times the minimum wage, the social quota still accounts for almost 30 percent of their total contribution to retirement savings under a publicly mandated but privately managed fund called an Administradora de Fondos de Retiro (AFORE). For affiliates earning 10 times the minimum wage, the social quota equals almost 9 percent of the contribution—a figure that actually understates the importance of the social quota because by law, no fee can be charged on its flow. However, it does not prevent funds from charging fees on the balance.

Subaccounts

Each affiliate must contribute to two principal subaccounts: the Sistema de Ahorro para el Retiro (SAR, or the Retirement Savings System) and the Instituto de Fondo Nacional de la Vivienda para los Trabajadores (INFONAVIT, or the government-run housing credit agency). Affiliates can also make voluntary contributions to SAR on top of their required contribution. During the period 2001–5, SAR received about 65 percent of total contributions, and the rest went to the housing subaccount. Policy-makers had hoped that workers would make substantial contributions to the voluntary account, given the tax break, but total contributions so far have been relatively small, less than half a percent of total contribution.

Coverage

Historically, most PAYGO pensions systems in industrialized countries have covered the vast majority of workers—but not in Mexico. When social security became compulsory in Mexico in 1942, it had very low rates of coverage of the labor force: in 1946, less than 3 percent. By 1952 coverage was still less than 5 percent, and in 1970 it was a little more than 25 percent. By the mid-1990s, the IVCM still covered only about 30 percent of workers (an additional 8% of the labor force was covered by special regimes for government employees). These figures stand in sharp contrast to coverage in more developed countries. In the USA, for example, social security coverage from 1935 to 1940 went from 0 to 63.7 percent, and by 1951, it was 93.7 percent.

When the new system was instituted in 1997, it started with less than 30 percent of the EAP—in the same range as the old IVCM. However, over the next 8 years the number of affiliates grew tremendously, both in absolute numbers and as a percentage of the labor force (see Table 10-1). By the end of 2006, 87 percent of the labor force was affiliated with AFOREs, a remarkable figure considering the slow progress of coverage over the previous 60 years.

Distribution of Unattached Accounts

A closer examination of the rapid growth of coverage reveals a different picture. For example, from 2000 to 2001, the number of affiliates rose from almost 18 million to more than 26.5 million, a steep rise. Table 10-2 contains monthly data from December 2000 to December 2001. During most months in this period, the number of affiliates did not rise more than 2.5 percent—with one stark exception. In the month of June 2001 the number of affiliates rose a whopping 35 percent.

TABLE 10-1 Affiliation and the Labor Force

End year	*Affiliates*	*EAP*[a]	*Affiliates/EAP*[a] *(%)*
1997	11,188,144	38,584,394	29
1998	13,827,674	39,562,404	35
1999	15,594,503	39,648,333	39
2000	17,844,956	40,161,543	44
2001	26,518,534	40,072,856	66
2002	29,421,202	41,085,736	72
2003	31,398,282	41,515,672	76
2004	33,316,492	43,398,755	77
2005	35,276,277	41,880,800	84
2006	37,408,828	42,846,100	87

Sources: CONSAR and INEGI.

[a] EAP is an abbreviation for economically active population.

To see why, we have to go back to the regulatory changes that took place in 1997, when the government allowed each worker to choose his or her own AFORE. Many workers made no selection, so their accounts were put into a separate 'concentrated account' (*cuenta concentradora*), administered by the Banco de Mexico (Mexican Central Bank). In June 2001, the Bank announced that it would transfer these concentrated accounts to the AFOREs by the end of the month. The Comisión Nacional del Sistema de Ahorro para el Retiro (CONSAR) devised a formula for distributing these accounts to the 25 percent least expensive AFOREs. Congress

TABLE 10-2 Monthly Rise in Affiliates (12/00–12/01)

Month	*Affiliates*	*Growth (%)*
December 2000	17,844,956	1.28
January 2001	18,018,358	0.97
February 2001	18,221,289	1.13
March 2001	18,444,190	1.22
April 2001	18,657,474	1.16
May 2001	18,865,906	1.12
June 2001	25,555,664	35.46
July 2001	25,665,592	0.43
August 2001	26,297,659	2.46
September 2001	26,353,396	0.21
October 2001	26,417,113	0.24
November 2001	26,471,301	0.21
December 2001	26,518,534	0.18

Sources: CONSAR and IMSS.

modified this formula in March 2007, stipulating that the assignment must take into account not just the management fees but also the AFOREs' rates of return.

From 2002 to 2004, more than one-and-a-half million accounts were distributed to the lowest cost AFOREs; during 2005 to 2006, another million and a half accounts were distributed. Did these accounts have anything in common? Most of them, as it turned out, had small balances along with low density of contributions. Contributions to them had been sporadic, because workers had either been working temporary jobs or switching back and forth between the formal and informal sectors. Theoretically, each person should have just one account, but evidence exists that several million workers have more than one. Consequently, the number of accounts does not necessarily correspond to the number of affiliates.

CONSAR's tabulations also reveal that these accounts have had low density of contributions. Specifically, more than 85 percent of the assigned affiliates have contributed less than 50 percent of the time. Given such infrequency, these workers will never have enough money to retire.[1]

A closer study of these assigned accounts also reveals that the affiliates are not necessarily receiving the lowest cost funds. The formula that CONSAR devised to allocate affiliates ranked all funds according to their charges for one year. However, the calculations do not account for the fact that companies with the lowest charge for a year do not necessarily have the lowest charges over longer periods—charges over a period of twenty-five years might show a very different picture. For example, as Table 10-16 shows, Inbursa had the lowest equivalent charges on balance over one year as of December 2006. However, if the period of affiliation goes up to twenty-five years, the equivalent charge on the balance would make Inbursa one of the more costly AFOREs. Given that affiliates tend to stick to default options, these assignments can have important ramifications, even when affiliates have the option to change their funds.

Affiliate Contributions

In addition to coverage, it is important for a pension system to achieve regular contributions by affiliates—an area where we see a divergence between the number of affiliates and the number of contributors (see Table 10-3). Soon after the 1997 reform, more than 60 percent of affiliates contributed regularly to the system. However, this proportion has since fallen to less than 40 percent. The number of regular contributors has stayed stubbornly under fourteen million while the number of affiliates by the end of 2006 soared to over thirty-seven million, compared to the twelve million in the old system in 1996. This sharp rise in the number of affiliates contrasts with

TABLE 10-3 Affiliates versus Contributors (1997–2006)

	Contributors (C)	*Affiliates (A)*	*Ratio of C over A (%)*
1997	7,769	11,188	69.0
1998	879,979	13,827,674	64.0
1999	948,855	15,594,503	61.0
2000	10,379,823	17,844,956	58.0
2001	11,864,672	26,518,534	45.0
2002	12,292,152	29,421,202	42.0
2003	12,660,999	31,398,282	40.3
2004	13,042,997	33,316,492	39.1
2005	13,557,086	35,276,277	38.4
2006	13,919,377	37,408,828	37.2

Sources: CONSAR and AMAFORE (Association of AFOREs).

the number of people contributing to the system. Specifically, the labor force rose by over four million while contributors rose by two million, an indicator that the informal sector is employing more people than is the formal sector.

Table 10-4 shows that not all AFORE affiliates contribute at the same rate. For example, Principal is one of the largest AFOREs in terms of affiliates, with more than 3.3 million affiliates at the end of 2006. However, only 23.4 percent of its affiliates contribute, compared to 40.7 percent of Banamex affiliates. Some AFOREs that started operations in 2006—such as Coppel and Scotia—initially showed contribution rates of 100 percent. However, these high rates were expected to diminish substantially over time.

Distribution of Funds

Table 10-5 provides the market share for each AFORE in terms of funds rather than the number of affiliates or contributors for that year. Banamex and Bancomer emerged as the largest AFOREs in 1997 and continue to dominate the market.

Table 10-6 shows how much money each affiliate had on average in each AFORE in December 2006. To allow comparison across countries, the figures are expressed in US dollars. The large funds—Bancomer, Banamex, Inbursa, ING, and Profuturo—have the largest balances on average per affiliate. Large AFOREs seem to contain a larger proportion of affiliates contributing regularly, suggesting that bigger funds have managed to attract clients with more consistent employment. Newer funds are also showing large balances, which will decline over time as their proportion of contributors fall.

TABLE 10-4 Affiliates versus Contributors (2006)

AFORE	*Total Registered*	*% of Contributing*
Actinver	1,248,442	35.2
Afirme Bajío	422,615	55.2
Ahorra Ahora	155,942	65.8
Argos[a]	No account yet	n/a
Azteca	1,270,951	41.3
Banamex	5,596,232	40.7
Bancomer	4,255,568	41.4
Banorte Generali	3,282,539	37.9
Coppel	203,834	62.5
De la Gente[b]	21	100.0
HSBC	1,767,775	41.7
Inbursa	3,630,280	37.4
ING	2,314,651	30.3
Invercap	833,415	57.7
Ixe	184,673	36.5
Metlife	112,833	88.7
Principal	3,326,545	23.4
Profuturo GNP	3,403,090	40.3
Santander	2,996,067	31.9
Scotia[c]	673	100.0
XXI	2,402,682	20.8
Total	37,408,828	36.8

Sources: Various.
Note: Figures are for December 31, 2006.
[a] Argos started operations on December 7, 2006.
[b] De la Gente started operations on November 15, 2006.
[c] Scotia started operations on November 1, 2006.

Examining all AFOREs that existed at the end of 2006 in terms of contributors rather than affiliates reveals that the average balance per contributor is US$4,625,[2] compared to US$1,721 for an average account balance for all affiliates. This nearly threefold increase in balances is not surprising given that there are almost three times as many affiliates as contributors (as shown in Table 10-3).

Number of Companies

The number of pension fund firms has fluctuated over the past decade. Out of the initial forty-four applicants, seventeen started operating when the system was inaugurated in July 1997; fifteen were operating in 2005. Five new funds have been given permission to operate during 2006: Coppel, de

TABLE 10-5 Market Share for Each AFORE (in %) (2001–6)

AFORE	*2001*	*2002*	*2003*	*2004*	*2005*	*2006*
Actinver	0	0	0	0	1	3
Afirme Bajío	—	—	—	—	—	1
Ahorra Ahora	—	—	—	—	—	0
Allianz Dresdner	4	4	3	0	0	0
Argos	—	—	—	—	—	0
Azteca	0	0	0	1	1	3
Banamex Aegon	15	24	23	22	21	15
Bancomer	22	22	21	20	20	11
Banorte Generali	6	6	6	7	7	9
Coppel	—	—	—	—	—	1
De la Gente	—	—	—	—	—	0
HSBC	0	0	0	4	4	5
Garante	9	0	0	0	0	0
Inbursa	7	7	7	8	9	10
ING	9	9	9	10	9	6
INVERCAP	0	0	0	0	0	2
IXE	0	0	0	0	0	0
METLIFE	0	0	0	0	0	0
Principal	2	3	4	4	5	9
Profuturo GNP	10	10	10	10	10	9
Santander Mexicano	9	9	9	8	8	8
Scotia	—	—	—	—	—	0
Tepeyac	1	1	0	0	0	0
XXI	6	6	7	6	6	6
Zurich	1	0	0	0	0	0
Total	100	100	100	100	100	100

Source: CONSAR.

Note: A figure of 0% may mean that the AFORE did not exist for that particular year.

la Gente, Ahorra Ahora, Scotia, and Argos. The total number of AFOREs is now twenty-one. At the end of 2005 Metlife was given permission to operate.

Originally, each AFORE was allowed to have only one investment portfolio (known as a Sociedad de Inversion en Fondos de Retiro, or SIEFORE) (see Table 10-7). Starting in 1999, AFOREs could offer funds for voluntary contributions (with tax breaks added in 2003). The larger companies Banamex, Bancomer, and Profuturo were the first to do so. Then in 2004 AFOREs were allowed a second SIEFORE, and investment funds followed suit. Basic SIEFORE 2 has a less restrictive investment regime than does Basic SIEFORE 1. While each fund can invest in stocks and foreign debt instruments, they cannot do so directly. Rather, they must invest using derivative instruments (or structured notes) as long as the principal is

TABLE 10-6 Balance in Each Fund (2006)

Fund	*Amount (thousands of US$)*	*Affiliates*	*$ per Affiliate*
Actinver	797,936	1,248,442	639
Afirme Bajío	150,086	422,615	355
Ahorra Ahora	7,000	155,942	45
Argos	—	—	
Azteca	1,364,866	1,270,951	1,074
Banamex	11,970,446	5,596,232	2,139
Bancomer	10,923,333	4,255,568	2,567
Banorte Generali	4,484,208	3,282,539	1,366
Coppel	48,532	203,834	238
De la Gente	331	21	15,762
HSBC	2,628,937	1,767,775	1,487
Inbursa	7,682,668	3,630,280	2,116
ING	4,589,110	2,314,651	1,983
Invercap	826,684	833,415	992
Ixe	240,327	184,673	1,301
Metlife	974,294	112,833	8,635
Principal	2,854,169	3,326,545	858
Profuturo GNP	6,758,434	3,403,090	1,986
Santander	4,240,470	2,996,067	1,415
Scotia	7,704	673	11,448
XXI	3,824,206	2,402,682	1,592
Total	64,373,740	37,408,828	1,721

Source: CONSAR.

Notes: The table does not include INFONAVIT funds. Rate of exchange is 11.1MXP per US dollar.

TABLE 10-7 Types of Funds at the End of Each Year

Year Year	*Basic SIEFORE 1*	*Voluntary SIEFOREs*	*Basic SIEFORE 2*
1998	17	n/a	n/a
1999	14	3	n/a
2000	13	3	n/a
2001	13	3	n/a
2002	11	3	n/a
2003	12	3	n/a
2004	13	3	13
2005	15	3	15
2006	17	6	17

Source: CONSAR.

TABLE 10-8 Evolution of Market Share of Number of Affiliates (%) (1997–2000)

Fund	*02/1997*	*07/1997*	*12/1997*	*12/1998*	*06/1999*	*06/2000*
Atlantico	0.00	1.38	1.77	1.03	*	*
Banamex	31.31	16.12	12.23	11.34	11.65	12.24
Bancomer	28.28	22.23	16.76	16.10	15.85	16.06
Bancrecer	0.06	4.07	4.67	4.39	4.22	3.90
Bital	4.00	9.84	9.20	9.44	9.92	10.20
Capitaliza	0.00	0.07	*	*	*	*
Garante	0.78	8.32	10.96	11.09	11.00	10.83
Genesis	0.04	0.67	1.06	*	*	*
Inbursa	0.49	2.62	2.63	2.68	2.58	2.36
Previnter	0.04	2.07	2.33	*	*	*
Principal	0.00	0.48	0.61	2.18	2.89	2.88
Profuturo	16.03	11.79	12.55	13.96	13.57	12.62
Santander	13.99	12.46	14.73	14.24	13.79	13.99
SBN[a]	4.99	4.89	6.76	8.61	8.49	8.82
Tepeyac	0.00	0.52	0.85	1.02	1.42	1.69
XXI	0.00	2.22	2.71	3.06	3.09	3.14
Zurich	0.00	0.25	0.18	0.86	1.24	1.27
Total	100.00	100.00	100.00	100.00	100.00	100.00

Source: CONSAR.

Note: An asterisk (*) indicates that the fund ceased to exist independently.

[a] SBN = Solida Banorte Generali.

protected. (Very few AFOREs have used this instrument.) In addition, only workers who are younger than 55 years can participate in them.

Table 10-8 shows the evolution of market share in the first four years of the operation of the new privatized pension system. (Some funds, like Atlantico, Genesis, Previnter, Tepeyac, and Zurich, never captured significant market share and folded.) In an effort to ensure a competitive market, CONSAR stipulated that the market share of any AFORE could not exceed 17 percent of affiliates. However, using headcounts rather than portfolio value is a misguided way to enforce competition, given the wide range in account balances. For example, Bancomer had 21.7 percent of total affiliates, thus temporarily exceeding the market share limit imposed by CONSAR. Table 10-9 shows that the top 4 firms had nearly 54 percent of the market in 2002, but by December 2006 their share had fallen somewhat to 45.60 percent.

Distribution of Contributors

It is critical to know the distribution of the contributors in terms of salary levels because ultimately what retirees will receive depends on what they

TABLE 10-9 Evolution of Market Share (%) (2002–6)

AFORE	*2002*	*2003*	*2004*	*2005*	*2006*
Actinver	*	1.24	2.21	2.51	3.4
Afirme Bajío	*	*	*	*	1.1
Allianz	4.28	3.92	*	*	*
Ahorra Ahora	*	*	*	*	0.4
Argos	*	*	*	*	*
Azteca	*	1.42	2.47	2.84	3.4
Banamex	17.91	17.87	17.48	16.93	15.1
Bancomer	14.8	13.79	12.98	12.67	11.5
Banorte	8.87	8.87	8.71	8.67	8.8
HSBC	*	*	4.3	4.66	4.8
Garante	*	*	*	*	*
Coppel	*	*	*	*	0.5
De la Gente	*	*	*	*	0.0
Inbursa	6.57	6.76	7.54	8.07	9.8
ING	9.21	8.57	7.88	7.4	6.2
Invercap	*	*	*	0.36	2.2
IXE	*	*	0.49	0.54	0.5
MetLife	*	*	*	0.04	0.3
Principal	7.47	10.22	9.69	9.63	9.0
Profuturo GNP	9.95	9.95	10.09	10.06	9.2
Santander	11	10.33	9.53	9.06	8.1
Scotia	*	*	*	*	0.0
Tepeyac	3.2	*	*	*	*
XXI	6.74	7.07	6.64	6.57	6.5
Zurich	*	*	*	*	*
Top 4	53.66	52.21	50.63	48.72	45.60

Source: CONSAR.

Notes: For each year during 2001–6, percentages are measured at the end of December. An asterisk (*) indicates that the fund does not exist independently. The potential market estimated by CONSAR as of December 2006 is US$36,097,411.

contribute. Table 10-10 shows that in 2005 nearly 33 percent of contributors earned less than 2 times the minimum salary, and almost 55 percent earned less than 3 times the minimum salary. At 5.5 percent of the minimum salary, the government contribution for the majority of contributors is therefore significant.

AFORE Transfers

Table 10-11 shows the transfers that have occurred each year as a percentage of the number of affiliates. In 1998 only 0.03 percent of affiliates

TABLE 10-10 Distribution of Contributors by Salary Level (2005)

Salary	*Contributors*	*Percentage*
0 to 1	153,674	1.20
1 to 2	4,179,468	32.67
2 to 3	2,820,322	22.05
3 to 4	1,592,271	12.45
4 to 5	999,463	7.81
5 to 6	700,488	5.48
6 to 7	443,700	3.47
7 to 8	362,324	2.83
8 to 9	254,860	1.99
9 to 10	183,627	1.44
10 to 11	145,153	1.13
11 to 12	125,036	0.98
13 or more	832,295	6.51
Total	12,792,681	100.00

Source: IMSS.
Note: Salary is expressed in multiples of minimum salary.

transferred, but by 2006 a substantial 9.15 percent had. If we calculate the transfers as a percentage of contributors, nearly one in four contributors have transferred from one AFORE to another. The number of transfers is gaining momentum now that the process has since been simplified and the penalty for moving from one fund to another has been reduced to a minimum.

TABLE 10-11 Transfers as a Percentage of Affiliates (1998–2006)

Year	*Transfers*	*Affiliates*	*Percentage of Affiliates Transferred*	*Contributors*	*Percentage of Contributors Transferred*
1998	3,535	13,827,674	0.03	879,979	0.40
1999	44,038	15,594,503	0.28	948,855	4.64
2000	91,653	17,844,956	0.51	10,379,823	0.88
2001	106,220	26,518,534	0.40	11,864,672	0.90
2002	120,089	29,421,202	0.41	12,292,152	0.98
2003	420,791	31,398,282	1.34	12,577,265	3.35
2004	1,199,293	33,316,492	3.60	12,751,029	9.41
2005	2,819,444	35,276,277	7.99	13,557,086	20.80
2006	3,423,554	37,408,828	9.15	13,919,377	24.60

Source: CONSAR.

TABLE 10-12 Pension Funds in 2001

AFORE	*SIEFORE*	*Value*	*Share*
Allianz Dresdner	Allianz Dresdner I-1	8,930.9	3.6
Banamex Aegon	Banamex No. 1	36,997.0	14.9
Bancomer	Bancomer Real	53,843.8	21.7
Banorte Generali	Fondo Sólida Banorte Generali	14,092.1	5.7
Garante	Garante 1	21,598.9	8.7
Inbursa	Inbursa	18,327.4	7.4
ING	ING	21,430.1	8.6
Principal	Principal	6,081.3	2.5
Profuturo GNP	Fondo Profuturo	23,648.6	9.5
Santander Mexicano	Ahorro Santander Mexicano	22,605.5	9.1
Tepeyac	Tepeyac	2,825.9	1.1
XXI	XXI	15,472.0	6.2
Zurich	Zurich	2,322.5	0.9
Total		248,176.1	100.0

Source: Notisar (2001). (Notisar was a precursor of CONSAR.)

Where are affiliates moving? A report by CONSAR suggests that over 80 percent are moving to cheaper AFOREs in terms of fees, and nearly 20 percent are moving in the opposite direction. There are two possible reasons why an affiliate might go to a more expensive fund. First, the costlier funds might be offering higher returns. Second, they may be offering better service. Of course, there may be a third reason: the expensive funds may be marketing their AFOREs more successfully.

Portfolios of AFOREs

When AFOREs first formed, they were allowed to have one SIEFORE each, and they had to have most of their investments in short-term government bonds. However, over the past eight years, the investment regimen has been relaxed. Table 10-12 shows the market share of each fund in 2001. As noted earlier, the market share according to the value of each AFORE does not correspond to the market share according to the number of affiliates. For example, while Bancomer had less than 13 percent of the affiliates, it controlled 21 percent of the market with respect to investments.

Table 10-13, which shows the investment profile for each AFORE in 2006, reveals that over 75 percent of all investment was in government bonds, largely in an indexed, short-term bond called Bonde 91. Private-bond investment was 8 percent of the total, lower than what was actually allowed by law, even though private bonds had much higher rates of return. The reason private-bond investment is low is because investment was only

TABLE 10-13 Investment Profile (2006)

AFORE	*SIEFORE*	*Value*	*Share*	*Govt.*	*Private*	*Bank*	*Others*[a]
Actinver	Actinver 1	2,381.3	3.32	94.3	0.7	1.5	3.5
Afirme Bajío	Afirme Bajío Siefore Básica 1	502.3	0.70	87.2	—	3.3	9.5
Ahorra Ahora	Ahorra Ahora 1	109.4	0.15	96.7	—	—	3.3
Argos	Argos 1	9.5	0.01	100.0	—	—	—
Azteca	Azteca Básica 1	2,397.2	3.34	84.5	5.5	2.1	7.9
Banamex	Banamex Básica 1	8,105.8	11.29	76.7	4.9	4.9	13.5
Bancomer	Bancomer Protege	10,175.7	14.17	76.9	12.8	3.3	7.1
Banorte Generali	Fondo Sólida Banorte Generali Uno	4,051.7	5.64	67.0	10.8	11.5	10.8
Coppel	Coppel Básica 1	147.6	0.21	74.8	9.3	9.2	6.6
De la Gente	De la Gente Básica 1	22.7	0.03	93.2	—	—	6.8
HSBC	HSBC-B1	3,025.5	4.21	85.3	7.6	3.8	3.3
Inbursa	Inbursa Básica	11,218.1	15.62	88.7	4.5	1.9	4.8
ING	ING Básica 1	4,493.0	6.26	70.0	8.5	9.0	12.5
Invercap	Invercap	1,143.3	1.59	34.4	22.3	22.5	20.7
Ixe	Ixe 1	462.5	0.64	93.0	—	4.5	2.5
Metlife	Metlife Met1	627.3	0.87	67.9	8.0	12.8	11.3
Principal	Principal 1	7,120.3	9.91	75.7	8.2	5.6	10.5
Profuturo GNP	Fondo Profuturo1	4,927.9	6.86	51.8	12.3	12.7	23.2
Santander	Ahorro Santander Básica 1	3,961.9	5.52	74.7	8.0	4.6	12.7
Scotia	Scotia Siefore Básica 1	23.6	0.03	91.0	—	6.0	3.1
XXI	XXI SB1	6,918.9	9.63	65.7	8.3	14.4	11.7
Total	—	71,825.4	100.00	75.3	8.1	6.4	10.2

Source: CONSAR.

[a] Includes government papers and instruments issued by states, municipalities, and government-related companies, as well as international papers.

possible in mxAAA- or better-rated private bonds, which are in short supply.

Thus, by 2006, AFOREs had reduced their holdings of government bonds from 88 to 75 percent, a proportion similar to that in El Salvador and Uruguay but much larger than in Argentina, Bolivia, and Chile.

TABLE 10-14a Accumulated Funds in AFOREs (2006)

AFORE	*Obligatory*	*Voluntary*	*Voluntary/ Obligatory (%)*
Actinver	4,648.3	29.6	0.64
Afirme Bajío	6.2	0.1	0.80
Azteca	8,637.2	6.4	0.07
Banamex	114,721.9	462.1	0.40
Bancomer	109,159.7	499.5	0.46
Banorte Generali	38,274.7	114.3	0.30
HSBC	24,973.5	18.3	0.07
Inbursa	61,171.6	201.8	0.33
ING	47,154.0	81.2	0.17
Invercap	1,798.3	0.9	0.05
IXE	1,206.9	4.0	0.33
Metlife	4,206.0	8.3	0.20
Principal	26,369.4	18.2	0.07
Profuturo GNP	57,462.8	169.6	0.30
Santander Mexicano	42,467.9	72.5	0.17
XXI	34,750.3	309.8	0.89
Total	577,008.7	1,996.5	0.35

Source: CONSAR.

Notes: Figures are in thousands of pesos. Includes only retirement funds.

Voluntary Contributions

Since 2003 affiliates have been able to invest in one of two voluntary funds. They can invest beyond the 6.5 percent of salary stipulated by law in the AFORE accounts that they already have or in a separate voluntary account (discussed above). Tables 10-14a and 10.14b examine additional voluntary contributions in the existing obligatory accounts. For the system as a whole, the voluntary contribution is very small: only 0.3 percent of total contribution comes as voluntary contributions.

What are the benefits of the separate voluntary fund? Because contributions are tax-deductible up to a limit, this segment was created to encourage workers to save more for retirement. Under current law workers can withdraw the funds after 6 months with a penalty of 20 percent tax payment, which means that individuals with a higher than 20 percent marginal tax rate can use this fund to reduce their tax burden.

Cost of the New System

There are different ways to examine the new system's costs:

1. At the basic level are the commissions charged by AFOREs.

TABLE 10-14b Investment Regimes of Voluntary Accounts (2006)

Fund	*Value*	*Percentage*	*Government Bonds*	*Financial Institutions*
Actinver 3	57.5	8.96	93.1	—
Banamex de Aportaciones Voluntarias	198.2	30.92	100.0	—
Banamex de Aportaciones Voluntarias Plus	0.7	0.10	100.0	—
Ahorro Individual Bancomer	235.5	36.72	100.0	—
ING AV3	23.0	3.59	92.6	6.0
Metlife Met3	30.4	4.74	100.0	—
Fondo Profuturo 2	93.9	14.65	89.0	0.4
Fondo Profuturo 3	2.1	0.32	100.0	—
Total	641.2	100.00	97.5	0.3

Source: CONSAR.

Notes: Figures are in millions of pesos. Investment portfolios are expressed as a percentage of total.

2. At the macro level is the cost of transitioning from the old to the new. The introduction of the new system means that those now receiving benefits under the old system will not be contributing. Consequently, substantial resources must be allocated to these retirees.
3. The new system also promises a floor plan. Those who would not have enough in their account under the new system will receive a minimum guaranteed pension.

Commissions

Commissions can be assessed over the flow of funds, on account balances, and over the rate of return. In 1997 most funds charged commissions on flow. Some funds charged on both the flow of funds and account balance. Inbursa charged only on the real rate of return, not charging anything if the real rate was negative. However, in 2000 Inbursa changed its commission structure. As the current structure stands, the commissions are not constant over time; they vary with the number of years an affiliate stays in the fund. AFOREs offer a discount for loyalty, which can accumulate for 25 years or more, depending on the fund.

Because charges are assessed differently from AFORE to AFORE, it is not easy to compare charges. Table 10-15 illustrates the charges as advertised by each fund. In 2006 each AFORE charged on flow (contribution) and, in most cases, on the balance as well. Principal, for example, charged 1.6 percent of wages and an additional 0.35 percent on the account balance.

TABLE 10-15 Commission Structure (2006)

AFORE	*Commission on Contribution*	*Commission on Balance*
Actinver	1.02	0.20
Afirme Bajío	0.62	0.24
Ahorra Ahora	0.90	0.20
Argos	1.07	0.33
Azteca	0.90	0.40
Banamex	0.75	1.48
Bancomer	1.20	0.50
Banorte Generali	1.25	0.40
Coppel	0.92	0.30
De la Gente	0.90	0.31
HSBC	1.40	0.40
Inbursa	0.50	0.50
ING	1.32	0.30
Invercap	1.03	0.20
IXE	1.10	0.33
Metlife	1.23	0.25
Principal	1.60	0.35
Profuturo GNP	1.64	0.50
Santander	1.28	0.50
Scotia	1.22	0.26
XXI	1.30	0.20

Source: CONSAR.

Note: Charges are expressed as a percentage of income in the case of contribution and on the balance in the last column.

For each additional year, an affiliate stays with Principal, these charges are reduced. With such a fee structure, it is clearly no easy task to compare the charges across AFOREs, although some direct comparison is possible.

In general, commission charges on balances increase over time as affiliates accumulate more wealth. For example, XXI charges lower commissions than does Profuturo on both contributions and balances. Thus, we can clearly rank XXI above Profuturo in terms of commissions. Using the same criterion, we can rank Actinver over XXI. However, given the variable discount structures of fees, any comparison must be specific to scenarios that depend on many factors, including initial balance, base wage, wage growth rate, interest rates over time, and inflation rate. Sinha, Martinez, and Barrios (1999) performed such a comparison using different scenarios in Mexico. However, because the number of AFOREs has changed over time, such calculations are moving targets.

To get an idea how much an affiliate pays in commissions, consider the following simple example. Suppose that a person earns the average wage (around 3 times the legal minimum wage in Mexico) and pays the 6.5 percent contribution to his or her retirement fund. Banamex would charge 1.68 percent of salary. Therefore, as a percentage of contribution, the charges would amount to 25.85 percent (1.68/6.5). However, it would be wrong to assign 25.85 percent as charges because there is the social quota—5.5 percent of minimum wage—that must also be considered. For this worker, who earns three times the minimum wage, the social quota would amount to 1.83 percent (5.5/3) of salary. This person's actual contribution is 6.5% + 1.83% = 8.33%. By law, charges do not apply to the social quota, so the actual charges amount to 20.17 percent (1.68/8.33) of the flow. Further complicating the picture is the discount AFOREs give depending on the number of years a worker stays with a fund, which means that this charge would fall over time. Flores (2004) devised a crude calculation showing that commissions as a fraction of contributions averaged around 19 percent during 1999–2004.

CONSAR provides information from each AFORE on how much they will charge in the form of an equivalent to a percentage of salary (but not as a percentage of contribution). Table 10-16 shows that, for some AFOREs, equivalent commissions rise over time. Others, like Banamex, fall over time because they charge only on flow, and this amount decreases as an affiliate stays with Banamex. The complexity of the charges makes a simple rule of thumb useless. Consider the following example. For Actinver, the commission equivalent first falls and then rises. For Profuturo, on the other hand, the commission equivalent keeps rising as a percentage of base salary. However, it is impossible to guess such outcomes simply by examining the fees structures.

In 2004 CONSAR emphasized how charges are falling over time, advertising it as a triumph of free market competition (Budebo 2004). For example, Pineda (2005) quotes Budebo, saying that this dramatic fall can be ascribed both to more competition among AFOREs and to the regulatory change that has allowed easier movement from AFORE to AFORE. The claim behind CONSAR's reports of falling charges is flawed for several reasons. First, the average charges reported are not for the date on which it is reported. Specifically, charges reported in Figure 10-1 for January 2002 do not apply during January 2002. Rather, they are the average charges that would apply (expressed as an equivalent of charges on the balance) if the affiliate were to stay with the same AFORE for the next 25 years. Thus, a new entrant to the system in January 2002 would pay much more than Figure 10-1 reports.

Second, as the law stood in January 2002, jumping from one AFORE to another meant that an affiliate would lose the discount for staying with the

TABLE 10-16 Commission Equivalent as a Percentage of Base Salary (2006)

Fund	*1 Year*	*5 Years*	*10 Years*	*20 Years*	*25 Years*
Actinver	0.94	0.95	0.94	0.99	1.05
Afirme Bajío	0.73	0.76	0.80	0.91	0.96
Ahorra Ahora	0.95	0.93	0.92	0.97	1.02
Argos	1.23	1.21	1.20	1.20	1.24
Azteca	0.94	1.00	1.01	0.97	0.98
Banamex	1.16	1.10	1.10	1.05	1.07
Bancomer	0.95	1.05	1.18	1.27	1.37
Banorte Generali	1.14	1.19	1.26	1.41	1.50
Coppel	1.06	1.12	1.20	1.34	1.42
De la Gente	1.05	1.11	1.19	1.34	1.41
HSBC	1.47	1.47	1.43	1.32	1.27
Inbursa	0.74	0.84	0.98	1.15	1.26
ING	1.43	1.39	1.38	1.39	1.47
Invercap	1.05	1.05	1.06	1.10	1.13
Ixe	1.16	1.17	1.18	1.27	1.34
Metlife	1.29	1.30	1.29	1.26	1.29
Principal	1.68	1.67	1.65	1.61	1.62
Profuturo GNP	1.41	1.50	1.63	1.81	1.91
Santander	1.52	1.45	1.33	1.33	1.42
Scotia	1.28	1.33	1.40	1.32	1.35
XXI	1.40	1.40	1.40	1.44	1.47
Simple average	1.17	1.19	1.21	1.26	1.31

Source: CONSAR.

Note: These figures are calculated for a person earning average salary with a real rate of return of 5%.

same AFORE. Thus, any movement would have meant a higher charge. If changing a provider causes a person to pay higher fees, in what sense would the standard argument of price competition apply? However, a 2004 change in law removed penalties for workers who switch but stay in the system, but every new entrant still must pay the highest possible fee of that AFORE.

Third, the average charges do not take into account the number of affiliates in each AFORE. Thus, a new AFORE gets the same weight as the established old AFOREs with millions of accounts. In reality, the average charges are not falling that rapidly for the affiliates and the charges will only be as reported in Figure 10-1 over a period of twenty-five years if there are no new entrants to the system.

What this all means is that charges with the discount do not apply to the time frame they refer to, and it is therefore not possible to compare these charges with other countries, as other countries do not report them in the prospective basis of the next twenty-five years.

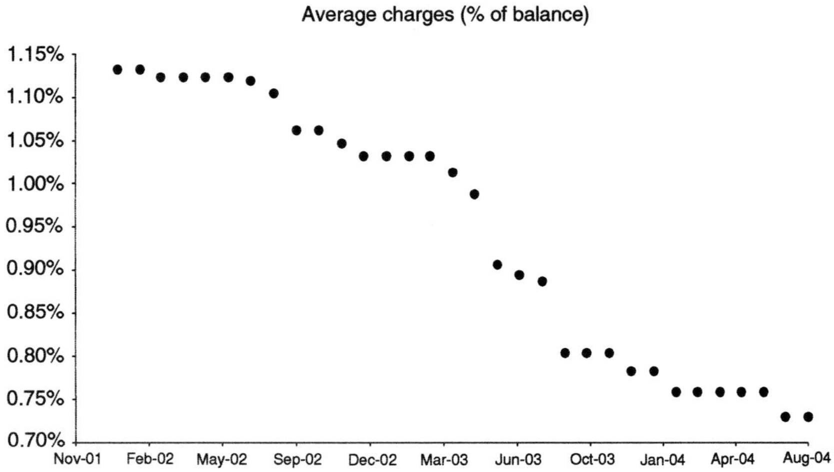

Figure 10-1. Reported average charges (01/02–08/04) (*Source*: CONSAR).

On March 29, 2007, Congress passed a law making charges on flow illegal. If the law is not overturned in the courts by an AFORE legal challenge, the structure of management fees will change dramatically.

Transition Costs

Moving from the old to the new system requires payment to two populations: (*a*) all the people owed benefits under the old system, and (*b*) all the affiliates under the new system who would not have accumulated enough capital in their savings accounts to receive a pension equal to one minimum wage (as determined in July 1997). Note that CONSAR forecasts assume a 5 percent annual real rate of return, as well as a flat 5 percent real rate of return. The forecasts concerning transition costs also require a rate of growth of wages over time as well as the rate of growth of real GDP.

CONSAR reported two series of payments over the next fifty years. A close look at the series shows that the cost is higher during the first two decades of the reform, then it falls below the forecast without the reform. Without reform, the cost is low at the beginning and gradually rises over the decades (see Sinha 2005). The only way to compare these numbers is to convert the series into their present values. However, we have no clear guide to choosing the discount rates. Table 10-17 reports the present value with different discount rates. Strikingly, for any discount rate above 3 percent,

TABLE 10-17 Present Value of Cost Without and With Reform

Discount Rate (%)	*Without Reform*	*With Reform*
0	$10,679.41	$4,462.17
3	1,965.85	1,984.38
6	776.09	1,338.12
10	361.55	690.01

Source: Authors' calculations, based on CONSAR's figures.

the present value of cost without reform is lower than the present value of cost with reform. This raises an important question: Was the reform financially a necessary one from a macroeconomic point of view? Casal and Hoyo (2007) recalculate the cost of the reform. They show that under a discount rate of 3.5 percent the transition seems to save around 20 percent of GDP. Since they assume a different discount rate (3.5%) and consider a different number of years (starting in 2006 and ending in 2090), the information that Table 10-17 presents is not strictly comparable.

Cost of the Guarantees

As noted above, the government offers two kinds of guarantees. First, for the transition workers (those who joined the system before July 1, 1997), the government guarantees that if an annuity bought by the affiliate using the AFORE balance does not exceed what he or she would have received under the old regime, the affiliate can choose to retire under the old regime. In this context, Feldstein (2005: 47–8) notes the incentive problem this guarantee creates:

> The notoriously high administrative costs in some Latin American countries reflect an incentive structure that causes individuals to disregard costs when choosing among plans.... Since someone who was 50 years old or older when the new system began could not possibly accumulate more in his investment account than he would be entitled to under the old rules, the cost and return in the personal accounts was irrelevant. Any promotional gift or other incentive to choose a particular plan or to change plans could therefore draw individuals to a high cost plan.

This guarantee does not apply to affiliates who join on or after July 1, 1997. However, these workers have a different guarantee: they will receive at least the equivalent of one minimum salary prevailing on July 1, 1997, adjusted for inflation. This guarantee amounts to a floor value of the new pension plans under the AFOREs. From the government's point of view,

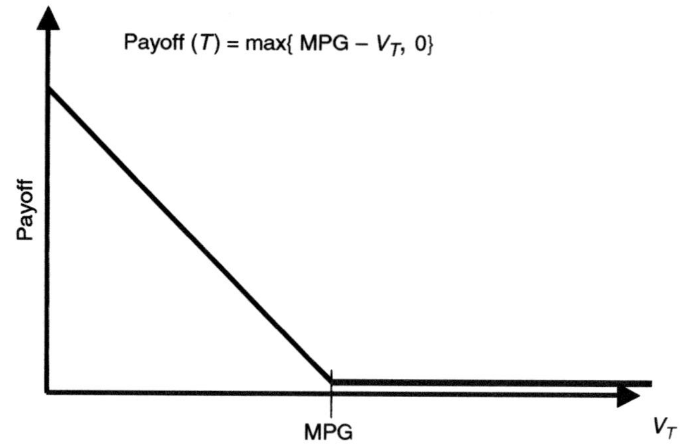

Figure 10-2. MPG as an option. (*Source*: authors' own calculation.)

this guarantee is equivalent to a standard put option, where the strike value is the MPG offered by the government. If the accumulated value is such that it amounts to a life annuity of the minimum pension, the government has zero liability. However, as Figure 10-2 illustrates, if the accumulated amount is less than what would amount to a minimum salary, the government has to make up the deficit.

Will the government have to chip in to make good the promise? Obviously, the answer to this will depend on the income levels of the affiliates. Intuitively, if affiliates have high incomes, the money in their accounts would be sufficient to pay for the minimum pension. To get a feel for the rate of return required at each level of salary, we calculated that rate for three different levels of salary for workers with contributions over twenty-five years—the minimum period of contribution to have the right to the MPG (see Table 10-18). For workers earning one minimum salary, the required real rate of return is 14 percent annually. For workers earning twice the minimum salary, the required rate of return is still 11.6 percent. For workers with the economywide average salary of 3 times the minimum salary, the required rate of return is 9.8 percent. To put it differently, it is likely that for more than half the people in the system, the government will have to top up the minimum pension, as promised under the new system. At present, no provision is being made for such financial contingencies in the government budget.

So far, we have not addressed the variability of the rate of return, nor the question about the likelihood of the government stepping in (from a probabilistic point of view). The next section explores this question further.

TABLE 10-18 Return Required to Receive the MPG

Multiples of Minimum Wage	*RRR*[a]
1	14.0
2	11.6
3	9.8

Source: CONSAR.

Note: Calculations are based on twenty-five years of contributions, with the assumption that a married couple receives the benefits, and the wife is five years younger than the husband.

[a] Required rate of return.

Investment Regimes

This section explores investment regimes in more detail, including how they have changed over time and how Mexico's investment regime compares with those in other countries.

Returns versus Fees

Do charges in different AFOREs justify their higher fees? Some AFOREs have argued that their higher charges are justified because they offer higher returns. As noted earlier, the charges are moving targets. However, this exercise takes the average charges of each AFORE over a period of twenty-five years. Because not all AFOREs have been around since 1997—making it difficult to compare performances—we consider only those that have been in existence since the beginning. Figure 10-3, which plots the twenty-five-year commission for each AFORE against its gross real rate of return over the past eight years, shows a positive relationship between charges and returns. It is clear that higher rates of return are associated with AFOREs with higher fees.

Does that mean that affiliates should be happier with the AFOREs that charge more because they get higher rates of return? The real issue is whether the extra return more than compensates for the higher fees. The answer is *no*. Any additional benefits offered in the form of higher returns are more than offset by higher fees. Each percentage point rise in rate of return requires a 50 percent rise in fees. Affiliates clearly would be better off by staying with the AFOREs that charge the lowest fees. Moreover, the higher returns also come with higher risks (Sinha 2002). Note that the fund with the lowest fee depends on the specific circumstances of the affiliates: salary level, growth of salary, time spent in the system, and real rate of return all can affect the value of the benefits.

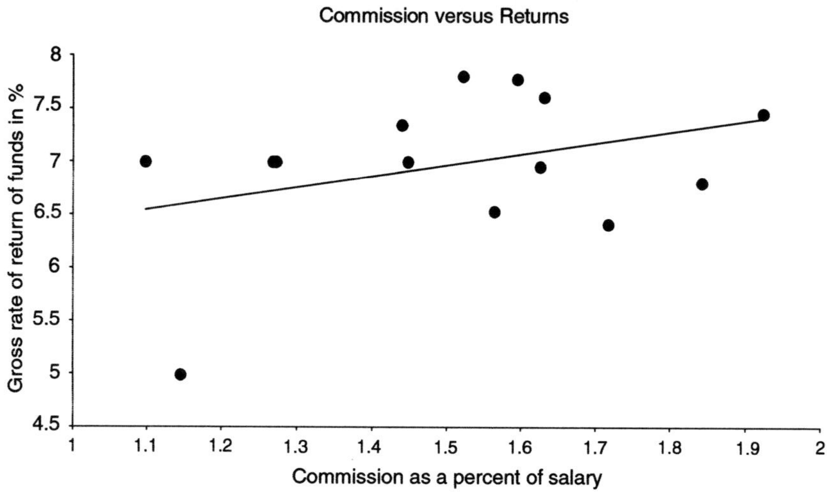

Figure 10-3. Relation between commissions and returns of the AFOREs. (*Source*: authors' own calculation.)

Structured Notes

In 2004, a new investment regime for the AFOREs took effect. With the new regime, AFOREs can now invest in domestic and foreign stock market indexes along with derivative instruments (they cannot invest directly in derivatives). Specifically, AFOREs can have two separate portfolios for each affiliate. The first portfolio is more conservative than the second, which can be invested not only in bonds but also stocks along with derivatives. Only workers aged 55 or younger are eligible to choose Fund 2, and there are restrictions on the investments in the stock markets. The AFOREs have to ensure that such investments guarantee the value of the principal. In other words, if 100 pesos are invested, the maximum that an affiliate can lose is the return earned over 100 pesos. This regime is called 'structured notes'. Perhaps because of the complexity, the AFOREs have not invested more than 1 percent of their portfolio in structured notes.

Payout Phase

The success of any pension system depends on how well it delivers benefits. Therefore, it is critical to examine how the payout phase is functioning. The system in Mexico is still immature, so it is not possible to see all the elements of the payout phase. Nevertheless, examining the basic building blocks of the payout phase can be revealing. This section examines the

TABLE 10-19 Number of Annuities Authorized by IMSS

Year	*Total Number*
1997	4,213
1998	23,257
1999	24,680
2000	27,108
2001	30,621
2002	15,361
2003	5,798
2004	6,124
2005	7,921
2006	7,828

Source: AMIS.

annuities markets, the results of the different rates of contribution for men and women, and future risks of insufficient money in the AFOREs.

Annuities Markets

The development of an annuities market is a critical element of any private system. When the new system began, the IMSS was supposed to buy a single premium annuity for everyone who became eligible. The rules stated that eligible workers would solicit offers from among the dozen insurance companies who offered the annuities. The eligible worker would then pick an offer, which would be communicated to the IMSS, who would then authorize a single premium for the annuity. To make the deal attractive, insurance companies offered various additional benefits.

Table 10-19 shows the number of people who became eligible. There were 4,213 annuities during 1997, the first year. By 2001, this number had reached 30,621. Approximately half of the benefits were authorized to persons with total and permanent disabilities. Another half of the benefits were authorized to widows and orphans of affiliates.

Something peculiar began to happen in 2002. Instead of rising, as we would expect with a maturing system, the number of authorized annuities started to fall dramatically, then seems to have stabilized after 2003. The reason for this unexpected decrease lies with the rules of annuities authorization. During the first four years, the IMSS authorized annuities without any delay. However, starting in 2002, the agency introduced a two-year probationary period for most cases. This meant that for the short run, the IMSS would not make a large single premium payment on behalf of

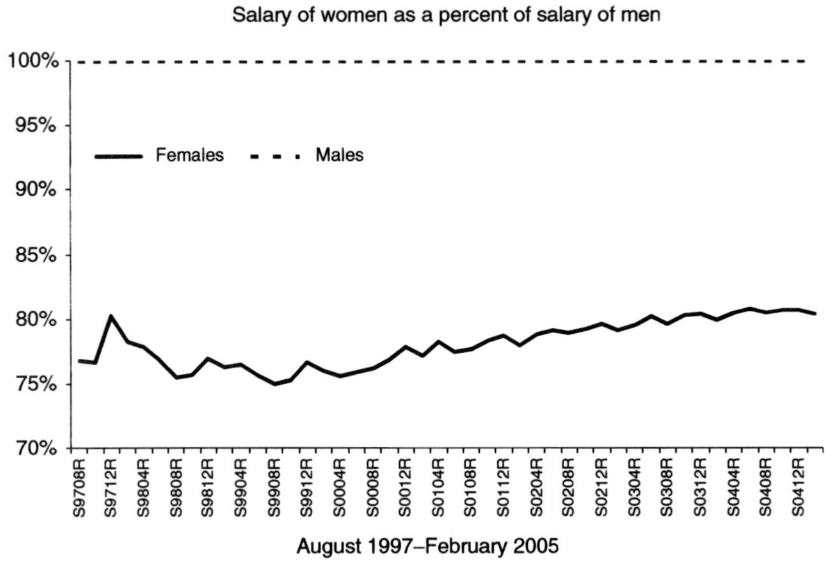

Figure 10-4. Average salary of women in AFOREs (08/1997–02/2005). (*Source*: authors' own calculation.)

these annuitants to the firms selling annuities. Rather, they simply made the payment themselves to eligible individuals from its current budget on a PAYGO basis. Given that the IMSS had lost a major segment of its income stream after the introduction of individual accounts, it has sought various ways to reduce current expenditures. Many observers in the industry see this clampdown as a direct result of such belt-tightening.

The Gender Issue

In many countries, women, on average, earn less than men. Mexico is no exception. CONSAR made a special tabulation of salaries of all persons who have contributed regularly during 1997–2005 (the tabulation excludes everyone who has contributed to their AFOREs only intermittently), separating them by gender. Figure 10-4 displays the average salary of men as 100 percent and calculates the average salary of women for each 2 months. During the 8 years, the average salary of women fluctuated between 75 and 80 percent of the average salary of men, which implies that at best, the average pension for women would be no larger than the corresponding average pension of men. In fact, the pension would be lower, as women have greater longevity. The annuity women can buy will take into account their greater longevity and therefore pay lower benefits per year, on the order of another 20 percent. Ultimately, this means that women with the same contribution density as men will receive a 40 percent smaller pension.

Likelihood of Future Shortfalls

The section above that discussed the cost of the guarantees examined how a number of affiliates (depending on their level of salary) would end up without enough capital in their accounts to ensure a minimum salary. In this section, we report the results of Sinha and Renteria (2006), who discuss the likelihood of this shortfall depending on investment patterns and levels of salary. The results of this study are discussed below.

This exercise requires that we make a number of assumptions about the investment regimes. We consider only AFOREs that can invest in different proportions in stocks and bonds without restrictions, and assume that the future rates of return of the stocks and bonds in Mexico (in real terms) will follow exactly the same pattern as during the past 8 years.

Suppose the affiliate (male with a wife four years younger) spends forty years in the system. The results show that if this affiliate has less than two times the minimum salary and if his or her investment regime allows investment only in Mexican government bonds, the likelihood that he will not have at least a minimum salary equivalent of retirement benefits is equal to one. This likelihood falls rapidly as the proportion of investment in the stock market rises.

If we repeat this exercise for an affiliate with 25 years in the system and an income of less than 2 times the minimum wage, we find that the likelihood of this person's not having enough to get the minimum guarantee is higher than 50 percent for all levels of investment in the stock market. Thus, amplification of the investment regime is unlikely to solve the problem for low-income individuals. It is realistic to assume that many low-income individuals will not spend the required minimum of twenty-five years in the formal labor market. Indeed, other studies have demonstrated that individuals with low income go in and out of the formal labor market (Maloney 1999). Perhaps the only reason why the MPG might not be expensive for the government would be because many low-income affiliates will not meet the twenty-five-year contribution minimum. Levy (2006: Table 5) calculates that the density of workers with 2 times the minimum salary is less than 47 percent, which means that workers at this level of income will need to be in the labor force for more than 50 years to be eligible for the minimum guaranteed pension.

Conclusions and Recommendations

When the new system was introduced, the federal government emphasized certain benefits that it would offer. However, many of the benefits have not materialized, despite some claims to the contrary. In fact, in many ways, the new system may be no more efficient than the old. To sum up:

1. The new pension system was supposed to reduce the informal segment of the market and increase coverage, historically low in Mexico. Indeed, a simple headcount of AFORE affiliates shows that the formal sector does appear to have grown significantly since the reform. Yet a closer examination of the proportion of affiliates who actually contribute reveals that the numbers of covered individuals are actually falling.
2. Creation of a voluntary account to encourage contribution has not worked very well. The voluntary accounts are empty for most people. Only those who seem to be contributing are the ones who could get some immediate tax benefits.
3. The new system was designed to allow workers to provide contributions to finance their own retirement, at least in the long run. As in Chile, it was felt that this factor would be incentive enough to bring more workers into the formal system. However, it is becoming clear that many low-income individuals will not have enough in their own accounts to support themselves in retirement—leaving the government to cover the deficit. To date, no financial provisions have been made to meet this impending shortfall.
4. The new system was intended to reduce costs associated with retirement but has proven to be costly. Approximately 20 percent of the resources are being eaten up in commissions during the buildup phase (both on flow of funds and on balance in the accounts).
5. Privatization of Mexico's pension system was projected to lighten the fiscal burden of the government. There are two ways this could be undermined: (*a*) the transition costs could turn out higher than anticipated, and (*b*) government guarantees may prove to be costlier than anticipated. It is still unclear how much more than what has been budgeted it will cost at the payout phase if the government has to provide a subsidy for the low-income affiliates without enough in their accounts to get one minimum salary equivalent.
6. A comparison of the transition costs of the new system to the costs of the old system indicates that the new system might not save much money in the long run, and in fact may turn out to be more expensive.

Notes

[1] i.e. enough in the sense of achieving the minimum salary equivalent promised by the government for all affiliates who comply with the minimum twenty-five-year contribution period.

[2] The 13,919,377 contributors (see Table 10-3) had a total contribution of $64,373,740,000 (see Table 10-6), making the average balance per contributor US$4,625.

References

Budebo, Mario Gabriel (2004). 'Diez Años de CONSAR', paper presented at the Tenth Anniversary of the Comisión Nacional del Sistema de Ahorro para el Retiro (CONSAR), CNSF, Mexico City, October 5.

Casal, José Alfonso and Carmen Hoyo (2007). 'Costo Fiscal de la Reforma a la Ley del Seguro Social', unpublished document, CONSAR.

Comisión Nacional del Sistema de Ahorro para el Retiro (CONSAR). www.consar.gob.mx/

Feldstein, Martin (Spring 2005). 'Structural Reform of Social Security', *Journal of Economic Perspectives*, 19(2): 33–55.

Flores, Raul (2004). 'Comen AFOREs 19% de las aportaciones', *El Reforma*, August 10.

Instituto Mexicano del Seguro Social (IMSS) (1995). *Diagnostico*. Mexico City: IMSS.

Instituto Nacional de Estadística, Geografía e Informática (INEGI). www.inegi.gob.mx

Levy, Santiago (2006). 'Social Security Reform in Mexico: For Whom?', Paper presented at the World Bank conference on Equity and Competitiveness in Mexico, November 27–8.

Maloney, William (1999). 'Does Informality Imply Segmentation in Urban Labor Markets? Evidence from Sectoral Transitions in Mexico', *World Bank Economic Review*, 13: 275–302.

Notisar. www.notisar.com [Notisar was a government-run Website but is now defunct.]

Pineda, Romina Román (2005). 'Disminuirán más las comisiones que cobran Afores', *El Universal*, December 27.

Sinha, Tapen (2002). 'Retrospective and Prospective Analysis of the Privatized. Mandatory Pension System in Mexico', Society of Actuaries Monograph.

—— (2005). 'Algunos comentarios sobre las AFOREs', in Mexican Congress (ed.), *Actualidades y Futuro de los Sistemas de Pensiones*.

—— and Alejandro Renteria (2006). 'Minimum Pension Guarantee', *ARCH*, (1): 123–46.

—— Felipe Martinez, and Constanza Barrios (1999). 'Performance of Publicly Mandated Private Pension Funds in Mexico: Simulations with Transactions Cost (or, My Pension Fund is Better than Yours: Lies, Damn Lies and Statistics)', *ARCH*, (1): 323–54.

Chapter 11

Pensions in Brazil: Reaching the Limits of Parametric Reform in Latin America

Milko Matijascic and Stephen J. Kay

Brazil is an outlier with respect to pension reform in Latin America. Countries throughout the region, including Southern Cone neighbors Chile, Argentina, and Uruguay, have introduced structural reforms that include private individual investment accounts designed to complement or replace state-run PAYGO systems (see Matijascic and Kay 2006). Brazil has instead engaged in parametric reforms. Inspired by the Swedish and Italian reforms, Brazil has instituted DCs without the funded accounts seen in the rest of the region.

The history of social security in Brazil is also distinct from that of its neighbors. Among other factors, social security is codified in the 1988 Constitution, its broad coverage and benefits structure make it the single largest national antipoverty program in the region, and a significant private pension fund sector had already developed even in the absence of mandated individual accounts. Although a few political leaders have favored private accounts (most notably ex-President Cardoso), individual accounts never received much political traction in Brazil, in part because moving to a private-funded system while still honoring commitments in the public system would entail prohibitively high transition costs, equal to 201 percent of GDP (ECLAC 2006: 127).

Brazil's 1988 Constitution includes several measures that universalized and raised social security benefits. It doubled rural pensions, recalculated pension levels to make up for value eroded by inflation, introduced indexing against inflation, and made the minimum wage the minimum pension level. It also permitted social security to be financed through taxes on gross revenues, financial transactions, and net profit. While codifying benefit levels in the Constitution provides greater legal protection for beneficiaries, these benefits have proven difficult to finance, especially because funds earmarked for social security have been used to fund a range of nonsocial-security-related public expenditures. Furthermore, because benefit levels

Opinions and errors are solely those of the authors and do not reflect views of the institutions with whom the authors are affiliated.

are defined in the Constitution, revisions require a constitutional amendment, which in turn requires a three-fifths majority in the Chamber of Deputies.

This chapter describes Brazil's social security system and the highly contentious process of reform, and concludes with an assessment of current policy dilemmas.

From Social Insurance to Social Security

Retirement coverage in Brazil harks back to the colonial period, when in 1554 the Santa Casa de Misericórdia in Santos first provided pensions. After the installation of the Portuguese Court in Rio de Janeiro in 1808, coverage was provided to select civil servants. This pattern of segmented coverage endured until the early twentieth century. In 1919, after the formation of the International Labor Bureau, accident insurance was provided via mandatory contributions. These developments mirrored those in neighboring countries and represented the beginnings of what eventually became identified as social security.

Later milestones include the 1923 creation of the Caixas de Aposentadorias e Pensões (CAPs, or Pension and Retirement Funds), which were DB programs funded with contributions from employees, employers, and the state that provided coverage for disability, illness, premature death, and time of service. In 1933 CAPs began to be replaced by the Institutos de Aposentadorias e Pensões (IAPs, or Retirement Pension Institutes), which ceased to exist in 1966, when they were centralized. The basic institutional characteristics of Brazilian pension programs since 1923 are outlined in Table 11-1.

Social security legislation since 1919, summarized in Table 11-2, reflects increasing state intervention, centralization, and universalization of coverage for workers in more precarious occupations—all of which was foreseen in 1945 but not enacted until the early 1970s. Initial regulations were tightly linked to Brazil's labor code, but over time most elements began to be seen as social rights and took on their own juridical identity.

The impact of the 1988 Constitution, which specified the parameters of social protection, is critical to understanding how events unfolded in subsequent years. There was considerable controversy over specific language in the Constitution that critics viewed as inefficient and financially onerous but that supporters viewed as necessary to reduce Brazil's perennial inequality. For the first time, universal coverage guaranteeing equal treatment of all workers was enacted. In addition, rural workers were given the right to retire five years before urban workers, and women have the right to retire five years before men or with five fewer years of service. A

TABLE 11-1 Institutional Structure of Social Security (1923–2006)

Structure	*CAPs 1923–31*	*IAPs 1931–67*	*RGPS since 1967*
Financing	Collective capitalization and DB	—	PAYGO and DB
Benefits	Uniform	By labor category	Uniform
Management	Sponsoring firms	State	—
Coverage	Authorized firms	Select occupations	Universal (after 1974)
Civil servants	By institution	IPASE	IPASE (until 1978) and by statute
Regulation	Finance Ministry	Labor Ministry	Social Security Ministry

Source: MPAS (2002).
Notes: RGPS = Regime Geral de Previdência Social, or General Social Security Regime; IPASE = Instituto de Previdencia e Assistencia dos Servidores do Estado, or State Employees Social Security Institute.

critical feature of the pension system since the Constitution was enacted is the 1991 linkage of pensions and the minimum wage.

To confer credibility on these new reforms, the government created the Social Security Budget (Orçamento de Seguridade Social, or OSS) and funded it from multiple sources—including payroll taxes, taxes on earnings and profits, and, beginning in 1993, a tax on financial transactions. The purpose of the OSS was to fund pensions, health care, and social assistance. This lumping together of all these issues under a new legal definition of security (*seguridade*, in Portuguese) could presumably insulate social spending from political interference by the Finance Ministry and provide policymakers with resources to better address social issues.

During the 1990s, Brazil instituted a number of parametric reforms while its neighbors largely engaged in structural reform. The process is by no means complete, and it is difficult to forecast what reforms will look like a generation from now, or even when current impasses in the reform process will be overcome.

A Process of Continuing Reform

Legislation since 1989 reflects a search for the means to improve revenue collection and achieve greater fiscal balance, while at the same time extending coverage, especially for those segments of the population in the greatest need (recent legislation is summarized in Table 11-3). Higher revenue was achieved through new taxes and higher tax rates.

TABLE 11-2 Principal Social Security Legislation (1919–88)

Year	*Legislation*	*Status*
1919	Signature of ILO Convention on accident insurance (insurance contracts)	Until 1967
1923	Eloy Chaves Law ratified, creating CAPs	Until 1966
1931	Labor Ministry created (responsible for social security)	Until 1974
1940	Minimum wage created—the basis for social security benefits	Current
1943	Labor laws consolidated, guaranteeing right to a pension	Current
1945	ISSB created—unified and universalized social security	Not in effect
1947	Unification of IAPs proposed	Not in effect
1952	First statute enacted consolidating civil service pensions	Current
1953	CAPs incorporated into IAPs	Until 1967
1960	LOPS enacted	Current
1962	Minimum age for time of service pensions eliminated	Current
1963	Pensions for rural workers created (PRORURAL)	Not in effect
1966	IAPs consolidated into INPS	Current via INSS
1967	Ministry of Labor and Social Security created	Until 1974
1967	Incorporated worker accident insurance into the INPS, ending insurance contracts	Current via INSS
1971	Pensions for rural workers created (FUNRURAL)	Until 1988
1974	Created Ministry of Social Security and Social Assistance	Current
1977	Closed and open pension funds legislated	Current
1978	Ended IPASE; distinguished between civil servants with and without INSS coverage	Until 1988
1982	Created FINSOCIAL, currently COFINS	Current
1988	Constitutional guarantee of social security rights	Current (in part)

Source: MPAS (2002).

Notes: ISSB = Instituto de Serviços Sociais do Brasil, or Brazilian Social Service Institute; IAP = Institutos de Aposentadorias e Pensões, or Retirement Pension Institutes; LOPS = Lei Orgânica da Previdência Social, or Organic Law of Social Security; PRORURAL = Previdência do Trabalhador Rural; INPS = Instituto Nacional de Previdência Social, or National Social Security Institute; FUNRURAL = Fundo de Assistência ao Trabalhador Rural; INSS = Instituto Nacional do Seguro Social, or National Institute of Social Insurance; FINSOCIAL = Fundo de Investimento Social, or Social Investment Fund; COFINS = Contribuição para o Financiamento da Seguridade Social, or Social Security Finance Contribution.

TABLE 11-3 Evolution of Social Security Legislation (1989–2005)

Year	*Legislation*	*Status*
1989	Created CSLL	Current
1990	Approved special pension regimes (RPP) for all public-sector employees	Current
1991	Approved new financing and benefit laws	Current (in part)
1993	Ended transfer of payroll tax resources for health	Current
1993	Created financial transactions tax (CPMF) to finance health expenditures	Current
1994	Created constitutional revision authorizing transfer of social security funds	Until 2007
1996	Created a special tax regime for small- and medium-sized businesses (SIMPLES)	Current
1998	Approved Constitutional Amendment 20	Current (in part)
1999	Created Social Security Factor (notional defined accounts)	Current
1999	Created contribution for retired civil servants (rejected by Supreme Court in 1999)	Current
2003	Approved Constitutional Amendment 41 (civil servant pensions)	Current (in part)
2003	Lowered age for receiving old-age benefit via LOAS from 67 years to 65 years	Current
2005	Social security revenue collected by the Treasury	In transition

Source: MPAS (2000–5 editions).
Notes: CSLL = Contribuições sobre o Lucro Líquido, or Contribution over Liquid Profits; RPP = Regime Próprio de Previdência; CPMF = Contribuição Provisória sobre Movimentações Financeiras; LOAS = Lei Orgânica da Assistência Social, or social security law; SIMPLES = Sistema Integrado de Pagamento de Impostos e Contribuições das Microempresas e Empresas de Pequeno Porte.

These legislative changes reflect a process of retrenchment of social protection that is best understood within the context of the constitutional reforms undertaken by the Fernando Henrique Cardoso administration presented in Table 11-4. As in the rest of Latin America, Brazil was moving toward a greater role for the market, cost containment, and what Pierson (2001: 425) refers to as 'recalibration' (adapting rules to new constraints).

In the wake of Constitutional Amendment 20, which was passed in 1998 during the Cardoso administration and which some critics considered too timid a reform, President Lula's administration sought to reduce the differences in civil service pensions and pensions for private-sector workers covered by the Instituto Nacional de Seguro Social (INSS) (Berzoini 2003).

TABLE 11-4 Principal Reforms of the Cardoso Administration (1995–8)

Parameters	*Situation in 1995*	*Proposals (PEC 33-A)*	*Approved by Congress (EC-20)*
Ordinary—35 years service men, 30 women	Time of service	Time of contribution	Time of contribution
Proportional—30 years of service men; 25, women	Available	Eliminate	Eliminate for new workers
Special for professionals	Normal (after 15 years of service)	For occupations deemed hazardous	For hazardous occupations and primary/secondary teachers
Minimum age	None	60	Civil servants: 60 men, 55 women. None for INSS
Old-age retirement	65 men, 60 women	65	65 men, 60 women
Rural old-age retirement	60 men, 55 women	65	60 men, 55 women
Benefit floor	Minimum wage	Delink from minimum wage	Minimum wage
Benefit ceiling	10 CWs	Reduce value	10 CWs
Basis of benefit calculation	Final 36 months	Entire career	Wages earned after July 1994 (Plano Real, or Real Plan)
Calculation formula	100% of contributions, price-indexed	Time of contribution	Notional defined accounts; age and time of contribution (social security factor)
Financing via payroll	All social security programs	No mention	Tied exclusively to the general regime
Special regimes (RPP)	Last salary	Match with INSS	Last salary
Complementary pension funds for RPP	None	Would create	Expected, not yet implemented
Employer participation in state-owned firms	No limit	Up to 50%	Up to 50%
Complementary pension fund portability	None	Not included	Implemented in 2001: Laws 108 and 109
Vesting in complementary pension funds	None	Not included	Implemented in 2001: Laws 108 and 109

Sources: Laws 108/2001 and 109/2001, Law 8.213/91, Proposed Constitutional Amendment 33-A, and Constitutional Amendment 20.

Notes: PEC = Projeto de Emenda Constitucional (proposed constitutional amendment); EC = Emenda Constitucional (constitutional amendment); CW = contribution wage.

Table 11-5 outlines these reforms and compares the situation before the 1998 Cardoso reforms and the changes proposed by President Lula in 2003.

Table 11-5 shows that the most important change was the possibility of creating DC pension funds for new civil servants, which introduced an important change with respect to pension funds in Brazil. Formal guarantees for these new workers would be limited to no more than the INSS benefit ceiling. The new rules would eliminate parity between pensions and active civil servants' salaries for new workers, while maintaining parity for those already receiving benefits,[1] and would require current civil servants to stay on the job until aged 60 years to avoid any reduction in pensions. It is important to note that these new rules exempt military and police pensions.

The creation of DC individual accounts was delayed. The regulations for EC-41 were postponed in part due to the difficulty of financing the transition costs in a climate of urgent fiscal adjustment. Disagreement over how such a system would be organized was also politically contentious, since contributions on retirement benefits would mean reduced pensions. The process remains incomplete, and pension reform will no doubt continue to be a significant policy challenge in the decades to come.

Structure and Coverage

In the section below, we describe the current state of Brazil's pension systems as well as key issues from current debates over reform.

Institutions and Benefits

The federal social security system, compulsory for all salaried workers and optional for the self-employed, has two regimes:

- The *General Social Security Regime*, managed by the INSS and encompassing all urban and rural private-sector employees, employees in government-owned firms, and the self-employed.
- The *Statutory Social Security Regimes for Civil Servants*, covering all federal employees serving in the executive, judicial, and legislative branches. (State and municipal employees have their own pension systems.)

Table 11-6 describes the main rules for eligibility and benefits in the special pension regimes for civil servants. The ceiling for contributions and benefits in the main system in 2007 was 2,802 *reais* equivalent to 7.6 times the minimum monthly wage (US$1,381.50 in 2007). In other special programs, the pension is equal to the worker's final monthly wage, with no predefined

Table 11-5 Special Civil Servant Retirement Regimes (1998–2003)

Parameters for Age and Value of Benefits	*Until 1998*	*1999–2003 EC-20*	*PEC-40 Sent by Lula Administration*	*EC-41 Approved in the National Congress*
Time of contribution in public service for integral retirement	None	10 years in the office, 5 on the job	35 years in public service, 20 in the office, 10 on the job	20 years in public service, 10 in the office
Minimum age for integral retirement	None	53 year for current workers, 60 for new	Unchanged	Unchanged
Time of contribution to social security	35 years of service	35 years of contribution	Unchanged	Unchanged
Access to benefits for women	5 years less service	5 years younger, 5 fewer years of contribution	Unchanged	Unchanged
Value of integral benefits	Equal to final salary	Equivalent to final salary	Average of all contributions	Average of all contributions since July 1994 (start of Real Plan)
Value of benefits at age 53	Equal to final salary	Equal to final salary	Reduced by 5% per year since 2006	Reduced by 3.5% per year
Value of public-sector survivor pensions	Equal to final salary	Equal to final salary	Minimum reduction of 30% for values above 1,058 *reais*	70% of values, benefits, or salaries above 2,802 *reais* (2006 INSS ceiling)
Benefit ceiling for civil servants	None	Close to 11,000 *reais*, never implemented	Approximately 12,700 *reais*	Undefined (around 20,000 *reais*)
Contributions by retired and survivor Pensioners	None	None	11% for all	11% for pensions over 1,200 *reais* (states and municipalities); 1,440 *reais* (federal); and 2,400 *reais* (survivor pensions)
Complementary benefits for civil servants	None	Integral pensions included	For new contracts and earnings over 2,400 *reais*	New contracts and earnings above 2,400 *reais*. DC plans under public management

Sources: Law 8.112/90, Constitutional Amendments 20 and 41, Proposed Amendment 40a.

TABLE 11-6 Eligibility for Primary Benefits (Special Regimes)

Benefit	*Eligibility*	*Length of Contribution*	*Replacement Rate*
Full retirement for time of contribution (ATC)	Age 60 for men and 55 for women in the civil service. No minimum age in the general regime	35 years for men and 30 for women	Average of 80% of the highest contributions for INSS[a] since July 1994 and 100% of all civil servants' salaries
Retirement based on the proportional number of years of contribution	Age 53 for men and 48 for women. Not available for new contributors since December 1998	30–34 years for men and 25–29 for women	Between 70 and 94% of the total retirement pension for the full contribution period
Retirement based on age	Age 65 for men and 60 for women, with 5-year reduction for rural workers	15 years (regular occupation for rural insured)	Same as ATC requirements (1 minimum monthly wage for rural insured)
Retirement due to permanent disability	Medical examination	12 months	Same as ATC without the social security factor
Survivor's pension on death	Death of the insured		91% of the formula adopted for permanent disability
Sick leave allowance	Medical examination	12 months	50% plus 1% for each year of contribution
Maternity aid	Birth of child	10 months	100% of the last wage for 120 days
Aid to the aged	Age 65 and older living in families with per capita income less than 25% of the minimum wage	None	1 monthly minimum wage
Benefits due to labor accidents	Medical examination	None	100% of last contribution wage

Sources: Laws 8112/90 and 8213/91.

[a]Multiplied by the social security factor (only for the INSS insured), which includes the record of contributions, the age of the insured and the expected longevity (without gender discrimination) at the retirement age, a similar formula as that used in Sweden and Italy. The formula adopted for Brazil is:

$$f = \frac{T_c \times a}{E_s} \times \left[1 + \frac{(I_d + T_c \times a)}{100}\right]$$

where f = social security factor; E_s = life expectancy at retirement; T_c = time of contribution at retirement; I_d = age at retirement; and a = contribution quotient of 0.31.

ceiling. The floor benefit in both programs is 1 minimum monthly wage (approximately US$181 in 2007).

The system also includes two supplemental regimes:

- *Closed* private pension programs (Entidades Fechadas de Previdência Complementar, or EFPC) are for workers (or a category of workers) in a given firm. The majority of these programs are DC. Supervision is the responsibility of the Secretary of Supplemental Pensions of the Ministry of Social Security (Secretaria de Previdência Complementar, or SPC).
- *Open* complementary private pension programs (EAPC, or Entidades Abertas de Previdência Complementar), also generally DC, are open to any worker seeking supplemental retirement savings. Benefit levels vary by plan and are under the supervision of the Superintendency of Private Insurance (Superintendência de Seguros Privados, or SUSEP) at the Ministry of Finance.

Table 11-7 summarizes these supplemental systems. Despite a relatively low rate of worker participation, the capital invested in these funds is a significant percentage of GDP given the relative concentration of income in Brazil.

With the passage of Constitutional Amendment 20 in 1998, firms began to contribute increasingly to open over closed pension funds. In 2005 open

TABLE 11-7 Indicators and Coverage of the EFPC and EAPC (December 2005)

Financial Indicators	*Closed (EFPC)*	*Open (EAPC)*
Funds as a percentage of GDP[a]	13.8	3.8
Contributors (millions)	1.73	6.08
Designated beneficiaries (thousands)	3.984	NA
Beneficiaries (thousands)	560	248
Contributors as a percentage of the economically active population (EAP)	2.72	6.33
Designated beneficiaries as a percentage of the EAP (IBGE)	4.73	NA
Beneficiaries as a percentage of total INSS beneficiaries	2.65	1.18
Market share as percentage	69	31
Fund with highest market share (percentage)	25.9	41.7
Market share of largest 5 funds (percentage)	49.0	79.2

Sources: SPC (2006), SUSEP (2006), and IBGE (2007).

Note: IBGE = Instituto Brasileiro de Geografia e Estatística, or Brazilian Institute of Geography and Statistics.

[a]GDP data are from the 2007 GDP data-set revision (see IBGE 2007).

TABLE 11-8 Principal Benefits Offered by Closed Pension Funds (2005)

Ordinary retirement	99%
Early retirement	43%
Disability	86%
Spousal pension	72%
Pensions for dependents	55%
Death benefit	41%
Vesting	67%

Source: Towers Perrin (2005).

funds received 31 percent of total employer contributions compared to 18 percent in 1994. Changes in income tax laws in 2002 provided an additional stimulus for firms to contribute to open funds. However, despite the influx of funds, the system continues to be characterized by a low density of contributions, with very few workers drawing benefits.

Table 11-8 shows that closed pension funds offer a range of benefits accessible after a vesting period, including the withdrawal of funds, that somewhat resemble a traditional life insurance policy. Table 11-9 demonstrates that replacement rates tend to be higher in closed funds for employees of state-owned firms and lower for other employees (especially in foreign firms).

In this respect, the coverage of the public systems and the closed complementary funds for workers in state-owned enterprises tend to offer better guarantees than do other programs because they offer higher replacement rates and are usually DB.

Financing Pensions

The question of how to finance the PAYGO pension programs has been a major policy challenge. Some workers contribute regularly, but about

TABLE 11-9 Replacement Rate of Closed Pension Funds (2005)

Replacement Rate	*Private Firms (National)*	*Private Firms (Foreign Owned)*	*State-Owned Firms*
80–100%	20%	1%	38%
60–80%	26%	24%	26%
40–60%	24%	8%	12%
Up to 40%	2%	1%	—

Source: Towers Perrin (2005).

50 percent of the working population, including rural workers, domestic employees, and workers in the informal urban economy, generally do not. The financing arrangements established in the 1988 Constitution are intended to compensate for workers' differing abilities to contribute by redistributing funds collected by levies on a broader revenue base. It classified the heterogeneous conditions of each benefit as:

- conditions of a contributive character, such as retirement based on time of contribution, which does not tend to involve transferring funds between generations;
- conditions of a partially contributive character, such as retirement by age, which requires a certain degree of redistribution of funds between generations; and
- conditions of a universal nature, such as welfare benefits, which do not call for contributions and have an explicitly redistributive character.

The system for funding health, welfare, and social security benefits reflects this mix of contribution-based and universal benefits.[2] The sources of funds for social security are captive, and based on four principal sources (see Table 11-10). The Constitution requires that a specific budget be drawn up, distinct from the federal fiscal budget, with exclusive sources of funds to finance social security.[3] Over time, the social security budget has also begun to receive revenue collected on financial transactions.[4]

In the civil servants' systems, employees must contribute a minimum of 11 percent of their wages. Their employers (federal, state, and municipal governments) contribute up to 11 percent or more, depending on the region, and must cover the difference between what is collected and spent on benefits.

Closed pension plans are increasingly moving from DB to DC systems. In 1994 43 percent of the closed plans were either DC or mixed systems with both DC and DB. By 2004, 89 percent of the funds were straight DC or mixed. Employers were beginning to shoulder less of the administrative costs. In 2000, 8 percent of affiliated employees paid administrative fees on closed pension funds, while by 2004 that figure had risen to 17 percent.

Coverage and Contributors: The Origin of the Problem

The principal source of the financial disequilibrium in Brazil is that benefit coverage for senior citizens is nearly universal, while the total number of workers contributing to the system is quite limited. This trend becomes clear in Table 11-11, which compares coverage levels among persons aged 60 years or older with the economically active population and

TABLE 11-10 Sources of Financing for Social Security Expenditures

Contribution	*Levying Base*	*Rate*
Contributions from employees	Gross wages up to a ceiling of approximately 10 CWs	7.65% to 1 CW, 8.65% from 1 CW to 3 CWs, 9% from 3 to 5 CWs, 11% from 5 to 10 CWs
Contributions by employers	Payroll	20% over the total, 1–3% to cover labor accidents, 15% when contracting self-employed workers
Contributions by self-employed workers	Income up to the ceiling of 10 CWs	20% over the class of income, subdivided into multiples of the CW, limited by the INSS floor and ceiling (11% for 1 CW)
Contributions by special rural, fishing and mining contributors (family economies)	Revenue from sales	2% plus 0.1% to cover labor accidents
Contribution for financing social security (COFINS)	Companies' monthly sales	7.6% for companies in general (financial institutions are exempted)
Contribution on companies' net profits (CSLL)	Companies' net profit	8% for companies in general and 18% for financial institutions
Funding from the federal government (National Treasury)	Fiscal budget	Depending on the need for financing
Income from lotteries	Net income	60% of all weekly revenue
Provisional contribution on financial transactions (CPMF)	Bank operations (with some exemptions)	0.38% on each transaction, 0.2% for health care, 0.1% to the INSS, and 0.08% to antipoverty programs
Integrated system for paying taxes and labor obligations by very small and small companies (SIMPLES)[a]	Sales by very small companies (minimum 5%) and small companies (up to 10%)	2–2.7% (depending on sales) as contribution of employers on payroll, 2% as COFINS, and 1% as CSLL
Other income	Income from bonds and securities or real estate	Depends on the earnings of each security, bond, or rental or sale of real estate

Sources: Law 8.212/91, updated by Constitutional Amendment 20/98 and Law 9.876/99.
Note: CW = contribution wages.
[a]The SIMPLES (tax) system replaces the COFINS.

TABLE 11-11 Benefit Coverage via Social Security Income Transfers (as % of Total Population)

Population Coverage	*1981–4*	*1985–9*	*1990–3*	*1995–8*	*1999–2002*	*2003–4*
Economically active	39.2	38.4	36.3	32.6	32.7	34.1
Family dependents	65.0	63.5	61.2	56.3	54.7	54.6
Old age (60 years+)	50.1	56.3	67.6	76.7	77.5	77.7

Source: IBGE.
Notes: Table does not include *Bolsa Família* (family allowance benefit). No data for 1991, 1994, and 2000.

their dependents. Direct coverage for individuals aged 60 years and older has tended to increase in recent years, while coverage for the other 2 groups has stagnated.

The coverage of those aged 60 years or older is high and increases with age. For instance, in 2001 70 percent of the population aged 65–69 years received a benefit, and an additional 20.8 percent of the population was covered through a family member. For those aged 70–74 years, those figures were 75.9 and 20 percent, respectively, according to Cordero (2005).

At older ages, coverage reaches very high levels—although not universal, it is nearly so. In recent studies, both the ILO and the World Bank have pointed to Brazil as an exemplary case with respect to coverage. However, the same cannot be said about the risks that affect current workers and their dependents; less than two-thirds of this population is covered and coverage rates remain low. As more workers enter the informal sector, the number of families with at least one member contributing to social security continues to decline. If this trend is not reversed, the system will experience growing costs and greater inequality.

Differing Diagnoses: Financing and Social Conditions

There is a wide-ranging debate over what actions are necessary to achieve pension reform in Brazil, a debate complicated by the lack of consensus about the reliability of basic social indicators. Issues in the debate range from the effectiveness of income transfers to the degree to which deficits or surpluses justify reform measures.

Social Conditions, Targeting, and Seguridade

Pension payments play an increasingly important role in reducing poverty for families with income below 50 percent of the per capita minimum salary. In 1992 49 percent of all Brazilian families would have had income below the poverty line if not for INSS payments that reduced the figure to 42 percent. There was a dramatic improvement by 2003, when 43 percent of families were below the poverty line without INSS payments and 32 percent were below after receiving benefits (according to Paiva, Passos, and Ansiliero 2005, based on IBGE data).

Despite the effectiveness of the INSS as an antipoverty program, if its purpose is to reduce poverty, then its benefits could be targeted more effectively. INSS benefit levels are linked to the minimum wage, but since only 30 percent of beneficiaries are below the poverty line, raising the minimum wage is not the most efficient way to target the poor. A 40-*real* increase in the *Bolsa Família* (family allowance), which benefits families in both the formal and informal sectors, would have the same poverty-reducing impact as a 10 percent hike in the minimum wage at two-thirds of the cost according to Barros and Carvalho (2005). Raising the minimum wage is not an effective way to combat poverty, they say, because the retired already receive an elevated level of income transfers, making it more effective to (*a*) transfer income to the poorest segments of the population, reducing retirement payments to the minimum level, and (*b*) raise *Bolsa Família* benefits for families with children up to 14 years old.

One element often overlooked in Brazil's social debate is the link between the 1988 Constitution and poverty reduction. The Constitution preserves (in part) the value of benefits, which has reduced the incidence of indigence and poverty among the elderly. Dain and Lavinas (2005) report that indigence among those older than 65 years fell from 3 percent in 1981 to 1 percent in 2003, while the absolute number of those older than 60 years living in extreme poverty fell by half. As Lavinas (2006) notes, when a benefit is not considered a 'right', the poor and indigent are not always identified because, beyond meeting the necessary requirements, they often lack information or voice (many of the poor lack required documents or even a postal address).

Targeted income transfer programs can generate inefficiencies, and not all of those eligible ultimately receive benefits. The recently launched Pesquisa Nacional por Amostra de Domicilios (PNAD, a national household survey) reveals that food security assistance reached only 18 million of 45 million households facing food insecurity. The PNAD survey also demonstrates that among indigent families with an income of 25 percent of the minimum wage or less, half have not applied for assistance. In other words, the coverage deficit is the largest in the most vulnerable groups. It is apparent that in Brazil, with its weak state capacity, profound social inequality, and large numbers of poor individuals with low education levels, targeting does not reach the most needy.[5]

Financing, Spending, and Long-Term Equilibrium

Many analysts suggest that reform efforts since 1993, while significant, have been insufficient, given projected actuarial shortfalls that could have grave macroeconomic implications in the future. Furthermore, the growing INSS deficits and rising expenditures on public servant pensions have brought on a fiscal crisis that has led to public spending being increasingly directed toward benefits rather than investment.

Giambiagi et al. (2004) demonstrate that the differences between revenue collection and expenditures are growing. Even though the deficit has grown faster for civil servants (because there is no specific contribution for the employer), INSS expenditures have expanded at an even faster rate (see Table 11-12).

Generous rules guiding benefits also contribute to financial shortfalls. According to the World Bank (2001) and Giambiagi et al. (2004), the relatively high value and long duration of pensions granted based on time of contribution are especially costly. Giambiagi et al. argue further that noncontributory pensions are relatively ineffective social policies that create a vicious cycle due to their high cost, which leads to high payroll taxes that in turn provide an incentive for joining the informal sector.

From this perspective, the solution is to adopt new constitutional reforms to guarantee benefits proportional to contributions and to avoid unrestricted spending on noncontributory benefits. Table 11-13 presents potential financial scenarios according to differing reforms, GDP growth, and minimum wages.

Giambiagi et al. (2004) say that reforms are necessary to contain costs, which could reach 10 percent of GDP, assuming moderate economic growth and a continued rise in the real value of the minimum wage. The authors point to acceleration in growth in assistance and time-of-contribution benefits, which will lead to worsening deficits unless a reform is enacted. The proposed reforms project that expenditures would fall to 6.9 percent of GDP assuming 3 percent annual GDP growth, and 5.6 percent of GDP with an annual GDP growth of 4 percent.

There are different perspectives on the link between the financial crisis and the reform process. According to Dain (2003) and ANFIP (2005), the 1988 Constitution requires that taxes on corporate earnings (COFINS, or Contribuição Social para Financiamento da Seguridade Social), profits (CSLL, or Contribuições sobre o Lucro Líquido), and payroll taxes were intended to finance pensions, health, and social assistance. Since the constitutional reform of 1993–4, the government has diverted more than 20 percent of COFINS, CSLL, and CPMF (Contribuição Provisória sobre Movimentação Financeira, literally 'temporary contribution on financial transactions') to other expenditures (see Table 11-14), and was authorized to do so through 2007. Critics argue that this practice deviates from the

TABLE 11-12 Pension System Operating Results (as a % of GDP)[a]

	1995	*1996*	*1997*	*1998*	*1999*	*2000*	*2001*	*2002*	*2003*	*2004*	*2005*	*2006*[b]
Operational imbalance	—	(0.1)	(0.3)	(0.7)	(0.9)	(0.8)	(1.0)	(1.1)	(1.6)	(1.6)	(1.7)	(1.8)
INSS revenue	4.6	4.8	4.7	4.8	4.6	4.8	4.8	4.8	4.8	4.8	5.1	5.3
Expenditure	4.6	4.9	5.0	5.4	5.5	5.6	5.8	5.9	6.3	6.5	6.8	7.1
Civil servants	(2.6)	(3.4)	(3.2)	(3.5)	(3.4)	(3.6)	(3.9)	(3.6)	(3.1)	(3.1)	(2.9)	(2.8)
Revenue	0.9	0.6	0.6	0.7	0.6	0.6	0.6	0.5	0.6	0.6	0.9	1.1
Expenditure	3.5	4.1	3.8	4.1	4.0	4.2	4.4	4.2	3.8	3.7	3.8	3.8
Total	(2.6)	(3.5)	(3.4)	(4.1)	(4.3)	(4.5)	(4.9)	(4.7)	(4.9)	(4.7)	(4.6)	(4.6)
Revenue	5.5	5.4	5.4	5.4	5.2	5.3	5.3	5.4	5.2	5.5	6.0	6.4
Expenditure	8.1	9.0	8.8	9.5	9.5	9.8	10.2	10.1	10.2	10.2	10.6	10.9

Sources: Giambiagi et al. (2004: 6), based on data from the Ministries of Plan and Social Security; IBGE (2007).

[a] GDP data are from the 2007 GDP data-set revision (see IBGE 2007).

[b] Preliminary data and authors' estimate.

TABLE 11-13 INSS Expenditure Projections Measured (as a % of GDP)

	Scenario without Reform				*Scenario with Reform*[a]	
	Minimum Wage Indexed to Inflation		*Minimum Wage Grows at Same Rate as Growth in Per Capita GDP*			
GDP	3.0	4.0	3.0	4.0	3.0	4.0
2005	7.8	7.7	7.8	7.8	7.8	7.7
2030	9.2	7.4	10.0	8.4	6.9	5.6

Source: Giambiagi et al. (2004: 34), based on data from the IBGE and Ministry of Social Security.

[a]Giambiagi et al. (2004) assume a minimum retirement age 55 years in 2010 and 65 years in 2025. During this period, the retirement age difference between men and women would be gradually reduced. In 2025, women would have a retirement age of 63 years with 33 years of required contributions. In addition, special benefits for preschool through middle-school teachers would be eliminated. Finally, the minimum benefit would be adjusted only for inflation. Old-age social assistance benefits would be set at 80% of the minimum pension and unlinked from the minimum wage, and granted at age 70 rather than at age 65, as is currently the case.

original 1988 Constitution, arguing that if all revenues had been spent on social security, revenues would have exceeded benefits, generating a huge surplus. In short, from this perspective, the INSS was not the source of the growing deficit.[6]

Others argue that these revenue losses occurred due to nonpayment of taxes, evasion, and fraud (see Table 11-15), facilitated by weak enforcement (ANFIP 2005). Revenue collection could be dramatically improved

TABLE 11-14 Annual Social Security Budget (as a % of GDP)[a]

	1995	*1996*	*1997*	*1998*	*1999*	*2000*	*2001*	*2002*	*2003*	*2004*	*2005*	*2006*
Revenue	7.6	7.7	8.3	8.3	9.1	10.1	10.4	10.7	10.4	11.4	11.6	11.9
INSS	4.6	4.8	4.6	4.8	4.6	4.7	4.8	4.8	4.8	5.1	5.1	5.5
COFINS	2.2	2.1	2.0	1.9	3.0	3.4	3.6	3.6	3.4	4.0	4.1	3.9
CPMF	—	—	0.7	0.8	0.7	1.2	1.3	1.4	1.4	1.4	1.4	1.3
CSLL	0.8	0.7	0.8	0.7	0.6	0.7	0.7	0.9	0.9	1.0	1.2	1.2
Expenditures	7.1	6.9	7.0	7.5	7.7	7.8	8.2	8.2	8.5	8.9	9.4	9.9
Pension (INSS)	4.9	5.2	5.1	5.6	5.7	5.9	6.2	6.2	6.6	6.7	6.9	7.2
Health (SUS)	1.9	1.7	1.7	1.6	1.6	1.7	1.8	1.7	1.6	1.6	1.6	1.7
Social assistance	0.1	0.2	0.2	0.3	0.4	0.3	0.3	0.4	0.4	0.5	0.8	1.0
Surplus	0.6	0.7	1.3	0.8	1.4	2.2	2.2	2.5	1.8	2.5	2.3	2.0

Sources: ANFIP (2007), based on data from the Ministries of Finance and Planning; IBGE (2007).

Note: SUS = Sistema Único de Saúde.

[a]GDP data are from the 2007 GDP data-set revision (IBGE 2007).

TABLE 11-15 Potential Social Security Revenue Collection (as a % of GDP, Rev. 2007 Data)

	1997	*1998*	*1999*	*2000*	*2001*	*2002*	*2003*	*2004*	*2005*
Nonpayment (*a*)	0.2	0.3	0.2	0.2	0.4	0.3	0.4	0.4	0.4
Fraud (*b*)	1.8	1.9	1.9	1.9	2.1	2.1	1.9	1.8	1.8
Evasion total ($c = a + b$)	2.1	2.2	2.1	2.0	2.5	2.4	2.3	2.2	2.2
Exempt (*d*)	0.8	0.7	0.8	0.8	0.7	0.7	0.7	0.8	0.6
Revenue collection (*e*)	4.7	4.7	4.6	4.7	4.8	4.8	4.7	5.0	5.0
Potential revenue collection ($f = b + d + e$)	7.3	7.4	7.3	7.4	7.6	7.6	7.4	7.7	7.4
Estimated losses ($g = f - e$)	2.6	2.6	2.7	2.6	2.8	2.8	2.6	2.6	2.4

Source: ANFIP (2007).
Note: Deflator: National Consumer Price Index (INPC—Indice nacional dos preços ao consumidor).

through increased compliance. Critics also argue that the granting of contribution exemptions, such as those given to philanthropic organizations and exporters, is questionable, given the fact that benefits are linked to contributions.

Note that policy assessments described in this section need to be viewed with caution, given the fact that they often rely on contradictory and erroneous data. Meanwhile, spending continues to rise, while average benefits do not satisfy basic needs. Policymakers face a clear agenda of improving the efficiency and equity of benefits while at the same time creating better conditions for business, investors, and labor.

Conclusions and Suggestions for an Alternative Agenda

Since the regional trend toward individual accounts took off in the 1990s, Brazil's path toward social security reform has differed significantly from that of its neighbors, focusing on universalizing benefit coverage and parametric reforms in the PAYGO public system rather than structural reform. As described above, policies in recent years have been shaped by the range of social protection codified in the 1988 Constitution, and the process of social security reform has required investments of tremendous political capital in order to amend the Constitution.

One conclusion that can be drawn from examining current debates in Brazil is that the immediate policy challenges of improving equity and efficiency can be met not only via constitutional reform, but, in the shorter

TABLE 11-16 Occupations as Proportion of the Workforce and Salaries in Selected Countries

Country	*Wages and Payroll/ GDP—2002*	*Occupational Structure 2002*			*Average Wage in Euros (2001)*[a]
		Employers and Self-Employed	*Salaried Workers*	*Domestic Household Workers*	
Brazil	36.1	30.0	61.3	8.7	5,138
Portugal	60.4	25.4	72.7	1.8	13,338
Spain	65.5	17.5	80.6	1.8	17,432
France	66.9	9.7	89.2	1.1	27,319
Germany	68.9	10.0	88.9	1.1	38,204
United Kingdom	65.2	11.4	88.1	0.3	37,677
Sweden	74.8	10.2	89.3	0.5	31,620
Eurozone	64.4	14.8	83.2	1.9	29,627

Sources: IBGE (2003), OECD (2003), and Eurostat (2003).
[a]Ten and more employees.

term through administrative reform, and improved regulatory and managerial performance.

Low levels of coverage for affiliates remain a basic problem in Brazil and the rest of Latin America (Gill, Packard, and Yermo 2004: 273–5).[7] Without higher salary levels, a largely formal and salaried labor sector, and a high density of contributions, social security benefits cannot provide a basic standard of living, nor is it possible to have a classic universal social security system functioning with an actuarial equilibrium based on a social insurance model (see Table 11-16).

With respect to current laws, changing survivorship rules and regulations would reap clear savings. In Brazil, lifetime survivorship benefits are given indiscriminately without regard to the age of the spouse, number of children in the family, or length of the marriage.[8] Such permissive benefits would be considered quite generous in the industrialized world, but seem altogether out of place in a developing country like Brazil (Coutinho and Ribeiro 2006).[9] In Sweden, for example, able-bodied workers are eligible for a universal survivor pension payable for 6 months after 5 years of marriage, or for as long as the survivor is caring for a child younger than 12 years. Sweden's six-month survivor pension stands in sharp contrast to the situation in Brazil, where even a young adult capable of working automatically receives lifetime benefits (see Table 11-17).

A similar principle exists with respect to disability: those capable of working should be expected to do so. However, in Brazil, nearly all of those classified as temporarily or permanently disabled are considered

TABLE 11-17 Comparison of Survivor Benefits in Select Countries

Country	*Requirements*	*Benefit*	*Termination*
Mexico	150 weeks of contribution	Private: 90% of the value of the disability pension Public: 90% of insured's pension (both for widow or dependent disabled widower)	Remarriage: 3-year lump sum
USA	6 of 13 quarters coverage prior to death	100% at retirement age, payable to widow(er) after minimum 10 years of marriage, 75% if disabled or caring for a child under aged 16	Age 18 for orphan children in school. Survivor retains pension if remarries after 60
Sweden	3-year residence	Maximum is 90% reduced base amount, 40% of earnings related pension (both for 6 months). Special survivor benefit if survivor ill or unemployed	Until dependent child is aged 12
Italy	5 years contributions, 3 in 5 prior to death	60% of insured's pension, 100% for spouse + 2 children, Income test if granted after September 1995	New marriage or age of majority
Portugal	Deceased met pension requirements	60% of insured's pension	5 years unless surviving spouse over 35 years of age, disabled, or caring for a child
Brazil	12 months of contribution	100% for spouses or dependents and up to 20% for orphans through age 16 (or 24 if in school). The pension is for life, regardless of age	Remarriage

Sources: Social Security Administration (2002, 2004).

totally disabled. Appropriately classifying partially disabled workers would encourage those who are capable of work to find suitable employment.

Another indicator that Brazil's disability pensions are alarmingly and disproportionately high is that expenditures associated with risk (disability and survival pensions) have remained steady for twenty-five years, despite the fact that the aged population has grown—and, since the constitutional amendment of 1988, has enjoyed more generous benefits. Under these circumstances, we would expect old-age pensions to increase as a proportion of overall pension expenditures. Nevertheless, disability and survival pensions only fell from 38.2 percent of expenditures from 1980 through 1984 to 34.8 percent of expenditures between 2000 and 2004.

Furthermore, many workers continue to be formally employed even while drawing pensions, a situation commonly justified by low benefits. Seniors are thought to have no choice but to return to work. Since 1981 the number of beneficiaries of retirement and survivorship pensions who are employed has increased, due not only to Brazil's rapid population growth (from 110 million in 1981 to approximately 180 million in 2004) and economic crises, but also because of the large number of people who sought early retirement ahead of the Cardoso administration's pension reforms. A growing number of these beneficiaries found employment in the informal sector, as the percentage of employed pensioners not contributing to the pension system expanded (see Table 11-18). Retired persons with lower benefits are less likely to be employed, while retirees receiving higher average benefits are more likely to be employed and to contribute to social security.

The general argument for permitting individuals to have multiple benefits is this: because benefit levels are so low to begin with, people should justifiably be able to accumulate more than one pension. However, that

TABLE 11-18 Retired and Survivor Pensioners' Work Status (% for Selected Years)

Beneficiaries	*Retirement Benefit*				*Survivorship Benefit*			
	1981	*1990*	*1995*	*2004*	*1981*	*1990*	*1995*	*2004*
Retired (not seeking employment)	80.9	76.9	65.2	67.0	73.5	72.4	66.5	70.7
Retired and unemployed	0.2	0.2	0.6	0.8	1.4	0.8	1.6	2.0
Employed and a contributor to pension system	6.4	6.2	6.4	6.0	14.0	13.0	11.2	8.9
Employed and a noncontributor	12.6	16.7	27.8	26.2	11.0	13.8	20.8	18.4

Source: IBGE (PNAD) (2004).

individuals receiving higher benefits tend to have multiple sources of income while those with lower benefits do not suggest that permitting multiple benefits leads to a higher concentration of income.

Although the population that retires relatively young and enjoys multiple benefits is significant, the vast majority receive only the minimum pension. The existence of this enormous population living in poverty raises the question of the effectiveness of targeting or lowering the benefit floor. Faced with a somewhat similar situation in Chile, the 2006 presidential advisory commission took a different approach to addressing the role of pensions in addressing poverty when it recommended a 'solidarity' pillar that would reach the bottom 60 percent of earners (Consejo 2006).

Policymaking is clearly hampered by the absence of accurate data, which is exemplified by conflicting data on worker mortality for those receiving benefits based on thirty years of contributions (these conditions are more typically met by workers in better remunerated jobs). Mortality is, of course, a key indicator for determining the duration of benefits and for projecting program costs. However, although workers tend to retire at relatively young ages in Brazil, the duration of benefits does not in itself appear to be the key problem for the private-sector workers pension system. Using Social Security Ministry data (from the DATAPREV database; see MPAS 2005), Table 11-19 shows that the average age when benefits are granted rose from 50 years for men and 48 years for women in 1997 to 54.8 years and 51.7 years in 2005, while the average age of cessation of benefits (i.e. death of beneficiaries) was 71.3/66.3 years.

The age at which benefits cease due to death is actually lower than overall average life expectancy, according to the 2004 government mortality tables, which show benefits ceasing at age 77.7 years for men and 80.8 years for women (after being granted at ages 55 and 52 years, respectively) (IBGE 2004). Comparing these numbers to the Ministry of Social Security numbers reveals a 6.6-year disparity for men and a 14.4-year disparity for women. This discrepancy exemplifies the lack of reliable indicators in Brazil, an especially serious problem for forecasting the long-term financing needs of the pension system.[10]

Some analysts emphasize the critical importance of raising the retirement age (Giambiagi et al. 2004), although retirement systems throughout the world permit early retirement in return for reduced benefits. However, as Table 11-20 shows, the issue in Brazil has more to do with high replacement rates relative to overall worker contributions. Furthermore, it has been possible since 1998 to alter how benefit formulas are calculated via ordinary law. This is not the case with raising the retirement age, which requires the very cumbersome process of constitutional reform. At the same time, 68 percent of the EAP and 44 percent of the working-age labor force work in occupations where social rights and legal protections are

TABLE 11-19 Average Age for Time of Contribution Retirement

Gender	*Benefit Status*	*1992*	*1993*	*1994*	*1995*	*1996*	*1997*	*1998*	*1999*	*2000*	*2001*	*2002*	*2003*	*2004*	*2005*
Men	First granted	53.6	53.4	53.1	51.8	50.2	49.7	50.7	52.9	53.1	53.3	54.3	54.8	54.8	54.8
	Average beneficiary	62.4	62.1	62.0	61.6	60.9	60.2	60.1	60.6	61.3	61.9	62.4	63.0	63.5	64.1
	Benefit ceases	69.2	68.8	68.3	68.0	68.0	66.6	67.9	68.8	69.4	69.9	70.5	70.7	71.0	71.3
Women	First granted	51.5	51.2	50.9	49.9	48.8	48.3	49.0	50.6	50.9	51.1	51.7	51.7	51.8	51.7
	Average beneficiary	60.3	59.5	59.3	58.7	58.2	57.4	57.3	57.6	58.2	58.8	59.2	59.6	60.1	60.5
	Benefit ceases	68.6	66.2	65.2	64.4	64.0	60.7	62.3	64.9	67.0	67.2	67.4	66.5	65.9	66.3

Source: MPAS (2005).

TABLE 11-20 Average Age, Legal Age, and Replacement Rates for Retirement Pensions in 2001

Retirement Pensions by Country and Type	*Average Retirement Age (Years)*	*Legal Retirement Age (Years)*		*Benefit as a Percentage of Salary*
		Men	*Women*	
Brazil (TC)	53.7	65	60	88/92[a]
France	58.7	60	60	75
Italy	60.4	65	60	65
Brazil (TC + urban, by age)	60.8	65	60	91/74[b]
Spain	61.4	65	65	65
Germany	61.6	65	65	75
Sweden	63.2	65	65	NA
United Kingdom	63.2	65	65	48
Portugal	64.5	65	65	54

Sources: MPAS (2001), IBGE (2001*b*), and Eurostat (2003); 2004 figures for Brazil INSS (excluding the special regimes).
Note: TC = time of contribution.
[a]Compared to salaried contributors. Figures come from two different sources (MPAS 2001 cites 92%; IBGE 2001*b* cites 88%).
[b]Compared to the employed workforce. Figures come from two different sources (MPAS 2001 cites 91% and IBGE 2001*b* cites 74%).

not respected (IBGE 2001*b*). The cost of the generous pensions enjoyed by a small percentage of retired workers is borne by that relatively small portion of the labor force that contributes at very high rates, which in turn encourages increased evasion.

The evasion problem could be solved with the adoption of a zero pillar/tier that pays a basic benefit to all workers, regardless of total contributions for old age. This kind of minimum income benefit could be complemented with a pension based on a classical social insurance scheme with DB and calculated strictly according to the effective contributions. For workers preferring higher income during retirement, market solutions including DC plans and voluntary saving could be encouraged. Such a scheme would be feasible with much lower contribution rates and an actuarially accurate formula that fixes replacement rates according to international standards. This solution would cover the needs of the retired without encouraging early retirement and the accumulation of multiple pensions by middle-class workers.

In coping with these challenges, it is important to emphasize that the lengthy process of constitutional reform is not the only nor necessarily the most effective method to reform social security and bring financial stability. Parametric reforms, including administrative measures, play an important role and could bring faster and more immediate results. Administrative reforms can present an effective financial solution without the political challenges of amending the Constitution.

Administrative measures could include:

- Eliminating risk-based benefits for those who do not need them. Partially disabled workers can continue to work in some capacity.
- Verifying more diligently disability status and ceasing total disability status for those capable of working.
- Preventing disability through better monitoring of workplace safety.

The following measures could be taken via ordinary legislative reforms:

- Imposing restrictions on receiving one or more pension benefits while still receiving wages from employment.
- In granting death benefits, considering the presence or absence of minor children and the capacity of survivors to be employed.
- Granting partial disability status when appropriate.

Arguments that Brazil's social expenditures are elevated given its stage of development (see Giambiagi et al. 2004) should be viewed with caution. Although Brazil's population is relatively young compared to European countries, its population is aging at a faster rate (UN 2004). As the rate of economic growth has slowed, income transfers have increased fiscal pressure. Table 11-21 suggests that Brazilian spending on old-age pensions could be considered relatively low compared to that in Mexico, which has a higher rate of growth, and the USA, which has a social protection system that assigns a greater role to the market and individual initiative.

As Gillion et al. (2000) point out, any analysis of social spending must consider total spending and not just public-sector expenditures. Spending should be viewed according to the age profile of the population to assess the level of spending with respect to the covered population. Such an exercise suggests that public expenditures on survivorship benefits in Brazil (3.1% of GDP) are overly generous (see Table 11-21). The rapid rise in spending on disability benefits and family income support in a population where fewer workers are contributing is also cause for concern.[11] Policymakers may wish to devote greater attention toward reforming rules over survivorship benefits.

Furthermore, the lack of integration among health, welfare, and pension policies creates duplication and waste, as does weak administration, which results in fraud. Operational costs (including personnel expenditures) in Brazil represent a relatively high 3.7 percent of total benefits.[12] Furthermore, up to 20 percent of benefits contain 'irregularities', and it is projected that annual losses are equivalent to 15 percent of total revenue

TABLE 11-21 Public Social Expenditures (as a % of GDP)[a]

	Germany		*Italy*		*Mexico*		*Poland*		*Portugal*		*Sweden*		*USA*		*Brazil*		
	1995	*2003*	*1995*	*2003*	*1995*	*2003*	*1995*	*2003*	*1995*	*2003*	*1995*	*2003*	*1995*	*2003*	*1995*	*2003*	*2006*
Old age[b]	10.3	11.3	9.4	11.3	0.6	1.0	6.5	8.8	6.5	7.0	9.9	10.1	5.4	5.5	4.2	4.9	5.4
Survivor[c]	0.5	0.4	2.2	2.5	0.2	0.3	1.9	1.0	1.3	1.6	0.7	0.7	1.0	0.8	2.0	2.5	3.1
Disability[d]	1.9	2.0	1.8	1.8	0.1	0,1	5.8	3.4	2.5	2.6	5.1	6.0	1.2	1.3	1.0	1.4	1.9
Family[e]	1.9	1.9	0.6	1.2	0.1	1.0	1.1	1.5	0.8	1.6	3.8	3.5	0.6	0.7	0.5	0.6	1.1
Total	15.8	16.3	16.5	17.0	3.9	8.1	17.1	17.0	11.2	13.1	19.4	17.9	8.2	7.6	7.7	9.4	11.5

Sources: IBGE (2007) and OECD (2007).

[a]GDP data are from the 2007 GDP data-set revision (see IBGE 2007).

[b]Old-age benefits include INSS old age and time of service pensions, and civil service pensions from the three branches of government for urban and rural workers. Some analysts view rural benefits as social assistance better categorized as family benefits, but according to Law 8.213/91 they are required to be integrated into Social Security (*Previdência Social*). In 1995 rural benefits were equal to 1.18% of GDP, and in 2005 they had risen to 1.24% of GDP.

[c]Survivor benefits include all INSS and civil service survivorship benefits.

[d]Disability includes INSS and civil service disability and sickness benefits.

[e]Family benefits include benefits for the aged who live in families considered poor, and also incorporates targeted assistance and income transfer programs like *Bolsa Família* and *Bolsa Escola*. Maternity and small child benefits are also included. Family benefits for workers with income below three contribution salaries are also included.

due to improper revenue collection and benefit payments. Because of these inefficiencies, elevated tax rates place an onerous burden on families and firms, stifling potential economic growth.[13]

Resolving these administrative and legislative challenges could facilitate political support for new constitutional reforms. Brazil's 1988 Constitution raised the benefit floor and facilitated access to benefits for the needy. Social security pensions were the primary government social program and played a key role in reducing poverty. As discussed above, significant steps can be taken to reduce overall pension expenditures in Brazil, primarily through addressing the benefits that are exceptionally generous by international standards without reducing basic benefits, which play a critical antipoverty role.

It is clear that the process of administrative and legislative reform at the subconstitutional level should be accelerated. It is also apparent, given the current distribution of benefits, that the pension system cannot be sustained by payroll taxes alone and that a strong basic antipoverty benefit is necessary given the significant number of workers earning wages at or close to the minimum wage. The creation of reserves or a system of partial capitalization could contribute to easing demographic transitions and stimulate market-led investment—which could also broaden the market for complementary pension funds geared toward professionals. However, any such reforms require transparency and must be done in such a way to minimize both risks and administrative costs.

Notes

[1] In July 2004 the Supreme Court ruled that retired civil servants have to contribute 11% of their pensions on the amount exceeding the INSS ceiling and that survivor benefits be reduced by 30% below the covered worker's retirement benefit only for pensions above the ceiling. Otherwise, civil servants would receive benefits lower than those of workers in the INSS even though contribution rates would be the same.

[2] Law 8.213 provides that civil and military federal, state, and municipal employees covered by specific statutes are exempt from paying into social security. Expenditures on these pensions were not part of the OSS seguridade budget that encompasses all the federal government's expenditures on health care, social assistance, and pension coverage, but were later added. OSS coverage of non-pension related expenditures was originally an interim measure, but will likely be extended.

[3] As mentioned above, the constitutional reform of 1994 allowed the administration to reallocate 20% of revenue to other areas.

[4] The provisional financial transactions tax (the CPMF) was introduced to help fund health-care expenditures when the resources that had been provided by payroll taxes or collected by the INSS were no longer directed toward health care.

[5] According to Lavinas (2006), among the poorest 10% of the population, 37% are single heads of households with children, with a median monthly family income of

12 *reais*, compared to 24 *reais* for 2-parent families (comprising 48% of the poorest 10%). Of these single-parent families, two-thirds are not covered by any type of income transfer compared to 50% of 2-parent families.

[6] The economic difficulties of the 1990s led to higher unemployment and informality, which led to a reduction in payroll tax revenue for financing social security. This ultimately led to a rise in taxes on profits, earnings, and financial transactions.

[7] Gill et al. (2005) see a positive correlation between higher income levels, the number of regular contributors, and contribution density. The authors point out, however, that coverage rates vary widely among countries with similar levels of income. This suggests that other factors, such as confidence in institutions or market incentives, can play an important role. The authors foresee an active role for government in reducing poverty levels among senior citizens.

[8] Benefits end upon remarriage.

[9] A court decision even permitted a woman to receive two state-funded survivorship pensions: one from her son and the other from her husband (Diário de São Paulo 2005).

[10] Furthermore, note that survivorship pension benefits are not taken into consideration when calculating the social security factor (described above). Because there is no minimum age to qualify for a benefit, the payout period can last for several decades. In fact, DATAPREV data does not include information on the duration of benefits or even the average age of the beneficiary. The lack of an INSS mortality table and the failure to include survivor pensions leads to gross errors and erroneous diagnoses based on inadequate data. Consequently, any financial projections using these assumptions are questionable, if not useless.

[11] Assembling crossnational indicators is complicated given differences in coverage, income supports, and the mix between private and public provision. These indicators serve as a reference to evaluate spending levels, which in turn can affect public finance and international competitiveness.

[12] Administrative costs of 3.7% of benefits are higher than in other countries. In the USA, administrative costs in 1992 were 0.7%; in Switzerland, 0.8%; in Japan, 0.3%; and in Italy, 3.4% (WB 1994: 312).

[13] Upon his resignation in March 2005, Social Security Minister Amir Lando argued that current benefits needed to be audited and that social security records should be compared with income tax and health records. Finance Minister Antônio Palocci later stated that reducing social security fraud and evasion would enable the government to increase the primary fiscal surplus without resorting to a constitutional reform of the pension system (see Agencia O Globo 2005).

References

Agencia O Globo (2005). 'INSS tem três milhões de benefícios irregulares', March 22.

Associação Nacional dos Fiscais de Contribuições Previdenciárias (ANFIP) (January 2005). *Previdência social e salário mínimo.* Brazil: ANFIP.

—— (2007). *Análise da seguridade social em 2006.* Brasília: ANFIP.

Barros, Ricardo P. and Mirela Carvalho (September 2005). 'Salário Mínimo e Distribuição de Renda', Seminários DIMACRO no. 196. Rio de Janeiro: IPEA.

Berzoini, Ricardo (2003). *Exposição de motivos do Projeto de Emenda Constitucional (40)*. Brasília: MPS.

Consejo Asesor Presidencial para la Reforma Previsional (2006). 'El Derecho a una Vida Digna en la Vejez: Hacia un Contrato Social con la Previsión en Chile'. Santiago: Presidencia de la República de Chile.

Cordero, Beatriz C. (2005). 'Universalização da Previdência Social no Brasil: uma questão ainda em aberto', Master's degree monograph. Campinas: Instituto de Economía, UNICAMP.

Coutinho, Mauricio C. and Jose O. L. Ribeiro (2006). 'Opções de reformas e o regulamento de benefícios segundo a experiência internacional com programas de Seguridade Social', unpublished paper. Rio de Janeiro, Brazil: IPEA.

Dain, Sulamis (2003). 'A diversificação da base de financiamento do RGPS no contexto da reforma tributária e do ajuste fiscal: velhas idéias e novos caminhos', in *Bases de Financiamento da Previdência Social: Alternativas e Perspectivas*, Série Estudos, vol. 19. Brazil: MPS.

—— and Lena Lavinas (2005). 'Proteção social e justiça redistributiva: como promover a igualdade de gênero', Versão Preliminar (preliminary research report), Relatório de Pesquisa. Rio de Janeiro: FASE.

Diário de São Paulo (2005). 'STJ garante duas pensões a viúva', November 30.

Economic Commission for Latin America and the Caribbean (ECLAC) (2006). *Shaping the Future of Social Protection: Access, Financing and Solidarity*. Santiago: United Nations.

Eurostat (2003). *Statistiques Sociales Européennes*. Luxembourg: Communautés Européennes.

Giambiagi, Fabio, K. I. Beltrão, J. L. Mendonça, and V. Ardeo (2004). 'Diagnóstico da Previdência Social no Brasil: o que foi feito e o que falta reformar?', Texto para discussão no. 1050. Rio de Janeiro: IPEA.

Gill, Indermit, Truman Packard, and Juan Yermo (2005). *Keeping the Promise of Social Security in Latin America*. Washington, DC: Stanford University Press, for the World Bank.

Gillion, Colin, John Turner, Clive Bailey, and Denis Latulippe (2000). *Social Security Pensions: Development and Reform*. Geneva: International Labour Organisation.

Instituto Brasileiro de Geografia e Estatística (IBGE) (2001*a*). *Microdados, Pesquisa Nacional por Amostra de Domicílios (PNAD)*. Rio de Janeiro: IBGE, www.ibge.gov.br

—— (2001*b*). *Microdados, Pesquisa Mensal de Emprego (PME)*. Rio de Janeiro: IBGE, www.ibge.gov.br

—— (2003). *Sistema de Contas Nacionais (número 12)*. Rio de Janeiro: IBGE, www.ibge.gov.br

—— (2004). Brazil: Tábuas Completas de Mortalidade-Sexo feminino e masculino.

—— (2007). System of National Accounts Series 2000–2006.

Lavinas, Lena (2006). 'Transferências de Renda: fatos e versões', Draft, May 30. Rio de Janeiro: Instituto de Economia da UFRJ.

Matijascic, Milko and Stephen J. Kay (2006). 'Social Security at the Crossroads: Toward Effective Pension Reform in Latin America', *International Social Security Review*, 59(1): 3–26.

Ministério da Fazenda (2005). Orcamento Social do Governo Federal 2001–2004. Brazil: Ministério da Fazenda.

Ministério da Previdência e Assistência Social (MPAS) (1992–2005). *Anuário Estatístico da Previdência Social (AEPS)*. Brasília: MPAS.

Organisation for Economic Co-operation and Development (OECD) (2003). *Compensation of Employees 1987–2002, Final Consumption Expenditures 1987–2002.* Paris: OECD.

—— (2007). Social Expenditure (SOCX) Database. Paris: OECD, http://lysander.sourceoecd.org

Paiva, Luís, Alessandro Passos, and Graziela Ansiliero (2005). 'Impactos da Previdência Social sobre a Pobreza', in *Informe de Previdência Social*, 17(3). Brazil: MPAS.

Pierson, Paul (2001). 'Coping with Permanent Austerity', in Paul Pierson (ed.), *The New Politics of the Welfare State.* Oxford: Oxford University Press.

Secretaria de Previdência Complementar (SPC) (March 2006). *Informe Estatístico.* Brazil: Ministério da Previdência Social.

Social Security Administration (2002). *Social Security Programs throughout the World: Europe.* Washington, DC: Social Security Administration.

—— (2004). *Social Security Programs throughout the World: The Americas.* Washington, DC: Social Security Administration.

Superintendência dos Seguros Privados (SUSEP) (April 2006). *Boletim Estatístico dos Mercados Supervisionados.* Brasília: Ministério da Fazenda.

Towers Perrin (2005). *Planos de Benefícios no Brasil, Pesquisa 24ª*. Rio de Janeiro: Towers Perrin.

United Nations (UN) (2004). World Population Prospects: The 2004 Revision Population Database.

World Bank (WB) (1994). Averting the Old-Age Crisis: Policies to Protect the Old and Promote Growth. Washington, DC: World Bank.

—— (2001). 'Brazil: Critical Issues in Social Security', Country report. Washington, DC: World Bank.

Chapter 12

Costa Rica's Pension Reform: A Decade of Negotiated Incremental Change

Juliana Martínez Franzoni

During the past two decades, Costa Rica has transformed its pension system and turned it into a 'mixed model' that combines collective and individual savings (Mesa-Lago 2004).[1] This chapter focuses on the structural reform approved in 2000 and in effect since May 2001 and the parametric reform approved in May 2005. The 2000 reform created a multipillar system, which included the Régimen de Invalidez, Vejez y Muerte (RIVM, or the Disability, Old-Age, and Survivorship Regime). The RIVM was created in 1943 and currently reaches nine out of every ten insured workers in the country. The 2005 parametric reform modified requirements and benefits of the RIVM and created new benefits while seeking to strengthen the collective capitalization system. Both reforms strengthened the administrative effectiveness of the RIVM.

This chapter discusses the main historical characteristics of the pension system, focusing on the RIVM; describes the political context for the design and adoption of the main reforms of the past five years; and explains both reforms in detail. It also examines the strengths and weaknesses of the implementation process and concludes with an exploration of tensions within the Costa Rican pension reform.

A Brief History of the Pension System in the Pre-reform Period

In the early 1990s, 64.5 percent of salaried and 5 percent of non-salaried workers were covered by all public pension systems compared to

A technical report commissioned by the Estado de la Nación (State of the Nation Project) provided me with the opportunity to organize the information regarding the 2005 reform process (Martínez Franzoni 2005*a*). I also thank Ana Catalina Ramírez for her meticulous support in completing information and bibliographic references, and Juan José Matamoros at SUPEN for his kind support in accessing and updating data. Stephen J. Kay and Tapen Sinha provided very helpful comments, and Stephen J. Kay patiently helped to edit a much longer version of this chapter. Flaws remain my own.

56.8 percent of salaried and 21.7 percent of nonsalaried workers in 2004 (Estado de la Nación 2005). Of those covered in the early 1990s, the RIVM paid benefits for 75.9 percent of retirees and 94.7 percent of contributors (Sauma 2004), and provided 3 types of pensions: (*a*) old age, for those who made the required number of contributions; (*b*) disability, for those who were forced to stop working; and (*c*) survivorship, for dependent family members of deceased-insured workers [Law 17 (Article 19); (CCSS 1994)].

Nineteen special regimes were operating alongside the RIVM, which operated in the public sector from the 1980s to the mid-1990s and covered groups such as teachers, legislators, and workers in the judicial branch. These programs offered privileged benefits, had enormous actuarial disequilibria, and were financed by the national budget. They received fiscal subsidies and had a regressive distributive impact that stood in stark contrast to the general lack of protection for the low-income sectors (Martínez Franzoni and Mesa-Lago 2003).

As the 1990s progressed, things began to change. In 1992 the pension law passed; in 1995 the teachers' pension system was restructured; and in 1996 Law 7605 abolished the special regime for legislators, making them part of the RIVM system. In fact, these reforms incorporated all public workers, except teachers and workers in the judicial branch, into the RIVM.[2] For that reason, current RIVM coverage is much higher among insured workers than pensioners. However, the financial weight of the regimes financed by the national budget (including teachers and the judicial branch) continued to grow because it has had to honor obligations previously contracted by the government. As Figure 12-1 shows, while the relative weight of the RIVM decreased from 9.2 percent of social expenditures in 1990 to 8.1 percent in 2003, special regimes went from 10 to 15 percent of overall social expenditures in that same period, corresponding to 40 percent of total pension expenditures in 1990 and 52.8 percent in 2003.

In contrast to most Latin-American pension systems and the Costa Rican special regimes, the RIVM was created as a partially funded DB system (called Capitalización Parcial Colectiva (CPC)) and has never operated as a pure PAYGO system. It has functioned on a scaled-premium system with considerable reserves, which if invested well could fund the system's costs along with worker's contributions. However, in 1998 it became apparent that in the medium term the system would face an actuarial disequilibrium, primarily due to an imbalance between benefits and contributions.

Several factors led to the RIVM's disequilibrium, including demographic, labor, design, and administrative problems (Martínez Franzoni 2005*a*). In demographic terms, the country had completed its transition. In other words, life expectancy increased while infant mortality has decreased,

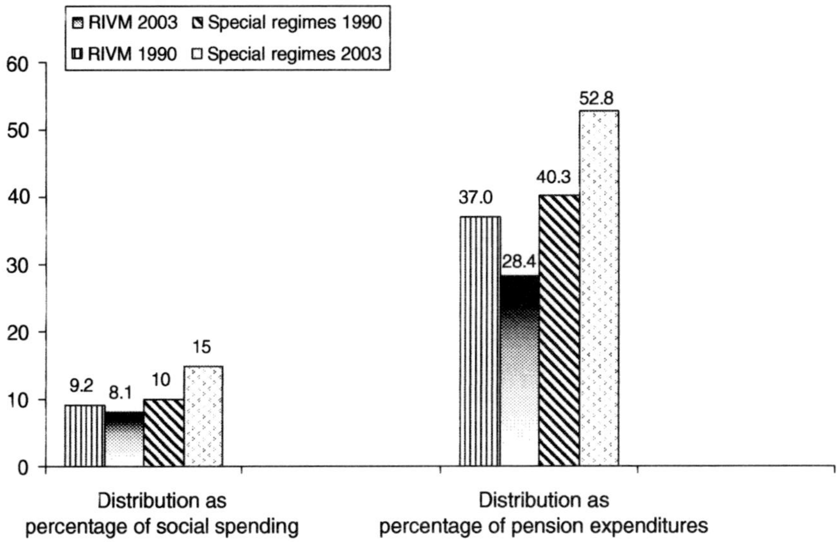

Figure 12-1. Structure and evolution of public social investments in contributive pensions (1990, 2003).

and, since 2001, population growth has been below the replacement rate (Estado de la Nación 2005). Today, there are 55 economically dependent people for every 100 paid workers. Toward 2018 the rate will be 44 per 100, and toward 2045 the composition of the dependent population will no longer be predominantly younger than 15 years but rather 65 years or older (Estado de la Nación 2003). This change will affect the labor market as well as pensions: while in 1970 there were thirty-two contributors per pensioner, in 2000 there were seven, and in 2040 there will be only three (CCSS 2004*a*).

Regarding labor, the growth of the informal sector, which by definition does not contribute to social security, weakened the system's finances. In 2003 five out of every ten new jobs were informal, three were formal, and two were agricultural (formal or informal) (Sauma 2003). Between 1990 and 2002, an average of 25,000 formal jobs and 20,000 informal jobs were created every year (Estado de la Nación 2003). Although informal sector employment is not necessarily low-wage work, a significant proportion of workers has not contributed to social security—not because they earn subsistence wages but rather because they lack information, do not see the point, or try to get a 'free ride'. In fact, 45 percent of all informal workers who have not contributed to social security (of which 7 of 10 are salaried) are fully capable of contributing, while the remaining 55 percent (of which

7 of 10 are self-employed) are partially capable (Trejos 2003). (Evasion among those workers with full contributory capacity was also indicative of the RIVM's administrative inefficiency.) The limited number of workers making regular contributions increased the demand for noncontributory pensions. Those below the poverty line could request noncontributory pensions from the Régimen No Contributivo (RNC, or Non-Contributory Pension Regime)—benefits equivalent to a basic food basket, insufficient for covering basic needs like housing, clothing, and transportation (CCSS 1995). In 2002, the RNC covered less than half of the target population (44.5%) and had an 11,000-person waiting list, primarily because the Ministerio de Hacienda (Ministry of the Treasury) cut resources due to the fiscal deficit (Castillo, Uzaga, and Carmona 2002; Durán 2002). Thus, the Caja Costarricense del Seguro Social (CCSS, or Social Security Agency) was granting one pension for every two retirement or survivorship applications, and it frequently takes years for an application to be processed (Martínez Franzoni and Mesa-Lago 2003).

Among the design issues that led to disequilibrium is the replacement rate, which remained at 60 percent nominal since the RIVM's creation. The rate was based on the highest 48 monthly salaries out of the last 60, with an additional 1 percent for every additional year of contributions over 240 contributions and a floor and ceiling fixed periodically by the CCSS board of directors. This formula encouraged underreporting of income during most of a person's working life (especially in the private sector) and overreporting (public as well as private) during the 5 years prior to retirement. The general contribution from its creation through 2005 was 7.5 percent, divided among workers, employers, and the government and distributed according to whether workers were salaried or self-employed and according to the degree of qualification of the self-employed (see Table 12-1).

Administrative weaknesses are apparent not only in the high levels of evasion but also in the way the system handled increased longevity of the population combined with stagnant rates of contributions.[3] The system is regressive to the extent that the higher the income level, the higher the amount of resources required from the collective fund. Because workers making fewer than 240 contributions were ineligible for old-age pensions, even at a reduced rate, they had an incentive to seek disability pensions. This situation resulted in more people receiving disability than old-age pensions, reaching a proportion comparable to a country at war (CCSS 2005*a*). It also reflected political clientelism and influence-trafficking; workers had to know the right people to access disability pensions.

The following reforms were designed to correct many of these problems.

TABLE 12-1 Contributions by Contributors, Pillars, and Type of Insurance as Percentage of Total Salary (2003)

Contributor	*Salaried*			*Independent*	*Insured without Remuneration*
	First Pillar IVM	*Second Pillar*	*Total*	*First Pillar IVM*	*Second Pillar*
Employers	4.75	1.75	6.50	n/a	n/a
Workers	2.50	2.50	5.00	7.25	5.5–7.25
				(State 0–2.5)[a]	(State 0–1.75)
State	0.25	0.00	0.25	0.25	0.25
Global	7.50	4.50	12.00	7.50	7.50

Source: Law 17, Article 33.
[a] Proportions established according to CCSS 2000.

Political Scenarios That Motivated the Reforms

Both the 2000 and 2005 reforms—as well as the creation of social security—took place under Social-Christian governments, now grouped under the Partido Unidad Social Cristiano (PUSC, or the Social-Christian Unity Party). The reforms can be considered consecutive since the second one facilitated changes the first one had not been able to make. Both reforms were planned by both government authorities and civil organizations, and they began after a failed reform effort, for which the Partido Liberación Nacional (PLN, or the National Liberation Party), under the José Figueres Olsen Administration (1998–2002), failed to get the approval of unions. In addition, unions supported both reforms, even though they had historically opposed adjustments to RIVM requirements and benefits and were ideologically opposed to the creation of a system of individual capitalization.

The 2000 Structural Reform: Creation of the Multipillar System

The prelude to the 2000 reform was the conflict that took place under the social-democratic Figueres administration (1994–8). Figueres opposed the Chilean-style reform promoted by the World Bank and proposed instead a modification to RIVM benefits and requirements, combined with the creation of a complementary individual savings pillar (Rodríguez and Durán 1998). However, the proposal did not get very far. In 1996, union demonstrators took over CCSS headquarters to show their opposition, particularly to the increase in the retirement age and the reduction in the replacement rate. They demanded that the government should improve the collection of social security fees and the financial management of RIVM investments before undertaking such drastic measures.

In 1998 Miguel Ángel Rodríguez won the presidential election by a narrow majority. His agenda included an ambitious set of economic reforms that would liberalize the telecommunication and electricity markets and incorporate private administrators in the management of mandatory complementary pensions. To that end, Rodríguez convened the Foro de Concertación Nacional (FCN, or the National Bargaining Forum) to begin negotiations about these issues. Government, business, and labor representatives whose organizations were represented in the CCSS board of directors participated, as did women's organizations and other groups representing new social movements. Although the government expected the FCN to strengthen support for its reform proposals, the alliance of organizations opposed to the reform actually grew stronger. To handle the opposition, the government changed the rules of the game, going from requiring a consensus to requiring a majority vote (Castro Méndez 2000). Still, in that volatile political environment, the pension reform unexpectedly survived, unlike all the other issues debated.

In September 1998 the pension agreement was the only one of the 96 agreements in the FCN's final report supported by all its members (Mesa-Lago 1998). Nevertheless, the law drafted in the legislature was far different from the one agreed on by the FCN, so revisions and intense deliberations in the Legislative Assembly went on for more than a year (Castro Méndez 2000). Finally, February 2000 saw the passage of the Ley de Protección al Trabajador (LPT, or Worker's Protection Law), which incorporated virtually all the agreements of the FCN (Law 7983).

The reformed pension system took effect in May 2001. Most notably from the government's perspective, the LPT omitted changes that the government had sought, including an increase in the retirement age and number of required contributions, and a replacement rate reduction. These parametric changes had been opposed by unions, cooperatives, women's organizations, and even the *solidaristas*,[4] which instead demanded, and achieved, long-expected measures to improve the administrative efficiency of the CCSS. Among measures aimed at collecting social security revenues were nonjudicial mechanisms, such as denying government contracts or shutting down firms not honoring social security contributions. Unions also agreed to create the capitalization pillar proposed by the government and the business sector, while the government agreed that pension fund administrators could be from either the public or private sectors (Jiménez 2000).

The 2005 Parametric Reform: Strengthening the RIVM

On February 18, 2004, the CCSS released its report on RIVM finances, forecasting that in 2005 contributions would be insufficient to finance pensions, interest from the reserves would be insufficient to pay pensions in 2015, and the fund itself would collapse in 2022. The ILO later confirmed this projection but forecasts that the collapse would hit instead in 2027. To address this financial problem, pension officials at the CCSS proposed creating a round of bilateral talks with interested civil society organizations largely representing businesses and workers. Cooperatives and unions persuaded the CCSS board of directors to create instead an advisory commission to identify proposals for re-establishing the financial sustainability of the RIVM. The brand-new Social Commission, also referred to as the Comisión Técnica Institucional (or the Institutional Technical Commission), would provide input to the CCSS board of directors ahead of any decision (Comisión Técnica Institucional 2004). This commission was made up of representatives from public institutions, chambers of commerce, and labor. Women's organizations and two public institutions, the Defensoría de los Habitantes and the Superintendencia de Pensiones (SUPEN, or Superintendency of Pensions), also participated as nonvoting members.

During the first four months after the commission's creation, external advisers and the CCSS assessed different aspects of the actuarial equilibrium. The ILO played a key role as an independent arbiter concerning the actual financial situation of the RIVM in order to reduce the initial distrust among some of the parties. Although projections varied by five years, the ILO validated key assumptions of the CCSS projections and, more importantly, helped civil society representatives understand why a parametric reform was much needed.

As mentioned above, longevity had increased—17 years since the 1960s—while the overall contribution to the RIVM had remained fixed at 7.5 percent since 1943. To compensate for this disparity, all parties agreed to increase contribution rates. They also agreed to discuss pension benefits for individuals retiring with more contributions than required. Based on these initial agreements, each sector defined what was or was not negotiable.[5] The main disagreements were over replacement rates.[6] The ILO's representative proposed an alternative, eventually supported by all parties, that would scale pension replacement rates according to workers' earnings; that is, the higher the income, the lower the replacement rate, and vice versa.[7]

The ILO's advisers created a working group, the Grupo Técnico para la Reforma de IVM (or the Technical Group) that worked with representatives from public institutions and civil organizations (but not the business sector or the *solidaristas*) to consolidate all of the measures that had been proposed up to that point (Grupo Técnico para la Reforma de IVM 2005). In 1995, after several meetings, the CCSS board of directors approved the proposal developed by the Grupo Técnico and supported by the Social Commission, with minor modifications. Table 12-2 compares the proposals in detail. The CCSS Pensions Management and Actuarial departments (not the government or the board of directors) had to retreat from a more severe adjustment in replacement rates and ended up maintaining different retirement ages for men and women.

Main Characteristics of the Adopted Reforms

The sections below explain the structural reform of 2000, address changes in requirements and benefits of the 2005 reform, and summarize measures adopted to improve administrative efficiency in both 2000 and 2005.

The 2000 Structural Reform [8]

After 2000, the LPT reform reorganized pensions around three complementary pillars, each based on five main parameters: (*a*) retirement age, (*b*) percentage of contribution, (*c*) number of contributions, (*d*) reference salary, and (*e*) pension replacement rates (FCN 1998). The percentage of contribution is distributed only among insured (third pillar), between employers and workers (second pillar), or among employers, workers, and the government (first pillar). The pillars are combined according to whom they cover: salaried population (first, second, and third pillars), self-employed (first and third pillars), or population in poverty (RNC) (see Figure 12-2).

The first pillar is DB and mandatory for salaried workers. With the passage of the LPT, it was set to become mandatory for self-employed workers as well. The second pillar is complementary, with mandatory DCs for salaried workers. The third pillar is complementary and voluntary, available to any person, employed or not. The RNC, targeted at people living below the poverty line, universalizes the first pillar for those aged 65 years and older who do not receive a contributive pension.

The first pillar is administered by the CCSS, the judicial branch, the Junta de Pensiones y Jubilaciones del Magisterio Nacional (National Teachers Assembly for Pensions and Retirement), the Instituto Nacional de Seguros (INS, or the National Insurance Institute), and, in the case of the transition system, the ministries of Labor and the Treasury. The second and third pillars are administered by corporations created by public (such as the

Table 12-2 Proposed and Adopted Measures for IVM Parametric Reform

Measures	*Pre-reform*	*Measures Proposed by the Business Sector*	*Measures Proposed by Labor Organizations*	*Approved*
(a) Normal retirement				
Retirement age	65	65	65	65
Number of monthly contributions	240	300	300	300
Contribution (distributed in a tripartite form)	7.50%	10.5% in 30 years; adjusted 0.5% for every 5 years	10.5% in 30 years; adjusted 0.5% for every 5 years	10.5% in 30 years; adjusted 0.5% for every 5 years
Reference salary	Best 48 out of last 60	Last 240	Last 240	Last 240
Real replacement rate (with 25 years)	56.55%	46.05%	Scaled, 58.70–46.50%	Scaled, 58.70–46.50%
Real additional amt after 240 installments	0.87%	1.30%	1.30%	1%
(b) Early retirement				
B.1 With more contributions	MRA differentiated by sex; 60 years for women and 62 years for men	Same requirements for men and women	MRA differentiated by sex; women make six fewer monthly contributions than men for all early retirement	MRA differentiated by sex; women make six fewer monthly contributions than men for all early retirement
B.2 With lower total pension	None	Only table for men and women	Differentiated table with 0.5% in favor of women	Differentiated table with 0.5% in favor of women

TABLE 12-2 (*Continued*)

Measures	*Pre-reform*	*Measures Proposed by the Business Sector*	*Measures Proposed by Labor Organizations*	*Approved*
(c) Reduced pension				
Reduced pension for those who contributed but did not reach required contributions for normal retirement	None	Yes, proportional to effective pension floor after 75% with 180 installments	Yes, proportional to effective pension floor after 75% with 180 installments	Yes, proportional to effective pension floor after 75% with 180 installments
(d) Measures for high-income sectors				
Incentives to make high-income sectors contribute	None	Eliminating pension ceiling	Establishing contribution ceiling	Pension management developed specific incentive plans

Sources: CCSS (2004*b*), CCSS (2005*a*), *Diario Oficial La Gaceta* (2005), and Grupo Técnico para la Reforma de IVM (2005).
Note: MRA = minimum retirement age.

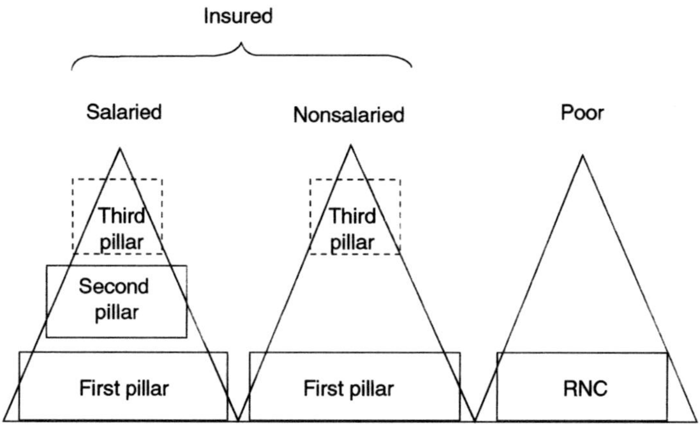

Figure 12-2. Multipillar system.

CCSS, Bancredito and Banco Popular) and private institutions. All are regulated by the state (Law 7983).

The First Pillar

Besides the RIVM, only four regimes provide first-pillar pensions: the judicial branch, the Régimen del Magisterio Nacional (teachers regime), the INS, and the transitional regime, financed by the national budget and closed to new contributors. Having relatively few special first-pillar regimes is a positive step, especially by Latin-American standards, toward achieving equal universal benefits because standard rules apply to as many people as possible. The two special regimes for judges and teachers have contribution and benefit rates higher than those in the RIVM.[9]

Formally, the RIVM promotes universalization and, along with the LPT, mandates insurance for self-employed workers (Law 7983). To that end, it offers both individual and collective insurance[10] and provides voluntary insurance to the non-EAP such as housewives and students.

The Second Pillar

The second pillar was created by the LPT as a mandatory complement to the first pillar for the salaried population. It is an individual capitalization regime—Fondo Obligatorio de Pensión Complementaria (FOPC, or Mandatory Complementary Pension Fund)—funded by 4.25 percent of a worker's total salary, with 3.25 percent coming from employers and 1 percent from workers (Article 9). Funding did not increase payroll taxes since contributions already made for other purposes were reallocated (Article 48). According to estimates, the FOPC will allow a replacement rate between 15 percent (for workers averaging less than 9 years of contributions) and 20 percent (for workers averaging 9 years or more of contribution) (SUPEN 2004).

The second pillar's funds are tax-exempt and belong to the insured, as is the case with third-pillar funds (see below). Workers can receive benefits as a life annuity or permanent annuity (Articles 68 and 73). The life annuity constitutes a monthly pension, from the day of the worker's retirement until his or her death (Articles 22–5 and Transitorio XIII). When the pensioner dies, the heirs do not receive any pension. The permanent annuity provides a pension during a period previously established with the insured—once it expires, the pension stops—along with an optional complementary disability and survivorship regime (Articles 27–9). If the pensioner dies before the end of this period, the total accumulated balance would be given to the beneficiaries (Article 29).

The LPT gives workers freedom of choice among administrators according to the limits and regulations determined by the SUPEN (Articles 2, 9, and 11). The administrators can be either privately or publicly owned firms and must be authorized by the SUPEN to operate.[11] They can be public institutions, public banks, social organizations, private banks, or occupational funds. The occupational funds created by state institutions or private companies can also become administrators (Article 75).

Since 2003 commissions have been assessed on both contributions and returns. Commissions range between 2 and 4 percent of a worker's contributions and between 6 and 8 percent of returns (SUPEN 2006).

In December 2006 there were eight administrators, six with ties to public banks and two to private banks (two of the original private administrators had merged). Workers who do not choose a fund are assigned to a designated public-sector administrator. Of the 1,542,151 affiliates in December 2006, 88 percent were with the state-owned public funds, Popular Pensiones and BN Vital (54.3 and 20.6%, respectively). Among privately held administrators, Interfin-Banex had the most affiliates, with less than 10 percent of the total (see Table 12-3).

Investments are mostly directed toward the public sector (85%). The law requires administrators to invest at least 15 percent in institutions belonging to the National Housing Financial System, which offers returns equivalent to the average return of other investments (Article 61).

If an administrator declares bankruptcy, an affiliate selects another administrator or is automatically assigned to one if he or she makes no selection (Article 44). If the administrator's assets are not enough to honor its obligations, the government must cover the remaining contributions

TABLE 12-3 Second Pillar Affiliation by Administrator: Absolute and Percentages (December 2006)

Administrators	*Affiliates*	*Percentage*
BN Vital	317,973	20.6
INS Pensiones	15,935	1.0
Popular Pensiones	837,882	54.3
Vida Plena	59,417	3.9
Interfin-Banex	127,552	8.3
BAC San José Pensiones	57,498	3.7
BCR Pensiones	106,369	6.9
CCSS OPC	19,525	1.3
Total	1,542,151	100.0

Source: SUPEN (2006).

and liquidate the administrator.[12] The government's guarantee is only partial since it does not include interest, and after 15 or 20 years of contributions, these will constitute the majority of the fund rather than the contributions.[13]

The Third Pillar

The third pillar has existed since 1995 (Law 7523), but the LPT brought it into the new multipillar system (Article 14 and following). It stimulates voluntary saving programs through fiscal benefits (Articles 69–73) and favors the creation of pension administrators, as was agreed in the FCN (1998, Agreements 63 and 87, described in Mesa-Lago 1998).

The 2005 Parametric Reform

The 2005 reform improved the equilibrium between the RIVM's contributions and expenses. The normal retirement age was kept at 65 years, but the number of required contributions increased from 240 to 300. Over a 30-year period, payroll contributions will increase from 7.5 to 10.5 percent, rising 0.5 percent every 5 years. Furthermore, workers now have an incentive to declare their wages because their benefits depend on their last 240 monthly real wages rather than the best 48 of the last 60 monthly nominal wages.

The primary innovation, however, concerns replacement rates. Before the reform, workers received a flat 52.2 percent of their real salary,

Table 12-4 IVM Contributors: Distribution and Shares of Total Income (2004)

Salary Group	*Workers*[a] *(%)*	*Total Salary (%)*
From 0 to < 2 minimum salaries	76	44
From 2 to < 4 minimum salaries	16	24
From 4 to < 6 minimum salaries	4	12
6 or more minimum salaries	3	20

Source: CCSS (2005*a*).
[a] The total is less than 100% due to rounding.

regardless of income levels. The reform scaled the benefits inversely to income levels—the lower the income, the higher the replacement rate—thereby making the system more progressive. The first salary group (zero to two minimum wages) includes almost 80 percent of CCSS contributors (who account for 44% of the CCSS income); 87 percent of all insured earn less than 3 minimum wages. On the other end, the top salary group (more than 6 minimum wages) includes 3 percent of the contributors (who account for 20% of total salaries). This very uneven distribution of income makes it possible to improve replacement rates among lower earners (see Table 12-4).

Table 12-5 presents the approved reform, distinguishing between the basic replacement rate with 240 contributions and the additional

Table 12-5 Benefit Levels According to Salary Scale in Adopted Parametric Reform (in %) (2005)

Salary Level, According to Number of Minimum Salaries	*Actual Real Basic Amount*		*Adopted Total Amount*	
	With 240 Contributions (20 Years) (a)	*With 300 Contributions (25 Years) (b)*	*Maximum Amount with 240 Contributions (20 Years) (c)*	*Maximum Amount. with Additional 1% (d)*
0 to <2	52.2	56.5	52.5	57.5
2 to <3	52.2	56.5	51.0	56.0
3 to <4	52.2	56.5	49.4	54.4
4 to <5	52.2	56.5	47.8	52.8
5 to <6	52.2	56.5	46.2	51.2
6 to <8	52.2	56.5	44.6	49.6
8 and more	52.2	56.5	43.0	48.0
Average amount	52.2	56.5	47.8	52.8

Source: CCSS (2004*b*).

replacement rate that includes an additional percentage for every 12 contributions beyond 240 (1% until 65 years of age and 1.6% afterward). A comparison of current and adopted replacement rates for people with 25 years of contributions shows that those who earn up to three minimum wages will have improved pensions. Columns (b) and (d) show an increase in pensions for up to 87 percent of the insured population, especially for the 78 percent with fewer than two minimum salaries. In these income brackets, the reform brings an average monthly increase of US$10 per insured person. The majority of workers with high incomes contribute for an average of 35 years. Therefore, their replacement rate effective loss will be less than that of those contributing for 30 years. Through a higher additional replacement rate, the reform provides an incentive for workers to contribute longer.

Early retirees get a full replacement rate if they make just under twice as many contributions as those required at age 65. This early retirement is useful for formal sector workers who start contributing very early in their careers, with high-average annual contributions, and who reach age 60 or 62 years with many more contributions than required at age 65 years. The reform maintained early retirement but improved differential tables for men and women: at every age, women are required to make 6 fewer monthly contributions than men, therefore acknowledging, even if minimally, women's unpaid work.

Prior to the reform, individuals who did not make 240 contributions lost the right to a contributive pension, unless they could prove disability, which explains the high proportion of disability pensions, as discussed above. The new reduced pension recognizes contributions below the 300 contributions required for normal retirement, if the worker has made 180 contributions or spent 15 years contributing. The reduced pension is calculated as a proportion of the current minimum pension, and it begins after 75 percent of the minimum pension with 180 contributions and complies with ILO Agreement no. 102, which Costa Rica ratified. Finally, high-income workers are required to make contributions based on their full wages. However, when they retire, their pensions have a ceiling, which creates an incentive to underdeclare wages.

The reforms took effect in November 2006, 18 months after being approved by the CCSS. The transition rules vary by age group. For those older than 54 years, contributions and benefits did not change. For people between aged 45 and 54 years, changes take place gradually. For those younger than 45 years, all changes apply (*Diario Oficial La Gaceta* 2005). These age groups are equivalent to 7, 17.5, and 75 percent of the contributive population, respectively (Estado de la Nación 2005).

TABLE 12-6 Overall Costs as a Percentage of Salaries, without Estimating Effects of Administrative Efficiency Improvements

Year	*Pre-reform Situation* (*a*)	*With Proposal Supported by the Business Sector*[a] (*b*)	*With Proposal Supported by Labor* (*c*)	*With Adopted Reform (with Adjusted Assumptions)* (*d*)
2005	7.4	7.1	7.4	7.4
2010	7.5	7.1	7.4	7.4
2015	8.2	7.6	8.0	8.0
2020	9.6	8.6	9.0	8.8
2025	11.4	9.7	10.4	9.9
2030	13.1	10.4	11.8	11.0
2035	14.7	11.1	13.2	12.4
2040	16.2	11.9	14.4	13.7
2045	18.5	13.2	16.3	15.6

Source: CCSS (2005*a*).

[a] Column (b) underestimates the costs of proposal because it considers that pensions are adjusted according to a rate lower than inflation and that pension upgrading corresponds to 80% of living expenses, while others consider such revaluation to be 100%.

Contribution rates are expected to rise gradually over time. The gradual rise will help keep the funds reserve from being depleted. Table 12-6 shows projected contribution rates according to different proposals presented at the negotiation table as well as the one approved by the CCSS. The only estimate that took into consideration increasing administrative efficiency is the one formulated with the assistance of the ILO, according to which in 2035 increased administrative efficiency would lead contributions to decrease from 13.2 to 12.6 percent of wages.

Table 12-7 shows how the reforms averted potential financial crises. The first critical moment is postponed by 30 years; the second by 24 years; and the third by 26 years. Because the increase in contributions is gradual over 30 years, there are several years in which contributions are insufficient yet balance out during the following years. The reform achieves actuarial equilibrium of the RIVM during the next four decades, without considering the result of improving administrative efficiency, through nonparametric measures (primarily through increasing revenue collection and coverage), investment returns, and better administrative controls.

Improvements in Administrative Efficiency, 2000 and 2005

The LPT introduced a set of measures to improve revenue collection. First, it established a set of mechanisms to reduce evasion and income

TABLE 12-7 Financial Sustainability Projections without Considering Increase in Administrative Efficiency

Critical Moments	*Prereform Situation*	*Proposal of Pensions Management, Businessmen, and solidaristas*	*Proposal of INAMU, Unions, and Cooperatives*	*Adopted Reform*
Contributions insufficient to finance expenditures	2011	2047	2036	2041
Total inflows insufficient to cover total expenditures; reserves start to decline	2022	2053	2041	2046
IVM funds reserves running out	2028	2060	2049	2054

Source: Grupo Técnico para la Reforma de IVM (2005).
Notes: Base scenario estimated by ILO based on CCSS Actuarial Department's. It was not possible for the Actuarial Department to replicate estimates under an efficient administration scenario as developed by ILO for one of the scenarios.

underreporting. These measures introduced or strengthened rewards and punishments and complement existing judicial measures. They include: (*a*) requiring firms to be in full compliance with social security obligations before receiving government contracts, being eligible for tax cuts, or accessing public records; (*b*) strengthening CCSS supervision; (*c*) creating the Sistema Centralizado de Recaudación (SICERE, or Centralized Collection System); and (*d*) allowing the CCSS to crosscheck information with other public databases (Castro Méndez 2000).

Second, the LPT established new parameters and regulations for investments, which eliminated for the CCSS the investment ceilings defined by the Ministry of Treasury and allowed them to invest up to 15 percent in the national mortgage system.

Third, the LPT established a five-year deadline to complete coverage of self-employed workers and an August 2000 deadline to complete the master plan to broaden coverage, which was 6 months after the LPT took effect. Although the master plan to broaden coverage was not yet designed, the law still mandated that total coverage had to be achieved by August 2005.

Fourth, the LPT required that up to 15 percent of public institutions' profits go to finance the expansion of coverage for self-employed workers.

When the Social Commission began negotiations, there were no estimates regarding how well the goals of these measures were being fulfilled. Existing evidence showed that progress was uneven, much more so with the implementation of the SICERE (which was especially necessary to begin the second pillar's operation). There was also little evidence that coverage was increasing among the self-employed. This situation began to change only in 2004, when negotiations to modify the requirements and benefits of the RIVM had already begun. This lack of evidence of progress generated distrust among Costa Ricans concerning the new reforms discussed in 2004 and adopted in 2005, especially for the unions, which had been their main advocates.

The Grupo Técnico reached a compromise agreement that would increase coverage, reduce evasion, improve investment management, control disability pension expenditures, and collect complementary public funding (of up to 15% of profits from public enterprises). It forecasts an increase in contributions in 2010 based on an increase in coverage (at least 50% of the annual increase of the economically active population over 5 years). The CCSS board of directors approved these changes, which was noted in the official record of the meeting. However, these policies are not reflected in RIVM regulations, which could weaken compliance (CCSS 2005*b*).

Considerations about Implementation

The 2000 reform was highly effective in its structural component. The 2005 reform, which addressed nonparametric issues that had already been passed in 2000 but had not been implemented, is too new to be assessed. The CCSS is supposed to lead accountability meetings every 6 months; the first was held only in July 2006.

The participation of Instituto Nacional de la Mujer (INAMU) in the 2005 reform reflected the greater attention to gender issues than took place during the 2000 reform. Although not all of INAMU's proposals were adopted, it raised issues that had not been previously considered, such as the economic dependency of women,[14] and it argued in favor of women having the option for early retirement.

The role of civil society organizations was very intense during the design and adoption phases but was diluted during implementation. The technical staff of the CCSS had to make significant compromises during the first two phases. However, they regained control of the process during the implementation of adopted measures. It is too early to assess the gap between policy design and implementation.

Possible Directions for Future Reform

Because of the 2000 and 2005 reforms, the Costa Rican pension system is a hybrid of the original pension system created during the 1940s and a Chilean-style system adapted by successive reforms in countries like Argentina and Uruguay. Costa Ricans took the experience of other countries with their reforms and combined this information with innovations based on their country's own institutional legacy. An example of this innovation is the financing of the second pillar in conjunction with the reform of severance payments, as it is the link between parametric and nonparametric measures. Beyond specific policy measures, however, it is the involvement of social, business, and, more recently, gender-sensitive actors in policy reform that makes the Costa Rican pension system highly distinctive.

Under the current model, Costa Rica could move further toward achieving the principles of universality, fairness, and solidarity established in its political constitution. However, doing so would require additional adjustments in requirements and benefits based on scaled replacement rates. Among these changes, it would be necessary to improve incentives so that high-income workers would contribute to the first pillar, rather than evade or underreport income. It would also be necessary to draw on collective insurance programs already available to expand contributory coverage and family insurance, especially for women in the informal sector.

Whether Costa Rica will follow this path or not is not clear. So far, Costa Rica's pension reforms have taken place at critical junctures, when societal projects conflict (Seligson and Martínez 2005). Some policymakers would want to increase the importance of individual savings; others would like to eliminate or reduce the role of individual savings. For instance, the business and financial sectors are not fully satisfied with the minor role of individual savings. Unions are not happy with noncompliance with measures legally established to strengthen collective accounts. The reforms represented a compromise approved only after lengthy and arduous negotiation among key stakeholders that could have potentially vetoed the reform.

Notes

[1] Argentina and Uruguay are the other two countries in the region with mixed systems. Ecuador designed a system of this kind but at the publication of this book had not yet implemented it (Mesa-Lago 2004). The mixed system exists in at least

twelve European countries, making it the most widespread system outside Latin America (Mesa-Lago and Hohnerlein in Mesa-Lago 2002).

[2] See Rodríguez and Durán (1998) for a detailed discussion of the introduced reforms.

[3] In 1940, life expectancy at birth was 46.93 years compared to 78.7 in 2004 (Central American Population Program, discussed in Méndez and Araya 2001; Estado de la Nación 2005).

[4] The *solidaristas* are worker–employer mutual support organizations. Unlike unions, they cannot negotiate collectively (Law 6970).

[5] Employers established 1% as the largest increase in contribution fees that they could afford without losing competitiveness. Unions opposed a general reduction in pensions, while the INAMU, the agency promoting women's rights, stressed the need to maintain different requirements for men and women.

[6] One proposal—defended by management at the CCSS Pension Division, the CCSS Actuarial Department, the business sector, and the *solidaristas*—consisted of reducing the old-age pension replacement rate from 52.2 to 46.5%, reducing the disability pension replacement rates, and eliminating the difference in the requirements for early retirement for men and women (Comisión Técnica Institucional 2004).

[7] This measure was supported by one government representative (from INAMU), unions, and cooperatives. They discarded the reduction in disability pensions and proposed maintaining early retirement differences for men and women. Because measures already established in the LPT to run the CCSS more effectively had so far not been fully implemented, these organizations demanded that parametric changes be conditioned to the implementation of nonparametric changes (ANEP 2004; INAMU 2004).

[8] In this section, all law references correspond to the LPT unless otherwise indicated.

[9] For teachers, the replacement rate is 80% and the contributions are 8% (workers), 6.75% (employers), and 0.25% (government) (Law 7531 1995, which reformed Law 2248). In the judicial branch, the contributions are 9% (workers), 11.75% (pensioners), 11.75% (employers), and 0.25% (government). They retire at age 62, after 30 years of service, with pensions equal to the average of the best 12 out of the last 24 salaries, or with the required years of service and/or under 62 years (Law 7333).

[10] Through 150 ongoing agreements, collective insurance only covers about 32,000 people, comprising 2% of the working population (Martínez Franzoni 2005*b*).

[11] LPT, Articles 30–8, 41, 42, 44, 45, 46, 54, 55, and 58–66.

[12] The law established the shared responsibility of the administrators and authorized social organizations for harm and damages that result from fraud committed by the members of its board of directors, employees, or promoters (LPT Articles 40 and 41).

[13] For example, after its ninth year, 38.47% of the funds are contributions and 61.53% are interest. It is projected that in its 30th year, 4.4% will be contributions and 95.6% interest (Castro Méndez 2000).

[14] Regardless of the growing number of women in the economically active population, women largely continue to access the pension system as economic dependents.

The RIVM discourages contributions from women because declaring a remunerated job, even if it is marginal, results in losing insurance as a dependent. Furthermore, it is likely that most women lack sufficient information to calculate the difference between the total pension for widowhood and their own contributive pensions. Among other proposals, the INAMU insisted on exploring the combination of contributive insurance (in pensions) and family insurance (in health).

References

Asociación Nacional de Empleados Públicos y Privados (ANEP) (December 2004). *Reforma de pensiones de IVM: Un consenso falso e ilegítimo.* San José, Costa Rica: ANEP.

Caja Costarricense del Seguro Social (CCSS) (1994). 'Reglamento del Régimen de Invalidez Vejez y Muerté, Mimeo.

—— (1995). 'Reglamento del Régimen No Contributivo, aprobado por Junta Directa en artículo 17', sesión 6921 y el artículo 4, sesión 6926, April 27 and May 23.

—— (May 2004*a*). 'Retos y perspectivas del seguro de Invalidez, Vejez y Muerte', in *Gerencia de Pensiones.* San José, Costa Rica.

—— (2004*b*). 'Valoraciones actuariales del seguro de IVM. Dirección Actuarial y de Planificación Económica', DAPE-323.

—— (2005*a*). 'Ajustes a la propuesta de reforma paramétrica del Régimen de IVM presentada por las organizaciones el 28 de febrero del 2005', GDF-13481.

—— (2005*b*). Artículo 12 de la sesión no. 7950, April 21.

Castillo, Marlen, Roxana Uzaga, and María del Rocío Carmona (2002). 'Cambios en el aseguramiento por el Estado y el Régimen no Contributivo', San José, Costa Rica: Curso de Régimen de Bienestar, Políticas Sociales y Cambios reciente en Costa Rica, Maestría de Economía de la Salud y Políticas Sociales, University of Costa Rica.

Castro Méndez, Mauricio (2000). *La Ley de Protección al Trabajador en Costa Rica: Proceso Previo y Análisis de Contenidos.* San José, Costa Rica: Oficina Internacional del Trabajo (OIT).

Comisión Técnica Institucional (2004). 'Propuesta de fortalecimiento y reforma del régimen de beneficios', San José, Costa Rica, December 10.

Diario Oficial La Gaceta (2005), No. 95, Wednesday, May 18.

Durán, Fabio (2002). 'Los programas de asistencia social en Costa Rica: el régimen no contributivo', in Fabio Bertranou, Carmen Solorio, and Woulter van Ginneken (eds.), *Pensiones no contributivas en Argentina, Brasil, Chile, Costa Rica y Uruguay.* Santiago: Oficina Internacional del Trabajo (OIT).

Estado de la Nación (2003). *Estado de la Nación en Desarrollo Humano Sostenible: Noveno Informe. San José,* Costa Rica: Proyecto Estado de la Nación.

—— (2005). *Estado de la Nación en Desarrollo Humano Sostenible: Undécimo Informe.* San José: Proyecto Estado de la Nación.

Foro de Concertación Nacional (FCN) (1998). 'Informe de la Comisión de pensiones al FCN', San José, Costa Rica, September 25.

Grupo Técnico para la Reforma del IVM (2005). 'Propuesta para la sostenibilidad del Régimen de Invalidez, Vejez y Muerte de la CCSS', San José, Costa Rica.

Instituto Nacional de la Mujer (INAMU) (2004). 'Comunicado conferencia de prensa', San José, Costa Rica, December.

Jiménez, Ronulfo (2000). 'El proceso de aprobación de la ley de protección al trabajador', in Ronulfo Jiménez (ed.), *Los retos políticos de la reforma económica en Costa Rica*. San José, Costa Rica: Academia de Centroamérica, pp. 247–70.

Law 17 Constitutiva de la Caja Costarricense del Seguro Social. San José, Costa Rica, October 22, 1943.

Law 6970 de Asociaciones Solidaristas, No. 6970. November 7, 1984.

Law 7333 Orgánica del Poder Judicial. May 5, 1993.

Law 7523 del Régimen Privado de Pensiones Complementarias. July 7, 1995.

Law 7531 de Pensiones y Jubilaciones del Magisterio Nacional (reform to Law 2248). July 15, 1995.

Law 7983 Ley de Protección al Trabajador (LPT). February 16, 2000.

Martínez Franzoni, Juliana (2005*a*). 'Reformas recientes de las pensiones en Costa Rica: Avances hacia una mayor sostenibilidad financiera, acceso y progresividad del primer pilar de pensiones', Informe técnico elaborado para el Proyecto San José: Estado de la Nación.

—— (2005*b*). 'La seguridad social en Costa Rica: Percepciones y experiencias de quienes menos tienen y más la necesitan', in *Banco Interamericano de Desarrollo*, WID 108, www.iadb.org/sds/wid/mainpublication_38_e.htm

—— and Carmelo Mesa-Lago (2003). *Reformas inconclusas: salud y pensiones en Costa Rica*. San José, Costa Rica: Fundación Frederich Ebert.

Méndez, Floribel and Olga Martha Araya (2001). 'Evolución de la esperanza de vida al nacimiento en Costa Rica, 1900–2000', Serie de estudios especiales 2. San José, Costa Rica: Instituto de Estadística y Censos.

Mesa-Lago, Carmelo (1998). *La Reforma de Pensiones en Costa Rica. San José,* Costa Rica: Fundación Friedich Ebert.

—— (2004). 'Las reformas de pensiones en América Latina y su impacto en los principios de la seguridad social', Serie financiamiento del desarrollo, no. 144 (March). Santiago, Chile: CEPAL.

—— and Eva Maria Hohnerlein (2002). 'Testing the Assumptions on the Effects of the German Pension Reform Based on Latin American and Eastern European Outcomes', *European Journal of Social Security*, 3(4): 285–330.

Rodríguez, Adolfo and Fabio Durán (1998). *Reforma de pensiones: los desafíos de la vejez*. San José, Costa Rica: Vicepresidencia de la República, Programa Reforma Integral de Pensiones.

Sauma, Pablo (2003). *Mercado de trabajo, distribución del ingreso y pobreza*. San José, Costa Rica: Proyecto Estado de la Nación.

—— (2004). *Perfil de los pensionados y cotizantes por regímenes*. San José, Costa Rica: Proyecto Estado de la Nación.

Seligson, Mitchell and Juliana Martínez (2005). 'Limits to Costa Rican Heterodoxy: What Has Changed in Paradise?', Prepared for delivery at the conference 'The Politics of Democratic Governability in Latin America: The Politics of Democratic Governability in Latin America: Clues and Lessons', Kellogg Institute, University of Notre Dame, October 6–8.

Superintendencia de Pensiones (SUPEN) (July 2004). 'Participación del régimen obligatorio de pensiones complementarias en la constitución de las pensiones individuales', presentation to the Comisión Técnica Institucional para la Reforma de IVM.

—— (2006). 'Estadísticas de los Fondos Administrados por las Operadoras de Pensión', www.supen.fi.cr

Trejos, Juan Diego (2003). 'El sector informal en Costa Rica a inicios del siglo XXI', Fundación Acceso/WIEGO. San José, Costa Rica.

Chapter 13

The Peruvian Pension Reform: Ailing or Failing?

Eliana Carranza and Eduardo Morón

In 1992 Peru followed the example of Chile and implemented a fully funded pension scheme, becoming the second country in Latin America to reform its pension system. The Peruvian reform shows three notable characteristics: (*a*) the public pension system was not closed—it continues to operate alongside the private one; (*b*) coverage is limited; and (*c*) competition in the privatized system appears to be limited.

First, the decision to maintain rather than eliminate the public pension system introduced several distortions to the overall functioning of the new mandatory pillar. These distortions have been obstacles to the reform's success. Political demands to return to the old public scheme are common—each year legislative initiatives are introduced to revise the private pension system. Most of these proposed reforms are aimed at reducing profits for the private pension funds rather than enhancing the performance of the private system, improving the fiscal situation, or meeting the needs of workers.

Second, the original objective of the pension reform was to provide more secure coverage than the public pension system. However, this objective has been met for only a small fraction of the workforce. In this respect, the government could participate more actively to expand coverage to individuals in the informal sector.

Third, Congress has discussed many initiatives to reduce profits in the private pension system rather than addressing the more urgent policy question of how to both increase competition and guarantee a secure pension benefit without creating excess market distortion. These challenges present no easy solution, as the government has the upper hand in the regulation process and the pension system provides an easy way to finance the fiscal gap. Consequently, the government has an incentive to trade long-term stability for short-term objectives.

Our gratitude to Lucero Burga, who helped with tables and figures, and to Tapen Sinha and Stephen J. Kay for their invaluable comments and suggestions. This paper represents only the personal views of the authors and not necessarily those of our institutions.

This chapter analyzes the pension system as a whole, considering both the mandatory private and public systems,[1] provides a preliminary assessment of the reform thus far, and analyzes potential reforms for the pension system.

The Pension System before the Reform

Government pensions date back nearly to Peru's independence. In 1850 the government sanctioned the Ley de Goces, or the Benefits Law, which created special pension benefits for a select group of public officials and citizens that served in the wars of independence.[2]

The mandatory public pension system started in 1936. Over the following decades, the system has undergone numerous modifications. Initially designed exclusively for private-sector workers, it was partially financed by taxes and contributions from employers, employees, and the government. In 1962 the system was extended to public employees; by 1973 most of the existing pension systems were consolidated into a single PAYGO public pension system called the DL 19990 regime.[3] There were two main exceptions: the Caja de Pensiones Militar-Policial, which still covers all military and police personnel, and the so-called Cédula Viva, a privileged pension scheme for high-ranking officers, which the government attempted unsuccessfully to close in 1974 by DL 20530.[4] Despite their differences, all the pension systems suffered from public pension fund mismanagement. Their sustainability was jeopardized by fiscally irresponsible governments that borrowed from pension funds to cover current expenditures and infrastructure projects, while high inflation wiped out the real value of pension funds.

In 1985 DL 19990 pensions covered only 34 percent of the EAP. The combination of a severe economic crisis and the reform of public-sector enterprises dramatically changed the labor market, tilting the coverage balance even more. Whereas, in 1990 two-thirds of the labor force had permanent jobs, one decade later this figure was just one-third. (Workers in the informal sector of course do not contribute to pension plans.) Growth in the informal sector is one of the most salient characteristics of the Peruvian economy.[5] By 1992 coverage had fallen to barely 21 percent of the EAP (see Carranza and Morón 2003: 21).

According to Mesa-Lago (1985), before the trough of the economic crisis in 1985, the Peruvian public pension system was already characterized as one in which (*a*) coverage was low (only 38% of the EAP, compared to 61% for Latin America as a region); (*b*) noncompliance with contributions was widespread; (*c*) the age structure of the affiliates was young (Peru had only 3.6% of its population older than 65 years, compared to 4.2% in the

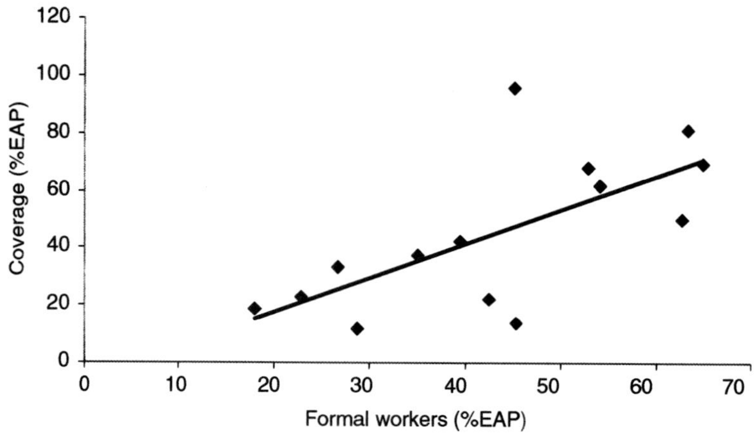

Figure 13-1. Coverage and informality in Latin America pre-reform (1985) (*Source*: Mesa-Lago 1985).

region); (*d*) pension benefit levels were not excessive—though this was not the case with the DL 20530 regime; (*e*) returns were significantly negative; and (*f*) recordkeeping was poor.

Low coverage is explained by the size of the formal sector: only 45 percent of the EAP were wage earners (Mesa-Lago 1985). The same pattern was true for the rest of Latin America (see Figure 13-1).

In sum, the public pension system suffered a severe mismanagement problem as the pension funds were subject to imprudent government policies. These problems were compounded when the demographic boom receded and a large share of younger workers migrated to other countries. Finally, government intervention in the market was biased toward the shrinking urban and formal labor market, which constitutes a minority of the workforce.

The Reform[6]

From a political economy perspective, some conditions are more conducive to reform than others. For example, it is easier to pass a reform if (*a*) the leader has an ample majority in Congress; (*b*) the president has recently been elected and is enjoying a honeymoon effect; (*c*) the group of beneficiaries will receive its benefits in the short run, whereas the costs are lumped in the long run; or (*d*) there is a clear consensus (see Brooks and James 2001). None of these four conditions were true in 1992.

Alberto Fujimori was elected president in July 1990 amid an economic crisis and the threat of increasing political violence. Given the desperate situation, he received political support for most of his political initiatives. However, Fujimori did not engage in dialogue with the legislature, nor did he pursue political alliances. He instead asked for special legislative powers to pass reforms, only explaining his decisions afterwards. Fujimori received ample legislative powers to pass a long list of reforms in the second half of 1991. In one week, the government issued more than fifty legislative decrees promoting private-sector participation in several sectors in the economy, including the pension reform (DL 724).

The early months of Fujimori's presidency were a time of major confrontation between the president and the Congress. Several decrees were changed or repealed.[7] One minister was censured and a motion to declare the presidency vacant was almost passed. These conflicts ultimately led to the April 1992 'self-coup', when Fujimori dismissed the Congress. In this complex political environment, the first attempt to reform the pension system did not succeed.

Mounting international pressure for a swift return to democracy forced the government to call for congressional elections. This put the pension reform in peril, as the issue lost importance in the political agenda. It was not until late 1992 that new legislation (DL 25897) was enacted to replace the first initiative.

The urgency of pension reform was justified in terms of the overall fiscal situation and the history of mismanagement of the public pension system. These two factors implied an inability to finance public pensions, and the pension reform was viewed as a way to avoid deeper fiscal problems. In this sense, replacing the PAYGO system with a system of individual accounts constituted one key element of the reform. Up to then, pensions were not linked to contributions and instead depended on the fortunes (or misfortunes) of the national treasury.

The reform did not bar workers from entering the public pension system, as in Chile,[8] due to mounting public opposition. The campaign to maintain the public system was assisted by favorable public opinion of Luis Castañeda, the manager of the agency running public pension and health programs (the Instituto Peruano de Seguridad Social, or IPSS, now called EsSalud). His managerial success undermined critics of the government's management of the pension system (although IPSS performance during his tenure was not representative of its past).

The manager's popularity explains why at that time it was considered positive to continue the operations of the public pension system. IPSS's coexistence with the AFPs or private pension fund managers was justified as a source of competition and as a way of disciplining the market.[9] Workers would voluntarily choose to join an AFP or the public pension system (El

Sistema Nacional de Pensiones, or SNP), but those who joined an AFP would also have to pay a solidarity contribution to the SNP to guarantee its financial sustainability.

One of the most significant design problems of the initial reform proposal was that workers had an incentive to stay at the SNP. The SNP offered several advantages, including a lower contribution rate, a lower retirement age, and an MPG—all of which the new system lacked. Meanwhile, recognition bonds to compensate those joining the new system for contributions made to the old public system were not implemented swiftly.[10] Additionally, workers who had chosen an AFP retained the option to move back to the SNP. Hence, the growth of the new system was slow (see Arce 2001). By the end of 1993, only 30 percent of workers with pension coverage were affiliated with the private pension system.

In 1995 most of the initial deficiencies were corrected. Under DL 26504 the contribution rate of the SNP was raised to match that of the Sistema Privado de Pensiones (SPP, or Private Pension System), the solidarity contribution was eliminated, and the retirement age was standardized for both men and women at 65 years. Also, the Oficina de Normalización Previsional (ONP, or Office of Social Security Normalization) was created to manage the SNP (replacing IPSS) and to expedite the recognition bonds process. Moreover, to tilt the balance toward the SPP, new employees had to select their affiliation preferences (SNP or a particular AFP) within a certain period; otherwise, they were automatically enrolled in an AFP.

Despite all the changes, some important issues still needed to be addressed, such as the implementation of a cap on mandatory contributions in the form of a taxable-wage ceiling, the possible phasing out of the SNP, and the introduction of an MPG for the SPP. Though included in the 1995 law, the MPG was not implemented until 2001. The reduction in the contribution rate from 10 to 8 percent that was intended as a temporary measure to attract more affiliates to the SPP became more of a permanent policy. Proposals to raise the contribution rate have been deferred year after year.

In summary, the initial reform introduced a fully funded DC system alongside an unfunded, fiscally unsustainable public system. The reform was incomplete, and there has been space for continuous revisions of the system. The politics of the reform have imposed great costs on the SPP: (*a*) the SPP has to invest significant resources in defending its existence; (*b*) its performance has been affected by changing the rules of the game; and (*c*) the SPP had to compete with the SNP to attract the same pool of workers but under unequal conditions and regulations. The experience of the past ten years suggests that a better strategy for the government would have been to complement the services provided by the private sector by extending coverage to sectors difficult to reach.

Evaluation of the Reforms

This section offers a preliminary evaluation of the pension system. A full evaluation is problematic given the fact that the system is still in a transition phase and is constantly changing.

Tables 13-1 and 13-2 provide a quick overview of the pension system as a whole. The most significant accomplishment of the reform is simply that it has endured, given the fact that policymaking in Peru is characterized by constant reversals (see Morón and Sanborn 2006). New governments have been prone to redo entire reforms regardless of the costs.[11] However, despite a strong and vocal group of opponents, the private pension system endures.

This resilience is notable. After a natural consolidation process that reduced the number of participants from eight AFPs to four, there was no effect on the affiliates (see Figure 13-2). Moreover, the pension fund has grown despite being tested by a series of major international economic crises during the late 1990s as well as a domestic political crisis following Fujimori's abrupt departure in 2000.

Evidence of the reform's progress can be found in the size of the funds managed by the private pension system: US$9 billion (more than 12% of the GDP). The rapid growth of pension fund assets has completely transformed the financial system. Banks have been displaced as the main providers of funding to the corporate sector. The government—after fixing major macroeconomic imbalances—was able to introduce a domestic bond market long awaited by the AFPs. Yet, in comparison with other reformed private pension systems, the Peruvian system has a much lower concentration in government bonds (see Table 13-3). Whereas the average in the region is close to 60 percent (in some countries, more than 80%), in Peru only 25 percent of the portfolio is in government bonds.

The excessive dependence on government bonds that characterize the rest of the reformed systems in the region highlights the fact that 'privateness' of the pension funds is relative. The only difference between those private systems and the old PAYGO systems is that now the workers' contributions go to their individual accounts instead of a common pool. However, the pension funds are still subject to regulatory capture and exposed to government whims. The limited investment in government bonds is one of the strengths of Peru's reformed system.

Of the main failures of the reform, the most pressing is the low coverage (see Table 13-4 for numbers on the region's coverage). In a recent World Bank study, Rofman and Carranza (2005) compute comparable coverage figures using Latin-American household surveys. The low coverage figures in Peru merit some explanation. First, Peru (along with Bolivia) is among the countries with the largest shares of informal workers in its labor force,

TABLE 13-1 The Peruvian Pension System after the 1992 Reform

	National Pension System	*Private Pension System*
Nature of the system	PAYGO	Individual capitalization account
Administration	National pension office (ONP)	Pension funds administration (AFP)
Mandatory contribution	13%	8%
Voluntary contributions	No voluntary contributions	Voluntary contribution up to 20% of the wage are deposited in the mandatory CIC
	—	Those in excess of 20% of the wage are deposited in separate voluntary retirement savings account
Fees as % of wage	None, but it is not clear how the 13% is distributed between retirement savings and administration costs.	Administration fee: 2.27%
	—	Insurance premium: 0.95%
	—	—
Maximum taxable wage	No ceiling	No ceiling
Maximum pension benefit	US$261	No ceiling
Minimum pension benefit	For all workers, according to the years of contribution:	Since 2002, only for workers that were born before 1945
	US$81 if less than 5 years	A benefit of US$125 is provided conditional on 20 years of contributions to any of the pension system
	US$93 if less than 10 years	—
	US$104 if less than 20 years	—
	US$125 if 20 years or more	—
Retirement pensions	According to the rules that consider the number and amount of contributions registered by the worker	As an annuity of the resources accumulated in the CIC: contributions and returns to the pension fund.

Source: MEF (2004).

TABLE 13-2 Pension System Indicators (December 2005)

	SNP		
	DL 19990	*DL 20530*[a]	*SPP*
Affiliates (in thousands)	1,154	60	3,637
Contributors (% affiliates)	41	—	36
Pensioners (in thousands)	4,133	262	27
Annual pension payment (in millions $)	1,050	1,318	86
Receive minimum pension (% pensioners)	27	—	3.5
Annual contribution collection (in millions $)	217	—	1,058
Pension Fund (in millions $)	—	—	9,931

Sources: Authors' own calculations based on data from ONP (n.d.), SBS (n.d.), and MEF (2004).

[a] The figures in this column are from December 2004.

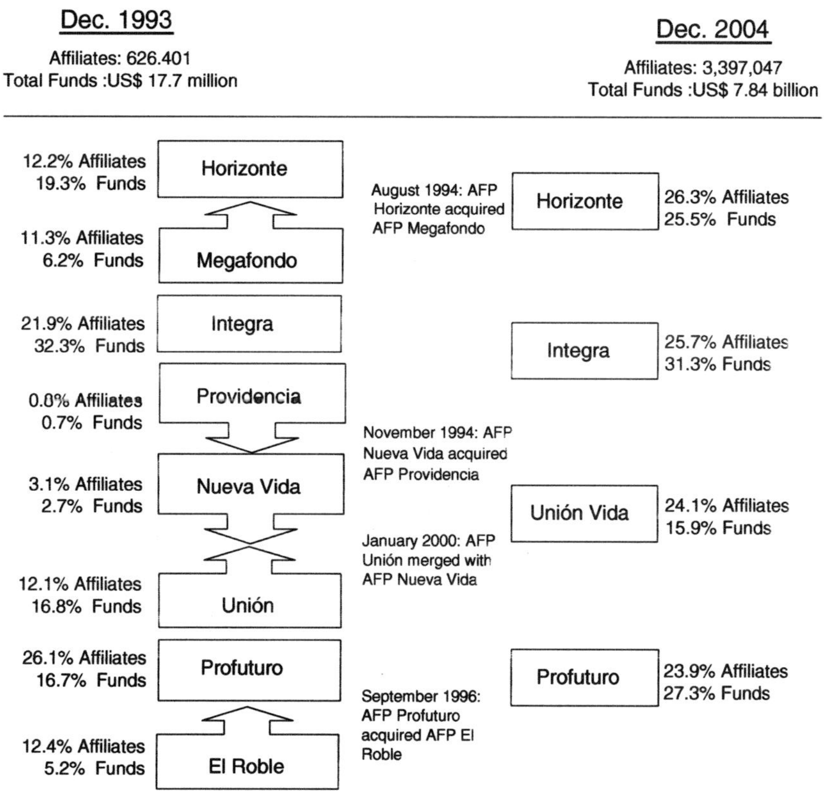

Figure 13-2. AFP mergers and acquisitions.

TABLE 13-3 Investment of Pension Funds (as of December 2004)

	Government Sector	*Corporate Sector*	*Financial Sector*	*Foreign Sector*	*Others*
Argentina	62.3	14.7	11.1	10.3	1.7
Bolivia	67.5	24.4	5.6	1.5	1.1
Chile	18.7	24.4	29.5	27.3	0.1
Colombia[a]	48.5	19.6	21.1	9.7	1.1
Costa Rica	77.2	11.4	11.5	—	—
El Salvador	83.5	0.3	10.5	5.5	—
Mexico	84.5	14.4	0.4	—	—
Peru	24.5	45.2	20	10.3	0.1
Uruguay	79	5.2	7.5	—	8.3
Average	60.6	17.7	13	10.8	2.1

Source: Author's own calculations based on FIAP (2005).

[a] The Colombian information includes only the mandatory pension system figures.

so the potential pension market is one of the narrowest.[12] Second, the reform law did not include incentives to increase coverage. For instance, Peru was one of the last countries to extend the MPG to the private pillar, and even then the guarantee is limited to affiliates born before 1945 with 20 years of contributions. Furthermore, contributions to the pension fund are still taxable in Peru.

By some measurements, pension system coverage has diminished since the introduction of the reform. However, measurements of coverage have a serious limitation: they do not control for the level or the certainty of

TABLE 13-4 Coverage Rates

	Contributors/ EAP	*Contributors/ Employed Persons*	*Contributors/ Wage-Earners*	*Beneficiaries/ Population Age 65+*
Argentina (2003)	34.6	40.3	54.7	68.3
Bolivia (2002)	9.9	10.9	29.0	14.7
Chile (2003)	58.2	63.4	77.3	63.8
Colombia (2002)	n.d.	n.d.	n.d.	18.6
Costa Rica (2000)	50.1	52.1	70.8	36.6
El Salvador (2000)	29.7	31.6	52.9	14.5
Mexico (2000)	38.5	39.3	62.2	19.2
Peru (2002)	13.9	14.4	31.3	23.7
Uruguay (2002)	55.3	65.0	78.6	87.1

Source: Rofman and Carranza (2005).

the pension provided.[13] In the past, the protection offered by the pension system was poor. The level of the pensions and the replacement rates were low and uncertain. In this sense, it is possible to argue that the law increased the cost of not participating in the system. However, the effects of these benefits were not extended to a larger group.

Another serious criticism of the reform is related to the level of competition in the private pension system. The perception in recent years has been that the four AFPs have behaved as an oligopoly and earned noncompetitive profits due to price agreements. The high return over equity (ROE) and concentration indices as well as the high and unchanging fees have been the fuel for dozens of legislative initiatives ranging from closing the private pension system to arbitrarily setting administration charges. They have also been the base of antitrust demands against each of the AFPs at INDECOPI (Instituto Nacional para la Defensa de la Competencia y de la Protección de la Propiedad Intelectual, or National Institute for the Defense of Competition and Protection of Intellectual Property), the competition watchdog. Nevertheless, all the demands were dismissed.

Typically, market concentration is measured by the Herfindahl-Hirschmann index (HHI). A first inspection of this indicator appears to support the position of the critics (see Figure 13-3), but the figures are deceiving as the number of firms is very small and not constant in the sample. To correct the problem, we compute an alternative indicator comparing the computed HHI with the lowest possible value it can take given a particular numbers of firms in the industry. The results in Figure 13-4 are the opposite of what Figure 13-3 shows. As the smaller firms were absorbed, the adjusted HHI of the remaining firms declined systematically. Given the number of AFPs, the market could not be less concentrated: the market shares of each AFP are almost 25 percent.

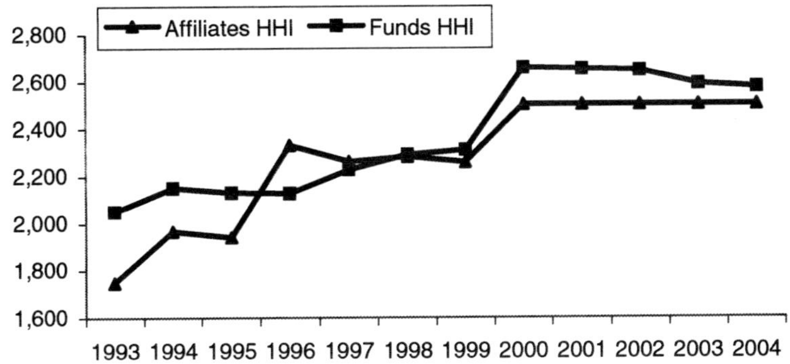

Figure 13-3. Herfindahl-Hirschman concentration indexes. (*Source*: Authors' computations based on SBS data n.d.)

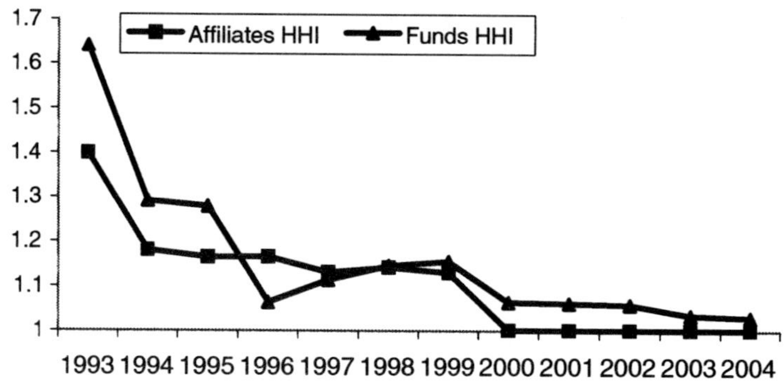

Figure 13-4. Herfindahl-Hirschman alternative indexes. (*Source*: Authors' computations based on SBS data n.d.)

Critics also frequently argue that the administrative fees charged by the AFPs reveal a lack of competition. Comparing Peru with other countries in the region, critics such as Campodónico (2005) claim that the Peruvian system is the second most expensive, just after the Argentine AFPs (see Table 13-5). However, a rapid inspection reveals that this conclusion is wrong. To rank the systems, the critics use the ratio of the administrative fee to the mandatory contribution rate. This indicator is flawed for two reasons. First, the ratio will be higher in those countries where the mandatory contribution to individual accounts is lower. In Peru, the level of this contribution is set by Congress, not by the AFPs. When Congress 'temporarily' reduced

TABLE 13-5 Contribution and Administrative Fee Rates (December 31, 2004)

Country	*Contribution Rate to Individual Account (1)*	*Administrative Fee*[a] (2)	*(2)/(1) (%)*
Argentina	4.47	2.53	56.8
Bolivia	10.00	2.21	22.1
Colombia	10.00	3.00	30.0
Chile	10.00	2.26	24.2
El Salvador	10.00	2.98	29.7
Mexico	4.88	1.38	28.9
Peru	8.00	3.19	39.9
Uruguay	11.95	2.90	24.7
Average	8.66	2.59	29.9

Source: Author's own calculations based on FIAP (2005).

[a] Only includes administrative fee charged as a percentage of wage.

TABLE 13-6 Average Commissions in Private Pension Systems (December 31, 2004)

Country	*Fixed Fee US$*	*Var. Comm. (% Wage)*	*Var. Comm. (% Wage)*		*Var. Comm. (% Pension Fund)*	*Var. Comm. (% RR)*
			AFP	*Ins. co.*		
Argentina	n/a	2.53	1.12	1.41	—	—
Bolivia	n/a	2.21	0.50	1.71	— [a]	—
Colombia	n/a	3.00	1.55	1.45	—	4.50
Costa Rica	n/a	—	—	—	—	7.25
Chile	0.95	2.26	1.27	0.99	—	—
El Salvador	n/a	2.98	1.78	1.20	—	—
Mexico	n/a	1.38	1.38	—	0.33	—
Panama	n/a	—	—	—	1.26	—
Peru	n/a	3.19	2.27	0.92	—	—
Dominican Rep.	n/a	1.50	0.50	1.00	—	28.75
Uruguay	0.43	2.90	1.94	0.96	0.002	—

Source: FIAP (2005).

[a] 0.2285 if the pension fund is less than US$1,000; 0.14 if the pension fund is more than US$1,000 but less than US$1,200; 0.067 if the pension fund is more than US$1,200 but less than US$1,500.

the rate of contribution from 10 to 8 percent in 1995, they made the system more expensive. Following this reasoning, by restoring the original rate, Peru would come close to the regional average.[14]

Second, the indicator is misleading, as it takes only the variable commission into account —that is, the fee charged as a percentage of a worker's wage. However, the AFPs across Latin America have differing administrative charges. Some also include a fixed fee, while others apply a fee on the size of the funds or on the return obtained by the funds (see Table 13-6). Consequently, this indicator underestimates fees on systems that depend less on the variable fees.

Carranza and Morón (2004) offer a better measure that allows comparisons among systems with different pricing schedules. Following James, Smalhout, and Vittas (2001), we compute equivalent annual fees, or the annualized value of all fee payments as a percentage of the workers' wages. The figures assume that the return on the funds and the mandatory contribution are the same across systems and over time. The results, in Table 13-7, show that while the cost of Peru's pension system was above the regional average, the discrepancy is not as high as previous studies have indicated. Furthermore, with the recent reductions in fees, the Peruvian system is among the less expensive ones in the region.

TABLE 13-7 Equivalent Annual Fees (% of the Individual Pension Fund) (December 31, 2004)

Country	*With Official Contribution Rate (1)*	*Assuming 8% as Contribution Rate (2)*
Argentina	0.760	0.424
Bolivia	0.523	0.597
Colombia	0.484	0.494
Chile	0.304	0.380
El Salvador	0.398	0.497
Mexico	0.707	0.560
Peru	0.532	0.532
Uruguay	0.390	0.487
Average	0.512	0.496
Memo: Peru (2006)	0.374	0.467

Source: Author's own calculations based on FIAP (2005).

Finally, pension fund firms have been criticized for excessively high ROE. According to a report prepared by Gerens (2005), the private pension industry has the highest ROE displayed in the past 10 years by any industry.[15] Furthermore, by that measurement, two of the AFPs rank as first and third best performers of the past decade.

Surprisingly, such a profitable market has not seen new entrants until this year. A typical explanation is that high barriers deter potential competitors, but the capital requirements for entry are not extremely large. Rather, other local factors hinder investor participation in this market. First, high uncertainty exists regarding the basic rules governing the system. Second, substantial limitations are imposed by the informal sector on the size of the potential market. Third, there is low price elasticity of affiliation and contribution. Fourth, switching from one AFP to other was an involved process in which the affiliate had to bear high transaction costs.[16] In such an environment, the most convenient method of entry was to buy an existing firm.

A weakness in the system is the effect of the temporary reduction of the contribution rate. Back in 1995, legislators were convinced that a reasonable way to attract more affiliates into the system was to reduce temporarily the contribution rate from 10 to 8 percent. However, they did not take the possible effects on replacement rates into account. Moreover, the temporary change has become a permanent one that has reduced projections of future pensions. A paper by Berstein and Ruiz (2004) suggests that frequency of contributions does not depend on the rate of contribution. If this is the case, then lowering the contribution rate will lead to lower replacement rates but not to greater compliance.

Another weakness is the inability to offer a response to the problem of the lack of compliance in contributions. More than half of the affiliates do not contribute regularly to their individual accounts. However, it is unclear whether this is because the worker is no longer employed or because the firm is not depositing the corresponding contribution. Both the SBS and the Ministry of Labor have a very limited ability to enforce compliance. Moreover, workers do not have the incentive to complain to their employers out of fear they might be laid off.

The Pending Reforms

As discussed above, the common view is that the reform failed to increase coverage, reduce administrative costs, or promote competition. The section that follows discusses proposals that tackle those issues.

Refocus Government Intervention[17]

The most pressing question for a country reforming its pension system is perhaps whether to close the old public system. This is a very difficult political decision, because the workers in the transition period are significantly affected. Compensating them increases the fiscal cost of reform but avoiding a complete phaseout of the public system reduces the efficiency of the private system and lessens the potential for reductions in administrative costs. The tradeoff is clear, because in essence the public and the private systems are serving the same clients.

In Peru, according to the most recent household survey, 77.5 percent of the population older than 60 years does not have pension coverage. Even if we include such informal social protection networks as retirees living with their children, 46.5 percent of people older than 60 years are still not covered against an income shock. This situation calls for a redefinition of the role and commitment of the government in the postreform period. Currently, its role is limited to supervising the private pension system and offering pensions to those affiliated with the public system. There is no effective universal MPG for the elderly. A World Bank report argues that current government programs should cover only those that comply with requisites of contributions and years of enrollment (WB 2004). Currently, the public provider duplicates efforts in that the SNP and SPP serve the same market in a situation in which the government is resource constrained and in which a large part of the population has no benefits whatsoever.

According to the report, pension system objectives require clarification. These systems should prevent poverty in old age and smooth consumption in old age. Those objectives could be achieved by: introducing a universal noncontributory means-tested pension; redefining pillar one as a mandatory pooling system with a crosssubsidized minimum pension; and creating individual capitalization accounts that provide affiliates with pensions consistent with their earnings. The report concludes that it is preferable that the government focus its attention and resources to meet the poverty-reduction objective through a collective system, whereas the private pension system takes care of consumption-smoothing through individual accounts. In this way, the pillars are clearly defined and complement each other.

Recently, Carranza (2005) and Morón, Ponce, and Tejada (2005) estimated the feasibility of adopting the World Bank proposal. Carranza finds that setting up a universal pension system will increase coverage from 15 to 40 percent, with the less expensive alternative costing around 0.6 percent of GDP annually. This does not take into account the administrative cost of running a pillar-zero program and the possibility of targeting problems that have swamped other social programs.[18] Both papers find that setting up an MPG in which the government fills only the gap not provided by individual contributions and the profitability of the funds managed by AFPs is fiscally feasible (costing around 0.05% of GDP annually). According to Morón, Ponce, and Tejada (2005), a restructured MPG program could be used as a source of additional funding to increase coverage for at least half a million workers. Asking individuals to fund at least a part of their future pensions will potentially free up government resources. However, phasing out the SNP will prove difficult for political reasons.

In our opinion, there is room for private-sector involvement in each of the pillars. The private pension providers could pay the universal benefits, manage the collective insurance, and administer the capitalization accounts. In this scenario, the role of the government would be restricted to providing funds for the universal pension, offering guarantees for a less restrictive MPG, improving the supervision and regulation of the AFP industry, and isolating the system from political risks.

Promote Competition with More Flexible Rules

Under the current regulatory framework and until the system matures, the dimension on which AFPs most often compete is price. Contrary to what happens in any other industry, the AFPs have not been able to differentiate their product by altering characteristics such as the liquidity of the retirement savings, the portfolio composition, or the returns on the pension fund. The administrative fee is the main differentiating factor, but this also has its limitations. The AFPs were not allowed to offer price incentives to loyal affiliates until 2004, and even in that case the elasticity of fee reductions is so low that this tool is ineffective.

Much of the current regulation was written during the early 1990s, when the only reference was Chile's groundbreaking experience. It was understandable that regulators were extremely cautious. For example, AFPs were required to invest only in investment-grade securities, and they had to attain a return similar to the average of the system. These restrictions promoted a copycat strategy among AFPs that was exacerbated in the context of a rather illiquid and underdeveloped financial market. In general, the strict limits on portfolio management have created a situation in which differences in the returns accumulated by the AFPs have to be measured using two decimal points.

Only since 2005 has the SBS changed its pricing policies. AFPs can now offer discounted fees to affiliates who sign contracts committing to stay with the same provider for a fixed term (1–3 years). Along the same lines, the SBS approved and regulated the creation of multifunds. In October 2005, the AFPs started offering three types of pension funds that may better meet the risk-return preferences of their affiliates. The previous scheme imposed too much risk on the old affiliates and offered moderate returns to the young. The new regulations allow individuals to invest voluntarily in an AFP other than the one in which they have their mandatory account. Nonetheless, if this initiative is not complemented with more flexible investment limits, the system will end up with three similar funds. Unfortunately, the Central Bank—which has the last word on portfolio regulation—has blocked the SBS proposal to raise the limit on investments in foreign markets.

Another way to introduce more competition is to promote the voluntary third pillar. For this, the SBS will have to introduce caps on contributions to the mandatory second pillar. The potential problem with this proposal is that if the ceiling is set too low, replacement rates may fall beyond reasonable amounts. On the contrary, if the ceiling is too high, the market for voluntary savings will be too thin to attract competitors beyond the AFPs such as mutual funds or banks.

Conclusions

In summary, the pension reform in Peru has been a partial success. The qualification is needed because the initial reforms were not as bold as they should have been. Could we say emphatically that the private pension system is safe from political interference in the near future? Unfortunately, the answer is a resounding *no*—it is a government-mandated, privately run system, not a private one. Sound policy requires taking a long-term perspective, an exercise that has never been an easy task for a government in which competing pressing needs and an unpredictable political scenario force policymakers to think myopically. Perhaps the size of the pension fund and its considerable influence on the financial system will be enough incentive to shift the policy debate toward long-term issues. Hopefully, as the pension system matures and grows exponentially, politicians will change their perspective.

The challenges ahead might seem insurmountable, especially regarding increasing coverage, which is clearly linked to the formalization of the economy and luring independent workers into the system. The system is vulnerable to multiple risks given that Peru is a developing country with a developing pension system. Nonetheless, the need for additional reforms is clear. For that to happen, it will require political will to lead a pension reform.

Notes

[1] Not included in this chapter is a discussion of possible reforms of the military and police pension systems.

[2] In fact, this legislation only rephrased older Spanish legislation (Real Cédula of February 8, 1803).

[3] DL is short for *decreto ley* (literally, 'law decree').

[4] There were attempts to end this system in both 1962 and 1974. This regime was to be restricted to employees who had entered the public sector before 1962. However, workers entered via special legislation in the 1980s (discussed below).

[5] According to Schneider (2005), Peru ranks among the world's top ten informal economies.

[6] An early but balanced account of the reform is found in Ortiz de Zevallos et al. (1999). A more personal and passionate account of the reform can be found in Roggero (1993). Roggero was a member of Congress until 1992 and the main proponent of the pension reform during the early stages of the process.

[7] Another set of legislative decrees were blocked by the constitutional court, which by all accounts was controlled by the Alianza Popular Revolucionaria Americana (APRA), the major opposition party. The pension reform (DL 724) was under review by this court when it was dismissed after the 1992 coup.

[8] A provision making the new system compulsory was part of the original executive proposal but President Fujimori removed it from the final bill. A proposal to charge higher fees in the public system (as an incentive for workers to join the private system) was also scrapped, as was a later 1995 attempt to require new workers to affiliate with the private system.

[9] In 1995 the World Bank proposed to unify both systems but the proposal was dismissed. See Kane (1995).

[10] Moreover, recognition bonds faced two problems: (*a*) reliable contribution records were absent and, (*b*) in most cases, actual salary records were also unavailable.

[11] For example, President García's regionalization process was completely dismantled by President Fujimori, only to be revived by President Toledo. All these changes happened in less than fifteen years.
[12] According to the ILO (2005), in 2004 58% of Peru's nonagricultural labor force was in the informal sector, compared to 66.7% in Bolivia and 47.4% in Latin America overall.
[13] Mesa-Lago (2001) discusses the pros and cons of alternative coverage measures.
[14] On the last day of the 2005 legislative session, Congress voted to return to the original 10% contribution rate.
[15] According to that report, the private pension system had an average 30.6% return over equity compared to a financial sector average of only 7.7% in nominal terms.
[16] This was changed in 2005 to allow affiliates to switch AFPs via the Internet and without having to wait six months to make a new switch. The new procedure has reduced the duration of the process from ten to two months.
[17] This section is based on Carranza and Morón (2004).
[18] Carranza (2005) simulates the cost of this program under two alternative targeting rules. In one case, the beneficiaries are all elderly people living alone in extreme poverty or in poverty and not receiving a pension benefit. In the other case, the restriction of living alone is lifted. In the less expensive case, the pension benefit is equivalent to 2/9 of the current minimum wage.

References

Arce, Moisés (Fall 2001). 'The Politics of Pension Reform in Peru', *Studies in Comparative International Development*, 36(3): 88–113.

Berstein, Solange and José Ruiz (2004). 'Sensibilidad de la demanda con consumidores desinformados: el caso de las AFP en Chile', Superintendencia de AFP.

Brooks, Sarah and Estelle James (2001). 'The Political Economy of Structural Pension Reform', in Robert Holzmann and Joseph Stiglitz (eds.), *New Ideas about Old Age Security*. Washington, DC: World Bank.

Campodónico, Humberto (2005). 'Las AFP Peruanas son las más caras de América Latina', *La República*, January 28.

Carranza, Eliana (2005). 'Improving Coverage in the Peruvian Pension System: Evaluation of the World Bank Reform Proposal', Paper prepared for graduation at John F. Kennedy School of Government, Harvard University.

—— and Eduardo Morón (2003). *Diez Años del Sistema Privado de Pensiones. Avances, Retos y Reformas*. Lima: Universidad del Pacífico.

—— —— (2004). 'Keeping Which promise, to Whom and How?', working paper, Universidad del Pacífico.

Federación Internacional de Administradoras de Fondos de Pensiones (FIAP) (2005). Informe Semestral No. 18, http://www.fiap.cl

Gerens (2005). *Competitividad Internacional y Rentabilidad de las Empresas en el Perú*. Lima: Gerens.

International Labour Organization (ILO) (2005). *Panorama Laboral 2005 América Latina y el Caribe*, Lima, Peru: Oficina Regional para América Latina y el Caribe.

James, Estelle, James Smalhout, and Dimitri Vittas (2001). 'Administrative Costs and the Organization of Individual Retirement Account Systems: A Comparative Perspective', Policy Research Working Paper 2554, Washington, DC: World Bank.

Kane, Cheikh (1995). 'Peru: Reforming the Pension System', ESP Discussion Paper Series, Washington, DC: World Bank.

Mesa-Lago, Carmelo (1985). 'Los Sistemas de Pensiones en el Marco de la Seguridad Social en América Latina', in Laura Morales and Javier Slodky (eds.), *La Reforma de la Seguridad Social. Análisis Comparativo del Perú dentro del Contexto Latinoamericano.* Lima: CIUP–Fundación Friedrich Ebert.

—— (2001). 'La cobertura de pensiones de seguridad social en América Latina. Antes y después de la reforma provisional', *Sociales,* (4), Rosario, Argentina.

Ministerio de Economía y Finanzas (MEF) (2004). 'Los Sistemas de Pensiones en Perú', Dirección General de Asuntos Económicos y Sociales.

Morón, Eduardo, Juan José Ponce, and Johanna Tejada (2005). '¿Tiene Sentido tener Sistemas Previsionales Paralelos en el Perú?', working paper, Universidad del Pacífico.

—— and Cynthia Sanborn (2006). 'The Pitfalls of Policymaking in Peru: Actors, Institutions and Rules of the Game', Research Network Working Paper R-511, InterAmerican Development Bank.

Oficina De Normalizacion Previsional (ONP) (n.d.). http://www.onp.gob.pe/

Ortiz de Zevallos, Gabriel, Hugo Eyzaguirre, Rosa María Palacios, and Pierina Pollarolo (1999). 'La economía política de las reformas institucionales en el Perú: los casos de salud, educación y pensiones', IADB Working Paper 348.

Rofman, Rafael and Eliana Carranza (2005). 'Social Security Coverage in Latin America', Social Protection Discussion Paper Series. Washington, DC: World Bank.

Roggero, Mario (1993). *Escoja Usted.* Lima, Peru: Tarea Asociación Gráfica Educativa.

Schneider, Friedrich (2005). 'Shadow Economies of 145 Countries All Over the World: Estimation Results over the Period 1999 to 2003', working paper, University of Linz.

Superintendencia de Banca y Seguros del Peru (SBS) (n.d.). www.sbs.gob.pe

World Bank (WB) (2004). 'Peru: Restoring the Multiple Pillars of Old Age Income Security', Report No. 27618-PE. Washington, DC.

Chapter 14

Uruguay: A Mixed Reform

Rodolfo Saldain

Introduction

Toward the late nineteenth century and the beginning of the twentieth, Uruguay was among the first countries in the hemisphere to introduce pensions. However, during the latter half of the past century, social insurance went through an extensive period of retrenchment as the maintenance of generous social security benefits became incompatible with chronic economic stagnation.

Although international organizations like the ILO urgently recommended reform as early as 1964, it was not until 1979—during the military dictatorship—that some parametric changes were introduced. By then, the relatively generous benefits combined with an aging population had resulted in the actuarial bankruptcy of the pension system. An insolvent social security system, covered by government transfers, represented around 2 percent of GDP during the 1970s, equivalent to a little more than 20 percent of central government expenditures (see Table 14-1).

In the beginning, the strategies for confronting the crisis included raising worker and employer contribution levels, which came to represent about 8 percent of GDP by the end of the 1970s. Funding was insufficient, however, and the purchasing power of pensions declined systematically. This ended in 1989 with a constitutional reform that increased the budget for pensions to approximately 15 percent of GDP.

In 1995 the third elected government after democracy was restored in 1985 approved a new structural reform. The new model is innovative in that it maintained continuity with the Uruguayan statist tradition yet still followed the regional trend toward privatization. The new system is mixed. The main component, or first pillar, is pure PAYGO with respect to contributions, benefits, and administration. The primacy of the first pillar will be maintained even after the mixed system reaches maturity, around the year 2020.

The author would like to thank economist Bruno Golembiewsci for his assistance with the tables, Larissa Bocanegra, who translated this document, and Stephen J. Kay and Tapen Sinha for their editing and comments.

TABLE 14-1 Central Government Expenditures on Social Security (1,000s of Nominal Pesos)

Year	*Central Government Outlays on SS*	*Central Government Total Indexed Outlays*[a]	*Weight of SS Expenditures on Central Government Nominal Outlay Structure (%)*
1974	103,594.35	438,426.11	23.63
1975	113,533.83	457,518.80	24.82
1976	115,718.16	505,420.05	22.90
1977	128,118.39	590,697.67	21.69
1978	157,635.47	667,816.09	23.60
1979	210,318.47	928,152.87	22.66
1980	506,923.08	1,439,252.75	35.22
1981	634,288.35	1,740,397.41	36.45
1982	870,237.24	1,977,217.83	44.01
1983	389,548.35	960,026.06	40.58
1984	298,485.12	901,067.55	33.13
1985	261,358.04	824,007.10	31.72
1986	276,970.14	965,530.85	28.69
1987	347,568.02	1,155,166.03	30.09
1988	396,553.07	1,254,071.50	31.62
1989	414,926.26	1,327,575.10	31.25
1990	378,246.02	1,322,066.52	28.61
1991	512,216.11	1,628,395.94	31.46
1992	709,677.27	1,987,605.18	35.71
1993	943,049.01	2,392,113.32	39.42
1994	1,238,793.63	2,934,836.78	42.21
1995	1,441,247.43	3,334,299.68	43.22
1996	1,712,481.27	3,681,136.15	46.52
1997	1,894,431.05	4,018,069.40	47.15
1998	1,972,784.57	4,132,022.44	47.74
1999	2,090,238.10	4,353,561.82	48.01
2000	2,056,682.64	4,269,617.13	48.17
2001	1,989,804.10	4,176,206.71	47.65
2002	1,439,320.12	3,169,018.31	45.42
2003	1,109,256.44	2,759,290.02	40.20
2004	1,154,658.82	2,992,841.55	38.58

Source: Author's computations, based on projections from the Instituto Nacional de Estadistica (National Statistics Institute).

[a] Does not include investment outlays.

Although the pension system survived the largest financial crisis in the country's history in 2002, it faced a political challenge when the left Frente Amplio coalition came to power in 2004. The Frente Amplio had systematically opposed the pension reform since its inception, and some sectors of the coalition demanded the abolition of certain structural components, such as the participation of *administradora de fondos de ahorro provisional* (AFAPs, or private retirement saving fund administrators). Thus far, there has apparently been no political attempt to alter the reform, as the government has focused on developing a hospitable environment for foreign and local investment.

Historical Evolution of the Pension System

In Uruguay's coverage of old-age, survivorship, and disability risks (Sistema de Invalidez, Vejez y Sobrevivencia, or IVS) started soon after independence in 1829. In 1896 the first protection system based on the Bismarckian model was created; it covered retirement for teachers, who were considered an essential human resource in the creation of the new nation-state.

After a series of armed conflicts ended in 1904, Uruguay went through an extensive period of democratic political stability—albeit with two limited episodes of instability in 1933 and 1942—distinguished by a multiclass and bipartisan political system.[1] In this context, a vast network of social security institutions developed that recognized workers' rights. All workers were gradually incorporated into this network. In 1943 rural workers were incorporated, representing the last large and significant sector of the labor force, and in 1954 coverage for old-age, survivorship, and disability was extended to all primary wage-earning employment.

After the foundation and development periods of the Uruguayan social security system, a long period of decline began in the mid-1940s, provoking a crisis in the system. The state apparatus became an arena of political conflict among the two traditional 'catch-all political parties', especially with respect to the social security system. During this period, several special pension systems were developed as a result of negotiations and bargaining processes, and political clientelism in the social security institutions covering IVS risks became common practice.

The Crisis

These circumstances, along with inefficient investment policies of the initial reserves, tax evasion, poor administration, and a demography characterized by low-birth rates and high life expectancy combined with economic stagnation and slow growth, led to the financial and social crisis of the system.

In 1963 an ILO report stated that 'it is no longer enough to apply palliative remedies to improve the situation. Instead there should be a radical change in the direction and implementation of social policy in order to avoid the total social, administrative, and financial collapse of the Uruguayan social security system' (OIT 1964: 64–71).

For at least three decades, the predominant policy was to maintain the formal–legal parameters of the social security system that promised access to generous benefits, while in practice the value of those benefits fell due to insufficient cost of living adjustments in an environment of high inflation. The political leadership typically denied the problem in order to avoid actions that would carry political or electoral costs. The government coped with the financial disequilibria of the pension system by (*a*) cutting the value of pensions in real terms,[2] (*b*) not paying all legally owed benefits, and (*c*) generating fiscal deficits in order to cover financial obligations.

During the military dictatorship that ruled from 1973 to 1984, there was a clear concentration of power. Although an important parametric reform in 1979 corrected some of the system's main shortcomings, there was no structural reform as in Chile. The regime that resulted from the 1979 reform (which endured through 1995) was pure PAYGO, with no accumulation of reserves. It was centralized in the executive branch and financed through worker, employer, and government contributions. The results of this reform still resonate among the retired population, and the worker/beneficiary ratio is likely to rise slightly through 2010, after which the ratio is expected to deteriorate at a constant rate, according to all projections.

The 1989 Constitutional Reform

In the early years following the return to democracy (1985–9), there were strong demands for benefits, in particular for pension increases. During that time, pensioner organizations emerged as a new social movement (see Papadopulos 1992: 158–77). These groups formed alliances with other political actors and demanded higher benefits, while at the same time radically defending the public PAYGO system.

In 1989 pension organizations and their allies successfully sponsored a plebiscite that amended Article 67 of the Constitution. Eighty percent of the electorate supported the initiative, which is still in effect today.[3] This article determined that pensions would be adjusted according to the variation in the median salary index and would go into effect concurrently with salary increases for employees of the central government. Fiscal balance was maintained only because of insufficient adjustment in a context of high inflation (which of course reduced the buying power of benefits). The new regulation altered one of the variables essential to the pension system's financial equilibrium: the ratio of the average benefit over the average contribution base salary.[4] In 1989 the average benefit was 58 percent of the average contribution base salary; this figure jumped to 77.5 percent in 1991, the first full year of reform. That rapid jump meant that additional resources equivalent to a 10-percent increase in the salary contribution rate were necessary. Consequently, the annual Banco de Previsión Social del Uruguay (BPS) pension budget rose from 7.7 percent of GDP in 1989 to 9.7 percent in 1991, and to more than 11 percent in 1994. (The BPS is Uruguay's Social Security Bank.)

There were only two administrative options to ease the excessive increase in the pension budget: (*a*) reduce the value of the national minimum wage, which was the measurement unit used to express pension ceilings and other social security benefits, or (*b*) moderate salary increases, especially for state workers, because of their direct impact on both the national budget and the median wage index, on which pension increases were based. To generate more income, the government declared a crackdown on evasion. Results were positive, though limited by the fact that structural conditions for evasion persisted.

Toward the 1995 Structural Reform

One virtue of the constitutional amendment of Article 67 was that it brought national attention to the challenges of social security reform. It was impossible to continue postponing difficult reform decisions by allowing inflation to limit benefits. The magnitude of the problem demanded that the government find the political will to implement difficult measures in the face of powerful interest groups opposed to reform. Various proposals were suggested based on foreseeable demographic trends and pension system indicators. By all accounts, the system appeared to be moving rapidly toward a financial crisis in the first decade of the next century.

After two failed attempts to introduce some parametric reforms in 1990, the Lacalle administration summoned political leaders and representatives of social sectors to discuss the magnitude of the problem, even though its major impact would largely fall on future governments. The administration proposed four objectives for the social security reform: (*a*) improve social equity and individual fairness, (*b*) establish total financial transparency, (*c*) achieve adequate financing of the programs administered by the BPS, and (*d*) improve the adequacy of the financial structure. They added four alternative proposals for analysis:

1. Maintain the current system, but modify the procedure used to calculate the base reference salary and the replacement rates;[5]

2. Create a new regime financed through individual capitalization. In this case, it would be necessary to define ways to finance transition costs[6] and the legal nature of the new pension fund administrators;
3. Create a new pension system based on individual accounts but financed via PAYGO;[7] and
4. Create a new two-tiered pension system that would include a state-managed PAYGO system with benefits clearly lower than those of the current regime,[8] and a second tier based on individual capitalization, with pension fund administrators operating in a competitive market.

In 1992 there was substantial progress toward reaching a political accord. However, the left-wing Frente Amplio systematically opposed all social security reform initiatives. Ultimately, the Chamber of Deputies did not approve the project. That same year, the legislature (without the support of the left-wing parties) agreed to modify the procedure to calculate pensions, but a 1994 plebiscite later reversed that modest reform and the Supreme Court found it unconstitutional.[9]

The 1995 Reform

Negotiations over social security reform began in January 1995, after Julio María Sanguinetti began his second term. An agreement soon resulted, though it again did not have the support of the Frente Amplio.[10] Political agreement was hastened by the fact that the technical and political teams working on the reform had worked together in prior years.

The Design of the 1995 Reform

The reform, centered on the idea of a mixed system, consisted of a traditional state-managed PAYGO pillar and a mandatory, private, individual saving accounts pillar under private management, with old-age, disability, and survivor's insurance financed out of savings.[11] In the new multipillar system, workers contribute to each fund according to where their income falls within a salary-level band. Additionally, the public sector participates by providing a basic safety net pension (PAYGO system) to complement the mandatory system of individual capitalization, administered by AFAPs and insurance companies.[12]

Studies conducted in 1991 and 1992, which analyzed the financial feasibility of the new mixed system, suggested the need to reduce the fiscal impact of the transition. As a result, the reform was oriented toward (*a*) the mandatory incorporation into the new mixed model of only the younger population (younger than 40 years), and (*b*) a PAYGO component large enough not to affect benefits for workers still acquiring rights—that is, those workers who had paid into the old system but had not yet qualified for benefits.[13] The ceiling proposed at the first level (PAYGO) was very similar to the one in the old system, but with more stringent conditions with respect to age and years of services. It was not necessary to acknowledge previous contributions because older workers and those who had contributed for a longer time could not be affiliated in the new system, unless they wanted to contribute to a voluntary supplemental account. In addition, the size of the first level—with relevant parametric changes—covered practically the entire sum of benefits owed under the previous regime, leaving unaffected the benefits that current workers were still acquiring.[14]

According to Caristo and Forteza (2003), the 1995 reform and later adjustments to the social security policy first increased and later decreased the financing that the BPS required.[15] In the first few years, the deficit increased by more than half a point of GDP, mainly as a consequence of decreasing the contributions withheld by the BPS. This situation changed in later years, since financial obligations decreased as outlays decreased. The improvement of the BPS financial results in the medium and long term is mainly a result of decreasing payouts to people who had obtained benefits without ever having contributed. According to the projections, from the second decade of this century on, central government debt will be less than if the reform had not taken place.

Multilateral credit organizations had a limited role in the conception and design of the reform initiatives. Even at the World Bank there was opposition to the proposed system at the beginning. On the other hand, at the end of 1994, a consultant group from the Inter-American Development Bank led by Francisco E. Barreto de Oliveira provided an important study of policy alternatives, including an analysis of the feasibility of a mixed system.

General Characteristics

The 1995 reform exclusively applies to BPS affiliates and provides for the existence of three regimes: the previous, transition, and mixed:

- For those affiliates with acquired rights in the old regime as of December 31, 1996, the old system was maintained with no risk of having the new regime applied to them, unless it would be more favorable;
- For affiliates aged 40 years or older by April 1, 1996, special transition rules were established through a parametric reform of the PAYGO system; and

- For affiliates younger than 40 years by April 1, 1996, for those entering the labor force for the first time, or for those (mentioned above) who voluntarily opted for it, the mixed model applies. The option for the mixed model is irreversible.

Regardless of the applicable regime, only work history registered after April 1, 1996 would be recognized. The BPS keeps this history—which includes time of service, remunerations, contributions, and other required information—and updates it monthly. According to the institutional organization of the 1995 reform, the Ministerio de Trabajo y Seguridad Social (MTSS, or Ministry of Labor and Social Security) is responsible for social security policy. The BPS is in charge of the previous system, transition system, and the first pillar of the mixed system. It is also responsible for collections, including contributions to the second pillar destined for individual accounts of the AFAPs' affiliates. The Banco Central del Uruguay (BCU, or Uruguayan Central Bank)—an autonomous organization with public resources—supervises the new social security participants (AFAPs and insurance companies) based on the creation of the mandatory individual savings pillar. For special services provided to specific groups, there are three parastatal pension funds (*cajas*),[16] as well as military and police pension funds.

The effective implementation of the reform was coordinated by the Planning and Budget Office through two ad hoc committees: the Evaluation and Follow-Up Committee and the Social Security Reform Program.

The Transition Regime

The transition pension system—for those not already retired under the old system or part of the new mixed system—includes a parametric reform. It is a modified version of the old system, and its regulations are similar to those of the first pillar in the mixed system. The new system (*a*) is based on a PAYGO system; (*b*) gradually increases the retirement age for women by 5 years until it is equal to that of men (60 years); (*c*) increases by 5 years the minimum number of years of service necessary to have pension rights (to 35 years); (*d*) increases to 20 years the period used to calculate the base reference salary;[17] (*e*) reduces the replacement rate; (*f*) increases by up to 120 percent the pension floor; and (*g*) progressively increases the pension ceiling by about 60 percent. This system, exclusively PAYGO, will apply to the great majority of new pensioners until about the year 2020.

The Mixed System

The first pillar includes, without exception, all affiliates in the mixed system for the first UY$12,524 of monthly earnings in 2005 values (equivalent

TABLE 14-2 General Regime

Remunerations (2005 values)	*Contributions*	
	BPS	*AFAP*
UY$12,525 (US$521)	Yes	Optional
UY$12,525–$37,573 (US$522–US$1,565)	No	Yes
UY$37,573 (US$1,566)	No	Voluntary

to about US$520 monthly in 2005). The second pillar includes BPS affiliates earning between UY$12,525 and UY$37,573 (between US$522 and US$1,565 monthly in 2005—see Table 14-2). It also includes affiliates with income lower than UY$12,524 who voluntarily opt to affiliate with the second pillar, depositing half of their contribution to each pillar (the decision is irrevocable).[18] There is also a third pillar for voluntary savings open to BPS affiliates for the band of salary over UY$37,573 per month. (All values are expressed in pesos, adjusted automatically according to the median salary index every time public salaries and pensions increase.)

Financing is based on the following:

- Employee contribution of 15 percent of salary up to the pension ceiling, with earnings up to UY$12,524 to the public pillar and earnings between UY$12,524 and UY$37,573 to an individual account.[19]
- Employer contribution of 12.5 percent—or 14.5 percent for public sector employers—up to UY$37,573 maximum earning deposited to the BPS (PAYGO system, first pillar).
- Central government contribution, if needed to supplement the finances of the BPS.

Current pensions and those to be paid in the future by the old rules, transition, and first pillar of the mixed system are paid by BPS.

The second pillar of the mixed system entitles only authorized insurance companies to issue life annuities. This component of the mixed system is fully integrated with the first pillar, since to have access to these benefits it is necessary to receive first pillar benefits. The only exception is for people older than 65 years, who can collect their second pillar benefits without contributing, while continuing their employment. If a worker dies without naming a survivorship beneficiary, the personal account balance can be inherited.

Benefits under the second pillar are the same as in the first pillar with two different procedures:

- Defined contributions, or individual savings, covering the risk of old age (ordinary retirement and extreme old age). In this case, the amount of the benefit is not legally defined, neither in absolute nor relative terms. It is calculated based on individual savings account balances to the date funds are transferred from the AFAP to the insurance company chosen by the affiliate, life expectancy according to general official tables, and life annuities' acquisition terms with the insurance company.

- Defined benefit, or group insurance, for disability and death-at-work coverage. In this case, the amount of the installment is legally defined in relative terms: a determined percentage from a determined calculation base. For the disability pension and the transitory subsidy for partial disability, benefits equal 45 percent of monthly base salary (on which contributions to an AFAP savings account were based on the past ten years of activity, or real time of contribution if less than ten years). For survivorship pensions, the same pension allotment percentages from the first pillar apply. This insurance is contracted by AFAPs with an authorized insurance company.

The BPS is responsible for paying all benefits in the first pillar, while insurance companies pay second pillar benefits, either those covered by collective insurance or the life annuities to be contracted by affiliates.

Retirement Saving Fund Administrators

As is discussed above, the AFAPs—single-purpose corporations authorized by the executive branch and the BCU—administer the private savings.[20] Each AFAP administers only one retirement savings fund. AFAPs are regulated by the superintendency of the BCU. They compete for affiliates, who can transfer their accounts from one administrator to other after contributing for at least six months. The AFAPs invest available pension fund savings and maintain updated individual savings accounts data. One hundred percent of fund investment returns are credited to the affiliates' accounts.[21] The investment funds are regulated as an administration trust. They are the property of the affiliates and are not part of the AFAPs' assets (and thus cannot be legally attached).

Collections are centralized under the BPS, which transfers affiliate contributions to the AFAPs. This method of organizing the collection process is considered one of the elements of cost rationalization, since it prevents duplication of effort for administrators and employers. In 2005 the BPS began to charge AFAPs for this service. AFAPs receive a commission for their work as the only payment from their affiliates for their services. Commissions are set freely according to the following rules:

- All affiliates are charged the same commission, except for bonuses for staying with an AFAP, as explained later;
- Commissions are charged only on mandatory contributions and voluntary deposits.
- Commission charges are not imposed on transfers from one AFAP to another, nor are they charged on account returns;
- Commissions can be a fixed amount, a percentage of the worker contribution, or a combination of these two; and
- AFAPs can provide bonuses for customer loyalty.

The law requires investment guidelines aimed at security, profitability, diversification, and term compatibility criteria based on objectives and investment limits found in the legislation (Table 14-3).

Implementation of the 1995 Reform

The 1995 reform implementation had to resolve several critical issues, some derived from the peculiarities of its own design, others from its partial introduction into the financial markets, and others due to its political and social acceptance.

Design Challenges: Central Role of Public Institutions

From an operational perspective, there were two especially relevant characteristics. The first—and most important—was the capacity of the BPS to administer the new mixed system. The BPS had six months to undertake a process in which it needed to account for the labor history of all active workers, establish adequate processes for collecting revenue, and create a process whereby contributions from affiliates in the mixed regime would be distributed to AFAPs according to individual choices. Unlike most reforms introduced in the region in the 1980s, which stressed the role of the private sector, the 1995 Uruguayan reform gave to the BPS, the central public pension administrative institution, the central role in the implementation and administration of the reform.

The second characteristic was the creation of a publicly owned AFAP, though it was fully governed by private law. This AFAP had to be fully operational when the reform took effect and could not repeat the classic inefficiencies of the public administration. From the start, workers flocked to the publicly owned República AFAP, making it the market leader. This leading role for a publicly owned AFAP has been one of the most notable developments of the reform implementation process.

TABLE 14-3 Social Security Savings Fund Assets Consolidated and by AFAP

	System		*Afinidad*		*Integración*		*República*		*Unión Capital*	
	Thousands of Pesos	*% s/total*	*Thousands of Pesos*	*% s/total*	*Thousands of Pesos*	*% s/total*	*Thousands of Pesos*	*% s/total*	*Thousands of Pesos*	*% s/total*
Resources available	4,705,871	9.98	589,794	7.01	322,912	8.12	2,887,196	10.87	905,969	11.1
National currency	820,278	1.74	51,622	0.61	91,751	2.31	610,110	2.30	66,795	0.82
Foreign currency	3,885,593	8.24	538,172	6.40	231,161	5.81	2,277,086	8.57	839,174	10.28
Investments	42,429,893	90.02	7,823,148	92.99	3,654,353	91.88	23,692,747	89.14	7,259,645	88.9
National currency	24,202,523	51.35	4,578,017	54.42	2,039,376	51.28	13,633,499	51.29	3,951,631	48.39
Uruguayan pesos	1,941,654	4.12	86,388	1.03	56,922	1.66	1,738,113	6.54	51,231	0.63
Ind. for Inflation	22,260,869	47.23	4,491,629	53.39	1,973,454	49.62	11,895,386	44.75	3,900,400	47.77
Foreign currency	18,227,370	38.67	3,245,131	38.57	1,614,977	40.61	10,059,248	37.85	3,308,014	40.51
Fund's total assets	47,135,767	100	8,412,942	100	3,977,264	100	26,579,946	100	8,165,614	100
Special reserve	240,911	0.51	43,059	0.51	19,913	0.5	136,160	0.51	41,779	0.51
FAP [a]	46,894,856	99.49	8,369,883	99.49	3,957,351	99.5	26,443,786	99.49	8,123,836	99.49

Source: Author's computations, based on BCU quarterly bulletins (*Memoria Trimestral del Régimen de Jubilación por Ahorro Individual Obligatorio*, various issues).

Note: Values to June 2005.

[a] FAP = *fondos de ahorro provisional*, or pension fund.

Introduction into the Financial Markets

The new capitalized pillars now required a complete introduction into the financial system. The system provided for a competitive market in which AFAPs would compete for affiliates, as in other countries in the region. When the reform took effect in April 1996, five AFAPs began operations; shortly after, a sixth firm entered the market. Since that time, only mergers have taken place; with severe barriers to entry in a small market with low new enrollment and few transfers, no other firms have entered the market. Today, there are four AFAPs: República, Afinidad, Unión-Capital, and Integración (see Table 14-4).

By June 2005, AFAPs administered US$1.678 billion, equal to 11.7 percent of GDP (see Table 14-5). República AFAP, which is owned by 3 state-owned firms, managed 56.5 percent of these funds, a share that was relatively constant during the 10 years after the reform. Fifty-three percent of the assets were in Uruguayan pesos and 47 percent in US dollars, while 81 percent of assets were invested in Uruguayan public debt titles. Since the system came into effect, the profitability of the funds in US dollars has been 9.59 percent annually and 12 percent in indexed Uruguayan pesos. Returns vary little among AFAPs due to legal regulations that led to the homogenization of investment policies and the lack of appropriate investment instruments, which in turn has contributed to a concentration of investment in instruments issued by the public sector.

For the 10 years after the reform, the 672,080 AFAP affiliates (as of June 2005) were distributed among the 4 AFAPs in a relatively stable pattern. República AFAP consolidated its lead, with slightly more than 37 percent of the affiliates. In looking at affiliate salary levels, República AFAP has been the leader among affiliates with higher salary levels. During the first four years of the reform, the AFAPs competed intensely to encourage affiliates to transfer to their firms. Firms employed large sales forces at very high costs and ended with essentially null results, as market shares remained stable. Toward the end of 2000, the six operating AFAPs agreed to end this strategy. Transfers came to a halt, making it clear that affiliation or transfer decisions are not sensitive to product differences. For example, there are differences in commission fees, but they do not seem to have an impact on an individual's decision to change or stay in the same AFAP.

AFAPs charge an administration commission, which since the beginning of the system has averaged from 1.58 to 2.25 percent of a worker's salary.[22] Since 1996, the group insurance for death and disability, which AFAPs contract for their affiliates, has ranged from a minimum value of 0.553 percent in 1998 to a maximum value of 1.165 percent in 2003. Charges from the second pillar of the mixed system do not have a regulated fixed ceiling. In

Table 14-4 Affiliate Distribution by AFAP: Market Concentration (through December of Each Year)

	1996	*1997*	*1998*	*1999*	*2000*	*2001*	*2002*	*2003*	*2004*	*2005*[a]
Tot. affiliates	300,798	442,903	499,865	531,190	565,324	593,736	613,432	632,330	655,204	672,080
Share by AFAPs										
Capital (%)	8.75	11.78	12.47	12.76	13.42	—	—	—	—	—
Comercial (%)	16.87	16.25	17.34	17.27	17.92	—	—	—	—	—
Integración (%)	15.93	15.02	14.29	13.61	13.29	13.22	13.27	13.59	13.98	14.16
República (%)	39.49	36.81	37.29	37.93	37.64	37.74	38.14	37.98	37.77	37.66
Santander (%)	13.49	14.48	12.85	12.64	11.93	—	—	—	—	—
Unión (%)	5.47	5.65	5.76	5.79	5.80	—	—	—	—	—
Afinidad (%)	—	—	—	—	—	29.72	29.51	29.41	28.89	28.65
Unión Capital (%)	—	—	—	—	—	19.32	19.08	19.02	19.36	19.53
Total (%)	100.00	100.00	100.00	100.00	100.00	100.00	100.00	100.00	100.00	100.00
Avg. HHI	0.239	0.223	0.225	0.228	0.227	0.286	0.287	0.285	0.283	0.282

Source: Author's computations, based on BCU Quarterly Bulletins.

[a] Values to June 2005.

TABLE 14-5 Social Security Savings Fund (FAP[a])

	1996	*1997*	*1998*	*1999*	*2000*	*2001*	*2002*	*2003*	*2004*
FAP[a] by AFAP in Thousands of Dollars									
Capital	3,146	13,011	25,420	40,320	70,356	n/a	n/a	n/a	n/a
Comercial	5,311	18,769	40,343	65,292	81,983	n/a	n/a	n/a	n/a
Integración	4,508	19,000	39,994	56,984	68,917	87,181	75,488	102,529	140,572
República	29,880	109,501	206,157	331,463	454,491	590,195	508,058	700,479	948,815
Santander	6,865	24,035	40,961	54,557	69,973	n/a	n/a	n/a	n/a
Unión	644	6,185	21,472	42,545	65,306	n/a	n/a	n/a	n/a
Afinidad	n/a	n/a	n/a	n/a	n/a	190,598	159,225	218,232	299,309
Uni. Capital	n/a	n/a	n/a	n/a	n/a	177,428	150,593	210,838	289,564
System	50,355	190,501	374,347	591,161	811,026	1,045,402	893,364	1,232,079	1,678,261
FAP as % of GDP	0.3	0.9	1.7	2.9	4.2	5.9	9.3	10.4	11.7
AFAP Market Share in Percentages									
Capital (%)	6.2	6.8	6.8	6.8	8.7	n/a	n/a	n/a	n/a
Comercial (%)	10.5	9.9	10.8	11.0	10.1	n/a	n/a	n/a	n/a
Integración (%)	9.0	10.0	10.7	9.6	8.5	8.3	8.4	8.3	8.4
República (%)	59.3	57.5	55.1	56.1	56.0	56.5	56.9	56.9	56.5
Santander (%)	13.6	12.6	10.9	9.2	8.6	n/a	n/a	n/a	n/a
Unión (%)	1.3	3.2	5.7	7.2	8.1	n/a	n/a	n/a	n/a
Afinidad (%)	n/a	n/a	n/a	n/a	n/a	18.2	17.8	17.7	17.8
Uni. Capital (%)	n/a	n/a	n/a	n/a	n/a	17.0	16.9	17.1	17.3
Sistema (%)	100.0	100.0	100.0	100.0	100.0	100.0	100.0	100.0	100.0

Source: Author's computations, based on BCU Quarterly Bulletins.

Note: Values are through December of each year. n/a=not applicable, because either the FAP has not been created or it has merged with another.

[a] FAP= *fondos de ahorro provisional*, or pension fund.

a small market such as Uruguay's—with only four participants—it is reasonable to think that price agreements or other anticompetitive practices are likely to occur.

Given the recent implementation of the system, benefits to be paid from the second pillar are still rare. Through June 2005, there were 4,002 cases, mainly survivorship pensions.

In 2002, six years after the reform, the second pillar successfully faced the deepest financial crisis in the history of the country. The crisis, which had two phases, could have severely damaged the reform. The first phase was based on criminal actions involving the management of two banks that owned AFAPs—100 percent of an AFAP in one case. The second was the result of the bank run that led to the closure of three of the largest banks, the public banks' failure to meet depositors' demands for withdrawals, and the fiscal crisis that forced a restructuring of long-term public debt as an alternative to default. The institutional structure of the second pillar meant that the criminal actions of the two private banks owning AFAPs had no impact whatsoever on pension funds. At the same time, the Batlle administration's solution to the 2002 fiscal crisis, which had the strong support of the US government and multilateral credit agencies, prevented damage to pension fund assets that were largely invested in Uruguayan public debt.

Political Opposition

From a political perspective, the reform had to overcome the strong opposition generated by the unions, pensioner organizations, and, especially, the Frente Amplio. These social and political organizations developed a campaign against the reform, but opponents fell just short in their campaign to collect enough signatures to turn the issue into a popular referendum.

Possible Future Trends

In March 2005 the leftist candidate, Tabaré Vázquez, assumed the presidency, and the Frente Amplio coalition won a legislative majority in both houses. This party has been highly critical of the 1995 reform. With a wide legislative majority, President Vázquez's administration could redirect policy. Questioning the social security reform was part of its political strategy, as it focused on restoring the classic characteristics of the Uruguayan welfare state, which has a strong hold on the Uruguayan collective imagination. During its ten years of opposition to the 1995 reform, the left did not provide an alternative project. During the 2004 electoral campaign some sectors of the leftist coalition—including their own candidate and the current president of the Republic—admitted that they would not abrogate the 1995 reform but would instead introduce some adjustments. This position was rejected by some members of the coalition, who continue to call for the reform's demise.

In its first two years in office, the Vázquez administration focused on improving the business climate. Maintaining the basic characteristics of the 1995 reform is an important step toward reaching that goal. Introducing adjustments to its design to improve the reform's efficiency is perfectly compatible with this goal. Among the options it could consider are (*a*) allowing for the administration of more than one investment fund, with different degrees of risk; (*b*) redefining voluntary savings regulations; (*c*) modifying insurance companies' regulations regarding life annuity calculations, including separating technical reserves into trusts separate from other insured risks; and (*d*) making the BCU superintendency of pension funds autonomous to avoid potential interference from other BCU sectors that have competing policy interests.

At the same time, AFAPs could be permitted to invest between 10 and 15 percent of funds outside the country. This measure, which is strongly supported by the AFAPs, has encountered stiff political opposition and does not currently seem viable.

A new administration considering socially oriented reforms could take two actions: make access to old-age pensions more flexible by allowing retirement after less than 35 years of service—for example, at age 65 years—and re-examine the income-tested noncontributory pension program, also administered by the BPS, and adapt it to the new context of contributive benefits, in which it will no longer be possible to easily obtain a pension without having contributed. With this perspective, it is necessary to guard against two risks: first, the temptation to direct the funds toward social spending at the expense of profitability and security and, second, to favor a greater market concentration, which would benefit República AFAP.

Indeed, if the new administration gives in to forces favoring the rollback of the 1995 reform, the most powerful tool to carry that out would be to promote market concentration, which would work to the detriment of the private administrators. Because it is better able than its competitors to reduce commissions, República AFAP could withstand this change. If competition among administrators disappears because of market rules, the model would lose part of its mixed character. Pension fund administration would be concentrated in the hands of public agencies, which would probably increase the political and financial risks inherent to the system.

If the political and legislative will were there, the relative weights of PAYGO versus savings components could be modified, giving PAYGO greater weight. In the short and medium term, this alternative could have a positive fiscal impact because BPS collections would immediately increase.

The design of the 1995 reform is flexible enough to adapt to changes in the relative weights of its two pillars, to either adjust exposure to different risks or to incorporate changes in the way the national community perceives the role of individuals, society, and the state. However, in the long term, with the current parameters of the PAYGO component, fiscal obligations would increase.

The risk of market concentration exists independently of an express policy in this regard. To avoid such concentration, it is necessary to decrease barriers to entry for new competitors. In fact, if the role of fiduciary administration is maintained (to ensure the inviolability of social security funds), the single-purpose requirement for administrators could be ended, thereby opening up competition to firms in related industries, always under an independent superintendency. Certainly, a measure of this kind would also reduce administrative costs considerably.

If an increase in population coverage is sought, it should not be oriented toward the second pillar but rather toward the first, since this is where mandatory coverage is accessed. The main limitations to be surpassed are exogenous to the pension system in that they are based on the labor market structure. Nevertheless, some endogenous actions—which are not exempt from fiscal impact—could influence the achievement of this objective. These include revising eligibility conditions of noncontributive pensions for the aged and reducing formal labor contracting costs, within the context of a tax reform.

The future of the 1995 reform depends especially on the balance between trends inside President Vázquez's own administration, which has expressed concern over preserving the investment and business climate. This goal, along with the lack of a viable alternative to the 1995 reform, suggests that the policy path with respect to pensions will be maintained, without precluding the introduction of advisable and necessary adjustments. In the coming years, social security will continue to be prominent on the national agenda, but without the urgency and dramatic tone of years past. This will foster improvement of the mixed system, which has already been consolidated. There is no doubt that a healthy, balanced social security system, which adequately integrates social solidarity and individual fairness, will continue to be one of the main instruments for the personal well-being and social development of Uruguay.

Notes

1 According to Hobsbawn (1995: 188), 'the list of solid constitutional states in the Western Hemisphere was small: Canada, Colombia, Costa Rica, and the United States and now the forgotten "South American Switzerland" with its only real democracy, Uruguay' (translated from Spanish).

[2] The real pension re-evaluation index, July 1962 = 100, was 34.29 in December 1973, reaching its lowest value in December 1985: 20.34. This index results from comparing pension increases with the Consumer Price Index.

[3] Only presidential candidate Jorge Batlle and the far-left Tupamaros National Liberation Movement opposed the initiative, for different reasons. In a second show of force, these organizations gathered enough signatures for another plebiscite initiative for constitutional amendment, this time to block the parametric reforms approved by the parliament in 1992. A new plebiscite was held during the national elections in 1994, and an ample majority approved the initiative, which declared unconstitutional the reforms previously introduced as part of the budgetary laws.

[4] After the amendment took effect and as a result of applying the constitutional reform, the real pension revaluation index went from 24.90 in December 1989 up to its highest value in 1999—41.64. Since then, that index has declined in line with the average salary decline.

[5] This parametric reform alternative was approved by the parliament in 1992. The Supreme Court later found it to be unconstitutional, based on the results of the November 1994 plebiscite.

[6] The team appointed by the Lacalle administration analyzed the financial feasibility of adopting a Chilean-style individual capitalization system and concluded that the transition costs would be prohibitive.

[7] This notional defined contribution alternative was the one developed for the project that the executive branch sent to the parliament in 1991. The project was given priority status but not approved.

[8] This was the selected alternative for the reform finally approved in 1995.

[9] It was sponsored by the Frente Amplio, the union and pensioner organizations, and also—strangely—by the political sector of ex-President Sanguinetti, who had originally approved the law.

[10] This coalition of political parties formed the main opposition force to those governments that approved and implemented the 1995 reform. It assumed the presidency in March 2005 with the support of more than 50% of the population and with an outright legislative majority.

[11] The design did not have the support of international credit organizations, and even the World Bank opposed it initially. However, after the operation began, the World Bank participated in the reform implementation process.

[12] The shares of one of the AFAPs are owned by three public institutions.

[13] Otherwise, social security benefit obligations accrued in the old system about to be repealed would have to be acknowledged (known as 'recognition bonds' in Chilean law).

[14] This total, based on the minimum wage and administered price levels, had already lost value in order to limit the system's financial obligations after the 1989 constitutional reform.

[15] Using a different methodology, Noya and Laens (2000) affirm that, in the long run, reductions of more than 2.1% of GDP are obtained in all cases. The reductions result from reducing social security expenditures in the PAYGO first pillar by 5.7% of GDP. The reductions are counteracted in part by diverting contributions equivalent to about 3.5% of GDP toward the capitalization pillar. In contrast, in the

short and medium term, the primary deficit increases, oscillating between 1.6 and 1.8% of GDP, the result of reducing PAYGO contributions as well as the expansion on social security expenditures introduced by the same reform.

[16] Caja Bancaria de Jubilaciones y Pensiones (Bank Employee Pension Fund), Caja Jubilaciones y Pensiones de Profesionales Universitarios (University Professional Pension Fund), and Caja Notarial de Seguridad Social (Notary Pension Fund).

[17] The previous system-based pensions on a reference salary covering the past three years in the labor force.

[18] These workers earning less than UY$12,525 retain the right to 75% of the benefit that they would have received in the public PAYGO pillar (even though half of their contributions go to an individual account).

[19] The contribution ceiling does not apply to those in the previous and transition systems.

[20] Policymakers stipulated that one AFAP was to be property of the BPS, by itself or jointly with the state-owned Banco de la República Oriental del Uruguay (BROU), Banco Hipotecario del Uruguay (BHU), and Banco de Seguros del Estado (BSE). República AFAP, the administrator with the largest number of affiliates and the highest total of administered funds, is owned by the BROU, BPS, and BSE.

[21] There is a minimum return requirement that if not met will eventually result in the liquidation of the AFAP.

[22] Today, República AFAP charges the lowest administration fees (fixed and variable commissions).

References

Banco Central de Uruguay (2005). *Memoria Trimestral del Régimen de Jubilación por Ahorro Individual Obligatorio* (quarterly bulletins of the Central Bank of Uruguay), various issues. http://www.bcu.gub.uy/a5954.html

Caristo, Anna and Alvareo Forteza (2003). 'El déficit del Banco de Previsión Social y su impacto en las finanzas del gobierno', Mimeo. *XVIII Jornadas anuales de Economía.*

Hobsbawm, Eric (1995). *Historia del Siglo XX. Crítica.* Grijalbo Barcelona: Mondadori.

Instituto Nacional de Estadistica (National Statistics Institute). http://www.ine.gub.uy/

Noya, Nelson and Silvia Laens (2000). *Efectos fiscales de la reforma de la seguridad social en Uruguay.* Santiago, Chile: CEPAL.

Organización Internacional del Trabajo (OIT) (1964). *Informe al Gobierno de la República Oriental del Uruguay sobre Seguridad Social, Programa Ampliado de Asistencia Técnica.* Ginebra: OIT/TAP/Uruguay.R.5.

Papadopulos, Jorge (1992). *Seguridad Social y Política en el Uruguay.* Montevideo: CIESU.

Chapter 15

The Pension System in Argentina

Rafael Rofman

Introduction

Founded more than a century ago, Argentina's pension system is one of the oldest in the world. Natural maturation and legislative changes progressively converted what was initially a highly fragmented contributive scheme into a mostly integrated model (see the discussion on system fragmentation later in this chapter). The current pension system enjoys growing fiscal support but declining coverage.

The 2001–2 fiscal and financial crises in Argentina created special interest in its pension system as many wondered about the resilience of the new funded schemes. Looking back a few years, to the worst of the crisis, it is clear that while the system and its beneficiaries suffered from the institutional confusion and financial turmoil, there are no lasting concerns arising from the crisis. The main challenges of the pension system continue to be around coverage, institutional design, pension fund managers' efficiency, and fragmentation—the same problems that a paper written in the late 1990s would have listed.

The Prehistory of Pensions in Argentina

The pension system in Argentina originated at the onset of the twentieth century, when in 1904 the government created a regime to cover civil servants. In 1915, with the creation of a program to benefit rail workers, the system began to expand to other sectors. By 1944 six autonomous national pension funds existed, covering approximately 7 percent of the labor force. Workers were able to retire as young as 47 years and could receive benefits close to 90 percent of their pre-retirement salaries. Not surprisingly, several of these funds had serious financial problems.

The legal and actual coverage of the pension systems expanded rapidly from 1945 to 1955, a period that saw a large number of social reforms. By 1956 almost every sector of the economy was covered by a pension scheme, and the proportion of the labor force effectively enrolled in the pension system was close to 30 percent. That same year, the number of beneficiaries was still relatively low, at around 500,000, or 25 percent of the population aged 55 years or older.

While the early programs had been designed as funded DC schemes, increasing financial problems and government interventions forced a conversion into PAYGO schemes. By the late 1960s most national programs were integrated into three centralized schemes: for civil servants, private employees, and the self-employed. To increase the financial sustainability of the schemes, the government adjusted the regulations. This reform was relatively successful; the system operated under reasonable conditions during most of the 1970s and early 1980s. However, by the mid-1980s, because of the continued aging of system participants and increasing informality in the economy, the system began to experience deficits. The government adopted a risky strategy that eventually backfired; to maintain financial stability, administrators ignored or 'reinterpreted' benefit indexation rules, which linked benefits to active workers' salaries. These actions resulted in a decline of the real value of benefits and the replacement rates. Beneficiaries' lawsuits against this practice rapidly multiplied, overwhelming the legal system and forcing the government to declare a state of emergency.

By the early 1990s the system was unsustainable, so the government proposed a structural reform. The debate about the proposed reform was difficult, as differences in ideologies and interests were large. However, after two years of debate, legislators approved a new law in October 1993 introducing a deep structural reform to the national pension system.

The Reforms

The 1993 pension reform was approved as the country was emerging from its most serious macroeconomic crisis in decades, having experienced two episodes of hyperinflation in 3 years; growing unemployment, informality, and poverty; and a sharp 15 percent decline in per capita GDP. The reform was partly inspired by Chile, where a funded scheme had replaced the old PAYGO system in the early 1980s.[1] The new design (SIJP, for Sistema Integrado de Jubilaciones y Pensiones, or Integrated Pension System) is a mixed model, with participation from the government and the private sector in its management, a combination of DB and DC components in the benefit formula, and financial arrangements that include PAYGO, funding, and tax financing elements.

The new model requires all workers in the private and the national public sectors (including the self-employed) to contribute 11 percent of their salaries; employers contribute 16 percent.[2] All workers must participate in the Regimen Previsional Público (the public pension scheme). They can also enroll in a funded, privately managed scheme. As a result, benefits have several components (see Figure 15-1).

	Public scheme	Private scheme	
Pillar II	Additional benefit ('PAP')	Annuity	Scheduled withdrawal
Pillar I	Basic universal benefit ('PBU')		

Figure 15-1. The integrated pension system (SIJP): benefit structure.

A worker retiring from the national system will receive a basic benefit (PBU, for *prestación básica universal*, or 'universal basic benefit'), equivalent to approximately 27 percent of the average wage at the time of the reform, as well as a benefit from the newer, smaller, publicly run PAYGO scheme (PAP, for *prestación adicional por permanencia*, or 'additional benefit'), or a benefit financed by his or her accumulated contributions paid in the form of an annuity or as a scheduled withdrawal.

The reform changed many aspects of the system, including its institutional setting, participation rules, risks distribution, and financing. These changes comprise four basic dimensions, which can be considered independently, although their implementations are deeply connected and sometimes mutually necessary due to political economy considerations.

The first dimension is a *parametric reform*. Most parameters in the system were modified, including:

- contribution rates, which changed from 10 to 11 percent of wages for workers' contributions;
- retirement age, which increased by 5 years for both sexes, to 60/65 years for female/male workers;
- required number of years with contributions to retire, which increased from 20 to 30;
- the benefit formula, which went from 70 percent of average of best 3 years for those retiring at the minimum age to an estimated 60–65 percent; and
- the indexation formula, which continued to be based on salaries but had stronger links to collection.

These changes, which increased revenue or reduced expenditures, were intended to improve the system's finances. Their implementation reduced both the expected number of beneficiaries and their average benefits, limiting coverage of the system.

The second dimension is a *benefit formula reform*. For many workers, the new system introduced a new level of uncertainty by switching part of the benefits from the traditional DB model to a DC scheme, or, more appropriately, an 'undefined benefit' model.[3] With the introduction of individual accounts, the state transferred to workers some risks, including those related to financial volatility and population aging. While these changes clearly improved the medium-term prospects for the state, transferring risks to workers was a change that could be considered problematic, as the pension system was also supposed to protect workers from those risks. Three characteristics of the new scheme were aimed at limiting the impact of these changes in workers: (*a*) the requirement to annuitize benefits at retirement (or to choose a schedule withdrawal calculated as an annuity), (*b*) the basic protection received by all workers from the PBU benefit, and (*c*) the minimum return regulation that reduces financial volatility in the system.

The third dimension affected the *financial scheme*. Since the mid-1960s, benefits had been financed by current contributions and treasury transfers, either through earmarked taxes or direct transfers. The new scheme, implemented in July 1994, reintroduced a funded scheme, with part of workers' contributions accumulating in individual accounts and used to pay benefits in the future. By diverting part of the contributions to the new pension funds, the reform further increased the system's dependency on transfers from the central government, at least in the short and medium term.

The fourth and final dimension of the reform introduced new actors in the system from the *private sector*. The newly created private companies would manage the pension funds for a fee. These managers are specialized companies, responsible for administering the individual accounts, investing funds, and paying benefits. They are also required to cover the cost of disability and survivor's benefits, for which they must get insurance from an outside provider.

Each of the four dimensions described above could have been implemented independently. The government could have addressed fiscal problems by simply adjusting the parameters of the system. It could have reduced its exposure to financial risks by introducing a variable benefit formula, as in the notional defined contribution schemes adopted in Sweden and other European countries. Similarly, it could have created funding to improve long-term financial sustainability without switching management or using individual accounts. The private management of these accounts was not a technical prerequisite for any of the other reforms.

Acknowledging that the pension reform in Argentina was in fact several reforms implemented at once allows for a clearer analysis of each of them and their outcomes, as well as the links between them. Several analysts (Kay 2001; Brooks 2002) have studied Argentina and other countries in the region, considering the pension reform processes from a political science viewpoint, and many public statements by those involved in the process are available. While the debate is far from being settled, it seems clear that the parametric reform would have had a small chance of being approved if proposed as an independent piece of legislation. However, because it was bundled with other reforms that involved potential benefits to capital markets and provided better alignment of interests for workers (due to the individual accounts) and managers (due to the participation of the private sector), it responded to the prevailing political climate in the early 1990s and received sufficient support to be approved.

The Impact of Reforms and the System in the Past Decade

Assessing the impact of the pension reform is a difficult task. Differences of opinion arise from the relatively short time that has elapsed since its 1994 implementation (given that it covers a lifecycle of 60 or more years), the lack of consensus regarding the actual goals of the reform, differences in relevance assigned to short- and long-term effects (which are in some cases contradictory), and a myriad of changes in the economic and social context as well as in the postreform legislation. Most debates about the reform and its impacts in Argentina rapidly evolve into a discussion on whether some particular trend can be attributed to the reform or to other social processes that have taken place in the same period, or whether the current system design is actually the result of the 1993 reform or the accumulated adjustments applied since that date.

In that context, this chapter considers the evolution and current state of the pension system in three separate dimensions, discussing the possible determinants of the observed changes, including the reforms of 1993 as a contributing factor. The dimensions are:

- fiscal, where changes in current and expected fiscal impacts of the pension system in the last decade are analyzed;
- coverage, where the role of the pension system as a provider of social protection is considered; and
- other indirect impacts, through institutions or markets.

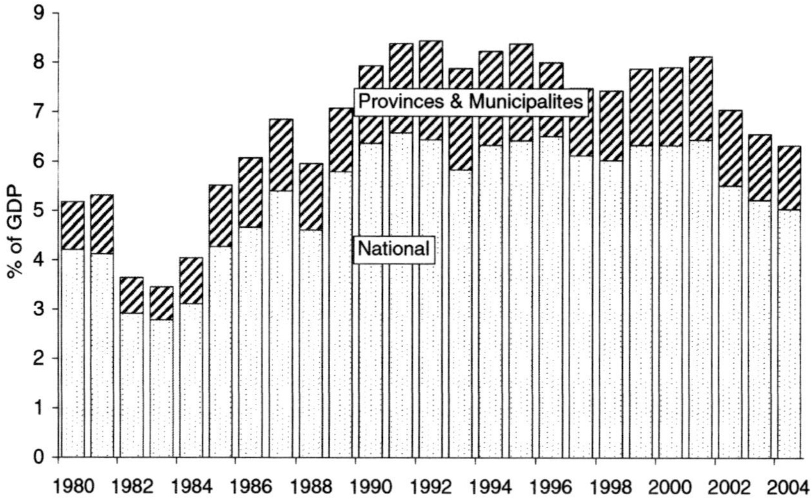

Figure 15-2. Pension spending by government level (1980–2004). (*Source*: Ministry of Economy 2005.)

The Fiscal Dimension

As discussed earlier, growing fiscal pressures were among the main triggers that initiated the pension reform process in the early 1990s. Pension expenditures at the national level had risen from less than 3.5 percent of GDP in the early 1980s to almost twice that number 10 years later. Aggregated expenditures (including provincial and municipal schemes) showed a similar trend, reaching almost 8.5 percent of GDP in 1992. Figure 15-2 shows that, with some volatility, expenditures after the reform stabilized at around 6.2 percent at the national level and 7.5–8 percent at the aggregate level. In addition, most projections show that expenditures should start to decline, as old retirees die and new beneficiaries receive benefits under the reformed legislation. As a result, expenditures should decline in the medium term, reaching 2–2.5 percent of GDP by 2025.[4]

While the reform appears to have already slowed down expenditures, the overall fiscal impact must be assessed considering the availability of funds to finance them. As in any country that replaces a PAYGO with a funded scheme, Argentina had a short-term cash flow problem that had to be solved. Because benefits of workers who were already retired continued to be paid and those retiring soon after the reform received a transitional benefit, the decline in expenditures has been a slow process. Moreover, when the funded scheme was introduced in 1994 the public system immediately lost revenues as individual contributions began to be directed towards the pension funds.

This 'transition cost' had to be financed until the system reached a new equilibrium. Some analysts (e.g. Baker and Weisbrot 2002) have argued that this cost was the main cause of the fiscal and financial crisis of late 2001 in Argentina. They estimated that if no reform had been enacted, the country's fiscal situation would have been much more solid, with small fiscal surpluses in most of the years between 1993 and 2001. These estimates, published soon after the crisis, received wide media attention and had significant political impact, yet they have some important flaws that cannot be ignored.

Baker and Weisbrot (2002) assumed for their calculations that the transition cost was stable at 1 percent of GDP during the whole period. They did not derive this figure themselves. Rather, they took it from an IMF (1998) report that introduced it without any discussion of how it was derived. An appropriate measurement of transition costs should consider the losses in revenue, which slowly grew as active workers switched from the PAYGO to the funded scheme, reaching 1.4 percent of GDP by 1999–2001. The measurement should also consider the savings produced by the parametric reform and the introduction of the funded scheme, which started paying some benefits soon after 1994. While this last figure is difficult to estimate, since no definitive counterfactual is available, there is no reason to assume it is negligible, especially considering the sudden stop in spending growth observed after the reform. Table 15-1 shows an estimate of these values. Column (ii) shows the difference between actual spending and a projection based on the growth of the elderly population and the growth of average benefits. (The negative values for 1994 and 1995 are the result of an increase in retirements immediately after the reform.) It is apparent that the transition costs between 1994 and 2001 went from a maximum of 0.9 percent of GDP in 1995 to 0.1 percent by 2001.

The transition cost in Argentina was actually manageable, and lower than in other countries in the region. However, the general fiscal pressures, increased by political conflicts and inflexible monetary policies, resulted in a major crisis in late 2001. In this context, the experience of Argentina indicates that a pension reform, as any other policy that requires important financial resources for several years, should only be implemented if this financing is guaranteed, or at least feasible.

The Coverage Dimension

The heated debates during the early 1990s about the fiscal implications of the pension system, or whether a funded scheme would operate more or

TABLE 15-1 Transition Costs and Other Related Policies in % of GDP (1993–2001)

	Transition Cost		
	Revenue Loss (i)	*Spending Reduction (ii)*	*'Pure' Transition Cost (iii) = (i) + (ii)*
1993	0.0	0.0	0.0
1994	0.3	−0.6	0.9
1995	0.8	−0.1	1.0
1996	1.0	0.2	0.8
1997	1.2	0.4	0.7
1998	1.3	0.6	0.7
1999	1.4	0.8	0.6
2000	1.4	0.9	0.5
2001	1.4	1.3	0.1

Source: Rofman (2006).

less efficiently than a PAYGO model, or whether the private sector would be more or less efficient than government, overlooked the topic of coverage, which should always have been in the center of the debate. Pension systems are social schemes designed to provide income protection to the elderly, under the assumption that if the task were left to them, most individuals would not be able to save enough during their active years. The problem of providing goods and services to the elderly has been present for most of mankind's history and was solved, with many instances of individual failure, through family or community support networks. It was only after the combined effect of the demographic transition (which resulted in smaller families) and the definition of labor as a marketable ability that could be exchanged for money that the traditional arrangements began to lose effectiveness. Social security systems were created to replace those schemes, due to the initiative of unions, employers, and lawmakers. In any case, and with many variations in design and implementation, the systems created during the last century were developed to provide income security to the elderly.

Due to its origins and a conceptual approach based on the Bismarckian model, the pension system in Argentina has been mostly contributive. The rationale is quite simple: pensions are payments designed to replace earnings when workers are forced to retire. Thus, the best way to assign these payments is by identifying those who were receiving payments for their work, and then replace these payments in a reasonable proportion.

While the early system designers focused on specific groups of workers, the system rapidly evolved into a national scheme. By the late 1940s it was clear that access to social security was considered a basic right of any citizen. In fact, a constitutional amendment approved in 1949 established the 'right to social security'. With this goal, new laws were approved to extend social security coverage to all workers, assuming that all workers would participate and the system would become universal. Logically, legal coverage extended much faster than effective coverage.[5] The number of workers contributing to the pension system expanded for several decades but as the system matured and labor market problems became more prevalent, the increase lost momentum. In the Buenos Aires metropolitan area, the percentage of salaried workers with contributions to social security was close to 80 percent in 1980 but declined to around 75 percent in 1985, 70 percent in 1990, and 66 percent in 1993—the time of the reform. This effect was compounded by the increase in unemployment.

Analysts have argued that the introduction of funded individual accounts in a pension system should result in higher participation, as a response to the incentives created for workers (Piñera 1991). However, opposing effects appear to have been much stronger, as the trend on coverage since the reform has continued to be negative. Figure 15-3 shows the proportion of the labor force contributing to a pension system in Argentina from 1992 to 2004.[6] The declining trend discussed earlier continued after the reform, as the percentage of the labor force paying monthly contributions to social security decreased from more than 45 percent in the early 1990s to less than 35 percent in the early 2000s. This decline was caused partly by growing unemployment, but the trend among occupied workers and even wage earners was similar.

The decline in participation since the early 1990s has been important, but the composition of this decline has become a serious problem, as Figure 15-4 shows. In the early 1990s participation by income among occupied workers was homogeneous, as the rates varied from 40 percent for the poorest to 60 percent for the fourth quintile. As the overall rate declined, the composition of the contributors changed dramatically. The two richest quintiles improved their participation rates, by 7 percentage points in the case of the fourth quintile and 17 points for the richest quintile. On the other extreme, the poorest workers saw their participation decline rapidly, as the second quintile reduced its participation from almost 60 percent to less than 20 percent, and the poorest went from 40 percent to under 2 percent.

Because the pension system in Argentina is mostly contributive, the proportion and composition of workers participating is important, since these factors determine workers' future right to receive benefits. However, the most relevant variable to assess the performance of a pension system is the percentage of the elderly receiving benefits, because the goal of the system is precisely to provide these benefits.

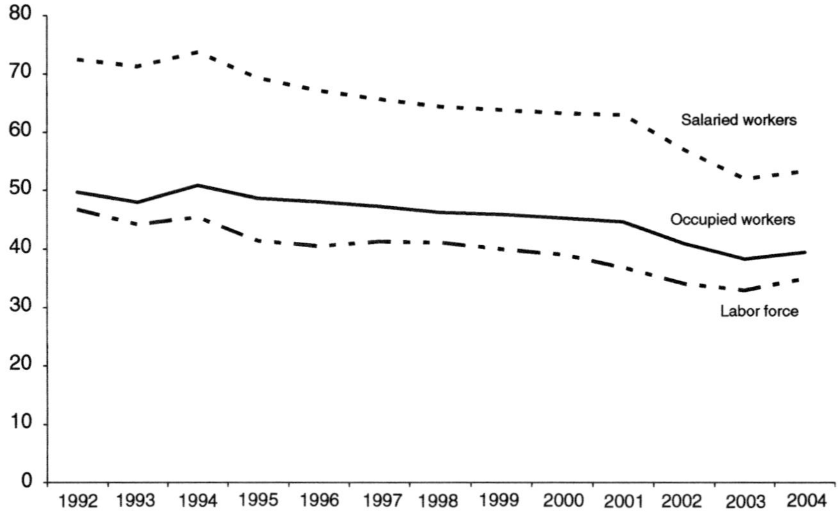

Figure 15-3. Rate of contribution of labor force, total and by income (1992–2004). (*Source*: Rofman and Lucchetti 2006.)

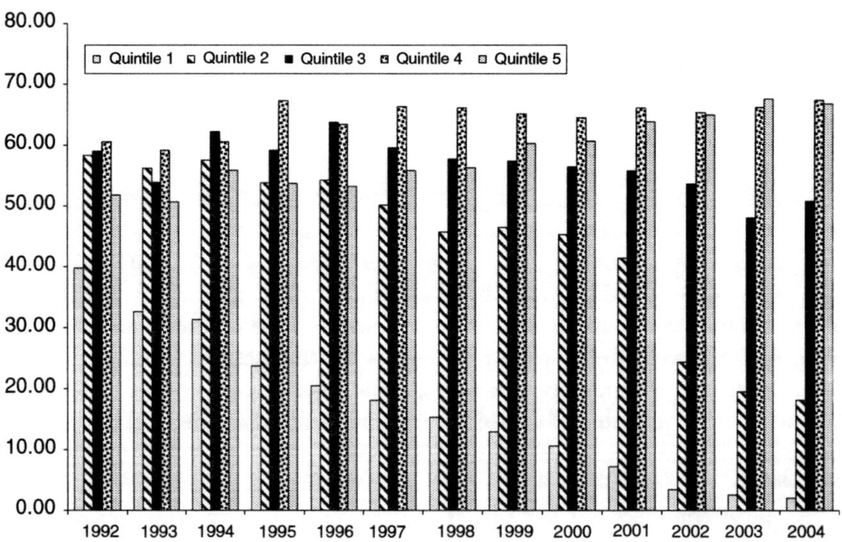

Figure 15-4. Participation of occupied workers by income decile (1992–2004). (*Source*: Rofman and Lucchetti 2006.)

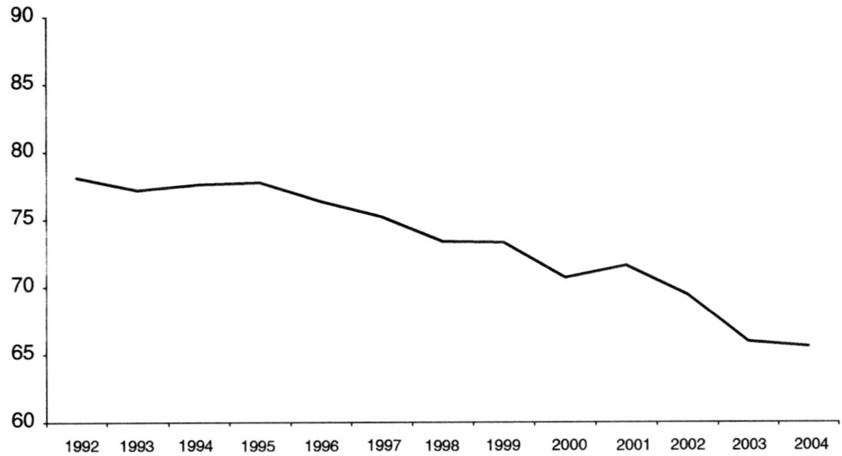

Figure 15-5. Coverage of the pension system among the elderly (1992–2004). (*Source*: Rofman and Lucchetti 2006.)

Data obtained from urban household surveys since the early 1990s show that coverage among the elderly reached a maximum by 1993–5, when 77 percent of the elderly were receiving a pension benefit, and then began to decline, by almost 1 percentage point per year, to 65 percent by 2004. This reduction was caused by the long-term negative trend in labor force participation and the introduction of stricter requirements in the system with the 1993 reform. It is important to mention that this data is not limited to the SIJP but considers as covered all individuals receiving benefits from other national or subnational schemes, including the noncontributory program (see Figure 15-5).

Other Impacts: Institutions and Markets

The creation of the funded scheme in the national pension system introduced several new areas of concern for analysts and regulators. Among the most relevant problems that deserve careful attention are (*a*) the role and performance of the institutions at the policy design, supervision, and operational levels; (*b*) the development of market conditions, competition, and costs; and (*c*) the investment policies, including regulations, managers' strategies, impacts on capital markets, and response to the financial crisis of 2001.

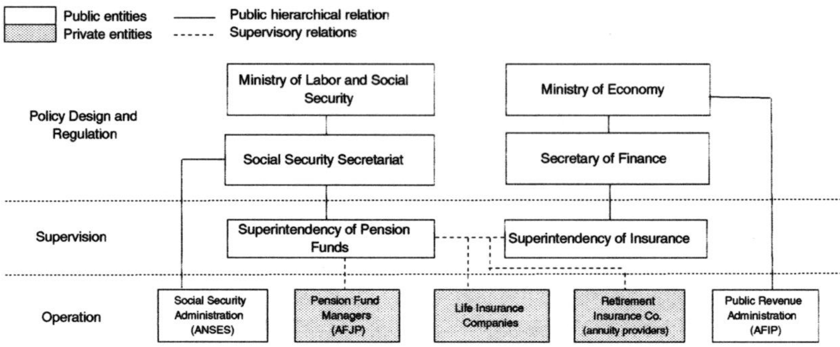

Figure 15-6. Institutional framework of Argentina's national social security system. (*Source*: author's own.)

The New Institutional Setting

When the new system was created in 1994, several institutions had to be organized or adapted to cover three functional levels (see Figure 15-6).

1. Policy design and regulations became the responsibility of the Ministerio de Trabajo (MT, or Ministry of Labor), through the Secretaría de Seguridad Social (SSS, or Social Security Secretariat), and, in some aspects, the Ministerio de Economía (ME, or Ministry of Economy), through the Secretaría de Finanzas (SF, or Finance Secretary).
2. Two public institutions, the newly created Superintendencia de Administradoras de Fondos de Jubilaciones y Pensiones (SAFJP, or Superintendency of Pension Funds) and the existing Superintendencia de Seguros de la Nacion (SSN, or Superintendency of Insurance), became responsible for overseeing activities of the private agencies and issuing lower-level regulations.
3. Finally, four groups of institutions took operational responsibility:
   a The Administración Nacional de la Seguridad Social (ANSES, or National Social Security Administration), an autonomous agency under the SSS, continued to manage the residual PAYGO scheme, including paying benefits to retirees under the old system, paying PAYGO benefits to those that chose the public scheme for the second pillar, providing basic pensions for all new retirees, and paying transitional benefits to those with contributions before the reform.
   b Specialized companies, Administradoras de Fondos de Jubilaciones y Pensiones (AFJP, or pension fund management companies), became responsible for managing the new pension funds. Directly supervised by the SAFJP, they manage individual accounts, invest assets, and process and pay benefit requests.

c Existing or newly created insurance companies, under the direct supervision of the SSN and, for some tasks, the SAFJP, became responsible for managing insurance schemes, including disability and survivor's policies for the AFJPs and annuities for beneficiaries.
d Finally, the Administración Federal de Ingresos Públicos (AFIP, or Federal Public Revenue Administration) continued to collect all contributions and distribute them to ANSES and the pension funds.

The performance of these institutions since 1994 has varied. At the policy design level, the role of the Ministry of Labor and the Social Security Secretariat was weaker than originally expected. Many policy initiatives came exclusively from the Ministry of Economy, and the political space of the SSS slowly declined, as they lost staff and budget. The 'emergency mode' that defined most policy decisions in the late 1990s and early 2000s in Argentina reduced the relevance of analytical areas in the government, a trend that was particularly damaging for the social security system. Hierarchical lines were rarely respected, and in many cases the Ministry of Economy or the president appointed authorities to ANSES and the Superintendency of Pension Funds without consulting the Ministry of Labor.

While the supervisory agencies have an autonomous status that should preserve their independence from political pressures, the experience during the first 10 years of the new pension system shows that this independence is limited when pressures are strong enough. The role of the SAFJP has been different from that of SSN, as the former has made important efforts to be proactive and focus its attention on protecting the workers' interests while the latter has had a more traditional approach, preserving 'system integrity' even if that means affecting beneficiaries' rights.

At the operational level, since the mid-1990 ANSES has had a strong record of implementing institutional improvements and simplifying processes. They have increased transparency and reduced delays in granting benefits, and taken some steps to reduce fraud. However, ANSES still has much to do in terms of achieving efficiency, transparency, and political independence. The agency manages a huge budget—nearly 40 percent of the total national budget—which unavoidably makes it the focus of many political interests.

Much controversy surrounds the role of AFIP, as the sole institution responsible for collecting and enforcing contributions to the social security system. Supporters of this arrangement have argued that, because AFIP manages all contribution databases for national taxes and social security, it has the advantage of being able to crosscheck information and enforce payment. Opponents, on the other hand, have argued that social security is too low in the AFIP's priorities, as most salaried workers are employed by relatively small firms or are independent workers. Meanwhile, AFIP efforts are focused on a small group of high contributors who are responsible for as much as 80 percent of revenues from income and value-added taxes. However, because they are not labor-intensive companies, their share in social security contributions is much smaller. There have been many proposals to separate the collection of taxes from social security contributions, including plans that would transfer this function to ANSES or to a new independent agency. The government implemented this last proposal in 2001, with the creation of the Instituto Nacional de Recaudación de los Recursos de la Seguridad Social (INARSS, or National Institute for Collection of Social Security Revenue), but this institute was never fully functional and closed a couple of years later.

Market Development: Competition and Costs

When the government instituted the new private system in 1994, 24 managing companies started operations. These AFJPs were owned by a diverse group of stockholders, including banks, insurance companies, government-owned agencies, health services providers, individuals, and even a soccer club. Almost 85 percent were from financial institutions, and 69 percent were domestic. The evolution of the market composition has been rapid. By the end of 2005 there were only 11 AFJPs. Of stockholders, 76 percent were from financial institutions, and only 58 percent were domestic. Concentration has also evolved. In 1995 nearly 50 percent of affiliates were enrolled in the four largest funds. By late 2001, this percentage had grown to 75 percent, falling to 61.5 percent by early 2007 (SAFJP 2007).

Although the new funded scheme was optional—workers could choose between it and the second pillar—whenever a worker did not make an explicit choice, administrators would assign the worker to an AFJP. During the first year of the new system, nearly 50 percent of workers registered in the SIJP had chosen an AFJP, 41 percent had chosen the PAYGO scheme, and 9 percent had been randomly assigned to an AFJP. Over the next 9 years, the proportion of assigned workers steadily grew; by mid-2005, 4 out of every 10 workers affiliated with an SIJP had entered the system through this channel.

As in other Latin-American countries, market competition has been a serious concern for regulators. Demand has shown low price elasticity, and the managing companies' returns became extremely high, particularly in the late 1990s. From the introduction of the system to late 2001, average fees were stable, at around 3.5 percent of wages. Meanwhile, operational costs declined as early investments were amortized and economies of scale realized. Consequently, returns in the industry grew rapidly: by 1999 and

2000 returns on equity were over 20 percent. However, these rates declined and became negative in 2002 and later, mostly because of poor financial management.

The history of competition among the AFJPs has been strongly defined by changes in regulations. We can identify 4 different periods, with different determinants and outcomes. The first period goes from mid-1994, when the AFJPs began enrolling workers, until the end of that year, when efforts to attract individuals to the funded scheme ended. During this period, the managers focused on capturing the largest possible share of the new market, developing large networks of branch offices and sales forces and making large marketing expenditures. The tight link between commercial expenditures and the number of affiliates each AFJP obtained shaped the future distribution of the market. Regulatory decisions reinforced this trend by randomly assigning workers who did not explicitly choose a company in proportion to the market share of each fund.

By early 1995 AFJPs entered a second phase when they were authorized to transfer affiliates. Consequently, the number of salespeople declined by nearly 75 percent, and a new period of relative calm but growing competition began. The ratio of annual transfers went from 19 percent in 1995 to 26 percent in 1996 and 32 percent in 1997. As the trend was accelerating (the annualized rate for the second semester of 1997 reached 38 percent), expenditures in sales force rapidly increased and concerns about the 'inefficient spending' of the industry became widespread. After many discussions, the Superintendency of the AFJP issued new regulations complicating transfers. Most AFJPs responded by rapidly reducing their marketing efforts.

From early 1998 to late 2001 the market was very calm, with few efforts to expand the overall contributor base and even fewer efforts to attract affiliates from other AFJPs. Only one AFJP showed significant net gains in affiliates, increasing its market share by an annual rate of 10–15 percent. The overall ratio of transfers to contributors sharply declined to one-third of its previous value. Marketing costs, which in 1997 had accounted for more than 50 percent of operational costs, also declined, by nearly 40 percent in 3 years.

The most recent period began when the fiscal and financial crisis of 2001 directly affected the AFJP industry. The economic turmoil created confusion, and two important reforms enacted in November of that year altered market conditions: (*a*) workers' contribution rates went from 11 to 5 percent of gross wages, and (*b*) a change in insurance policies brought these costs to nearly zero in the short term. Reacting to these changes, AFJPs sharply reduced their fees, which resulted in little change in competition or transfers. Other changes, such as the creation of a new AFJP in 2001 and the differential impact of the financial crisis, had some minor effects, though by mid-2005, transfers were still very low.

The insurance industry has had a different history. Insurers that provide death and disability protection do not compete to attract workers. Rather, they sell their policies to the AFJPs, usually within the same economic group. While analysts, policymakers, and industry experts have discussed the determinants and evolution of AFJP costs, the analysis of the life insurance market has been less intense, probably because the supervisory agency has a less proactive attitude. Regulations state that AFJPs must select their insurer through a competitive process, whereby they publicly request bids every year. However, with very few exceptions, AFJPs hire insurance companies within their economic group at rates that are not transparent.

Designers of the funded scheme expected the cost of death and disability insurance to be around 1 percent of taxable wages. In the early years of the system, mortality was much lower than expected, and market analysts disagreed on whether these numbers were in line with the long-term expected rates or whether there was a delay in claims processing that would eventually catch up. As claims increased over the next few years, so did rates. These rates in part reflected the higher actual payments but, given the observed delay, they were also affected by concerns about future increases in claims. By 2001 the average insurance costs had grown by 60 percent compared to the 1995 rates. Most analysts agreed that these costs would continue to grow.

In late 2001 the government enacted a new regulation allowing insurance companies to disregard expected payments. Consequently, costs rapidly declined to less than 0.5 percent of salaries but then began to grow again. By early 2007 they had reached their highest level ever, at 1.41 percent of salaries (SAFJP 2007). Although some analysts have argued that the growing costs are because the medical boards responsible for assessing disability claims are overly lenient, a report from the Superintendency of Pension Funds shows that these boards have been very consistent over the years, with an approval rate of around 60 percent of claims (SAFJP 2004). Furthermore, the data show that the absolute number of claims has been stable since the comparable data was collected in 2000.

The Investment Policies: Regulations, Strategies, Crises, and Responses

Asset management under the new funded scheme has also been the target of controversy. The law and regulations were restrictive regarding diversification—setting maximum investment limits by type of instrument and issuer—and required minimum risk ratings to increase security. Regulations also limited international diversification, as in other countries in the region. Following Chile, the Argentine system also includes a guaranteed minimum return, defined as either 70 percent of the market average or the average minus 2 percentage points, whichever is lower.

Portfolios have been highly concentrated in domestic government securities, nearly always at the established limit of 50 percent, or even higher because of valuation changes and short-term regulation adjustments. The high incidence of public debt during most of the period can be explained by the high returns generated by these instruments. However, during the 2001–2 crisis, when authorities actively promoted and sometimes required that the AFJPs increase their exposure, this percentage went well beyond the limit (see Table 15-2).

Regulations on diversification have not been binding, except in a few particular cases. This is also true for investments in foreign assets, as the maximum limit has been 17 percent of the funds' value and actual investments never exceeded 10 percent. On the other hand, the minimum return guarantee has had an important effect both directly—several AFJPs have had to compensate their affiliates for low returns—and indirectly—pension fund managers tend to replicate their investment strategies to avoid falling below the minimum return.

Despite the controversies over the impact of the 2001–2 crisis on the financial status of the pension funds, real returns in the system have been reasonable over time. Analysts and fund managers predicted in early 2002 that the government default would result in a catastrophic loss for the pension funds, by as much as 45 percent.[7] These assessments were exaggerated, the result of comparing nominal dollar values of assets before and after the default and negotiations. The actual evolution of pension funds' real returns should be measured in local currency. The pension funds have produced an average real return of nearly 10 percent per year since 1995. While volatility has been important, in some cases it can be attributed to a delay in adjusting valuation to the actual conditions of the market (see Figure 15-7).

What Is Next?

The pension system in Argentina appears to have survived the worst of the 2001–2 crisis in relatively good condition, but several problems that preexisted it were somewhat worsened and require urgent attention. Public debate about the pension system has been focused on topics that appear to be relevant in the short term but have little if any importance in terms of long-term strategy. Meanwhile, some of the most important structural problems—such as declining coverage, dysfunctional institutional design, weak competition, high costs in the funded scheme, and residual fragmentation—have been neglected.

Table 15-2 Portfolio Composition of Pension Funds (in %)

	1995	*1996*	*1997*	*1998*	*1999*	*2000*	*2001*	*2002*	*2003*	*2004*	*2005*
Cash	2.3	2.2	1.4	1.4	1.9	1.1	0.7	2.3	0.9	2.5	1.5
Government bonds	51.5	51.8	49.3	44.6	51.3	53.0	53.3	77.8	75.2	67.4	59.6
Bank deposits	27.1	17.6	16.4	23.0	18.1	15.2	15.4	2.1	3.2	4.2	7.4
Equity	2.0	13.5	21.8	20.9	17.3	16.6	11.5	8.3	8.2	10.4	13.0
Corporate bonds	6.8	10.7	4.8	2.3	2.3	2.4	2.3	1.3	1.3	2.1	2.1
Mutual funds	4.2	1.5	4.1	5.5	6.5	5.5	11.6	1.0	1.1	2.7	4.7
Foreign assets	2.8	0.4	0.4	0.4	0.2	4.4	3.4	5.6	8.3	9.4	9.9
Other	3.4	2.4	1.8	1.9	2.3	1.8	1.7	1.6	1.8	1.4	1.8
Total	100.0	100.0	100.0	100.0	100.0	100.0	100.0	100.0	100.0	100.0	100.0

Source: SAFJP (2005).

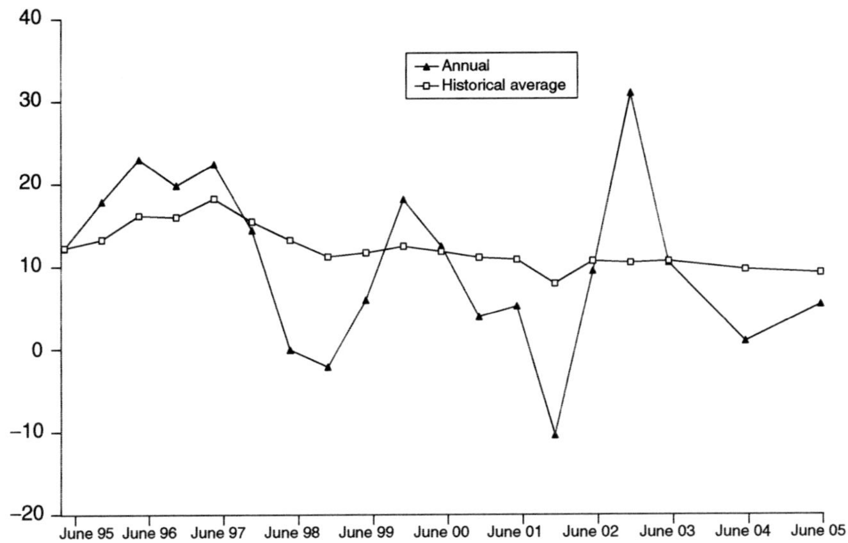

Figure 15-7. Pension fund real annual returns. (*Source*: SAFJP 2005.)

Coverage

As discussed earlier, workers' participation in the pension system has steadily declined in the past two decades, a process that reflects deep changes in the economic structure and the labor market at the national level. This decline cannot be fully explained, nor can it be fixed with reforms. However, to continue performing its role as a provider of income security to the elderly, the system must adapt to the new reality.

There are several areas where policymakers might have an impact, and each of them should be carefully considered. First and foremost, at the national level, Argentina has a fragmented model that could be better integrated to improve coverage and reduce gaps. The 3 schemes of basic benefits—the PBU, or basic benefit for those retiring under the standard system, received at age 60 or 65 years with a minimum of 30 years of contributions; an 'old-age' benefit, received at age 70 years with a minimum of 10 years of contributions; and a noncontributory benefit—are sometimes inconsistent and exclude many potential beneficiaries. Several measures in recent years have attempted to repair these inconsistencies, including reforms in the noncontributory pension scheme and a simplification of rules for back payments for the self-employed (a de facto reduction in the requirement of 30 years with contributions). However, these changes are not part of a clear strategy to expand coverage, especially for the poorest.

As of 2005, nearly 60 percent of expenditures were being financed with taxes or transfers, and this proportion is likely to decline in the future. Given that the public system has clearly moved away from a purely contributive financing scheme, the division between contributive and noncontributive schemes has become somewhat artificial, and a serious discussion of the reasonability of continuing to discriminate among beneficiaries on this basis is necessary. While sharp changes in the benefit structure are not possible or desirable for political, social, and legal reasons, authorities could try to focus the debate in the system design for the medium and long term, and discuss the transition mechanisms to reach that model later.

Institutional Design

The institutional design of the pension system at the national level in Argentina is good, with clear separation of policymaking, supervisory, and operational roles among institutions. However, these roles are not always respected, and the limits between these three levels are often blurred.

Correcting this problem is not simple, as political forces tend to override normative structures, yet it might be possible to improve it by reinforcing the existing model and by prohibiting officials and institutions from going beyond their assigned functions. Legislation could be made clearer regarding the definition of ANSES as an operational agency with no policymaking responsibilities, or authorities could reinforce the independence of the Superintendency of AFJP. However, taking these steps would certainly require strong political commitment from current and future authorities.

Alternatively, the government could redesign the institutional structure, reducing the number of agencies and abandoning specialization as the main organizing principle. Thus, ANSES could take on both policy design and operational functions, which would give it a much higher status in the government structure, perhaps at the level of a ministry. Other countries have taken this approach, which has some advantages, as it eliminates the source of institutional conflicts, but also carries risks, as it concentrates too much unsupervised power in one institution.

Competition in the Funded System

By bringing in multiple private providers to manage the pension funds, the system designers had hoped that market competition would bring about improved services and declining costs. However, the providers have focused most of their competitive efforts on marketing, with only a few cases where differences in costs, services, or returns had a relevant role.

Inadequate incentives for participants are the primary cause for this lack of competition. Affiliates have shown little interest in switching to the least expensive or more profitable pension fund, and system regulations have done little to reverse this situation. The original legislation made switching pension funds difficult, and regulations made the task even more so.

Because the government creates the rules to assign workers who did not choose an AFJP, it has a powerful tool for promoting competition. However, until 2001 the criterion used to assign workers was not pro-competitive. Originally, they were distributed in proportion to the number of workers enrolled in each AFJP. Nearly 3.7 million workers were assigned following these criteria. In 2001 legislators implemented a new criterion whereby 'undefined' workers were enrolled in the least expensive pension funds, at a time when the flow of new affiliates was much smaller—only 1.1 million workers were assigned with this criterion between 2001 and 2005.

Experiences in other countries show that enhancing demand awareness is difficult but some actions, such as public information campaigns, can increase it. Others, such as simplifying switching procedures, can facilitate switching. Peru recently changed its regulations to permit switches through the Internet and enabled managers to sign workers to long-term contracts. This change was immediately followed by the entrance of a new provider in the market and a sharp reduction of fees by all participants. In Chile some have proposed allowing group and long-term contracting. Other countries have implemented more ineffectual changes. In Colombia, for example, policymakers tried to set up a maximum fee, but all managing companies adjusted to the maximum fee without any competition.

System Fragmentation

The pension system in Argentina was born as a fragmented model, with many institutions and schemes operating in parallel. For most of the twentieth century, each government, knowing that fragmentation had led to inequities and sustainability problems, tried to integrate these pension schemes. In this context, the reform of 1994 and the transfer of provincial civil servants to the national system was aimed at unifying the social insurance system at the national level.

The integration trend lost momentum in the late 1990s, and more than 100 independent schemes that cover provincial level civil servants or professional groups still exist, with insufficient supervision and coordination. Many of these programs are very small, with their own rules and financial schemes. While many are well managed and requirements are stricter than in the national system, workers usually suffer due to problems of portability, and the medium- and long-term sustainability of the programs is not clear. Recent legislation appears to be intensifying fragmentation, with the creation of several new civil servant and professional funds at the provincial level and the reinstatement of special schemes within the national system for occupational groups.

As in any social insurance scheme, integration of systems appears to be a desirable strategy. Larger pools are better able to distribute risks, and multiple systems unavoidably generate inequities across the population. Policymakers should renew the drive towards integration, either institutionally—that is, progressively integrating all systems into the national SIJP—or by developing a better coordinated supervision system, ensuring access, sustainability, and equity across the system.

Recent Changes

In late 2005 Argentina's government began to refocus its interest in the pension system. Several reforms approved since then have had and will have a significant impact on the system's operation and performance. In 2005, under a generous financial agreement, the government approved a program that would allow individuals who had been self-employed before 1994 but had failed to make contributions to pay off their debt. This program originally seemed like a minor collection measure but turned out to be a de facto universalization of the system. Lower-level regulations established that all these workers could apply for retirement benefits immediately after making the first installment of their payment plan, and that they would receive benefits as long as they continue to pay their monthly obligation. Though no official data is available, it has been estimated that by December 2006, 1.5–2 million new beneficiaries had been added to the system, nearly doubling the number of beneficiaries.

In early 2007 the government announced a legislative reform expanding the role of the public system by automatically assigning unaffiliated new workers to the public system, raising its replacement rate, and allowing workers in the private system to switch back to the state-managed system. Other changes proposed in this reform include the elimination of disability and survivors insurance, as these benefits would be financed directly by the pension funds, and the introduction of a maximum fee for AFJPs to reduce costs.

While it is still too soon to assess the impact of these proposals on the pension system in Argentina, they will probably result in a much smaller private pillar, with a role limited to providing complementary benefits to a relatively small proportion of middle- and high-income workers.

Notes

[1] The Argentine reform also included elements from the Peruvian system. For a full discussion of that system and the Chilean system, refer to Carranza and Morón (this volume) and Arenas de Mesa et al. (this volume).

[2] The system includes more than 80% of the labor force; the only workers not covered under the national scheme are the police, the military, civil servants at the provincial level in 14 of the 24 provinces, and independent professional workers (lawyers, engineers, medics, etc.) working at the provincial level.

[3] This concept was proposed in an international workshop by Elsa Rodriguez Romero, an Argentine expert on pension law, who noted that the new schemes are characterized not by the fact that the contribution is known, but rather by an unknown future benefit.

[4] Rofman, Stirparo, and Lattes (1997) estimate that, by 2025, the national system would be spending 2% of GDP; Grushka (2002) estimates expenditures of 2.4%; and the SSS (2005) estimates expenditures of 2.15%.

[5] Measuring coverage in pension schemes is a complex issue. Problems in definitions, availability and quality of data, and interpretation of indicators have produced controversy and confusion. This chapter considers that workers who contribute to a pension system are covered by it during their active years, and coverage among the elderly is estimated by comparing the number of individuals aged 65 years and older with retirement benefits with the total population of that age. For a discussion of problems, limitations, and caveats in definitions and data, see Rofman (2006).

[6] The household surveys in Argentina do not ask about contributions of the self-employed. Data shown in this chapter assumes that all self-employed are uncovered, an assumption that underestimates coverage but not significantly. According to registration data, the proportion of the self-employed contributing to social security has been around 10%, which would increase the overall coverage by approximately 3 percentage points.

[7] This figure was included in a press release issued by the UAFJP in March 2002, as reported by Cronista (2002).

References

Arenas de Mesa, Alberto, David Bravo, Jere R. Behrman, Olivia S. Mitchell, and Petra E. Todd (2008). 'The Chilean Pension Reform Turns 25: Lessons from the Social Protection Survey', this volume.

Baker, Dean and Mark Weisbrot (2002). *The Role of Social Security Privatization in Argentina's Economic Crisis*. Washington, DC: Center for Economic and Policy Research.

Brooks, Sarah (2002). 'Social Protection and Economic Integration: The Politics of Pension Reform in an Era of Capital Mobility', *Comparative Political Studies*, 35(5).

Carranza, Eliana and Eduardo Morón (2008). 'The Peruvian Pension Reform: Ailingor Failing?', this volume.

Cronista (2002). 'Las AFJP se presentaran ante la justicia contra la pesificacion del Gobierno', March 14, p. 10.

Grushka, Carlos (2002). *Proyecciones Previsionales de Largo Plazo. Argentina 2000–2050.* Buenos Aires: SAFJP.

International Monetary Fund (IMF) (1998). 'Argentina: Recent Economic Developments', IMF Staff Country Report No. 98/38. Washington, DC.

Kay, Stephen J. (2001). 'Politics, Economics, and Pension Reform in the Southern Cone', paper presented at the Social Security and Pension Reform Conference, Instituto Tecnológico Autónomo de México (ITAM), March 2.

Ministry of Economy (2005). 'Series de Gasto Público Consolidado por Finalidad-Función, 1980–2003', Buenos Aires.

Piñera, Jose (1991). *El Cascabel al Gato: La Batalla por la Reforma Previsional.* Santiago: Editora Zig-Zag.

Rofman, Rafael (2006). 'El Costo del Sistema de Pensiones en Argentina', in María Cristina Vargas de Flood (ed.), *Política del Gasto Social: La Experiencia Argentina.* Buenos Aires: La Colmena.

—— and Leonardo Lucchetti (2006). *Pension Systems in Latin America: Concepts and Measurements of Coverage.* Washington, DC: World Bank.

—— Gustavo Stirparo, and Pablo Lattes (1997). *Proyecciones del Sistema Integrado de Jubilaciones y Pensiones.* Buenos Aires: SAFJP.

Secretaría de Seguridad Social (SSS) (2005). *Prospectiva de la Previsión Social.* Buenos Aires: SSS.

Superintendencia de Administradoras de Fondos de Jubilaciones y Pensiones (SAFJP) (2004). *El Régimen de Capitalización a Diez Años de la Reforma.* Buenos Aires: SAFJP.

—— (2005, 2007). Boletín Estadístico Mensual, 13(2), February. Buenos Aires: SAFJP.

Chapter 16

Epilogue: The Future of Retirement Systems in the Americas

Olivia S. Mitchell

Lessons from Pension Reform in the Americas

Financing retirement is actually a very simple concept—at least in theory. That is, people are supposed to set aside money during their work lives, and then draw down the interest and principal during the retirement period. The problem, of course, is in moving from theory to practice. Workers are not particularly well informed about their lifetime earnings paths; they are often financially illiterate about capital market investments; and most do not know when they will die, so are unable to formulate the necessary optimal asset buildup and drawdown paths. Most people also lack the remarkable self-control and predictable lives that saving for retirement takes, and instead are often tempted or forced to draw down their savings for consumption needs, housing, or other emergencies (Mitchell and Utkus 2004).

These realities are typically the rationale for government-provided, or government-mandated, old-age retirement programs. From this perspective, having an old-age system is seen as a necessary self-control device, one that operates on the 'if you don't see it you won't spend it' principle. Old-age programs are therefore a way to get workers to pay today, so that funds will be there in the future to support their old-age consumption. In most of the Americas, the first pillar of old-age support is often called 'the Social Security system'.

Precision in Speaking and Thinking Matters

But what exactly is social security? One of the lessons I have learned from many years of working on pension reforms in Mexico, Uruguay, Bermuda, Brazil, Japan, and the USA is that precision in speaking and thinking about social security is essential but too often ignored. In fact, sometimes we are the six blind men of myth who confronted the elephant. When each man felt a different anatomical feature of the beast, he concluded that the ear, the trunk, or the tail defined the animal in its entirety. If we fail to understand and appreciate key aspects of a country's old-age system, we also run the risk of standing in the way of, or even subverting, ways to engage in successful retirement system reform.

As one example, there are wide differences of opinion about what social security is and what it should be. When I was working on administrative costs and expenses of social security programs in Latin America, I found enormous cross-country differences in costs—which only made sense when I noticed the wide variation in tasks that these systems are asked to carry out (Mitchell 1998). As an example, most countries have old-age benefits included, but after that, there is huge diversity. Sometimes social security goes on to include disability as well as survivor and dependent benefits. Often in the Americas other risks are also included—for example, unemployment and severance pay, health care and maternity leave, poverty-alleviation measures, and, in some cases, even housing and educational subsidies. As a result, being clear about vocabulary matters, since how people talk about their system reveals what they expect from a reform—and this might be very different from how others conceive of the system and its objectives. Until we fully understand what the system is asked to do in a given country, it is impossible to figure out if it is doing it efficiently, cost effectively, and equitably.

Another example of when precision in speaking and thinking has been inadequately precise is in the discussion around 'replacement rates'. All the literature on the topic uses the term, but just a moment of thought confirms that it means very different things to different people. For instance, the current US Social Security system links workers' old-age benefit accruals to their own lifetime earnings. This is justified as a means to maintain a given 'own lifetime earnings replacement rate', by which is meant that a retiree's benefits replace a fixed percent of his own lifetime pay; after retirement, benefits are indexed to prices, not wages, so they fall relative to active workers. Whether this is affordable is, of course, a debate in the USA, but it is by no means a unique definition of the replacement rate concept. In contrast, in Europe and some Latin-American countries, retiree benefits are set up so they are tied to payroll rather than prices after retirement, either formally or informally. For instance, the pension of a public-sector retiree in Brazil rises every time the person now holding the retiree's job gets a raise. This is an entirely different concept of replacement rate, yet nobody pays attention to the vastly different and more expensive financing implications.

When I served on the President's Commission to Strengthen Social Security (see www.csss.gov), we proposed bringing the national DB system into balance rather than wage-indexing the benefit accrual path (Cogan and Mitchell 2003). This would lead to lower 'own lifetime earnings replacement rates' for many, but it would enhance the system's solvency and ensure that no benefits would fall in purchasing power, compared to today. It also permitted us to identify money to raise benefits for low-wage workers and poor widows. Hence our proposal would have brought about a solvent, sustainable, and more equitable result, with higher lifetime replacement rates for low-wage workers. Over the long haul, this would mean that eventually everyone would get a flat benefit amount, producing high lifetime earnings replacement rates for the poor and lower ones for the highly paid.

A third arena where clearer thinking would be invaluable has to do with the use of the term 'transition costs'. Many critics of reform have argued, incorrectly, that reforming retirement systems always means new and expensive 'transition financing'. In fact, those who complain about 'transition costs' due to reforms are usually wrong. The sensible way to think about it when a country has an insolvent social security or pension program follows.

First, figure out how much promised benefits are worth, ideally computed using an open-ended horizon and sensible economic and demographic assumptions. Then, figure out how much future system revenues can be expected to be, and difference the benefits and the revenue. What remains is the unfunded liability of the system; this is the hole to be filled.

Next, determine projected revenue and benefit streams given a specific reform plan. To the extent that this reform reduces the system's unfunded liability, the reform generates a *saving*, not a cost.

In practice, many reform critics focus exclusively on the financing needs of the reform, but remain oblivious to (or at least silent on) the size of the hole to be filled if there were no reform. In the US case, many charged our commission's proposals as having high transition costs; the reality is that our plan generated transition *savings*, by moving to a new system. Much more clarity along these lines is required in the future.

Retirement Reform Is a Process, Not an End in Itself

A second lesson I have learned after many years of pension reform in the Americas is that reforming retirement systems takes patience and, in fact, the process is never over. So if you are a young, eager, and energetic reformer, the good news is that you have steady employment prospects. The bad news is that there will be political and economic risk, and your job is never done.

This is a frustrating message to many economists, particularly because we often see wasted opportunities and little problems turn into big ones, for lack of action and attention. As my mother used to say, 'Time is money', and so, too, is it here. Each day reform is postponed, the workforce ages, the number of retirees grows, and the more insolvent become many of the systems on which so many people rely for survival. In the case of the USA, everyday Congress does nothing means that pensions and social security will be that much more difficult to fix in the future.

This observation also applies to the individual accounts programs that so many Latin-American nations have developed over the past two decades, in variants of Chile's personal accounts approach. The political and implementation process has tended to focus too often on getting the 'front-end' of the reform going—the accumulation phase, having the money flow into the accounts. However, often there is too little attention paid to common elements needed to support the new system, such as tax reform, health-care reform, and capital market reform. Without these, the new pension system may fail to inspire trust, for example, when it forces people to hold government bonds in their accounts, or unduly encourages mortgages rather than diversifying participants' holdings (Bodie, Mitchell, and Turner 1996). In most of the Americas, governments have devoted too little attention to the regulatory, supervisory, and payout mechanisms—for instance, overlooking the need to restructure the insurance and annuity markets so that workers gain the confidence that they will not run out of money in retirement (Brown et al. 2001).

The inevitable constraints of time, money, and political energy may imply that retirement reforms will often be gradual and sequential in nature, particularly in poor countries where there are urgent claims on resources. However, in the retirement system arena, it is important to underscore that the challenge is to announce a reform and keep on a steady path. After all, we are asking participants to make decisions about working, saving, and investing that will affect their financial wellbeing 60 or 80 years into the future. Even the most coldly rational consumer is unlikely to believe that today's retirement system will be identical to that in place one to two decades from now. As Carranza and Morón (2008) note, 'policymaking in Peru is characterized by constant policy reversal... new governments have been prone to redo entire reforms without caring how costly it was to implement them'. This has been a more general problem with pension reform in the Americas. While stability is a virtue, at the same time it is essentially impossible to tie the hands of future policymakers. In fact, it could even be a bad idea to force people to continue under a legacy system designed for a different era but which now falls far short for the evolving economy. As an example, the fact that many retirement systems in the Americas induce early retirement, particularly for women, is a good example of a shortsighted and outmoded practice that must be changed in order to better target retirement security in old age.

Suggestions for the Future

One of the most critical consequences of the aging revolution in the Americas is that all of us must think more creatively if we are to find new ways to ensure that our older citizens have a decent standard of living. As more of us survive to older ages, it will become more and more difficult to tax increasing fractions of the younger population's earnings. At the end of the day, then, the real question is: 'What needs to be done to make retirement systems more resilient?'

First, making accumulation easier and more automatic will help. To boost saving, employers and governments must get young people 'in the habit' of saving at a very tender age. Habit-formation effects are substantial, and will help loosen constraints later.

Second, a serious and country-specific debate is required to explore how much can be afforded for minimum benefits: what can be financed and how it is an essential exercise that should not be delayed. This includes all groups in society—and yet a major challenge for the next decade throughout the Americans is to figure out ways to fold in public-sector workers—such as federal or state employees, the military and police, and other 'special' groups who have enjoyed above-average benefits that are now unaffordable.

Third, more research is needed on the capital market so we have better ideas about how to configure the environment for more cost-effective and efficient pension offerings, disability and survivor offerings, health insurance, and even retirement guarantees. Much remains to be learned about these key issues.

Fourth, policymakers and analysts desperately need more microeconomic individual-based household data to make sensible retirement policy. The Encuesta de Previdencia Social (EPS) in Chile, the HRS in the USA, and Mexico's Mexican Health and Aging Study (MHAS) are some shining examples. Such micropanel data help illuminate people's financial knowledge and expectations, along with their assets and debts; these illustrate where governments, employers, unions, and educators should concentrate their efforts in designing their plans, and then on executing them. As Peter Drucker said, 'Plans are only good intentions unless they immediately degenerate into hard work.'

Conclusions

In serving on the President's Bipartisan Commission to Strengthen Social Security, I was pleased to share with the commission the lessons of Latin-American pension reform for the USA. Though the USA has not yet taken steps to reform its system, we still stand to learn much from the numerous alternative reforms undertaken by our Latin neighbors, and to follow their useful examples.

The commission devoted enormous energy and collegiality to clarifying concepts, identifying future spending burdens, and developing solutions. Since the commission submitted its report, I have continued to spread the message that the US system is running short of funds to pay promised benefits, and this will happen soon. I was proud to be able to develop and support reform proposals that would enhance the safety net for old age in the USA, while permitting some diversification out of the traditional PAYGO system.

President Franklin D. Roosevelt once remarked: 'Old age is like everything else. To make a success of it, you've got to start young.' This leaves a substantial task for those of us in the policy and planning business. The goal in the retirement security arena is to help people 'do what they know they should'—save more, invest wisely, work longer, and avoid outliving their assets. Education is critical, though sometimes a hard sell—a lesson I learned from personal experience, when I tried to convince my teenage daughter to save part of her summer earnings in a retirement account. Financial institutions must help more as well, by developing more attractive, sensible, and low-cost ways to meet retirement objectives. Last but not the least, our elected officials must take up the challenge to make retirement security a national goal and to structure a more coherent environment for workers and retirees of the future.

References

Bodie, Zvi, Olivia S. Mitchell, and John Turner (eds.) (1996). *Securing Employer-Provided Pensions: An International Perspective.* Philadelphia, PA: University of Pennsylvania Press.

Brown, Jeffrey, Olivia S. Mitchell, James Poterba, and Mark Warshawsky (2001). *The Role of Annuity Markets in Financing Retirement.* Cambridge, MA: MIT Press.

Carranza, Eliana and Eduardo Morón (2008). 'The Peruvian Pension Reform: Ailing or Failing?', this volume.

Cogan, John F. and Olivia S. Mitchell (Spring 2003). 'Perspectives from the President's Commission on Social Security Reform', *Journal of Economic Perspectives,* 17(2): 149–72.

Mitchell, Olivia S. (1998). 'Administrative Costs of Public and Private Pension Plans', in M. Feldstein (ed.), *Privatizing Social Security.* Chicago, IL: University of Chicago Press, pp. 403–56.

—— and Stephen P. Utkus (eds.) (2004). *Pension Design and Structure: New Lessons from Behavioral Finance.* Oxford, UK: Oxford University Press.

Index

Figures, notes and tables are indexed in bold, e.g. 260**t**. More than one figure/table on a page is indexed as **(a)** or **(b)**.